The Transformation
of Plato's *Republic*

The Transformation of Plato's *Republic*

Kenneth Dorter

LEXINGTON BOOKS

A division of
ROWMAN & LITTLEFIELD PUBLISHERS, INC.
Lanham • Boulder • New York • Toronto • Oxford

LEXINGTON BOOKS

A division of Rowman & Littlefield Publishers, Inc.
A wholly owned subsidiary of The Rowman & Littlefield Publishing Group, Inc.
4501 Forbes Boulevard, Suite 200
Lanham, MD 20706

PO Box 317
Oxford
OX2 9RU, UK

British Library Cataloguing in Publication Information Available

Library of Congress Cataloging-in-Publication Data

Dorter, Kenneth, 1940–
    The transformation of Plato's Republic / Kenneth Dorter.
        p. cm.
    Includes bibliographical references and index.
    ISBN 0-7391-1187-6 (cloth : alk. paper)—ISBN 0-7391-1188-4
    (pbk. : alk. paper)
        1. Plato. Republic. I. Title.
    JC71.P6D67 2006
    321'.07—dc22   2005024186

Printed in the United States of America

♾ ™ The paper used in this publication meets the minimum requirements of American
National Standard for Information Sciences—Permanence of Paper for Printed Library
Materials, ANSI/NISO Z39.48–1992.

For Gregory and Amanda

Contents

~

Preface

The *Republic* is Plato's most comprehensive dialogue, but whether it is coherent as well as comprehensive has been the subject of considerable debate. The character of the argument changes abruptly after Book 1, and again, although less so, before and after Books 5–7, and once again in Book 10. The changes in direction and method have prompted speculation about whether in some or all of these cases the *Republic* has been compiled from material written at different times. One of the aims of the present study is to show how what appear to be discontinuities are intrinsic parts of an overall design.

The comprehensive design and the significance of each of its elements—the whole and the parts—cannot be understood apart from each other. On the one hand, the generality of any overview of the dialogue has to emerge from its details rather than from broad speculation. Plato's arguments are always carefully constructed, and the care that went into their construction calls for equal care in analyzing them. But on the other hand, analysis alone will not be enough. If the progressive changes in the character of the dialogue reflect a movement from simpler but less adequate formulations to more adequate but more difficult ones, any inadequacy in argumentation may be intended to reflect the limitations of the current approach, rather than being simply unsuccessful. In a dialogue where Socrates' methods are disparaged not only by the sympathetic figures of Glaucon (357a) and Adeimantus (487a–c), but even by Socrates himself (354a–c, 435c–d), more is going on than an attempt to construct sound arguments. The dialogue must therefore be approached synthetically as well as analytically, by trying to discover the way each argument, good or bad, functions within the development of the argument as a whole. It is always possible, of course, that an unsound argument may simply be misconceived rather than designedly flawed, and we shall have to keep that possibility in mind as we proceed. Even arguments that succeed on their own terms, however, often leave some readers dissatisfied, since all philosophers rely on presuppositions and intuitions that their readers do not always share, and not least Plato. We should not ignore the controversial nature of some of the *Republic*'s presuppositions, but we should also make every effort to evaluate the achievement of the dialogue on its own terms.

I am grateful to the Social Sciences and Humanities Research Council of Canada for research grants that aided the completion of this project in many ways, and to the University of Guelph for a sabbatical leave that enabled me to complete the project years sooner than otherwise would have been possible. I especially want to thank David Gallop, Cristina Ionescu, and Emily Jaklic for their valuable comments on an earlier draft of this work; and Douglas Al-Maini, Giorgio Baruchello, Antonio Calcagno, Cristina Ionescu, Roopen Majithia, and Julian Meynell for their help in searching and retrieving the relevant materials. I owe more than I can say to a great many people over the years who have contributed to my understanding of the *Republic*. Apart from the authors of the books mentioned in the bibliography, I am indebted to my teachers, to my students over many years, to audiences where I have presented this material, and to readers and editors for the venues where the material listed below was published.

Some of the material has previously been published in a different form in the following works, and appears here with the permission of the original editors: "The Divided Line and the Structure of Plato's *Republic*", *History of Philosophy Quarterly* 21 (2004): 1–20; "Free Will, Luck, and Happiness in the Myth of Er", *Journal of Philosophical Research* 28 (2003): 129–42; "Philosopher-Rulers: How Contemplation Becomes Action", *Ancient Philosophy* 21 (2001): 335–56; "'One, Two, Three, But Where is The Fourth?': Incomplete Mediation in the *Timaeus*", in Z. Planinc, ed., *Politics, Philosophy, Writing: Plato's Art of Caring for Souls* (Columbia: University of Missouri Press, 2001), 160–78; "Wisdom, Virtue, and Knowledge", *Review of Metaphysics* 51 (1997): 313–43; and "Socrates' Refutation of Thrasymachus and Treatment of Virtue", *Philosophy and Rhetoric* 7 (1974): 25–46.

~

Introduction

Conceptual Models

The *Republic* is a book of contrasts, built on oppositions between the just and unjust life, rationality and appetite, necessary and unnecessary appetites, being and becoming, knowledge and opinion, originals and images, blindness to dark and blindness to light, and the evolution and devolution of political and psychological constitutions, among others. Beyond these internal oppositions are further contrasts between the *Republic*'s message and its method: it employs encyclopedic breadth to extol the virtues of narrow specialization, and presents an evolving point of view to establish the primacy of what is unchanging. The evolution of the *Republic*'s point of view is less evident than the other examples, but it can be discerned at three levels: 1) transformation of models, 2) overall structure, and 3) dialectical method, which also provides the basis of Plato's interest in oppositions.

In the first case, on several occasions in the dialogue Socrates presents clear and simple models to help us grasp fundamental distinctions, but the clarity of the models is purchased at the price of oversimplification, and once the distinctions that are illustrated by the models have been established, Socrates begins to introduce nuances that complicate the models, rendering them more subtle and sophisticated but more difficult to conceptualize.[1] The most obvious instance is the model of the city as "the soul writ large" (368c–9a). The model at first seems intuitively acceptable and relatively unproblematic except for the lack of amenities that Glaucon complains of (372d), but as it develops in complexity it gradually reaches the point where Socrates deliberately suppresses some of the emerging implications because they are so counterintuitive that they would threaten to undermine the entire enterprise (450a–51a).

In other cases the transformation of simple models into complex or subtle ones is less explicit. After Socrates introduces the model of the tripartite soul (436a–41c), for example, he does not call attention to the way its clear distinctions between appetite, spiritedness, and rationality become increasingly ambiguous in what follows, but by Book 6 the whole is conceived as a single force that flows in different directions: "when the appetites strongly incline toward some one thing they are thereby weakened toward others, like a stream from which there is a diversion into another channel. . . . So when they flow toward learning and all such things, they will be concerned, I suppose, with the pleasures of the soul itself by itself, while those that come through the body it will abandon" (485d–e).[2] Here rationality (love of learning) is no longer opposed to appetite but is a kind of appetite. Although Socrates did not call attention to the gradual transformation of the first model into the second, he introduced the tripartite soul with the warning that the model was not one that they could rest satisfied with: "we will never get an accurate answer using our present methods" (435c). Socrates proceeds only when Glaucon insists.

A third example is the "two worlds" model that Socrates introduces in Book 5. The world is divided into the two discontinuous realms of being (the forms) and becoming (visible things); and our soul has two equally distinct faculties: knowledge which is set over being, and opinion which is set over becoming (477c–80a). Here again the original clear, simple, division between these apparently discontinuous realms becomes increasingly blurred until this model too is gradually reduced to one in which the original ontological distinction, and the distinction of faculties, become only differences in the direction in which a single faculty is turned: "When the soul is turned to what is illuminated by truth and being it understands and knows them and appears to have reason, but when it is turned toward what is mixed with darkness— what comes to be and passes away—it opines" (508d). In this case too, Socrates does not call attention to the transformation of the model as it occurs, but as with the model of the tripartite soul he prefaces it with a warning: "It would not at all be easy to tell someone else, but you I think will agree to this" (475e). We can read this as saying, 'In our discussion of the tripartite soul you were willing to accept avowedly oversimplified analyses, so I think you will accept this one where someone else would not'. We will be able to trace the development of these models from simple oppositions to more nuanced conceptions.

The Structure of the *Republic*

The structural principles on which the *Republic* is organized are never made explicit, and the stages in its development can all too easily appear to be juxtapositions of disparate material written at different times and not completely integrated. The sections that are most often thought to be incompletely incorporated into the whole are Book 1, Books 5–7, and Book 10.

Book 1

The relationship between Book 1 and the remaining nine books has long been a subject of controversy, with many scholars taking the first book to be an early work to which the remainder of the dialogue was subsequently added. However, even those who regard it as an earlier dialogue concede that it must have been revised when Plato incorporated it into the *Republic*,[3] in which case there is, at least, no reason to treat Book 1 in its present form as a separate dialogue that can be interpreted independently of the remaining books, as is sometimes done. There is historical interest in the question of whether an earlier form of Book 1 was originally an independent dialogue, but our concern here will be with the *Republic* in its present form. There is no denying that in its contentious tone and method of argument the first book is different from the rest of the dialogue, and resembles the early dialogues[4] that are characterized by Socratic elenchus or refutation, but there are good reasons for that which follow from the structure of the *Republic* itself and do not need to be supplied in an external way. There is no need for an explanation that undermines the unity and integrity of the dialogue.

If we look at the content of Book 1 rather than the style, the continuity between it and the rest of the *Republic* is obvious. The conversations with Cephalus and Polemarchus are mostly elenctic—Socrates' emphasis is on refuting their claims rather than affirming views of his own—but in the conversation with Thrasymachus he makes a number of positive assertions. Most of them are defended in so polemical a way that both Socrates (354b–c) and Glaucon (357a–b) conclude that however much the arguments may seem to establish their conclusions, nothing more than an appearance of plausibility is attained. Nevertheless each of the claims is resurrected in the following books, where they turn out to be crucial for the argument of the dialogue as a whole, as can be seen from the following side-by-side comparison of some of the chief instances.

1. Rulers seek the good of their subjects rather than seeking their own good at their subjects' expense (342e).

   The rulers do everything for the good of the subjects and nothing for themselves (419a–b).

2. Accordingly, no one is willing to rule without getting something in return, and since the best people will not be tempted by normal rewards they must somehow be compelled to rule (346e–347d).

   The philosophers will be reluctant to rule because of the sacrifice it entails, and must be compelled to do so by an appeal to their indebtedness to the city that nurtured and educated them (520a–d).

3. Justice and knowledge have the same attributes and are therefore the same (350c).

   Justice is equivalent to the rule of knowledge within us (442b11–d1, 443b1–2).

4. We can understand the nature of justice in the individual by seeing how it operates in a group (351c–352a).

   We can understand the nature of justice in the individual by observing it in the city (368c–369a and *passim*).

5. Virtue consists in performing well the function for which we are suited by nature (352d–353c).

   The city's virtues lie in the proper performance of the functions for which the members of the three classes are suited by nature (433a–b, 443c–e; cf. 608e–611a).

Plato could have used these connections to establish a smooth transition to Book 2, by having someone point out that there are crucial assumptions that need to be justified, and ellipses that need to be filled in. Socrates could then treat the ensuing argument as a justification of the previous one. Instead Plato does the opposite, making it seem as if the arguments of Book 1 are to be completely discarded, and Thrasymachus' challenge to be addressed anew rather than as a continuation of the previous argument. He has Socrates say at the end of Book 1 that he became distracted from the question of the nature of justice by other questions about justice, so that "the result of the discussion for me is that I know nothing. For since I do not know what the just is, I shall hardly know whether it happens to be a virtue or not, or whether someone who possesses it is unhappy or happy" (354a). The next speaker,

Glaucon at the beginning of Book 2, asks, "Do you want to appear to have persuaded us or truly persuade us?" (357b). Rather than presenting Book 1 as a first step in the overall argument Plato presents it as something that has left us back where we started and in need of a new beginning. It is hardly surprising then that many scholars take Book 1 to be an early work to which the remainder of the dialogue was subsequently added.

Books 5–7

The middle books seem to have been grafted between Books 4 and 8 so awkwardly that some scholars have supposed them to be a later addition as well.[5] In some ways they are clearly discontinuous with the surrounding books. For example, they drop the paradigm instituted in Book 2 (368d–369a), and so strongly emphasized in Books 4 and 8, that the model of the just city is meant to show us what justice is like in the soul. Unlike the features of the city that are introduced in Books 2–4 and 8–9, the distinctive features introduced in Books 5–7 are relevant only to the city, and instead of drawing a city-individual parallel as he does in Books 4 and 8, Socrates evades the question by saying, "No doubt it's also clear what we'll say the individual is like" (541b). But, in fact, it is far from clear.[6] Nothing in the soul corresponds to the "Three Waves"—the requirements that women rule equally with men (457b–c), that families be replaced by communities of men, women, and children (457c–d), and that philosophers should rule (473c–d).[7] The requirement in Book 4 that the rational class should rule fits in with the city-soul correspondence, for we have a rational faculty within us; but we do not literally have a philosopher within us.

Plato emphasizes rather than minimizes the breaks before and after Books 5–7, as he did with the break between Books 1 and 2. At the beginning of Book 5 Socrates could have said in effect, "Now let us proceed to investigate the longer road we spoke of [435c–d] that leads to a more precise answer and to an even more beautiful city and man [cf. 543d]". Instead Plato has him attempt to skip directly to the material of Book 8 and enumerate the stages of the previous city's decline; and resist plaintively when questions from Polemarchus and Adeimantus force him to reexamine the issues "as if from the beginning" (450a). And Book 8 could have begun with Socrates simply proposing to examine the stages of the philosophical city's decline, but Plato has him say instead, "Let's recall the point from which we digressed [ἐξετραπόμεθα] to here, so that we may proceed again along that same path" (543c). The implication is that they are now going back to the end of Book 4 as though nothing happened in between. In fact, the subsequent books presuppose some of the material of Books 5–7, so the latter are not a digression at all, but Plato emphasizes the discontinuity of the transitions rather than minimizing it. In some places he even calls attention to the lack of integration between the material in Books 2–4 and the material in Books 5–7, rather than simply adjusting them to agree with each other, such as when Socrates says, "In the earlier part of our discussion we chose old men, but in this one we cannot accept that. . . . All the preparatory studies for dialectic must be put before them when they are children" (536c–d).

Book 10

By the end of Book 9 the work of the *Republic* seems to be over, but at the beginning of Book 10 Socrates says, "Many other considerations regarding the city assure me that we were entirely right in organizing it as we did, not the least of which, I claim, is poetry" (595a), and then he returns to the themes of Books 2 and 3. There is no continuity with the immediately previous argument, nor any attempt by Plato to provide a connecting link. In this case it is hard to see how such a link is even possible. The material at the end of Book 10 (immortality and the rewards and punishments of the afterlife) could have followed quite naturally from the discussion of virtue and vice in Book 9, had Plato not interposed the examination of art between them. Not surprisingly, then, Book 10 is sometimes taken to be a later addition, as Book 1 has been taken to be an earlier work.[8]

Not only are the themes of Book 1 adumbrations of the themes of the dialogue as a whole, but Book 1 also functions as a symmetrical counterpart to Book 10, together with it framing the *Republic*'s arch structure.[9] The overall argument of the *Republic* is most obviously seen as a gradual progression to a climax in Book 9 where the victory of justice over injustice is finally established, followed by a consolidation of that victory in the second half of Book 10. But other patterns are at work as well. For example, the thematic motifs that accompany the progression of the argument are organized in symmetrical pairs around an apex: 1) An introductory book that precedes the beginning of the main argument. 2) An upward path in the form of an investigation in Books 2–4 of the rise of the city and the nature of justice. 3) At the apex a portrait in Books 5–7 of what Socrates calls the kallipolis (beautiful or noble city: 527c). 4) A downward path consisting of an investigation in Books 8–9 of the decline of the city and the nature of injustice. 5) A concluding book that follows the resolution of the main argument.

The symmetry between Books 1 and 10 is not limited to their negative quality of not being part of the main argument. Each book falls into two parts whose themes mirror the parts of the other. The first part of Book 1 and last part of Book 10 are both concerned with religious motifs and the connection between afterlife and virtue; and the last part of Book 1 and first part of Book 10 are both concerned with the production of the appearance of knowledge without the presence of actual knowledge. In the first case, the religious motifs at the beginning of Book 1 which culminate in Cephalus' remarks about his impending death and the importance of virtue for the afterlife (330d–e), are balanced at the end of Book 10 by the proof for the immortality of the soul followed by a depiction of the afterlife and the importance for it of virtue (608b–621d). In the second case, Socrates' confession, despite his apparently successful demonstration, that "the result of the discussion for me is that I know nothing" (354a), is mirrored by his contention in the first part of Book 10 that practitioners of the fine arts give the appearance of knowledge but in reality know least of all (e.g., 601a–b). The fine arts, like the art of polemical argument that was displayed in Book 1, provide only empty appearances. Glaucon's complaint that Socrates' arguments give the appearance of persuasiveness without the reality of persuasive reasons (357a–b) perfectly parallels what Socrates later says of the poets.

The narrative follows a symmetrical arc, rising through a consideration of the nature and origin of justice to a vision of the good itself, that reaches its peak in incommunicability (533a) before descending again through a consideration of the nature and origin of *injustice* to a conclusion that mirrors the beginning:

Table I.1

Book 1	Books 2–4	Books 5–7	Books 8–9	Book 10
a. Morality & afterlife	Rise of City; Justice	Best City	Decline of city; Injustice	a. Persuasion without knowledge (poetry)
b. Persuasion without knowledge (disputation)				b. Morality & afterlife

The *Republic* as a whole extends in both directions the ascending and descending trajectory of *noesis* (511b–c) generally, rising to and returning from *noesis* as *noesis* rises and returns within itself, even as in other respects the dialogue continually moves forward in its inquiry.

The modes of thinking through which the dialogue passes during its rise and return exemplify the different levels of thought processes classified under the Divided Line. We will see that Book 1 exemplifies *eikasia* (thinking in images about the visible world), Books 2–4 *pistis* (observing the visible world itself), Books 5–7 *dianoia* (images of the intelligible world) and as much of *noesis* (intellectual intuition) as can be put into words.[10] The progress from

Books 1 to 7 thus parallels the liberated prisoner's ascent to wisdom, while the philosopher's subsequent return to the cave is echoed by the second half of the dialogue, which returns from *noesis* to *dianoia* in Book 7, to *pistis* in Books 8–9, and to *eikasia* in Book 10. In these latter cases the higher forms are kept in view during the return to the lower ones, much as the philosopher-rulers keep their experience of true reality in mind when they descend again into the cave to govern. There was an innocence in the way *eikasia* is employed in Book 1, *pistis* in Books 2–4, and *dianoia* in Books 5–7—as if they were unaware of their own limitations—but the return to *dianoia* in Book 7 is made in the awareness of something higher, the return to *pistis* in Books 8–9 is explicitly regarded as a degeneration, and *eikasia* returns in Book 10 as the subject of intense criticism by contrast with the wisdom described in Books 6–7.

The *Republic*'s opening words, "I went down", are sometimes taken to be an allusion by Socrates to the philosopher's descent back into the cave in order to help the prisoners see the light. On the present interpretation it is not only a general allusion, but a precise reflection of the dialogue's beginning at the heart of the cave, *eikasia*; while the dialogue as a whole provides an image of the progress of the prisoners who ascend through stages to a vision of the ultimate principle and, transformed by that vision, return to the cave to benefit their successors.

Within this larger structure local structural principles permeate the argument at every level. The apparent casualness of the conversation is constantly underpinned by ordering patterns so that the narrative becomes an image of the world itself, in which the apparently random flow of becoming implicitly exhibits the ordered rationality of being (616b–617c).

Dialectic in the *Republic*

The great variety of subjects that the *Republic* traverses in pursuit of a single question illustrates the difference between Plato's approach to philosophy and that of almost every Western philosopher after him. Instead of mapping the territory of a particular subject matter, and remaining as far as possible within the boundaries of a single division of philosophy or science—logic, psychology, biology, physics, metaphysics, ethics, politics, poetry, rhetoric—Plato's Socrates speaks instead of following the argument wherever it leads, and it frequently leads across the borders that separate one philosophical discipline from another. Nowhere is that more true, or as true, as in the *Republic*. The governing concern of the *Republic* is moral theory, but its investigation takes the form of political theory (including along the way discussions of contract theory, eugenics, gender equality, and the family), which is then applied to psychology (the city is the soul writ large), along with extensive investigations into philosophy of art (music, poetry, and visual art), metaphysics, theory of knowledge, and religion.

Paradoxically, as we noted earlier, the *Republic* is not only the dialogue in which the breadth of Plato's scope is at its most expansive; it is also the dialogue which most emphatically insists on the benefits of a limited focus: the key to a healthy city is narrow specialization (370b), the key to justice is not to busy oneself with too many things (μὴ πολυπραγμονεῖν: 433a8–9), and the arts are reproached for their unrestricted subject matter (596d–e). But it is the approach of Aristotle's treatises and their successors, rather than Plato's dialogues, which reap the benefits of thematic specialization, specifically in the form of thoroughness of treatment and wealth of detail. It is not that Plato violates the principle that is recommended in the *Republic*, for specialization as it applies to philosophy means primarily that love of wisdom must not cross over into love of wealth or power; but he applies it only to philosophy's external relations to other pursuits and not to its internal distinctions. There is much to be gained by Plato's approach in panorama and synopsis, but also a price to be paid in thoroughness and detail. We can get a clearer sense of the advantages and limitations of Plato's method, both in general and with reference to the *Republic*, by examining his use of dialectic.

Together with his avoidance of strict specialization, Plato presented his philosophy not technically but contextually, varying his vocabulary and terms of reference from one dialogue to another in accordance with the question under consideration and the people participating in the discussion. For that reason we must be cautious about asking global questions like what Plato means by "dialectic", a term that he seems to have been the first to use.[11] From the following sampling of his use of the term *dialektikē* we can see that it has several different senses, whether disparate or complementary:

1. *Cratylus* 390c (cf. 398d): Dialectic means knowing how to ask and answer questions.

2. *Meno* 75d: Dialectic answers not only truly but also in terms of the admissions of the person being questioned.

3. *Republic* 532a–b (cf. 534b): Dialectic discerns the essence of each thing until it reaches the essence of the good itself.

4. *Republic* 533c–d. Dialectic overcomes the hypotheses of *dianoia* and progresses to the first principle.

5. *Republic* 537c: Someone who can see synoptically is a dialectician.

6. *Phaedrus* 266b–c: Practitioners of the methods of collection and division are dialecticians.

7. *Phaedrus* 276e: By means of dialectic we can implant intelligent words into suitable partners in conversation.

8. *Sophist* 253d: A dialectician divides according to classes and neither thinks that the same form is different or that a different form is the same.

9. *Sophist* 253e: Only someone who philosophizes with purity and justice can be a dialectician.

10. *Statesman* 285d: Employing the method of division to find the statesman also makes us better dialecticians generally.

11. *Philebus* 16e–17a: Dialecticians do not proceed from the one to the unlimited without taking note of all that lies between them.

These passages lend themselves to the following generalizations: a) In passages 1, 2, and 7 dialectic most has its original sense of a *dialogue between two people*, with the addition that it must be performed well. b) Passages 3 and 8 credit dialectic with *discerning the essence of things* (cf. *Statesman* 285a–b). c) In passages 3, 4, 5, 6, 8, 10, and 11 dialectic is understood as a *bridge between the one and the many*, either by ascending through intermediates to a first principle or by descending from a unifying principle through intermediates. d) According to passages 3 and 9 dialectic is *inseparable from goodness*.

In passage 3 we can see that all but the first of these four characteristics are present in the *Republic* (not necessarily in the same way that they are present in other dialogues) and are given the name dialectic there. Nothing that corresponds to the first characteristic is explicitly called dialectic in the *Republic*, but the procedure is present nevertheless. The kind of asking and answering that the *Meno* refers to in passage 1 is the Socratic elenchus, the distinctive style of refutation that Socrates regularly displays in the early dialogues.[12] Socrates begins by eliciting from his partner a definition of one of the virtues—justice, courage, piety, self-control,[13] wisdom or knowledge, or virtue itself—and then draws out what seem to be the inevitable consequences of that definition, combined with appeals to our normal intuitions, at the end of which an answer is reached that is the opposite of what was originally proposed. Unlike the usual form of refutation, elenchus does not merely lead to a conclusion that the proposed definition is too broad or too narrow (although such claims are made along the way) but that the very opposite of the original definition is the case.[14] As Adeimantus puts it: "when all their small concessions are added together at the end of the discussion, a great falsehood appears which contradicts what they said at first" (*Republic*, 487b). The most dramatic example is at the end of the *Protagoras*, when Socrates says:

It seems to me that the present outcome of our argument is accusing and ridiculing us as if it were human, and if it could acquire a voice it would say, "You are strange men, Socrates and Protagoras. You, on one hand, after saying previously that virtue is not teachable, now are eager to contradict yourself by trying to demonstrate that everything is knowledge—justice, self-control, and courage—in which case virtue would seem most of all to be teachable. . . . Protagoras, on the other hand, who at that time supposed that virtue was teachable, now seems eager to show on the contrary that it is almost anything rather than knowledge; and thus it would least of all be teachable". [361a–c]

If Socrates showed simply that a given definition was too narrow or too broad, the speaker would feel that all that was needed were some further adjustments. But by having the original definition lead imperceptibly to its own contradiction (here we return to the theme of contrast and opposition with which we began), Socrates produces not merely dissatisfaction with the original, but bewilderment. The elenchus is meant not simply to lead the other person to a better definition but to leave him at first with nothing at all, and the dialogues in which it is employed typically end in aporia or impasse. A question is raised to which the interlocutor thinks he knows the answer, but Socrates shows how the familiar answers lead to contradictions, and the dialogue comes to an end in perplexity. When Meno compares Socrates to a stingray that numbs its prey (*Meno*, 80a), Socrates replies that the first step in achieving true knowledge is when our false knowledge leads to an impasse from which we must seek a different way out (84a–c). If the negative aspect of the breakdown of the familiar is the discouraging feeling of being at an impasse, the positive aspect is the sense of wonder that may accompany it. Socrates says in the *Theaetetus*, "This feeling—wonder—very much pertains to philosophy. For there is no other beginning of philosophy than this" (155d).[15] Elenchus is the type of dialectic that Socrates employs throughout Book 1 in his refutations of Cephalus, Polemarchus, and Thrasymachus, although it is never called dialectic there; there is even some slight reason to hope that Thrasymachus may have been inspired with philosophical wonder, given the more favorable references to him later on (450a, 498c9–d1).

The elenchus is not only deconstructive, however; it provides more than perplexity and wonder. The elenctic dialogues leave us with an opposition whose paradoxical character invites us to find a way to reconcile the opposites by embracing them within a higher conception. In the case of the *Protagoras* passage cited above, for example, the contradiction within Socrates' position can be resolved within a higher conception of knowledge that embraces a species of knowing that is not teachable, one which is explicitly acknowledged in the *Republic* (533a) and may well be implicit in the *Protagoras*. The *Meno*, too, suggests that virtue can be taught only if it is a kind of knowledge (87c), but proceeds to argue not that virtue is a kind of knowledge but that it is a kind of wisdom (98d). The paradox of its aporetic conclusion points to a resolution in a higher conception of knowing that embraces and distinguishes between a knowledge that is teachable but does not entail virtue, and wisdom that is not teachable but does imply virtue.

In Book 1 of the *Republic* the distinctions that Socrates makes in the course of his refutations point toward positive doctrines that will be formulated in later books. When he refutes Cephalus by distinguishing a counterexample to the principle that we ought to pay what we owe and tell the truth, Polemarchus understands that what is necessary to resolve the contradiction is to distinguish between what is good and what is not good: we are obligated to repay good things that we owe but not harmful ones (332a), a distinction that points to the very heart of the *Republic*. His own reformulation runs into other kinds of difficulties, the most striking of which is that justice turns out to be a *techne*[16] of thievery (334b). That aporia is left unresolved, but Book 4 makes clear in retrospect that the elenchus turned on a failure to make a further distinction, between character and skill, or virtue and *techne*. In the case of Thrasymachus too there are multiple refutations, but the turning point is when Socrates forces him to make a distinction within the *techne* of ruling between the *techne* itself and payment received for it (345e–346e), a distinction that will figure importantly in the description of the lives of the philosopher-rulers.

The way that elenchus points toward distinctions provides common ground between it and the sense of dialectic that underlies the method of division.[17] The method of division makes explicit the implicit presupposition of elenchus that we can understand the subject of our inquiry by making appropriate distinctions. However, it proceeds systematically rather than ad hoc, and aims to provide not only a definition based on genus and differentia, but a genealogy of the concept sought that shows its location on a conceptual tree. The fundamental features of the tree are inclusion and opposition: a genus divides into species by the opposition introduced by the differentia (the genus of animals can be split into winged and non-winged), while in the reverse direction species are united within a genus that provides a common denominator (fliers and walkers are both animals). The method of division is never formulated in the *Republic*, although the technique of making progressive distinctions until the precise nature of the quarry has been specified is employed by Socrates in his progressive halving of the ground beneath Thrasymachus' feet until it becomes clear precisely where Thrasymachus stands.[18]

If the method of division is never explicitly present in the *Republic*, Socrates nevertheless shows great interest in the relation of opposition that is so fundamental to that method. In two places he uses the principle of opposition ("nothing can be precisely in opposition to itself") to divide apparent unities into opposed species in order to further his inquiry—namely in produc-ing the divisions of the tripartite soul and the primary division of the Divided Line. In the first case he employs the principle to distinguish oppositions between rationality and appetite, appetite and spiritedness, and spiritedness and rationality (436a–441c). In the second he employs it to distinguish a con-tradiction between the way a finger is perceived by the senses, as a coherent unity, and the way it is perceived by the mind, as an incoherent combination of apparently inconsistent relations—a contradiction that reveals the funda-mental opposition between physical and intelligible reality (523a–524c), which is the basis of the Divided Line. In a similar spirit the training that Par-menides prescribes to Socrates as a propaedeutic to defining "the beautiful, the just, the good, and every one of the forms" (*Parmenides* 135c) is a thirty-page meditation on opposition, the most sustained passage of abstract reasoning in the dialogues.

A related procedure in the *Republic*, but which moves in the opposite direction, is the sense of dialectic provided by the fifth passage above, that to be a dialectician is to see things synoptically. The dialectician moves from the axiom-governed special sciences like arithmetic, plane and solid geometry, astronomy, and harmony, and unifies them by moving from the least inclusive (arithmetic) to the more inclusive (astronomy and harmony) until they reach their fundamental unity in the Idea of the good (531a–532b). Nowhere are Plato's reasons more clear for preferring his synoptic approach, to the spe-cial sciences approach. At that point we can descend again from this unity by means of a higher version of the method of division, to see how the special forms proceed from it (511b–c).

The narrative organization of the *Republic* itself displays a progressive ascent through oppositions in the direction of greater inclusiveness, which is perhaps intended as a literary image of the *noetic* dialectic that Socrates just spoke of. 1) The dialogue begins with Cephalus' conception of justice ("tell the truth and pay what you owe") as something which benefits its practitioner, but which turns out to apply only in peaceful situations (331c). 2) When Cephalus' son Polemarchus defends his father's view, the resultant conception ("help friends and harm enemies") applies in war-like situations but not peace-ful ones (332e–333e). 3) When the examination of Polemarchus' view results in the conclusion that (in peacetime) we ought only to help others, not harm them, it leads to Thrasymachus' pronouncement that justice is always the good of another, and is therefore harmful to the practitioner and inferior to injustice (335b–d). 4) In reply Socrates argues that justice does indeed benefit its practitioner (and injustice harm its practitioner) because justice is the inner harmony of virtue while injustice is the disharmony of vice (353a,

443c–444b). We can see from this summary how the argument moves through a series of oppositions: from the positive pole of peace to the negative pole of war, from the positive pole of justice to the negative pole of injustice, and back again at a higher level from the negativity of injustice to the positivity of justice. What is especially striking is that the oppositions arose from an attempt to continue in the same direction: Polemarchus' intention of simply defending Cephalus led first to the reversal of Cephalus' peace-centered conception, and then to a reversal of Cephalus' belief that justice benefits its practitioner.

At the same time another kind of progression takes place. Cephalus and Polemarchus represent opposite poles of a deontological approach to the question of justice: one reduces justice to a rule that presupposes peace, the other to a rule that presupposes war. When Thrasymachus contemptuously dismisses all of the preceding discussion (336b–d) his contempt springs in part from the fact that his own views are based on consequentialism, and deontology strikes him as naïve (343a–344c). Socrates then transforms the terms of reference from Thrasymachus' consequentialism to virtue ethics. These three approaches to morality stand in mutual opposition like the three corners of a triangle: consequentialism looks to the results of an action, while deontology and virtue ethics look to the ground of it; deontology takes the form of an absolute command, while virtue ethics and consequentialism respond ad hoc to fluid situations; virtue ethics depends on imprecise criteria, while consequentialism and deontology depend on precise ones. The relation of these three oppositions in the *Republic* is not one of mutual exclusion but one of progressive inclusion. When Socrates turns from the consequentialism of Thrasymachus, which is revived by Glaucon and Adeimantus in Book 2, to virtue ethics, he assimilates consequentialism to virtue ethics by showing how the condition of virtue outweighs any other consequences.[19] Deontology has its place as well, most notably in the principle that we must each do our own work.[20] Rules and consequences are still relevant to the discussion, but they are no longer the governing principle. Even the particular rules proposed by Cephalus and Polemarchus are taken up into the larger narrative: Polemarchus' injunction to help friends and harm enemies becomes the basis of the warrior ethic of the original guardians (375b–c), and Cephalus' principle of paying what we owe becomes the basis for compelling the philosophers to take their turn as rulers (520a–d).

This kind of progression through opposition can be found in other dialogues as well,[21] and it helps account for the encyclopedic breadth of Plato's philosophy that led to Whitehead's famous characterization of the history of philosophy as a series of footnotes to Plato. We saw, for example, how within the first book alone different speakers advocate each of the three major species of prescriptive ethics: deontology, consequentialism, and virtue ethics. If Plato's expositions followed a linear path they still could have achieved a grandeur and depth, as Spinoza did in his *Ethics*, but they would be less likely to achieve the panoramic diversity that prompted Whitehead's hyperbole. Plato's expositions advance by tacking from side to side in a systematic meander, in the fashion of a serpentine river,[22] canvassing lateral territory as it moves forward.

More than a narrative strategy is involved, for the narrative strategy reflects Plato's conception of the way opposites naturally arise out of one another. The general principle was articulated in the *Phaedo*, in a provisional formulation that is later taken as established: "Let us examine whether it is necessary for everything that is opposite to something, that they come from nowhere else than from their opposite" (70e). In Book 8 of the *Republic* Socrates puts forward a version of that principle in order to explain how each type of constitution comes to be destroyed: "anything that is done to excess is wont to produce a correspondingly great opposite reaction" (562b–564a). In Book 1 he did not call attention to the reversals of direction that we have noted, except when they produced an elenchus (as at 334e3–4), but in Book 3, at the point in the city's ascent that corresponds to the point in its later decline where Socrates put forward the principle just quoted, he announces: "By the dog, without noticing, we have been purifying the city that we just said was luxurious (399e)". They had been allowing the city to grow in size and luxury as appetite continued to seek more and more varieties of gratification, but at some point the direction tacitly changed from indulgence and expansion to discipline and contraction.

The principle of reversal is now known as the "pendulum theory", but in the absence of pendulums Plato's model was the wheel. Every point on a wheel (κύκλος, cycle) alternates between moving forward and backward as the rim rotates and the wheel as a whole moves forward. This is the basis of the Greeks' cyclical view of history, and the metaphor that Socrates uses in describing both the growth and the decline of the city. In his description of its growth the metaphor emphasizes the forward motion of the wheel: "The regime, once it starts out well, proceeds like a wheel (κύκλος) in its growth", for sound nurturing and education produces better natures in the next generation (424a)—i.e., it is cyclical because each generation will be able to improve on the previous one as better nurturing produces better natures and better natures produce better nurturing. The notion of reversal implicit in the wheel metaphor becomes explicit when Socrates introduces the city's inevitable decline: "Not only for plants that grow in the earth but also for animals that live upon it, fruitfulness and barrenness in their soul and bodies come about when in each case the revolutions of their cycles (κύκλων) complete their orbits" (546a).[23]

Although the narrative dialectic of the *Republic* and the dialectic of the method of division both have their basis in the relation of opposition, they differ in two fundamental ways: the *Republic* passes through oppositions consecutively rather than displaying them concurrently as species within genera; and the *Republic* moves from partiality to inclusiveness while the method of division moves in the opposite direction. In two other ways, however, their purposes converge. First, passage 10 above, where the Eleatic visitor says in the *Statesman* that employing the method of division to find the statesman also makes us better dialecticians generally, suggests that there is more to the method of division than definitions; and passage 11 from the *Philebus* tells us what it is: "The wise among us today make a one and a many in a haphazard way, faster or slower than they ought to, going from the one directly to the unlimited. But they omit the intermediates, and it is they that make the difference between whether the discourse that we engage in with one another is dialectical or eristic". In other words, the purpose of dialectic, including the dialectic of the method of division, is to discover how each of the many stand in relation to the one, which is also the function of the *Republic's* synoptic dialectic (passage 5).

The second way that the method of division converges with the dialectic of the *Republic* may be seen from passage 9: "You will certainly not grant that the activity of dialectic belongs to anyone who does not philosophize with purity and justice". If all that were at stake in the methodology of the *Sophist* were definition and classification there would be no need for this stipulation; people's moral character does not enter into their ability to distinguish species within genera. The suspicion aroused by this remark, that there is something more to the nature of dialectic than what we are being shown in the *Sophist*, is confirmed in the *Statesman* when the Eleatic visitor says that there is something about the method of division that he is not able to explain to them (262c). The fullest description of dialectic that Socrates gives in the *Republic* does have a unifying upward component and a diversifying downward component that may represent the highest level of the kind of thinking that the method of collection and division is meant to instill in us. He says that dialectic uses the hypotheses of the special sciences mentioned above, as stepping-stones "to reach the unhypothetical first principle of everything. Having grasped it, it once again hangs onto the things that depend from it, and proceeds downward to a conclusion, making use of nothing at all visible but only of forms themselves, from them to them, and concludes in forms" (511b–c).

The *Republic* presents this conception not as a doctrine but as a goal. It cannot be a finished doctrine, partly because of human limitations and partly because what is experienced cannot be put into words. In the first instance Socrates insists that he does not understand these things himself, and can do no better than offer tentative opinions about them like a blind man who might hit upon the right road (506b–e). And in the second, when Glaucon asks him to explain how this power of dialectic functions, what species it falls into, and what paths it follows, Socrates replies:

> You will no longer be able, my dear Glaucon, to follow me, although for my part I would not willingly omit anything. But you would no longer see an image of what we are saying, but the truth itself. . . . And the power of dialectic alone can reveal it to someone who is experienced in the things we just went through, and it is not possible in any other way. [533a]

It may be that the method of division that is introduced in the *Phaedrus* is, among other things, a propaedeutic for the kind of thinking by which we can proceed from a vision of the Idea of the good to all the other forms. But the actual state of mind for which it is a preparation could no more be put into words in the *Phaedrus* (276e–277a) or the *Statesman* (262c) than it could in the *Republic*.

The aporetic character of Platonic philosophy is evident not only in Plato's refusal to declare any teachings in his own name, but also in his representation of Socrates, the main speaker in most of the dialogues, as insisting on his own ignorance (e.g., *Republic* 506b–e). Plato further undermines Socrates' authority by showing how little Socrates' own audience is convinced by him. Simmias still has reservations at the end of the proofs of immortality in the *Phaedo*, and others are openly skeptical or even hostile to what Socrates says—Philebus, Meno, Anytus, Callicles, Polus, Gorgias, Protagoras, and Thrasymachus, among others. In fact, Plato has members of Socrates' audience cast doubt not only on Socrates' conclusions but on the very reliability of his methods. He has Callicles tell Socrates that most people distrust what Socrates says: "Somehow what you say *appears* to be right, Socrates, but I feel the way most people do: I'm not really convinced by you" (*Gorgias* 513c). Not only Callicles, but "most people" think Socrates' arguments only appear convincing, and ultimately lack credibility. We might take this to reflect on *hoi polloi* ("most people") rather than on Socrates, but in the middle of the *Republic* Plato puts the same charge into the mouth of his own half-brother Adeimantus, who unlike Callicles is sympathetic to the conclusions that Socrates is trying to establish. Adeimantus says:

No one, Socrates, could contradict the things you say, but on each occasion that you say them your hearers are affected in some such way as this: they think that because of their inexperience in asking and answering questions they are led astray by the argument, a little at each of your questions, and when all their small concessions are added together at the end of the discussion, a great fallacy appears which contradicts what they said at first. Just as inexperienced checkers players are in the end trapped by the experts and can't make a move, so they too are trapped in the end and have nothing they can say in this different kind of checkers which is played not with counters but with words; yet they don't believe the conclusion to be in any way more true for that. [487b–c]

To have one's characters repeatedly express doubts about the tactics and persuasiveness of one's "spokesperson" is not the mark of an author who wants us to regard his writings as established doctrine. If such disclaimers mean that Plato cannot be regarded as a foundationalist, the intensity and thoroughness with which the ideas are presented shows that they are nevertheless meant to be taken very seriously. What it means to take them seriously without taking them as foundational is something that we shall have to discover in the course of pursuing their implications.

Notes

1. Cf. Grace Hadley Billings: "One of Plato's favorite methods of developing a theme [is that a] partial or superficial view of the subject is first presented, only to be superseded or supplemented by further discussion. The *Republic* [is among the] notable examples of this method" (*The Art of Transition in Plato* [Menasha, Wis.: George Banta, 1920]: 21 & n64).

2. All translations are mine unless otherwise stated.

3. The view that Book 1 was originally an independent dialogue has been especially prominent in the German tradition, which often refers to it as the *Thrasymachus*, but the view is by no means limited to that tradition and has been persistent. Already in 1920 Billings believed that "The philosophic and structural unity of the *Republic*, attacked by Hermann, Krohn, Pfleiderer, Rohde, and other German scholars has been established beyond a doubt by the arguments of Hirmer, Zeller, and Campbell" (1920, 33); but the attack has continued nevertheless. Holger Theleff, for example, writes, "surely we underrate Plato if we consider him unable to transform a separate sketch into an introduction" (*Studies in Platonic Chronology* [Helsinki: Societas Scientiarum Fennica, 1982], 107; cf. 137–39, 185–86). Paul Friedländer thinks it is "practically certain" that it was an earlier dialogue—"an assumption few would question today" (*Plato*, vol. 3, 1969 [1960] 63, cf. vol. 2, 1964 [1957] ch. 3)—and cites support for it going back to Schleiermacher, although he also mentions the disagreement of others. A. E. Taylor, on the other hand, regards the hypothesis as "fanciful"

and "inconceivable" (*Plato: The Man and His Work*, 6th Edition [Cleveland: World, 1956 (1926)], 264). Others who share Friedländer's view include Hans-Georg Gadamer ("Plato's Educational State" [1942], in Gadamer, *Dialogue and Dialectic* [New Haven: Yale University Press, 1980], 77); Gregory Vlastos (*Socrates, Ironist and Moral Philosopher* [Ithaca: Cornell University Press, 1991], 248–51); and Debra Nails (*The People of Plato: A Prosopography of Plato and Other Socratics* [Indianapolis: Hackett, 2002], 324). Those who, like Billings and Taylor, reject it include Charles Kahn (Review of Gilbert Ryle's *Plato's Progress*, *Journal of Philosophy* 1968: 368), W. K. C. Guthrie (*A History of Greek Philosophy* Vol. 4 [Cambridge: Cambridge University Press, 1975], 437), C. D. C. Reeve (*Philosopher Kings: The Argument of Plato's Republic* [Princeton: Princeton University Press, 1988], xi–xii), and Terence Irwin (*Plato's Ethics* [Oxford: Oxford University Press, 1995]), who suggests that "Book I sketches some of the conclusions that Plato means to defend; the rest of the *Republic* should show us how he means to defend them" (169). For Friedländer's acknowledgement that the "*Thrasymachus*" must have been revised see 1964, 2.63 & n15. The most obvious revisions would be the passages at 327a–328b and 347a–348b which feature Glaucon, who is prominent in Books 2–10, and who was presumably added to Book 1 to integrate it with what followed. Friedländer (following Pohlenz and von Arnim) believes that at least the latter passage betrays signs of being a later insertion. This is disputed by Thesleff (*Studies in the Styles of Plato* [Helsinki: Societas Philosophica Fennica, 1967], 97n1), who does not however deny that a revision took place, and suggests that the organization of Book 1 around 345b–348b, which "resembles a visionary central section . . . may be a further indication that book 1 was originally a separate work" (113).

4. For convenience I adopt the usual dating of the dialogues, but my conclusions would not be affected by alternative chronologies.

5. According to A. E. Taylor, that is how Henry Jackson and R. D. Archer-Hind respond to the fact that no reference is made to the doctrines of the middle books when the *Republic* is summarized at the beginning of the *Timaeus* (*A Commentary on Plato's Timaeus* [Oxford: Clarendon Press, 1928], p. 27). Also see R. L. Nettleship, *Lectures on the Republic of Plato*, 2nd edition (London: Macmillan, 1964 [1901]), 162, and Shorey 1937, 424 note c.

6. Cf. G. R. F Ferrari's attempt to supply what is missing and develop an individual parallel as far possible (*City and Soul in Plato's Republic* [Sankt Augustin: Academia Verlag, 2003], 110).

7. The most sustained attempt to show that the *Republic* is intended to represent *only* the soul writ large, and *not at all* political theory, is made by Robert Hoerber (*The Theme of Plato's Republic* [St. Louis: Washington University, 1944]), but even Hoerber does not claim any strict correspondence between the Three Waves and features of the soul. He only makes the general connection that the denial to the rulers, of private property, wives, and children, is to illustrate the principle that the "desires and pleasures of the appetitive element are not to influence the rational and high-spirited elements of the soul" (113), and to prepare "for the deduction that true happiness exists apart from the domination of desire and pleasure" (115). As for the require-

ment that women rule equally with men, Hoerber regards this as a reductio ad absurdum to show that the political dimension is not to be taken seriously (34–45). The equality of the sexes in the ruling class could have had a parallel in the soul only if Plato had distinguished masculine and feminine elements within the rational part (cf. Drew Hyland, "Plato's Three Waves and the Question of Utopia", *Interpretation* 18 [1990]: 91–109, esp. 107).

8. See, for example, Annas 1981, 335; Thesleff 1982, 185–86; and Gerald Else, *The Structure and Date of Book 10 of Plato's Republic* (Heidelberg: Carl Winter, 1972), 55–56. Alternatively, the reemergence of the subject of art has been ascribed to the carelessness of Plato's Alexandrian editors (Dennis Rohatyn, "Struktur und Funktion in Buch X von Platons Staat: Ein Überblick", *Gymnasium* 82 [1975]: 314–30, esp. 315).

9. The metaphor of a pediment, which has the advantage of not being anachronistic, is used by Thesleff 1982 (101) and Robert Brumbaugh, *Platonic Studies of Greek Philosophy* (Albany, N.Y.: SUNY Press, 1989) 20–21. Eva Brann employs the comparable metaphor of concentric circles ("The Music of the *Republic*", Agon 1 [1967] i–vi, 1–117: 2).

10. These terms will be discussed in chapter 6, 191–99.

11. See Charles Kahn, *Plato and the Socratic Dialogue: The Philosophical Use of a Literary Form* (Cambridge: Cambridge University Press, 1996), 325 & n52.

12. As Richard Robinson puts it, "It is so common in the early dialogues that we may almost say that Socrates never talks to anyone without refuting him" (*Plato's Earlier Dialectic*, 2nd edition [Oxford: Clarendon Press, 1953], 7). Surprisingly, Robinson's example of an exception is Cephalus, who is not only refuted but refuted in record time—perhaps it is the speed of his undoing that makes him seem an exception.

13. *Sōphrosunē*, commonly translated also as "moderation" or "temperance".

14. Cf. R. Robinson: "But at last Socrates says: 'Come now, let us add our admissions together' (*Prt.* 332D); and the result of doing so turns out to be the contradictory of the primary answer" (1953, 7).

15. Cf. Aristotle *Metaphysics* 982b12–27. Also R. Robinson: "The aim of the elenchus is not to switch a man from an opinion that happens to be false to an opinion that happens to be true. . . . The aim of the elenchus is to wake men out of their dogmatic slumbers into genuine intellectual curiosity" (1953, 17).

16. I prefer to leave the term *techne* untranslated because it has a range of meanings that no single English term can encompass—including art, skill, craft, and science—and plays a central role in the dialogue.

17. See above, passages 6, 8, 10, and 11.

18. See the table on page 35.

19. 613c–e, cf. 516d, 580a, 591a.

20. 370b, cf. 433a, 442e–443a, 551e, 554d, etc.

21. In the *Phaedo*, for example, Socrates defends the paradox that death is superior to life because only then can the soul fulfill its vocation of beholding truth unobstructed by the body, but suicide is wrong because we are servants of the gods and ought not to deprive them of our service; Cebes replies that Socrates' defense leads to

the opposite conclusion: if we are servants of the gods it makes no sense to praise death over life, since gods are the best possible masters. Socrates reconciles the opposites by saying that after death we will be subject to gods who are no less good than the ones here (62b–66d). Again, each of the speeches of the *Symposium*, although presented in an apparently haphazard order, conveys a view that either stands in contradiction to its predecessor or else reconciles a previous opposition. In the first speech, Phaedrus praises justice in terms of self-sacrifice, and is followed by Pausanias, for whom its value lies not in self-sacrifice but self-interest. Eryximachus follows these one-sided oppositions with a speech according to which the value of eros lies in its power to reconcile opposites. In the next speech too, that of Aristophanes, eros is a reconciling power; but where Eryximachus saw it as a corporeal force, Aristophanes portrays it as a spiritual one, piety. Agathon's speech, which follows, includes key aspects of all the previous speeches but opposes Aristophanes' divine-centered conception of virtue as piety with a human-centered conception of virtue as wisdom. Socrates explicitly rejects this in the next speech, and takes a position midway between Aristophanes' piety and Agathon's wisdom, by choosing a model of virtue that is in between them, namely of love of wisdom. For details see my article, "A Dual Dialectic in Plato's *Symposium*" (*Philosophy and Rhetoric* 25 [1992]: 253–70). Rosemary Desjardins discusses a different way that Plato uses the tension between opposites to evoke a higher unity (*Plato and the Good: Illuminating the Darkling Vision* [Leiden: Brill, 2004], 120–27).

22. The term comes from the Maiandros (Menderes) river.

23. Brumbaugh connects Socrates' reference to cycles in the growth and decline of the city with the cosmic cycles of the Myth of Er (*Plato's Mathematical Imagination* [Bloomington: Indiana University Press, 1954], 193).

CHAPTER ONE

~

Theories of Justice
(Book 1)

The Opening Scene (327a–328b)

The opening words of the *Republic*, "I went down to the Piraeus yesterday", have given rise to two questions: why the Piraeus, and whether the first three words allude to the philosopher's descent back into the cave in Book 7 to lead the prisoners out. Plato's unusual choice of the port settlement of Piraeus as the location of the *Republic* may be intended as a counterpart to the Myth of Er at the end of the dialogue, where the souls of the dead debark and embark from one life to the next. Since the myth functions as a kind of microcosm of the dialogue as a whole, as we shall see, Plato may have situated the dialogue in a place of transit beyond the city walls to allude to one in a different kind of beyond.[1] As to whether Plato is here alluding to the philosopher's return to the cave, that possibility becomes attractive when we notice that the kind of argumentation in Book 1 matches the later description of the kind of thinking that the cave represents as *eikasia* or "likelihood", the lowest of the four stages of the Divided Line. In the course of the first seven books of the *Republic* we will find Socrates leading his audience upward though all four stages.

The theme of an ascent from the darkness of the cave to the illumination of the sun is implicit not only in the levels of argumentation from Books 1 to 7, but also in the contrast between the dialogue's beginning and its end. The *Republic* begins and ends with references to goddesses, but the nature of goddesses is quite different on the two occasions. At the beginning Socrates has gone down to Piraeus to witness the first Athenian celebration of the Thracian goddess Bendis, who was worshipped with orgiastic rites similar to those of Dionysus,[2] and on this occasion an all-night festival with a torch race on horseback (328a). The goddesses at the end of the dialogue in the myth of Er are the Sirens and the Fates, who sing the harmony of the spheres, and Necessity the mother of the Fates, all of whom are in the midst of a brilliant light that stretches through heaven and earth (616b–617d). Not only does the dialogue move, then, from a goddess who is associated with the orgiastic rites of the appetites, to goddesses associated with the harmony of rational necessity; but just as in the allegory of the cave we move from the artificial firelight that illuminates the cave to the natural light that is the source of all being, so the dialogue itself moves from a goddess associated with the artificial firelight of torches to one associated with the natural light of the heavens.[3] In a dramaturgical parallel to all this, the conversation itself continues through the night and sees the dawn of the new day (the recitation alone would take some fourteen hours to read aloud).[4]

The four main speakers in Book 1—Socrates, Cephalus, Polemarchus, and Thrasymachus—have clearly been chosen with care. Their basic characters are sharply delineated and distinguished from one another, and their views are carefully matched to their characters. The complacent and comfortable Cephalus defends a view of justice that proves incompatible with violence, while his aggressive son Polemarchus defends one that is hard to reconcile with peaceful situations, and the self-aggrandizing Thrasymachus extols the self-aggrandizing qualities of *injustice*. The principle underlying the choice of those four types of speaker does not emerge until Book 4, when Socrates distinguishes the tripartite classification of character types. The first three speakers—Cephalus, Polemarchus, and Socrates—represent the appetitive, spirited, and rational types of person distinguished there, while the fourth speaker, Thrasymachus, is a counterpart to Socrates in another way, as the unjust stands in relation to the just. His faculty of reason is highly developed, but rather than ruling in him as it does in Socrates, Thrasymachus regards rationality[5] as an instrument to serve our appetites. Thrasymachus and Socrates anticipate the two types that Glaucon and Adeimantus will challenge Socrates to compare with regard to the happiness of their lives.

Cephalus (328b–331d)

Cephalus is wealthy (329e), eager to make sacrifices to the gods (328c, 331d), and glad to converse with Socrates (328c–d). At first it seems conceivable that he might belong to any of the three classes that will later be distinguished: as a money-maker he would fit in with the appetitive class; but since he is wealthy he might be a spirited, competitive money-maker for whom, like Thrasymachus, wealth is a means to power; while his devotion to the divine and to Socrates' conversation may mark him as a lover of truth. He turns out to be not very spirited, however, and makes an excuse to leave the first time Socrates challenges him (331d). His wealth was due not to any ambitious enterprise on his own part, but to that of his grandfather, and he himself added only slightly to what he inherited (330b). As for his apparent devotion to truth, not only does he escape as soon as Socrates tries to make him think, but he readily admits that the only reason he is interested in Socrates' conversation is that he has become too old to enjoy the physical pleasures that he used to pursue. Conversation is for him not a means to discover truth, but a kind of pleasure for which we can develop an appetite when other appetites fail: "as the bodily pleasures wither away, the appetites and pleasures of conversation increase to the same extent" (328c–d).[6] Nevertheless he does not regret the loss of his youthful appetites the way others might, but agrees with Sophocles that it is not so much a loss as "an escape from a frenzied and savage master"—although his replacement of Sophocles' singular "master" with the plural "very many raving masters" seems to mark him as more appetitive than Sophocles (329c4–d1). The story that Plato has him tell about Sophocles concerns sexual appetite in particular, and so ushers in the theme of eros that will figure so importantly throughout the dialogue[7] (although it never becomes the focus of attention as in the *Symposium* and *Phaedrus*). In fact, the difference between the just and the unjust person will turn out to be expressible in terms of the direction in which their eros is turned.[8]

Everything about Cephalus points to a man of appetite. Even his piety results not from a love of the divine but from fear of the painful punishments that might otherwise await him in the afterlife (330d–e). That fear is what convinces him of the importance of avoiding injustice, and what he most values in wealth is that it gives us peace by enabling us to avoid having to deceive anyone or cheat a person or god of their due. It allows us to die in peace without owing money to any person or a sacrifice to any god (331a–b). This is justice as it appears within an appetitive life—justice as a way of avoiding pain and as a money-maker's balance sheet. Is that what it means to be a just person, Socrates asks, to tell the truth and repay whatever we have received from someone? If someone lends us weapons when he is in his right mind and wants them back when he is raving mad, a just person would neither return them nor tell him the whole truth (331c). Cephalus agrees, and when his son Polemarchus steps in to help his father, Cephalus makes his escape.[9]

Polemarchus (327a–328a, 331d–336a)

In keeping with his name, Polemarchus (War Leader)[10] is portrayed as intimidating and belligerent. When he sees Socrates he decides to bring him home for what might be called a command performance: rather than calling out to him and inviting him back to his house, Polemarchus orders (ἐκέλευσε) his slave to insist (κελεῦσαι) that Socrates to wait for him. "Polemarchus insists (κελεύει) that you wait", says the slave, after getting Socrates' attention not by calling his name but by insolently grabbing his cloak from behind (327b). This technique, we later discover, he learned from his master who employs it to get Adeimantus' attention (449b). When Polemarchus catches up with Socrates, rather than inviting Socrates to stay and visit, Polemarchus points out how many people he has with him and tells Socrates that unless Socrates thinks he can overpower them he has no choice but to stay. However jocular this may be, it is a heavy-handed jocularity and it tells us something about Polemarchus' nature. When Socrates replies that persuasion might be another way for him to get Polemarchus to let him leave, Polemarchus merely says, "Can you persuade someone who won't listen?"[11] If Polemarchus cannot be persuaded, Socrates can; and when Adeimantus mentions the torch race on horseback in honor of Bendis, Socrates agrees that that will be worth staying for (327c–328a).[12] Plato's handling of this episode leaves us with the impression of a spirited personality who is not interested in listening to reason when he is in a strong enough position to get his way without it. He may seem at first to be associated with appetite because he begins by defending his father's appetitive definition of justice, but the definition soon evolves into one that is modeled on wars and alliances (332e), and after Socrates refutes that one as well, Polemarchus pronounces himself ready to be Socrates' "ally in battle" (335e).[13]

Polemarchus begins by pointing out that the poet Simonides attested to Cephalus' conception of justice when he said that it is just to give everyone what is owed to them (331e). But Simonides could not have meant it is just to return a weapon to someone in a rage, Socrates points out, and Polemarchus agrees. What Simonides really meant by "what is owed", Polemarchus concludes, is that what is owed to friends is something good and what is owed to enemies something bad, so justice means helping friends and harming enemies (332a–b, d). In introducing the concept of goodness to rescue his father from Socrates' counterexample, Polemarchus has correctly grasped the distinction that Cephalus failed to make (and anticipated the heart of the dialogue), but Socrates will soon show Polemarchus the difficulties involved in applying that concept within the present terms of reference.

Socrates' refutation of Polemarchus is far more elaborate than that of Cephalus. We are given four arguments that appear to follow each other in a casual way, but each of which is really an elucidation of its predecessor.

First Argument (332c–333e)

The first argument takes a familiar form that Socrates employs when he wants to deny the status of knowledge to something which, like poetry or rhetoric, lacks a specialized subject matter.[14] In such cases Socrates points out that for any claim to knowledge that one ascribes to the *techne* in question (for example, a poet's knowledge of warfare), there is always a specialized *techne* which has a greater claim to that knowledge (such as a general's knowledge of warfare). In the present case he asks what the *techne* of justice can do to help friends and harm enemies (332c–d). When Polemarchus maintains that the just person is most able to benefit friends and harm enemies in wars and alliances, Socrates asks him whether justice is therefore useless in peacetime. Polemarchus thinks it must be useful in peacetime as well, but Socrates points out that for every peacetime occupation there is always some kind of knowledge that can help friends and harm enemies better than justice can: for example, when buying a horse it is more helpful to consult a horse breeder than a just person. The just person turns out by default to be someone we can trust to keep our money safe when we are not using it, and nothing more. "Justice can't be worth much then, if it turns out to be useful only for useless things" (333e). Only in war does this kind of justice seem to have any value. It may seem odd that Socrates raised these objections about the peacetime uses of justice, but was willing to accept Polemarchus' claim that in war the just person could help friends and harm enemies by making alliances with friends and fighting against enemies. After all, Socrates could have raised the same kind of objection against this answer: "Who is better at harming the enemy a just man or an archer?" etc. Specialized *technai* like diplomacy, military strategy, horsemanship, archery, and swordsmanship can do more to help friends and harm enemies than can justice. Nevertheless it seems reasonable to say that in war it is clearer what we must do to help our friends and harm our enemies than it is in peacetime. Polemarchus' conception of justice, then, is suited to the portrait of him as spirited and aggressive.

It has often been noted that the definitions of Cephalus and Polemarchus, although they begin as identical, end up as opposites, the former plausible in peacetime but not in war, and the latter in war but not in peacetime. As we saw in the Introduction, it is common in Plato for an argument to progress by turning into its opposite and then turning back again, but in this case something else may be at work as well. Cephalus' definition goes too far in one direction, making justice function in peaceful but not violent situations, while Polemarchus' definition goes too far in the opposite direction. In view of the fact that justice will finally turn out to be a mean between extremes (619a), Plato may be signaling at the outset that conceptions of justice may miss the mark by going to one extreme or the other, and that, by implication, justice itself is a kind of mean—although it will not turn out to be a mean between the kinds of conceptions that Cephalus and Polemarchus offer, since both attempt to reduce justice to rules.

Second Argument (333e–334b)

The next argument is presented as an additional refutation, but it also gives us the clue to a weakness in the first argument. Socrates points out through a series of examples that a *techne* can be used either to help or to harm. For example, boxing teaches us to defend against blows as well as land them, and medicine enables us to make people sick as well as cure them. If justice enables us to keep other people's money safe, therefore, it must enable us to steal it, to keep it from them as well as to keep it for them. "The just person, it seems, has turned out to be a kind of thief, then".[15] The conclusion seems hyperbolic at first, since the reasoning implies only that justice makes thievery possible, not that it makes it actual. But since on Polemarchus' account justice means harming enemies as well as helping friends, it must do harm as well as good. The *techne* of holding money must not only involve taking possession of our friends' money in a way that helps them, but also taking possession of our enemies' money in a way that harms them. The just person must be a thief as well as a trustworthy repository, and Polemarchus can only reply that he no longer knows what he meant.

The general form of the argument is:
a) The same *techne* is used to help or to harm.
b) Justice is the *techne* of keeping money.
c) ∴ A just person keeps money in a harmful way as well as a helpful one, i.e., is a thief.

As is often noted, the problem arises with the second premise, which is doubly false: justice does not mean keeping money safe, and justice is not a *techne*. In fact, the argument is partly a reductio ad absurdum to demonstrate that justice cannot be a *techne*.[16]

It was Socrates rather than Polemarchus who called justice a *techne*, but Polemarchus did not object (332c–d), and his conception of justice as something which is equally capable of helping and harming fit the model of *techne* that Socrates proposes. Both Cephalus and Polemarchus had treated justice as a *techne*, something that could be attained by learning appropriate rules like "Tell the truth and pay your debts" or "Help your friends and harm your enemies", but whenever we try to reduce justice to one or more simple rules we can always find counterexamples to belie the universality of the rules. And now we are shown that if it really were a *techne* justice could be harmful in ways that neither Polemarchus nor we are willing to accept. It seems clear from all this that justice cannot be a *techne*, or at least not a *techne* that consists of the straightforward application of precise rules. But when we reach the discussion with Thrasymachus we will find that the relationship between justice and *techne* is more complicated.

Third Argument (334c–335a)

The conclusion of the second argument was counterintuitive but not impossible. People who believe that they have enemies who are unfairly exploiting them might well think that justice demands that they steal from their enemies to get even, and that a just person would be a thief in such cases. The third argument will show that the conception of justice as a *techne* is not only counterintuitive in its consequences, but impossible in principle. In a line of questioning that will reappear in his interrogation of Thrasymachus, Socrates asks whether "friends" means those who appear to be good for us or those who really are so, and similarly with "enemies". When Polemarchus says it means those who appear to be good, Socrates points out that we often make mistakes about whether people are beneficial to us or not. In such cases, when we misidentify our friends and enemies, the definition requires us to help our enemies who appeared to be our friends, and harm our friends who appeared to be our enemies. Faced with this reductio Polemarchus agrees that perhaps justice means helping just people whether or not they are our friends, and harming unjust people whether or not they are our enemies, but Socrates points out that in that case Simonides was wrong to conceive justice as helping friends and harming enemies.[17] Polemarchus realizes that these difficulties resulted from distinguishing between "friends" and "good people", that is, apparent friends and real friends, and so he now rejects the distinction and says that friends are those who both appear to be and really are good, and the reverse with enemies.

Instead of replying to Polemarchus' new formulation, Socrates introduces a new question: "Is it proper then for a just person to harm anyone at all?" Why did Socrates not respond to Polemarchus' new suggestion? The appropriate response to it is obvious: since Polemarchus agreed that we often make mistakes about whether someone is truly good for us, then it is impossible for us to reliably identify when our apparent friends—those who appear to be good for us—really are so, and we can never know whether to help them or harm them. We now see why justice cannot be a *techne* in the usual sense. Human beings are not completely knowable; unlike the materials of a carpenter, for example, they practice deception and behave foolishly, so they are always to some extent unpredictable, like the man in Socrates' counterexample against Cephalus, who lent a weapon when he was sane but wanted it back when he was raging. The clearest evidence for the unpredictability of human nature is our inability to reliably identify our true friends and enemies. If *techne* as normally understood is the application of universal rules in a predictable way, the theater of human action in which justice plays its role cannot adequately be addressed by *techne*.

Fourth Argument (335b–e)

Socrates' new question, whether it is ever proper for a just person to do harm, could have been posed at the very beginning of the discussion, as soon as Polemarchus spoke of harming enemies. But in that case the argument would have bypassed the discussion by which Socrates established why justice cannot be a *techne*. By saving this point until now, it takes on broader implications than if it had been raised earlier.

The first argument focused only on the difficulty of explaining how in peacetime justice can help our friends, while the next two arguments displayed tensions that arise from trying to satisfy both parts of Polemarchus' definition. The final argument balances the first by showing that the concept of harming enemies in peacetime is as problematic as that of helping friends. The power of the second refutation as a reductio ad absurdum followed from our belief that justice can never be harmful, and so a just person cannot be a thief; but the belief that justice can never do harm was an unexamined intuition which, as we saw, others do not always share. The final refutation will examine and justify that belief. At the same time it introduces a theme that figures prominently throughout the *Republic*—including the proof for immortality near the end of Book 10—the idea that every kind of thing has its characteristic way of being (i.e., its function) and has excellence or virtue to the extent that it functions well in that respect.

To harm, Socrates says, means to make something worse, that is, to reduce its excellence (ἀρετή); so to harm a person is to make that person worse in human excellence or virtue (ἀρετή). But the function of goodness is the opposite of harm, and a just person is good, so the function of a just person is the opposite of harming, and justice cannot mean harming enemies, at least not in peacetime. Just as "it is not the function of heat to make cold, but of its opposite; . . . and it is not the function of dryness to make wet, but its opposite; . . . it is not then the function of a just person to inflict harm, Polemarchus, neither on a friend nor an enemy, but of the opposite, an unjust person" (335d–e). That does not mean we cannot punish wrongdoers, but we must conceive the punishment as a means of reforming them or setting an example for others, or even disabling destructive behavior, but not as retribution. Just as moralists may tell us to condemn the deed but not the doer, here we may think of undermining a course of action, but not undermining a human being.[18] At the end of Book 9 Socrates will emphasize the importance of punishing wrongdoers, and will explain that, far from harming them, the punishment will help them by making them better people (591a–b).

Those who believe in retributive justice would have no reason to accept Socrates' identification of justice with helping. They could reply that the purpose of justice is to exact retribution on evildoers, and whether the person punished becomes more or less virtuous as a result is irrelevant. They could substitute other analogies for Socrates' analogy with cold and wetness: just as what is colored does not make other things colored, and what is hard does not make other things hard, there is no reason why a good person should make other people good.

As with most of the conclusions in Book 1, adequate premises must wait for the later books. In Book 3 Socrates says that only those can be entrusted with the care of the city who love the city as they love themselves, and make no distinction between what is good for the city and for themselves (412d); accordingly, in what follows Socrates institutes ever stricter measures to deny to the rulers property of any kind, including families, to prevent them from distinguishing their personal good from that of the city. If good and just people are those who perceive their own good as inseparable from what is good for the whole, and thus for other people, rather being in competition with them, then goodness and justice would indeed automatically extend themselves to the welfare of others, and Socrates' analogy with cold and water would be vindicated. Socrates goes on to narrate two myths that break down the citizens' sense of the discreteness of themselves and their good. In the Myth of the Metals he tells them that they all constitute a single family with common interests (414d–e), and in the Myth of Er the doctrine of reincarnation treats the souls of all things as interchangeable: one person becomes another, and members of any species can become members of any other species (617d–620d).[19] If wisdom necessarily perceives the connectedness between ourselves and others, and justice necessarily includes wisdom (443c–e), then it belongs to the nature of just people to seek other people's welfare. The myths are an improvement over the arguments from analogy insofar as they give us a persuasive image of the connection which the analogies with cold and wetness merely presuppose, but the Socrates who proposes the Divided Line can never be satisfied with images. His purely philosophical justification for the present conception of justice will have its basis in the universalizing quality of rationality, which is the basis of justice and which abstracts from all individual differences.

When Socrates says that just people would never harm anyone, is he only rejecting Polemarchus' claim that justice entails harming our enemies, or is he rejecting the very distinction between friends and enemies, and implying that we should not think of anyone as our enemy at all? Once again the problem must be limited to peacetime, for it is never suggested that killing enemies in wartime is unjust, despite the fact that killing people certainly makes them less capable of human virtue. When the guardian city is established one of the qualities looked for in the guardians is that they be gentle to their friends and harsh to their enemies in order that the city may survive (375b–c). If the just person is not to harm enemies in peacetime, is it because we should seek to help people even when they are our enemy, or because the concept of enemy has no place in peacetime at all? In Book 6 when Adeimantus suggests that Thrasymachus would disagree with what Socrates is saying, Socrates replies, "Don't slander Thrasymachus and me, who have just become friends, and we weren't enemies before either" (498c). It is a puzzling remark, for if the advocate of justice and the advocate of injustice were not enemies, what were they? What could "enemies" mean if not those who are diametrically opposed about the most fundamental issues of life? The answer is that the just person in peacetime does not think in terms of enemies at all, but thinks of everyone as a friend, as someone to be helped. Socrates does not disagree with Thrasymachus' claim that to be just is to benefit others. Not even the men who prosecuted Socrates to his death are his enemies. It is not necessary to read Socrates ironically when he addresses Meletus as "my friend" (ὦ φίλε Μέλητε: *Apology* 26d).

Thrasymachus' Defense of Injustice (336b–347e)

The dialogue proper began with Cephalus' claim that a) being just is beneficial to the just person because it leads to rewards instead of punishment in the afterlife, and b) justice consists in telling the truth and paying what we owe (330d–331b). We saw that the second of these turned into its opposite in the course of Polemarchus' attempt to defend it—from a position that made sense in peace but not in violence, to one that made sense in violence but not in peace—and now we find that the same thing has happened to the first half of the definition: what follows from the discussion now is that justice is beneficial to others, but not that it is beneficial to just people themselves. In this way Plato prepares us for Thrasymachus, who now states the antithesis of a) as starkly as possible: justice benefits only the recipient and is harmful to the practitioner, while injustice alone benefits the practitioner—precisely the reverse of what Cephalus had originally claimed. It will turn out to be the reverse of Polemarchus' claim as well, for in Thrasymachus' view just people not only benefit others, but they benefit their enemy, the unjust person, even more than their friend. The defense of Cephalus' claim led to its opposite in Polemarchus, and the defense of Polemarchus' claim leads to its opposite in Thrasymachus. They are opposites in another way as well: both Cephalus and Polemarchus conceived of justice in deontological terms, rules that were meant to be applied without exception; but Thrasymachus will reconceive the question in consequentialist terms, looking ahead to the results instead of looking back to the principle. At the beginning of Book 2 Thrasymachus' consequentialist formulation will be reformulated by Glaucon and Adeimantus, and in the course of responding to it Socrates will define the issue in terms of virtue ethics rather than either deontology or consequentialism, although in Books 9 and 10 he will argue that his conclusions ought to satisfy a consequentialist as well.

If we ask about Thrasymachus what we asked about his two predecessors—whether he embodies an appetitive, spirited, or rational nature—the answer to all three would be affirmative. His entry into the discussion could hardly be more spirited: when his neighbors are no longer able to restrain him from disrupting the discussion "he coiled himself like a wild animal and threw himself at us as if to tear us to pieces" (336b), and his belligerence continues until he suffers his defeat. At the same time he is also a lover of money: when Socrates asks for the answer about justice that Thrasymachus boasts of knowing, Thrasymachus refuses to divulge it unless he is paid (337d), and he values injustice for leading to monetary gain (343d–344a). But he is also a lover of rationality: as a sophist his profession is an intellectual one, and his ideal is not someone who dominates others by force alone but someone who does so by means of infallible knowledge (341a). Thrasymachus does not correspond to any of the pure tripartite types, but to the unjust person who is described in Book 4 as lacking in self-mastery, in whom rationality functions in the service of appetite rather than ruling over it (443d–444a, cf. 430e–431a), and the tyrant of Book 9, who is lacking in self-control and at the mercy of his appetites (579c). Both by his arrogant behavior and his admiration for the life of the tyrant as the happiest life (344a) he is the champion of tyranny. He represents the potentially rational and philosophical nature that is corrupted into the very opposite, the worst instead of the best (491b–492a, 495a–496a, 519a). So where the first two speakers exemplified the appetitive and spirited alternatives to the rational person, Thrasymachus exemplifies rationality in the service of injustice rather than justice. Socrates and Thrasymachus represent the alternative lives that the dialogue must decide between. The difference is adumbrated here in Socrates' response to the demand for payment: "I will when I have money"; while Thrasymachus proceeds only because Glaucon promises that the rest of them will pay for Socrates (337d). The contrast could not have been more stark: Thrasymachus charges money even to participate in a casual discussion, while Socrates has no money because he does not even charge his own students.

The answer worth paying for, in Thrasymachus' estimation, is that justice is the advantage of the stronger. This characterization is sometimes felt to be inconsistent with Thrasymachus' later claim, already referred to, that justice is what is good for someone else, the good of another (343c), because if we do something good for someone weaker than ourselves it will be just according to the second criterion, the good of another, but not the first, the advantage of the stronger. The two cannot both be definitions of justice, then, but Thrasymachus does not claim that they are. The first is called an answer (ἀπόκρισιν: 337d) but the second never claims to be more than an assertion about justice. Thrasymachus' claim of a bold new perspective on the subject makes sense only if we assume that the first claim is the more fundamental one, for there would have been nothing original about his claiming that when we are just we always benefit someone other than ourselves, but it is a novelty to claim that justice always provides an advantage for stronger people and never for weaker ones. Thrasymachus' point is that justice always benefits the recipient, not the practitioner, and injustice (selfishness) benefits the practitioner, so it is always in our advantage both to practice injustice ourselves and to be treated justly by others; but only the strongest people will be able to exact justice from others while dispensing injustice themselves.[20]

Until Socrates forces Thrasymachus to clarify what he means, the declaration that justice is the advantage of the stronger has a certain plausibility because it is almost a tautology. To be advantaged means to be stronger, so of course it is just that the stronger have an advantage. Everything depends on what kind of strength and what kind of advantage Thrasymachus has in mind. If he meant that justice itself is a source of strength and is advantageous to the just person because it is productive of happiness, then even Socrates would find nothing to quarrel with. The vaguer a definition, the less it means and the harder it is to evaluate or refute. The sophist trades on suppressing distinctions, Socrates on exposing them (although he is not above suppressing distinctions himself when it suits him). The argument can be divided into four sections: 1) Clarification of the definition (338c–347a), 2) A just person is more knowledgeable (349a–351a), 3) A just person is stronger (351b–352d), and 4) A just person is happier (352d–354a).

The first section is the most confusing part of the argument, and one of the most confusing passages in Plato.[21] That is partly because, although it seems that Socrates is merely trying to narrow Thrasymachus' claim down to a precise statement, he is doing two other things as well. First, he disguises the lines of classification that underlie his questions, to embarrass Thrasymachus by leading him to give answers that he will have to retract. Second, he creates an appearance of inconsistency in Thrasymachus' position, which later turns out to be a false appearance. Although the argument is generally read as an unsystematic series of claims and rejoinders by Thrasymachus and Socrates, or a kind of sparring in which the differences between their positions emerge in an informal way, it is actually governed by an organizational principle similar to what the *Phaedrus*, *Sophist*, and *Statesman* call the Method of Division. Socrates' questions force Thrasymachus to choose between a series of alternatives so that his originally vague claim is progressively disambiguated and narrowed until it is finally given a precise form.[22] The steps through which Socrates leads Thrasymachus can be schematized as follows:

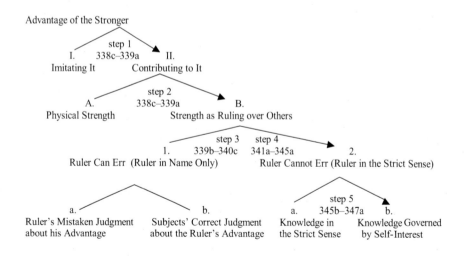

Steps 1 & 2 (338c–339a)

Socrates first eliminates the obvious: "Surely you are not saying this: if Polydamas the fighter is stronger than we are, and beef is advantageous to him for his body, this food is advantageous, as well as just, for us who are weaker than he is". Since the formula, "advantage of the stronger", has no verb, such as "contribute to" or "imitate", it is not clear what it is about this advantage that is supposed to constitute justice. Powerless people might approve of Thrasymachus' definition if they take it to express the egalitarian sentiment that "It is just for me to have the same advantages as those who are stronger". By asking whether "the advantage of the stronger" means "imitating the advantage of the stronger", Socrates forces Thrasymachus to distinguish within the general category of "the advantage of the stronger" the species of "contributing to it" from the species of "imitating it". At the same time he forces him also to distinguish political strength from physical strength within the genus of "stronger".

Step 3 (339b–340c)

Now that Socrates has narrowed the definition to something like "Justice is contributing what is advantageous to the ruler", he secures Thrasymachus' assent that it is therefore just to obey the ruler (339b). "Tell me whether rulers in the various cities are infallible or are capable of making mistakes", Socrates asks, and Thrasymachus replies that they indeed make mistakes (339c). So now the species of ruler has been subdivided into fallible rulers and infallible rulers, and Thrasymachus aligns his definition with fallible rulers. But that turns out to be a mistake for, as Socrates immediately points out, since Thrasymachus has agreed that we must obey the ruler, then if the ruler makes a mistake about what is in his advantage we must say either that it is not just to obey the ruler after all (but instead to do what is really in his advantage), or, if it is just to obey the ruler who is mistaken about his advantage, it is not always just to do what is in his advantage. Thrasymachus is faced with a crucial dilemma.

Step 4 (341a–345a)

Thrasymachus cannot accept either of these alternatives without trivializing his position. Obedience to what the ruler wrongly believes to be in his interest would be incompatible with Thrasymachus' view that justice means doing what is good for someone else. If we do what is bad for the ruler because he mistakenly thinks it is good, Thrasymachus' criterion is not met. On the other hand, doing what is in the ruler's advantage even if it means disobeying him, is simply benevolence, and the element of coercion is gone that is also an important part of Thrasymachus' claim. No one in the audience would suppose that the second, altruistic alternative represents Thrasymachus' actual view, but Cleitophon believes that the first alternative, obedience, does represent it (340b).[23] Thrasymachus sees more deeply, however, and realizes that both alternatives must be rejected if he is to salvage what is distinctive about his position, and thus that he took the wrong turn when he answered Socrates' question whether the stronger (i.e., the rulers) sometimes make mistakes. He now reverses himself: "Do you think I would call someone acting from error stronger when he is acting from error?" (340c). Thrasymachus proceeds to distinguish rulers in the strict sense, those who at any given time are actually in control and therefore not making a mistake, from rulers in name only, and to apply his definition only to rulers in the strict sense.

Step 5 (345b–347c)

Thrasymachus' claim has now been refined as: justice is doing what is in the advantage of the ruler in accordance with the ruler's knowledgeable decree. But thus far it is still not clear that it is a definition which Socrates would want to disagree with since, for him, the advantage of the true rulers is inseparable from that of the city (412c–e). If both Thrasymachus' and Socrates' rulers are acting from knowledge of the principles of ruling, how can Thrasymachus' position favor injustice and Socrates' favor justice? The difference lies in what is meant by the science (*episteme*: 340e) of ruling, and here is where their disagreement comes to a head. For Socrates it is obvious that rulers are like shepherds who align their own interest with the well-being of the flock; for Thrasymachus it is equally obvious that the goal of the *techne* (or *episteme*)[24] of the shepherd is not to promote the well-being of sheep but to promote the well-being of diners.

At this point Thrasymachus gives a fully candid account of his position: To be just is to do good for another, while to be unjust is to take something good from another; therefore an unjust person will always end up with more than a just person. People praise justice and condemn injustice not because they think it is better to be just to others but because they would like other people to be just to them. The only reasons why someone would be just rather than unjust are either because they are fools or because they have been coerced by someone stronger into serving the latter's interest. Consequently the happiest of all people is the tyrant, who coerces everyone into doing what benefits him at the expense of themselves (343c–345b).

Socrates' response is to force Thrasymachus to make one last distinction. Thrasymachus has surreptitiously changed his position, Socrates says (345b). He is not referring to Thrasymachus' change from the loose sense to the strict sense of "ruler" in step 4, but to a different kind of looseness. Thrasymachus said that a ruler in the strict sense is one who at any given moment is correctly applying the science of ruling, rather than being a ruler in name only. But Thrasymachus' strict sense now fails to distinguish between the pure science of ruling and the mixture of ruling with reward or getting paid. The person who herds sheep in order to eat them or sell them is combining shepherding with profiteering, and thus not being a shepherd in the strictest sense. In fact, the reason that people expect to get paid for practicing any *techne* is that a *techne* is always for the good of its subject, not its practitioner; something must be added to it if the practitioner is to benefit as well. We can say then that *techne* resembles what Thrasymachus said about justice: it is for the good of another. On Thrasymachus' own terms, therefore, the practitioner of a *techne*, includ‑ ing the *techne* of ruling, is just. *Techne* results in injustice only when it is not practiced in the strict sense, but in an impure sense as an instrument of profit to the practitioner (345b–347a). We are reminded again of the contrast between Thrasymachus, who will not even argue casually without payment, and Socrates, who does not accept payment even from his students.

It may seem that Socrates is unfair in accusing Thrasymachus of inconsis‑ tency, because what Thrasymachus meant by the strict sense was "infallible", not "infallible and disinterested", which is the strict sense at issue now; but there is more to it than that. Thrasymachus' position has been all along that Socrates is naïve: although people pretend to think justice is better than injustice, in the real world we can all see that injustice triumphs. Thrasy‑ machus considers himself to be a realist who takes an unflinching look at what actually happens, as opposed to Socrates the idealist, who sees only hopeful theories. But in order to escape the dilemma that Socrates sprang on him in step 3, Thrasymachus had to present an idealized version of a ruler who does not make mistakes, and now that Socrates shows that an idealized ruler is not self-interested but altruistic, Thrasymachus returns to arguments about how rulers actually behave (343b–344c).[25] Thrasymachus' final posi‑ tion is thus an inconsistent hybrid between realism and idealism. If he regards ruling as a science, then it cannot include self-interest, whereas if he regards it as "what rulers actually do", then it cannot be infallible. We shall see, how‑ ever, that the dilemma is not as devastating as Socrates makes it appear.

Plato could have given Thrasymachus a consistent position, as he does when Glaucon and Adeimantus restate the Thrasymachean point of view at the beginning of Book 2, so why does he not do so here? When Thrasymachus was faced with the dilemma of step 3, he retreated from B1 ("Rulers can err") to B2 ("Rulers cannot err"), on the grounds that someone who is in error is not at that moment a ruler because he is not acting from the science of ruling. Why did he call ruling a science, which left him vulnerable to Socrates' attack, instead of simply saying, "By ruler I mean whoever happens to be stronger at the moment"? For that matter, in step 2 when Socrates forced him to distinguish his sense of "stronger" from that which pertains to the muscular Polydamas, why did Thrasymachus insist on defining stronger as a ruler of cities, rather than simply whoever is in a control of a particular situation? The difference between his position and the one later put forward by Glaucon and Adeimantus, is that Thrasymachus wants to say more than that injustice pays better than justice. He also wants to say that there is a science of injustice, namely the science of ruling. As a sophist, Thrasymachus solicits payment to teach people how to achieve political success—success that is self-serving and in that respect unjust. If political success is teachable it must be a science. There is nothing adventitious about the hybrid position that Plato puts in Thrasymachus' mouth; it is a position to which he must be committed. To the extent, however, that Socrates' refutation turns on a tension between two views that Thrasymachus maintains simultaneously, rather than refuting one or both on their own terms, it is ad hominem. Consideration of the theory of injustice by itself, cleansed of its present conflation with the claim that it is a teachable science, will have to wait for Book 2. But that conflation is not mere obfuscation on Plato's part; it is a representation of the conflict of interest between theory and profit that is a distinguishing characteristic of the sophists.

Just as Socrates showed against Polemarchus that justice cannot be a *techne*, he needed to show against Thrasymachus that *injustice* too cannot be a *techne* (or *episteme*). He has now apparently done so by showing how injustice arises only from the contamination of *techne* by self-interest. Socrates proceeds to introduce an apparent incoherence into the discussion, however, in the way that he speaks of combining *techne* with self-interest. He could have left it at saying that because the *techne* of ruling benefits only the subjects and not the ruler, the ruler demands to receive pay (*misthon*: 345e6). But he goes on to say that this means the ruler is practicing not only the *techne* of ruling but also the *techne* of getting paid (*misthōtikē*), which provides the benefit of payment the way medicine provides health, and similarly with other *technai* (346a6–b1). This further step is problematic in itself, and it also severely complicates Socrates' position. It is problematic because in ordinary usage *misthōtikē* has the sense of "mercenary craft", and if someone asks what need is filled by a mercenary soldier, for example, we would say warfare, not money-making. Not only is it peculiar to say that the function of a mercenary craft is money-making—as if that is what the skill of a mercenary consisted in—but it undermines Socrates' entire argument. Having just argued that *techne* does not benefit its practitioner, he now calls something which does benefit its practitioner a *techne*. Why does Socrates call getting paid a *techne* when doing so violates not only the normal meaning of *misthōtikē* but the very requirements of his own argument?

Socrates' reply to Thrasymachus originally began with a reference to Polydamus the *pancratist* or all-around fighter (338c). How does the *techne* of *pancration* conform to Socrates' claim that "no *techne* or rule provides what is beneficial to itself but, as we have said for a long time, it provides and orders what is beneficial for the one governed, looking to its advantage because it is weaker, but not that of the stronger" (346e). In the case of a shepherd the *techne* is applied to the sheep, and it is reasonable to say that shepherds do what is best not for themselves but for the sheep. But in the case of fighting it would seem that the one to whom the *techne* is applied is the opponent, and fighters do not benefit their opponents by hitting them, rather than benefiting themselves. In the discussion with Polemarchus, when Socrates argued that any *techne* can be used for benefit or harm, one of his examples is that "the person who is most adept at hitting in a fight, whether in boxing or any other kind, is also the best at defending against it" (333e). If we apply this to the present case, neither of those two aspects of boxing, hitting and parrying, benefit the opponent; both benefit the fighter. The same is true of the *techne* of making war, which is so much a part of Polemarchus' position. It is clear then that *techne* does not always benefit the ones toward whom it is directed, rather than the practitioner. Can that be reconciled with Socrates' statement that no *techne* provides what is beneficial to itself but only to the one governed?[26]

Socrates' general principle seems justified—that since the purpose of any *techne* is to address a need in something, the beneficiary of the *techne* is what was in need, rather than the practitioner. But in the case of fighting, the one in need coincides with the practitioner rather than with the one to whom the practitioner applies it—the opponent. It is still the case that the *techne* does not benefit itself: the *techne* of fighting does not benefit the *techne* of fighting but the fighter. But why did Socrates make it seem that if a *techne* does not benefit itself it does not benefit its practitioner?

When Socrates explains what he means by payment, he says that in the case of a ruler it can take the form of money, honor, or a penalty for refusal, namely when the best people end up being ruled by their inferiors (347a–c).[27] We can generalize that principle beyond the *techne* of ruling by saying that payment can always be of three kinds (corresponding, as it later turns out, to the three parts of the soul): something that gratifies our appetite, something that gratifies our love of honor, and something that gratifies our rationality. If we apply this to the example of fighting, we can see that people who fight without being paid money to do so still receive payment because they fight for honor. But if when we fight for our honor we automatically receive (or at least hope to receive) payment in the form of honor, then we can say that the *techne* of fighting is a species of the *techne* of payment. In other words, when Socrates—seemingly in contradiction both with our intuitions and the requirements of his own argument—calls getting paid a *techne*, he is obliquely correcting a misdirection in his previous account. He is now acknowledging, however surreptitiously, that there are two kinds of *techne*—one kind that is transitive in that its practitioners do not benefit themselves (the beneficiaries of the shepherd are the sheep), and another that is reflexive in that the practitioners themselves are benefited (the beneficiary of fighting is the fighter). Socrates' paradoxical term, "the *techne* of getting paid" or "mercenary *techne*", makes sense when we see it as referring to the entire species of reflexive *techne*. By collapsing the distinction between saying "a *techne* never benefits itself" (which follows from his argument) and "practitioners of *techne* never benefit themselves" (which does not follow from it) Socrates obscured the species of reflexive *techne* from Thrasymachus and simplified his own argument. If he had acknowledged that although no *techne* benefits itself, some *technai* benefit their practitioners, Thrasymachus would have tried to place ruling within the latter category; ruling would not be a mixture of *techne* and getting paid, but a pure reflexive *techne* like fighting. But Socrates makes it look as if the conclusion, "no *techne* benefits its practitioners", followed from the premise "no *techne* benefits itself":

> It was because [no *techne* benefits itself], my dear Thrasymachus, that I just said no one would willingly choose to rule and take other people's troubles in hand to straighten them out, but everyone asks for payment because the person who is going to practice the *techne* well never does what is best for himself nor orders it when he orders according to the *techne*, but only what is best for the one governed. [346e–347a]

He then calls getting paid a *techne* in order to hint at what has been suppressed. Unless it was done as a covert allusion to the whole genus of *technai* that benefit their practitioners, his use of the term makes no sense in terms of the requirements of his own argument.

We can see then that Thrasymachus could have salvaged his position after all. When Socrates presented him with his dilemma—if ruling is an *techne* then it cannot include self-interest, and if it is "what rulers actually do" then it cannot be infallible—Thrasymachus could have tackled the first horn by showing that in some cases a *techne* can benefit its practitioner. Socrates may be guilty of oversimplifying matters, but he is not being dishonest. He certainly believes that ruling is a transitive *techne* rather than a reflexive one, so his concealing of the latter alternative does not affect the truth of the conclusion; but it does spare him from having to prove to Thrasymachus that ruling is not a reflexive *techne*.

We saw that Cephalus' and Polemarchus' positions represented the opposite extremes of peacefulness and conflict, and suggested that Plato may have been foreshadowing the later claim that justice is a mean rather than an

extreme. Something of the kind may be at work here as well. On Thrasymachus' view there are only two alternatives, the extreme selflessness of justice and the extreme selfishness of injustice (343c). The practitioners of
justice are fools or weaklings who sacrifice their own advantage in order to
serve the advantage of others. Consummate practitioners of injustice, on the
other hand, use the *techne* of ruling to exploit their subjects and to compel
them to serve the ruler's advantage. Socrates' insistence that *techne* includes
a *techne* of getting paid shows that there is a middle ground between these two
alternatives; it locates the justice of *techne* in contradistinction to both
extremes. On one hand those who practice altruistic *techne*, especially the
techne of ruling, insist on being recipients of the benefits of the counter-*techne*
of getting paid, and so are not self-sacrificing. On the other hand rulers who
behave as Thrasymachus describes, and do not aim at the benefit of their subjects, are not practicing a *techne* in the strict sense at all (345b–347a). By taking normal *techne* to be inseparable from the *techne* of getting paid, Socrates
portrays *techne* as a whole as being neither self-serving (as Thrasymachus
regards the *techne* of injustice or ruling) nor self-sacrificing (as Thrasymachus
regards the "*techne*" of justice) but as a mean between those extremes. Even
when we practice what Socrates called the *techne* of justice (332d) we receive
a kind of payment (cf. 588e–591b).

The claim that injustice is a *techne*, which Socrates refuted only by equivo-
cating between "no *techne* benefits itself" and "no *techne* benefits its practitioner", was only a subordinate element in Thrasymachus' position. His primary
claims about the advantage of the stronger and the superiority of justice have
not been refuted even apparently, but only forced to become more precise.[28]
Accordingly Socrates says a little later, "You seem to me now, Thrasymachus,
not to mock us at all, but to speak your opinions about the truth" (349a).

First Refutation: Knowledge (348a–350e)

It seems as though Socrates wants to begin by employing his familiar identification of knowledge with virtue to counter Thrasymachus' identification of
knowledge with injustice, for he asks whether Thrasymachus agrees that justice is a virtue and injustice a vice. But Thrasymachus replies, "That's likely,
you amusing man, when I say that injustice is profitable and justice isn't!"
(348c). Socrates replies, "If you had put it that injustice is advantageous, but
agreed that it is a vice or shameful, as some others do, we would be able to discuss it in a conventional way" (348e). But now it is obvious that some other
strategy must be found. Thrasymachus already agrees that virtue is knowledge; the question is whether justice or injustice counts as virtue, as human

excellence.[29] Socrates begins with an attack on Thrasymachus' connection between injustice and knowledge (*episteme*). On the contrary, Socrates argues, it is justice that belongs with knowledge, while injustice belongs with ignorance. The argument is dense and convoluted, in part because Socrates is springing a trap for Thrasymachus. It can be schematized as follows:

A. 1. Just people, behaving justly
   a. toward other equally just people, are not trying to outdo them by means of that behavior (349a–b).
   b. toward unjust people, are trying to outdo them (i.e., are trying to be more just) (349b–c).
2. Unjust people, behaving unjustly
   a. toward just people, are trying to outdo them (e.g., by cheating them) (349c).
   b. toward other unjust people, are trying to outdo them too (349c).
3. Therefore,
   a. just people try to outdo those who are unlike but not those who are like themselves (349c).
   b. unjust people try to outdo both those who are like and those who are unlike themselves (349c–d).
B. Each person has the qualities of the people whom he is like (349d).
C. 1. People are superior at what they know about (349d–e).
2. People are inferior at what they are ignorant of (349e).
D. 1. People acting only from knowledge
   a. are not trying to outdo others acting from the same knowledge (349e–350a).[30]
   b. are trying to outdo others acting without it (349e–350a).
2. People acting from ignorance
   a. try to outdo those who act from knowledge (350b).
   b. try also to outdo others who act from ignorance (350b).
3. Therefore,
   a. people who are knowledgeable and therefore superior (C1) try to outdo those who are unlike but not those who are like themselves (350b).
   b. people who are ignorant and therefore inferior (C2) try to outdo both those who are like and those who are unlike themselves (350b).
E. Therefore (from A3 and D3),
   1. A just person is like a knowledgeable and superior one (350c).
   2. An unjust person is like an ignorant and inferior one (350c).

F. And therefore (from E and B),
    1. A just person is knowledgeable and superior (350c).
    2. An unjust person is ignorant and inferior (350c).

Even in a schematized form the nineteen steps are not easy to hold in one's mind at once, but the key steps can be reduced to six:

    1. A just person is like a knowledgeable one and an unjust like an ignorant one (A3, D3).

    2. Being alike means having the same qualities (B).

    3. ∴ A just person has the same qualities as a knowledgeable one, and an unjust the same as an ignorant one (1, 2).

    4. ∴ A just person is knowledgeable and an unjust person ignorant (3).

    5. A knowledgeable person is superior to an ignorant one (C).

    6. ∴ A just person is superior to an unjust one (4, 5).

Several of the premises are open to question,[31] but most of them are defensible even if not fully demonstrable, namely those which argue that both in justice and in knowledge we recognize that there is a correct degree and to go beyond it is to go too far, while in injustice and ignorance there is no such recognition. The one step that is not merely questionable but indefensible is B: "Each of them [the just and unjust man] is of the same quality (τοιοῦτος) as the one he resembles" (349d). The premise is clearly an all or nothing fallacy—obviously people can resemble one another in some ways without being the same in other ways. Socrates himself later points out the absurdity of this kind of reasoning, when he says that the reason people are reluctant to believe that women can rule as well as men is that they are misled by eristic arguments which claim that if there is some difference between two kinds of thing they cannot be the same in any respect. One might as well say, he concludes, that since a bald person differs from a long-haired one, if bald people can be shoemakers then long-haired people cannot (454a–c). Then why does Thrasymachus agree to the premise instead of laughing it out of court?

The proof that Socrates is deliberately tricking him and not merely arguing carelessly is that the premise is introduced at the seventh step of the argument (B), but not brought into play until the eighteenth step (F). The only conceivable reason for Socrates to introduce it when he did, rather than waiting until its proper place in the argument, is that at that point it looks as though it will work to Thrasymachus' advantage, so it will be easy to secure his agreement. They are discussing Thrasymachus' correlation between injustice and wisdom, rather than Socrates' later correlation between justice and knowledge, so it appears advantageous to Thrasymachus to say that if the two are similar they are the same. By the time Thrasymachus has been forced to accept Socrates' parallel rather than his own, he has already swallowed the bait. Socrates camouflages his strategy even further by introducing the premise as a conclusion that follows from premises that Thrasymachus already accepts. He does not say:

1) An unjust person resembles a wise and good person.

2) Those who resemble each other have the same qualities.

3) Therefore an unjust person is wise and good.

Thrasymachus might have recognized the danger that Socrates could find a way to insert a different major premise. Instead Socrates starts with Thrasymachus' own contentions:

1) "An unjust person is wise and good, while a just person is neither".

2) "An unjust person also resembles wise and good people, while a just person does not".

3) "Then each of them is of the same quality as the one he resembles".

So the damaging premise is introduced as a harmless-looking clarification rather than a formal principle. Thus camouflaged, the trap remains invisible to Thrasymachus until Socrates finally springs it at 350c, and there is nothing left for Thrasymachus to do but to blush (350d) at being outwitted after all his condescension, and after his boast to Socrates, "You will neither be able to inflict damage surreptitiously nor overpower me in argument" (341a–b). Now that the emptiness of his boast has been exposed he tries to fall back on rhetoric, offering to make a speech in defense of his claims, an offer which Socrates predictably declines (350d–e).

What did Plato hope to gain by handing Socrates a victory so obviously tainted? Socrates' audience is not impressed with his victory (357a) and neither has been Plato's. The Divided Line, which Socrates introduces in Book 6 to represent four kinds of thinking, is first partitioned into two segments, one of which represents the intelligible realm and the other the visible realm, after which each is bisected again into perception of the image of an object and perception of the object itself. The result is a fourfold classification: *eikasia* (from the word for "likeness" or "image") perceives the images of visible things,[32] *pistis* perceives the visible things themselves, *dianoia* perceives the images of intelligible things, and *noesis* perceives intelligible things themselves (509e–510b). We shall see that the images represented by the first and third levels of the Line are, at least in part, images in words, and as we read through the dialogue we shall find that the course of the arguments takes us progressively through the four levels as far as possible. Book 1, then, is an illustration of *eikasia*, images (in words) of visible things, because it examines only what people say about just actions without examining the nature of just actions themselves. Accordingly, at the end of Book 1 Socrates will confess that he never got around to investigating what justice is, because he was distracted by questions about whether it is vice and ignorance, or wisdom and virtue; "Consequently for me the result of the discussion is that I know nothing, for if I don't know what justice is I will hardly know whether it happens to be a virtue or not, and whether someone who has it is unhappy or happy" (354c).

In the *Phaedrus* Socrates says:

> In the law courts no one cares anything at all about the truth of these things, but only about what is convincing; and this is the "likely" (*eikos*), to which whoever intends to speak with skill must apply himself. He must sometimes not even mention the facts themselves, if they did not happen in a likely way (*eikotōs*) but rather what is likely (*eikota*), both in prosecution and defense. And, whatever one says, one must pursue the likely (*eikos*) and say goodbye to the true. [272d–e]

What takes place in Socrates' refutation of Thrasymachus is similar insofar as it is concerned only with creating the semblance of demonstration, not with investigating the truth of the matter; "likelihood" (*eikasia*) is an apt term for it. Thrasymachus even accuses Socrates of being a *sukophantēs*, a person who persuasively brings false witness against someone in court (340d). It was mentioned that the *Republic*'s opening words, "I went down" are sometimes taken to be an allusion to the philosopher's descent back into the cave in order to help others see the light. On the present interpretation it is not only a general allusion, but a precise reflection of the dialogue's beginning at the heart of the cave, with *eikasia*. At this level there is argument but not real persuasion—Thrasymachus is defeated but not convinced. In order to convince his audience Socrates will have to raise their thinking through the stages of the Divided Line so that they can see the truth for themselves.

However flawed the argument is, its central claim is credible, namely that unjust people and ignorant people are not aware of any proper limit and go to extremes. So here, for the third time, and more explicitly than before, is the suggestion that justice is a kind of mean.[33]

Second Refutation: Strength (351a–352b)

Thrasymachus had argued that the strength of unjust people lies in their superior knowledge, so in the first refutation Socrates forced him to concede that knowledge dwells with justice rather than injustice. Socrates now hones in on Thrasymachus' larger claim, that "the stronger" who are benefited by justice are unjust people, while just people are weak victims who are only harmed by their justice. Thrasymachus, who has nothing but contempt for justice and fairness, has no intention of arguing in good faith but only of winning the argument: "What difference does it make to you whether I believe it or not, why don't you refute the argument?" (349a). Socrates had to defeat him, therefore, not by convincing him or by giving a cogent demonstration but only by outmaneuvering him. Things have not changed, and Socrates is determined to hold on to his tactical advantage. He prefaces the next refutation with the words, "since justice has been shown to be wisdom and virtue it will, I think, be easily shown to be also stronger than injustice, since after all injustice is ignorance—no one can any longer fail to recognize this" (351a). In fact, Socrates wants to establish the new conclusion independently of the previous argument, but the warning ensures Thrasymachus' cooperation in what follows. Thrasymachus saves face as best he can by adopting a patronizing air and humoring Socrates ironically. His answers are careful nevertheless, and when Socrates praises him for them he replies, "I'm trying to please you", to which Socrates responds, "You're doing well" (351c). Can it be that in accordance with his own principles Thrasymachus recognizes his obligation to contribute to the advantage of Socrates, who has shown himself to be the stronger? Or does he simply recognize Socrates' ability to embarrass him whenever Socrates finds it necessary, on the basis of the concessions that Socrates has already forced from him, and is saving face as best he can by patronizing Socrates?[34]

The new argument takes the following form:

1. A group whose members behave justly to one another is stronger than one whose members treat each other unjustly.

2. Therefore justice is a source of strength and injustice a source of weakness.

3. Injustice retains its propensity to induce weakness even when only a single individual is involved.

4. Therefore a just person will be stronger than an unjust one.

The questionable step is step 3. Socrates asks, "If injustice arises in one person will it lose its power or will it retain it undiminished?" and tame Thrasymachus replies obligingly, "Let it retain it undiminished" (351e). Thrasymachus knows perfectly well that the admission is not warranted, for the weakness of injustice that was established in the first premise followed from the dissention it creates within a group. To conclude that this same weakness must be present even apart from any group clearly does not follow. Whether we classify the fallacy as a false analogy or a fallacy of division, it is certainly invalid. But since Socrates began by pointing out that he can already establish everything he wants on the basis of the conclusion of the first argument, this second argument must be intended to provide something more than merely Thrasymachus' further defeat. Only when we get to Book 4 do we see that it is a foreshadowing of the doctrine of a multipart soul, and of the conclusion that justice is the harmonious condition of the soul in which the parts operate in concert, while injustice is the disharmonious condition in which the soul is at war within itself. On one level the argument presents an appearance of cogency together with a fallacious reality, while on another level it indicates where we must look for the strength and weakness of justice and injustice, namely in the way they produce unity and disunity respectively.

Third Refutation: Happiness (352b–354c)

This final refutation challenges Thrasymachus' claim that an unjust person will be happier than a just one. If the first part of the argument with Thrasymachus (345b–347a) picked up on the relationship between justice and *techne* that arose in the second refutation of Polemarchus, the final part elaborates a theme that arose in the fourth refutation of Polemarchus, namely that a just person would not harm anyone because to harm is to reduce the virtue or excellence of something, and justice cannot be the cause of a reduction in virtue. That argument spoke of the natural virtue by means of which something is good of its kind, and spoke of the function (*ergon*) of justice and injustice, heat and cold, and dryness and wetness. The new argument combines these concepts of function and virtue:

1. The function of a thing is what one can do only with it, or best with it. For example, we see only with the eyes and hear only with the ears, and although we can prune a vine with any kind of knife we can best do so with a pruning knife (352e–353a).

2. A thing can perform its function well only if it has the associated virtue or excellence rather than the corresponding evil; in the case of the eyes, for example, sight rather than blindness (353a–d).

3. The functions which pertain to the soul include caring for things, ruling, deliberating, and living, which it will do well if it has its proper virtue, but badly if it has the corresponding evil (353d–e).

4. The virtue of the soul is justice and its evil is injustice (353e).

5. Therefore a just person lives well (353e).

6. To live well is to be happy (354a).

7. Therefore a just person is happy and an unjust person is wretched (354a).

The most significant step as far as Thrasymachus' contribution is concerned is step 4, for when Socrates asks, "Didn't we agree that the virtue of the soul is justice, and its vice injustice?", Thrasymachus replies, "We agreed" (353e). And yet we saw that when Socrates had asked whether Thrasymachus agreed that justice is a virtue and injustice a vice Thrasymachus contemptuously denied it (348c). Having been outmaneuvered by Socrates, however, Thrasymachus now agrees to the proposition in an attempt to save face by patronizing him, and Socrates takes advantage of it. So from Thrasymachus' point of view the argument is hardly a convincing one. But what about those of us who do believe that justice is a virtue?

First of all, what does Socrates mean by "function"? He began by asking, "Does a horse seem to you to have a function?" Thrasymachus assents, and Socrates asks whether the function of a thing is "what one can do only with that thing, or do best with that thing" (352e). Thrasymachus does not understand, but instead of staying with the example of the horse, Socrates explains what his point is by means of less obscure examples: the function of the eye is to see, the function of the ear is to hear, the function of a pruning knife is to prune vines. Our soul has functions such as taking care of things, ruling, deliberating, and living. From their previous agreements it would seem that justice is indeed the virtue or excellence of such things, since it is the locus of knowledge and strength, but their previous agreements were coerced from Thrasymachus rather than free. It remains for the next eight books to show whether Socrates can provide us with reasons for accepting this conclusion freely.

But why did Plato introduce the concept of function with the example of a horse, if he uses quite different examples to explain the point? In the final argument with Polemarchus Socrates had established that when horses are harmed they become worse, specifically, worse in the excellence or virtue of horses rather than, for example, dogs (335b). Since we think of individual horses as better or worse instances of their species, we must have some conception of what it means for a horse to be good or bad of its kind; that is, what equine excellence or virtue consists of. And we could not have a conception of a distinctive equine excellence unless we had a conception of what a horse ought to achieve by virtue of being a horse—such as having a spirited nature, for example (375).[35] That is what Socrates means by its function. Like so much else in Book 1, this point seems to have been left undeveloped because it points to the succeeding books for its completion. There we will find that not only eyes, ears, elements, and irrational animals have a function and excellence or virtue, but so do different kinds of human beings.

Finally, there are significant ambiguities in steps 3 and 6. First, there is no clear unifying concept in the list of the soul's functions—caring for things, ruling, deliberating, and living—so it is not clear that Socrates is working with a coherent conception of soul. Second, when step 6 takes "living well" to mean "being happy", he is going beyond anything that was implied in the concept of "living" in step 3.[36] In step 3 "living" means being alive, so "living well" would mean no more than being healthy; but we can be healthy without being happy. In order to overcome this apparent equivocation we have to assume that the virtue of the soul includes also performing the other functions well—caring, ruling, deliberating—but not until Book 7, and perhaps even Book 10, will the soul be conceived in a way that unifies such seemingly diverse functions.

Notes

1. Brann (1967) writes that the typical use of the article when speaking of going "to the Piraeas" (εἰς Πειραιᾶ) is because "it meant the 'beyond-land', ἡ Περαία, the land beyond the river which was thought once to have separated the Peiraic peninsula from Attica". She suggests that it is here an allusion to Hades, which brings the beginning into relation with the concluding Myth of Er. Claudia Baracchi also takes the Piraeus to correspond to the site of the Myth of Er (*Of Myth, Life, and War in Plato's* Republic [Bloomington: Indiana University Press, 2002], 18). For other views see Ruby Blondell, *The Play of Character in Plato's Dialogues* (Cambridge: Cambridge University Press, 2002), 166; and George Rudebusch, "Dramatic Prefiguration in Plato's *Republic*" (*Philosophy and Literature* 26 [2002]: 75–83, 81–2).

2. Strabo, *Geography* 10.3.16.

3. Eric Vogelin, however, writes that Bendis is identified with Hecate, who conducts souls to the underworld, and that the Myth of Er thus echoes rather than contrasts the opening scene. In support of this he cites Kerenyi but without saying what Kerenyi's evidence is that so departs from Strabo (*Plato* [Baton Rouge: Louisiana State University Press, 1966], 54). Baracchi (2002), too, identifies rather than contrasts the goddesses evoked in the opening and concluding passages (222), on the grounds that Socrates makes the Fates the daughters of Necessity in the myth of Er, while Hesiod makes them the daughters of Night (192), and because the celebration of Bendis at the beginning of the dialogue includes an all-night festival (192n15[210]). But Socrates depicts Necessity not as nocturnal but as dwelling in the midst of brilliant rainbow-hued light (616b–c).

4. This is the first of several parallels that we shall notice with the *Symposium*, the only other dialogue to extend throughout the night and into the next morning (the *Laws* is a daytime dialogue which begins in the morning: 625a–b). There is no indication that the conversation of the *Republic* was further lengthened by interruptions for dinner or festivities like the torch race. Gadamer (1942) suggests that the point is that "the philosopher leads those who have stayed behind in the hopes of seeing something into a conversation *instead of* to a torchlight race on horseback in honor of the goddess. And therein we have precisely the philosophical event which occurs wherever Socrates is" (91; emphasis added).

5. "Rationality" translates λογιστικόν throughout, while "reason" is reserved for νοῦς. The former is associated especially (but not only) with the doctrine of the tripartite soul of Book 4, where it is opposed to appetite and spiritedness; while the latter term is employed more generally, with a range of meanings from "understanding" to "mind".

6. This remark anticipates Socrates' later observation that "when the appetites strongly incline toward some one thing they are thereby weakened toward others, like a stream from which there is a diversion into another channel" (485d).

7. Cf. David Roochnik, *Beautiful City: The Dialectical Character of Plato's Republic* (Ithaca: Cornell University Press, 2003), ch.2.

8. Compare 491d–492a with 486d–e and 572e–573e.

9. Rudebusch writes: "As Gifford has pointed out, the Socratic counter-example to the first definition of justice—that of Cephalus—is instantiated by Cephalus himself. . . . Cephalus was a weapons manufacturer—a fact publicized in a famous speech of Lysias (*Against Eratosthenes* XII). He supplied and therefore owed weapons to Athens, which was out of its mind with war anger (see Gifford, pp. 4–5, 9 [a reference to Mark Gifford, 'Dramatic Dialectic in *Republic* I', presented to the 1999 Pacific Division meeting of the American Philosophical Association])" (2002, 76). The resemblance between Cephalus' product and Socrates' counterexample is weakened, however, by the fact that the weapons that Cephalus manufactured were shields. See Nails 2002, 84.

10. "The name indicates that the polemarchos [sic] original function was to command the army. . . . Thereafter the polemarch's main functions were legal" (*Oxford Classical Dictionary*, 3rd edition [Oxford: Oxford University Press, 1996], 1203).

11. David Lachterman suggests that "In this way the opening scene contains in germ *the* major political question of *The Republic*: How can a multiplicity of individuals be persuaded to form a community of citizens?" ("What Is 'The Good' of Plato's *Republic*?", *St. John's Review* 39 [1989–90]: 139–71, 149).

12. Polemarchus' threat to force Socrates to stay has been taken as an anticipation of the compulsion that must be put on the philosopher to return to the cave to rule. The cases are not quite parallel because in the present instance Socrates is not compelled to go down but only prevented from leaving, but the fact that it is persuasion rather than force that compels him to remain does parallel the later episode (cf. 520b–e).

13. Cf. Blondell 2002, 177. For a more elaborate exploration of Polemarchus' character see Carl Page, "The Unjust Treatment of Polemarchus", *History of Philosophy Quarterly* 7 (1990): 243–67.

14. Cf. *Ion* 538b, *Gorgias* 453d, *Protagoras* 311b, 318c.

15. Although this functions here as a reductio ad absurdum, it also foreshadows Socrates' later claim that the very virtues of the philosophical nature enable that nature to become most vicious when it is corrupted (491b–e).

16. Whether or not justice is ultimately meant to be understood as a *techne* in the *Republic* is a matter of dispute. Those arguing in the negative include Cross and

Woozley 1964, 13–16; Leo Strauss, *The City and Man* (Chicago: Rand McNally, 1964), 72; Annas 1981, 24–8; C. D. C. Reeve, *Philosopher-Kings: The Argument of Plato's Republic* (Princeton: Princeton University Press, 1988), 8. Proponents of an affirmative answer include Rosamond Sprague (*Plato's Philosopher-King* [Columbia: University of South Carolina Press, 1976], 63–6); Parry 1996, 88 and 96; and Irwin 1995, 69 and 171 n. 14 (377). We shall see when we get to chapter 7 why it is difficult to give a straightforward answer.

17. Socrates is teasing Polemarchus: it was not Simonides but Polemarchus who made this claim. Simonides said only that it is just to give everyone what is owed to them. Blondell suggests that Socrates is inviting Polemarchus "to reject not just Simonides, but the whole poetic tradition" (2002, 175). The words of the poets should not be taken as authoritative pronouncements.

18. Theodor Gomperz believes there is "a confusion between 'to injure' in the sense of making unserviceable, and in that of causing pain or unhappiness" (*Greek Thinkers* [London: John Murray, 1905], III, 56). Similar criticisms are raised by Cross and Woozley, who think Socrates "exploited an ambiguity in the Greek word βλάπτειν" [harm]: Polemarchus may mean "harming" not by making someone worse but "by thwarting him, by interfering with his interests, by making life somehow more unpleasant for him" (20); and by Julia Annas (*An Introduction to Plato's Republic* [Oxford: Clarendon Press, 1981], 32–4). For a reply to Gomperz see H. W. B. Joseph, *Essays in Ancient & Modern Philosophy* (Oxford: Clarendon Press, 1935), 13–14. For a reply to Cross and Woozley and a general discussion of this passage see Andrew Jeffrey, "Polemarchus and Socrates on Justice and Harm", *Phronesis* 24 (1979): 54–69. Whatever Polemarchus may have had in mind, the argument shows in what sense just people cannot act against their opponents, but it does not rule out senses that do not reduce the virtue of the opponent.

19. Wang Yang-ming (1472–1529), the last of the great Neo-Confucianist philosophers, takes it one step further and extends this expanded view of the self even to what is inanimate: Each person forms "one body with Heaven, Earth, and the myriad things. Therefore when he sees a child about to fall into a well, he cannot help a feeling of alarm and commiseration. This shows that his humanity forms one body with the child. It may be objected that [this is not one body with Heaven, Earth, and the myriad things because] the child belongs to the same species. Again, when he observes the pitiful cries and frightened appearance of birds and animals about to be slaughtered, he cannot help feeling an inability to bear their suffering. This shows that his humanity forms one body with birds and animals. It may be objected that birds and animals are sentient beings as he is. But when he sees plants broken and destroyed, he cannot help a feeling of pity. This shows that his humanity forms one body with plants. It may be said that plants are living things as he is. Yet even when he sees tiles and stones shattered and crushed, he cannot help a feeling of regret. This shows that his humanity forms one body with tiles and stones. This means that even the mind of the ordinary man necessarily has the humanity that forms one body with all" (*Instructions for Practical Living* [NY: Columbia University Press, 1963], 659–60).

20. Also see G. B. Kerferd, "The Doctrine of Thrasymachus in Plato's *Republic*", *Durham University Journal* n.s. 9 (1947): 19–27; and "Thrasymachus and Justice: A Reply", *Phronesis* 9 (1964): 12–16. For a discussion of the controversy surrounding this issue see P. P. Nicholson, "Unravelling Thrasymachus' Arguments in 'The Republic'", *Phronesis* 19 (1974): 210–232.

21. Cornford (1941) does not translate it but replaces it with a paraphrase. Commentaries usually treat it as a series of statements that can be usefully commented on, but without an underlying structure. See, for example, Nettleship 1964 (1901), Gomperz 1905, Cross and Woozley 1964, Friedländer 1964, vol 2 (who calls the argument "verbal juggling", 62), Strauss 1964, Sparshott 1966, Bloom 1968. Murphy (1951) discusses the positions of Socrates and Thrasymachus without any reference to the argument itself.

22. Anthony Flew argues that Plato never does mount an attack on Thrasymachus' position, but merely counters Thrasymachus' "is" with his own "ought", without facing up to Thrasymachus' correctness in maintaining that moral people must make sacrifices that immoral people do not make ("Responding to Plato's Thrasymachus", *Philosophy* 70 [1995]: 436–47). While that is avowedly true of Book 1 (354b–c), all of Book 9 is devoted to showing the sacrifices that an immoral person inevitably makes, and Glaucon's acknowledgement that the unjust person sacrifices far more than a just one is completely plausible in context.

23. Cleitophon's position has been defended by George Hourani, who argues that "Thrasymachus' intended definition of justice is obedience to law (conventionalism or legalism" [110]) but that Socrates "forces him to modify this" ("Thrasymachus' Definition of Justice in Plato's *Republic*", *Phronesis* 7 [1962]: 110–120). If this were Thrasymachus' position, however, it is hard to see why he would express it in terms of "advantaging the stronger" rather than "obeying the law", and why he rejects Cleitophon's suggestion. See the replies to Hourani by Kerferd (1964), and Demetrius Hadgopoulos ("Thrasymachus and Legalism", *Phronesis* 18 [1973]: 204–8).

24. The terms *techne* and *episteme* are often used interchangeably. Cf. Aristotle, *Metaphysics* A.1. 981a3–b9.

25. As James Adam puts it, "The strength of Thrasymachus' theory lay in its correspondence with the facts (real or apparent) of experience; it is the temptation to defend his theory against the criticism of Socrates which leads him to abandon facts for ideas; and as soon as he is refuted on the idealistic plane, he descends to facts again" (*The Republic of Plato*, 2nd edition [Cambridge University Press 1963 (1902)], 33).

26. The problematic nature of Socrates' claim is widely noted; see, for example, Annas 1981, 47, and Reeve 1988, 19. Edward Warren seeks to resolve the problem by distinguishing between licit and illicit forms of *techne* ("The Craft Argument: An Analogy?" in John Anton and Anthony Preus, eds., *Essays in Ancient Greek Philosophy III: Plato* [Albany: SUNY Press, 1989], 101–115). But Socrates would not be able to make that distinction without begging the question.

27. Joseph (1935) suggests that since the *techne* of getting paid refers not only to money but to the appropriate reward for all three kinds of people, it "is really the same

as that of what Aristotle afterwards called ἀρχιτεκτονικὴ τέχνη [architectonic
techne]—the art of so ordering one's life as to secure happiness, or realize for oneself in
it . . . good" (26).

28. For a different view see T. Y. Henderson, "In Defense of Thrasymachus", *American Philosophical Quarterly* 7 (1970): 218–228.

29. T. D. J. Chappell argues that the fact that Thrasymachus puts injustice "in the
class (μέρει) of virtue and wisdom" (348e) does not mean that injustice is a virtue,
but only that it is a concomitant of virtue, namely of practical wisdom ("The Virtues
of Thrasymachus", *Phronesis* 38 [1992]: 1–17, esp. 9–13). I am not sure that this distinction is more than semantic, for even if Thrasymachus does not "simply mean acting unjustly . . . [but] as unjustly as you can get away with" (10), virtue too always
admits of degrees. The distinction does not affect our analysis.

30. As Allan Bloom points out, this argument, like the fourth against Polemarchus,
"serves to point toward a realm of noble human activity which is not essentially competitive" (*The Republic of Plato* [New York: Basic Books, 1968], 336; cf. 324).

31. See Cross and Woozley 1964, 51–55, Francis Sparshott, "Socrates and Thrasymachus", *Monist* 50 (1966): 421–59; and Annas 1981, 50–52.

32. "By images (*eikones*) I mean first shadows, then reflections in water and in all
compacted, smooth, and shiny materials, and all such things" (509e–510a).

33. Also see Nettleship 1964 (1901), 37–40.

34. As was noted in the Introduction, the more positive references to Thrasymachus in later books (450a, 498c9–d1) may even permit the possibility that he has
been inspired with philosophical wonder. Basil O'Neill argues that Socrates has
begun to convert Thrasymachus, and that even if the arguments are "unsound as an
abstract argument" they are "sound as a dialectical therapy for [Thrasymachus']
divided soul" ("The Struggle for the Soul of Thrasymachus", *Ancient Philosophy* 8
[1988]: 167–85, 178). O'Neill acknowledges that after Thrasymachus blushes he still
pronounces himself dissatisfied and wants to make a speech, but O'Neill believes that
Thrasymachus' decision to defer to Socrates' refusal to let him make one shows that
he is now willing to be guided by Socrates (181).

35. Cross and Woozley think Socrates should have explicated "function" in terms
of "purpose" (59), such as the purpose of a knife, but this would not be possible in the
example of the horse, which they do not consider.

36. Cf. T. M. Robinson, *Plato's Psychology* (Toronto: University of Toronto Press,
1970), 35–6.

CHAPTER TWO

~

The Origin of the City
(Book 2 to 376c)

Glaucon and Adeimantus

In Book 1 Cephalus, Polemarchus, and Thrasymachus represented three types of lives with which the rest of the dialogue is concerned—appetitive, spirited, and unjust. From now on with minor exceptions the interlocutors will be Plato's half brothers, Glaucon and Adeimantus.[1] If Socrates represents the best nature fulfilled and Thrasymachus the best nature perverted, the brothers represent this nature in a state of aporia (ἀπορῶ: 358c), poised to go in either direction, hoping that Socrates is right but fearing that Thrasymachus may be right.

Socrates describes Glaucon as courageous (357a) and Adeimantus calls him a lover of victory (548d), so he is sometimes taken to be the type of the spirited person. But spiritedness is not the only attribute that he displays. It is Glaucon who is unhappy with the first city because it does not offer enough pleasures for the appetite (372c), and it is he who pushes Socrates to explain the highest principle of philosophy, the good (506d), and becomes his partner in the central metaphysical discussions (506d–548d). So one can make a case for his appetitive and rational nature as well. Adeimantus' role is less prominent than Glaucon's, inasmuch as Glaucon is Socrates' partner both at the beginning and end of Books 2–10, and is on stage almost twice as long as Adeimantus—roughly 171 Stephanus pages to Adeimantus' 91—and of course Glaucon was in company with Socrates at the beginning of the dialogue while Adeimantus was with Polemarchus. For these reasons and others

Adeimantus is sometimes thought to represent a lesser type than Glaucon, but that does not seem to be supported by the text.[2] Adeimantus is Socrates' partner in the founding of the first city and in the education of the guardians of the second city; he is the one who challenges the credibility of the Socratic elenchus in principle (487a–d; Glaucon had earlier dismissed its results in Book 1: 357a), and he is Socrates' partner in the initial discussion of the nature of philosophy and the good.

Any attempt to distinguish between the two brothers seems arbitrary, and their combined roles may be merely a matter of verisimilitude. Near the beginning of the *Sophist* Theaetetus says that if he gets tired of answering questions for the Eleatic visitor his young friend (also named Socrates) can step in for him (218b), which is precisely what happens when the conversation of the *Sophist* continues in the *Statesman* (257c). Since Books 2–10 of the *Republic* are five times as long as the *Sophist* or *Statesman*, it is reasonable to expect more than one interlocutor. What tends to happen is that when one of them thinks his brother has become too accommodating toward Socrates he steps in to offer more resistance. Their respective contributions are summarized below.

GLAUCON	ADEIMANTUS
327a–328b. Accompanies Socrates, takes Polemarchus' side in urging Socrates to stay.	327a–328a. Accompanies Polemarchus, takes Polemarchus' side in urging Socrates to stay.
357a–362c. "Shows courage" in reviving Thrasymachus' position	
	362d–372c. Says Glaucon has not gone far enough: the opposing arguments must be rebutted. Founding of the first city.
372c–376d. Complains of austerity in the first city. Founding of the second city.	
	376d–398c. Interlocutor in the education of the guardians.
398c–417b. Does not agree that the principles covering songs and melodies are obvious. Examination of songs and melodies.	
	417b–427d. Complains of austerity for the rulers. Further discussion of the guardians' role.

Glaucon's Objection (357a–362c)

Socrates defeated Thrasymachus only with a semblance of persuasiveness,
Glaucon says. He revives Thrasymachus' argument by asking into which of
three classes Socrates would place justice: things that we value 1) for their
own sake and not for their consequences, like joy; 2) both for their own sake
and also for their consequences, like knowledge; and 3) only for their consequences, like medicine. Socrates places it in the second category—once again
a mean between two extremes—and Glaucon points out that most people
would place it in the third, because they think that in itself it is burdensome
but it brings us rewards. Since everyone agrees about the extrinsic rewards of
justice, and the dispute is about whether it is also intrinsically good, Glaucon
wants Socrates to show what justice and injustice are, and what their intrinsic power is, within us. He proposes to state Thrasymachus' case as strongly as
possible even though he does not agree with it, but he hears such arguments
often (Plato has already explored them in the *Gorgias*, especially in the mouth

of Callicles) and does not know how to reply to them. He thinks Socrates is the one most likely to be able to refute them. He will proceed by stating the common view 1) of the nature and origin of justice; 2) that justice is practiced reluctantly, as something necessary, not intrinsically good; and 3) that the life of an unjust person is better than that of a just one.

1) (358e–359b). Glaucon's explanation of the origin of justice foreshadows Hobbes' social contract theory:

> By nature,[3] they say, committing injustice is good, while being treated unjustly is bad, but the badness of being treated unjustly far exceeds the good of committing injustice. So when people treat others unjustly and are treated unjustly, and taste both, those who lack the power to avoid the latter and attain the former believe that it is to their advantage to make a contract with one another neither to commit nor suffer injustice. Then they begin to make laws and contracts, and they call the commandment of the law lawful and just. And this is the origin and essence of justice: in between the best, which is to do injustice without paying the penalty, and the worst, which is to be treated unjustly and be unable to take revenge. Justice is a mean between these two [358e–359a]

Here again justice appears as a mean, however inadequately understood from Socrates' point of view.

2) (359b–360d). The reason that justice is practiced only unwillingly is that "every nature by nature tries to outdo[4] others, which it considers good, but is perverted by law into honoring equality" (359c). If everyone were allowed to follow their natural inclination, then, we all would pursue injustice. None of us would act any differently than the ancestor of Gyges of Lydia, who, when he found a ring that rendered him invisible, did not hesitate to use this advantage to usurp the kingdom. And if anyone who had such power did not use it for personal advantage, people would think him a fool.

3) (360d–361d). In order to show that the just life is intrinsically better than the unjust, Socrates cannot appeal to extrinsic rewards, since that would tell us nothing about the intrinsic merits. On the other hand, since the whole point of *injustice* is the achievement of extrinsic rewards, the extrinsic rewards must be granted to the unjust person in describing the unjust life. This does not seem quite fair since Socrates classed justice as the kind of thing that is good both intrinsically and for its consequences, so he should not have to defend it as though it were good only intrinsically. But that is not all: to make sure that he receives no rewards for being considered just, the hypothetical just person must be perceived by others to be unjust, and indeed unjust in the extreme, and he must suffer the consequences of such a perception. Thus the just person must suffer every possible social affliction, even if that means

"being whipped, stretched on the rack, bound in chains, having his eyes burned out, and finally, after suffering every evil, being run through with nails" (361e). This is hardly the sort of "other things being equal" comparison that one would expect, but Plato does not make Socrates object—Socrates, the most just of all men (*Phaedo*, 118a), who was hounded to his death on charges of immorality. Seen in those terms the challenge makes sense: was Socrates' life with its tragic ending better or worse than that of a successful scoundrel? This does not mean, as it may at first seem, that the happiness of a just person does not depend at all on external circumstances. Socrates is only required to show that the just person, in no matter what condition, will be happier than the unjust person, in no matter what condition. He is not required to show that external goods and good fortune are entirely irrelevant to the happiness of a good person; and in the Myth of Er we will find that he does not claim they are irrelevant. When Aristotle says that the just and good person needs a certain modicum of external goods in order to be happy,[5] he is usually taken to be departing from a Socratic-Platonic claim that the just person requires nothing but justice in order to be happy. Whatever may be the case in other dialogues, the Socrates of the *Republic* never makes that claim in response to Glaucon and Adeimantus.[6]

As for the unjust person whose life is to be balanced against that of the just person, here too we must see it in its most extreme form. Since it is part of injustice to try to evade detection, the unjust person must be able to achieve the greatest possible injustice while having a reputation for the greatest justice. Like the skilled practitioner of a *techne* he must be allowed to operate from knowledge and not make a mistake; or if he does he can correct it. This is of course similar to Thrasymachus' "ruler in the strict sense", but the unjust person is no longer necessarily identified with a ruler, so the tensions in Thrasymachus' formulation between egoism and legalism have been eliminated. Thus conceived, the unjust person will achieve every material advantage imaginable. With his enormous wealth he will be able to help his friends and harm his enemies (thus achieving Polemarchus' goal); he will also be able to take care of people who are useful to him, and the gods, better than a just man, and will be rewarded for this by the gods (thus achieving Cephalus' goal) (362b–c).

Adeimantus' Objection (362d–367e)

However clear Glaucon's intentions in raising these objections may seem, Adeimantus believes that they need to be made clearer by examining the arguments on the other side. The case against justice can be made not only by arguing against justice, but also by showing the limitations of the arguments in favor of it. The double-sided procedure is analogous to the method that Plato's Parmenides will advocate: "not only must you examine what follows if what is hypothesized exists, but also if it does not exist" (*Parmenides* 135e–136a). Adeimantus mentions four connected arguments (363e365a).

1. When fathers praise justice to their sons, and when Homer, Hesiod, and Museaus praise justice to their audiences, they do not praise justice for itself but only for its consequences. They praise the rewards it brings and point out the punishments that injustice brings.

2. They admit that although justice is a fine thing it is burdensome and difficult while injustice is sweet and easy, and shameful only by opinion and law.

3. They acknowledge that when unjust people become wealthy they are honored despite their injustice, while the poor are dishonored despite their justice.

4. The most remarkable of all these arguments is that, according to Homer, Musaeus, and Orpheus, the gods can be influenced by sacrifices and priestly incantations to reward the unjust and harm the just; so a wealthy unjust man has nothing to fear.

The conclusion to which these arguments lead is that we would be happiest if we could be unjust without suffering the consequences, and that there are ways to avoid suffering the consequences. We can avoid civic punishment by joining secret societies and political clubs, and by learning rhetorical techniques to use in our defense, so that, "sometimes using persuasion, sometimes using force, we will overreach (πλεονεκτοῦντες) without being brought to justice" (365d). And we need not worry about punishment by the gods either, for they may not exist, or they may exist but not concern themselves with us. But if they do exist and do care about us, we ought to believe the poets who claim to know about them, and who tell us that the gods can be influenced by sacrifices purchased with our ill-gotten gains. No one, Adeimantus says, has ever praised justice for itself and condemned injustice for itself, but only for their consequences. Socrates must redress this by showing how the just person is advantaged by being just, and the unjust harmed by being unjust, without regard to extrinsic rewards and punishments. Otherwise only the reputation for justice will be seen to be good, not justice itself.

The brothers do not ask Socrates to show that justice is good even if it does not benefit the just person—they want to see that it does benefit the just person: "Show us what justice and injustice do to their possessor by themselves . . . so that the one is good and the other bad" (367e). Their challenge is to show that justice is good apart from any *extrinsic* rewards like gratitude, honors, and monetary awards.[7] Since there are still intrinsic rewards in the way justice benefits the just person, Socrates is still defending his original claim that justice belongs in the middle class (things which are good both for themselves and for their consequences) and has not been forced, by the brothers' extreme polarization of the alternatives, to defend justice as if it belonged instead to the first class (things that are good only for themselves).[8] Justice not only makes the world a better place (good in itself) but improves the lives of those who practice it.

Pistis and the Healthy City—Cephalus' Justice (367e–372d)

The strategy that Socrates suggests for discovering the nature of justice and injustice in the individual is to first seek the nature of justice and injustice in cities, and then see whether what they discover in that way is also applicable to the individual—just as, if we were trying to read small letters at a distance, and the same letters were written in a larger form close by, we might recognize that the smaller ones are the same as the larger. This approach was previously employed in the second refutation of Thrasymachus, where Socrates showed that justice strengthens a group while injustice weakens it, and then claimed that the same must be true even within a single individual (351c–352a). Socrates proposes to create a city in thought to see how justice and injustice enter into it, and then to see whether what they learn applies to justice in the individual as well.

There is an ambiguity in Socrates' analogy. Are the letters that represent justice in the soul difficult to read because they are small or because they are far away? Why are they described as both when either one would do, and both together make the example equivocal? If the contrast were only between small and large there would be no problem since an individual is smaller than a city, as Socrates points out; but if the contrast is also between near and far it seems we are being told that in some sense justice in the city is closer to us than justice in ourselves. But that seems counterintuitive since justice must come first to the individual and only subsequently to the city: the characteristics of a city are explained by those of its citizens, as Socrates later says (435e), rather than the other way around. A more likely explanation is that although justice in the individual may be prior to justice in the city in the order of being, justice in the city comes first in the order of knowledge, and is closer to us in that sense. And not only because a city is larger than an individual and therefore easier to look into—that was the previous point—but also because justice in the city is to be found in visible actions, while justice in the individual is found in the soul or self, which does not belong to the visible world (cf. *Phaedo* 79b). At this stage the dialogue is operating at the level of *doxa* ("opinion", the lower of the two main segments of the Divided Line), which is directed to the visible world, so the invisible soul is further from our knowledge than the visible city is. When the highest stage of knowledge is reached, in *noesis*, it will be the visible city that is furthest from our minds (519a–d).[9] Looked at in this way, the recognition of the farther letters by the closer ones parallels the recognition of the forms from the perception of the things that participate in them, according to the doctrine of recollection;[10] however there is only a parallel since the ever-moving soul is not at the level of unmoving forms.

Book 1 was an example of what the Divided Line calls *eikasia* or "likeness thinking", thinking by means of images of visible things, because it never examined the nature of just or unjust actions themselves but only refuted theories (images) about them. In proposing to examine the nature of justice by examining the development of cities, Socrates moves from *eikasia* to the next level of the Divided Line, the higher kind of *doxa*, namely *pistis* or "conviction", which is directed at visible things themselves. Cities give us visible examples of just and unjust actions. Glaucon evoked the term *pistis* in its verbal form at the beginning of Book 2 when he said, "Socrates, do you want to seem to have convinced (πεπεικέναι) us or to truly convince (πεῖσαι) us that it is in every way better to be just than unjust?" (357a–b). The greatest discontinuity in the cave is between *eikasia* and the other levels, because that is the only point at which the prisoners must be freed from their chains and forcibly turned around to face the opposite direction. It is perhaps for that reason that the greatest discontinuity in the *Republic* as a whole is between Book 1 and the remaining books, echoed by the return to *eikasia* in Book 10.[11]

On Socrates' account the genesis of the city is quite different from the social contract theory mentioned by Glaucon:

> A city comes into being because it so happens that each of us is not self-sufficient, but we are in need of many things; or do you think that any other principle establishes the city?
>
> Not at all.
>
> Thus when someone takes on one person for one service and another for another, since we are in need of many things, many people gather together in one place to live as partners and helpers. . . . When one person shares with another, if he shares, or takes from the other, he believes it to be better for himself. [369b–c]

Since Adeimantus was only a devil's advocate for the rival view, he has no hesitation in accepting this hypothesis, which diverges from the social contract theory in far-reaching ways. Our natural relationship to others is no longer one of outdoing and exploitation—in other words, of injustice—but of mutual need and benefit through exchange. Not the "wars and alliances" ethic of Polemarchus' "help friends and harm enemies", but the appetitive ethic of Cephalus' "pay each other what you owe". Thus when Socrates asks Adeimantus where justice and injustice are to be found in this city, Adeiman-tus surmises that "it is in some need that these people themselves have of one another". Here justice involves only exchange; laws and government will emerge only in the next city. Socrates' reply, "Perhaps what you say is right",[12] is guarded because mutual need is only one aspect of the justice that is oper-ative here. It does not yet include the principle of natural specialization. As Socrates puts it later, "The requirement that we imposed throughout the city when we began to establish it, that, I think, or some form of it, is justice, . . . [namely] that each one must practice one of the occupations in the city for which his nature is naturally suited" (433a).

If social justice is conceived in terms of a specialization of functions, then it is an image of metaphysical goodness not only in terms of its beneficent consequences but also formally: the city's natural division of itself into spe-cialized functions parallels the way the Idea of the good articulates itself into simple and pure paradigms (forms) of a single quality and function (509b).[13] The natural tendency, whether of intelligible or visible reality, is from unity to multiplicity, from generality to specialization. Thus as soon as the city is founded it begins to grow through further specialization.

1) It begins with the basic needs of food, shelter, and clothing, and there-fore with a farmer, a builder, and a weaver (369d).

2) A cobbler and doctor are immediately added (369d).

3) Further additions are made when Socrates raises what seems to be a new consideration, but was obviously implicit in what had already been said. He asks whether each person will provide all these things for himself, or whether each will specialize and produce the same thing for everyone. The latter turns out to be the better course for three reasons. "First, we are not all born alike, but we have different natures that suit us for different functions" (370a7–b2). Here the concept of "function" returns, that was introduced in the fourth refutation of Polemarchus and developed further in the final refutation of Thrasymachus. Second, people do a better job working at one *techne* than at many (b4–5). Finally, if someone who is working at a *techne* "lets the right moment (*kairos*) go by, the work is ruined" (b7–8), so it is better for people to be able to focus on a single *techne*. Accordingly we should not expect the craftspeople already mentioned to make their own tools, so we will need more citizens, including carpenters and metal workers, and shepherds and cowherds to produce animals for plowing and hauling, and hides and fleece

for clothing. We have now gone from the original city of three jobs to a city of at least nine.

Why did Socrates introduce the principle of specialization at this point, when it was clearly presupposed by the original founding principle that we are not self-sufficient, and the consequent division of the first city into a farmer, a builder, and a weaver? The same principle is proposed now as the principle not of origin but of growth. The founding principle, that specialized cooperation benefits us, is never satisfied once and for all, but constantly pushes us into cooperative relationships at increasingly complex and specialized levels. It is the fundamental principle of what we today call "progress", and will be the driving force that leads from this city to the next one. The motive force behind the principle of specialization is appetite: "things are produced in greater quantity, of better quality, and more easily, when one person does one thing according to his nature and at the right time (*kairōi*)" (370c). Our appetite for more and better things, and for doing things with less work, is insatiable, and will keep pushing us to go ever further in that direction. Only when the city is subjected to the deliberate self-discipline of spiritedness, with the introduction of the soldier-guardians, does the relentless expansion come to a halt, and even begins to reverse itself.

The word *kairos* (timely, fitting, in due measure) appears here twice. In the present context it seems innocent enough, but implicit in it is a tension that will turn out to be of fundamental importance for the concept of *techne*, which figured so prominently in the discussion of justice in Book 1. The ability to recognize the *kairos* cannot be reduced to the conceptual principles of a *techne*, because it is based on sense perception, the recognition of when the time is ripe for something. The rules governing a *techne* can be taught, but the ability to recognize the distinctive opportunities inherent in fluid situations that differ in subtle and indefinable ways cannot be taught; it is a product of personal experience and unselfconscious talent. Since it is nevertheless a necessary condition for employing any *techne* successfully, even if justice could be reduced to a *techne* (in Socrates' strict sense) the principles will not always be able to be applied successfully. That is why the best possible city, even if it can be established, will not be able to continue indefinitely: "Even though they are wise, those who were educated to be rulers of the city will not hit upon the fertility and barrenness of our race through calculation together with sense perception" (546a–b); sooner or later the rulers will apply an essential formula contrary to *kairos* (παρὰ καιρόν: d2).

4) (370e–372c). Next are added importers, more workers to make enough goods for export, merchants, sailors, retailers, and wage-earning laborers. There are now fourteen professions, with multiple members of each. Their

life will consist of working, eating, sleeping, and procreation, together with the rudiments of music and religion: they will sing hymns to the gods. Like Cephalus' world, theirs is a peaceful existence with no occasion for war (372c, d). For Socrates this is the true city, the healthy city (372e), which may seem surprising because it contains nothing of the examined life—there is no rational component. It is the "healthy" city because it is like a healthy body—its concerns are entirely corporeal.[14] And it is the "true" city not because it is the best city, but because it is the true beginning of cities, in contrast with the social contract envisioned by Thrasymachus.

5) (372c–d). But the principle of growth, the insatiability of appetite, speaks again, this time though Glaucon. He is dissatisfied because the simplicity of the food excludes delicacies. Socrates attempts to appease him by the addition of salt, olives, figs, and other such things, but without success:

> If you were founding a city of pigs, Socrates, what else would you fatten them on?
> How should it be, Glaucon?
> What is customary. They should recline on couches if they are not to be uncomfortable, and dine from tables,[15] and have delicacies and desserts as people do now. [372d]

This is the beginning of the transition from an appetitive to a spirited city, and it may be fitting that Glaucon breaks into the conversation to become the catalyst of that change since he himself is described in spirited terms as courageous (357a) and a lover of victory (548d), but we should also keep in mind that he has done so in the name of appetite.

The Fevered and Spirited Cities—
Polemarchus' Justice (372c–376c)

Socrates replies that what Glaucon now asks for is no longer the origin of a city, but the origin of a luxurious city, and he turns his attention from the healthy city to a "fevered" one. The city is now given an odd list of additional components, with prostitutes placed between perfumes and pastries: furniture, delicacies, perfumes, prostitutes, and pastries.

1) (373a). The previous city included only necessities (that was the basis of its health), but now we go beyond what is necessary and add painting, embroidery, gold, and ivory. How is painting not a necessity, when it seems to have been with us from earliest times? Only in Book 8 does Socrates finally explain the difference between the necessary and unnecessary appetites: "Those which we are not able to prevent would rightly be called necessary, as would those whose fulfillment benefits us . . . Those which someone could

eliminate if he practiced from youth, and which accomplish nothing good by being present in us . . . are not necessary" (558d–559a). And only in Book 10 will we learn why Socrates thinks that that painting may not be beneficial.

2) (373b–c). Now as before, the city does not stand still but continues to expand and to add more things that go beyond necessity: hunters, practitioners of the various arts, manufacturers, especially of women's cosmetics, additional servants, tutors, wet-nurses, nannies, beauticians, barbers, chefs, cooks, swineherds, additional cattle because they will now be eaten, and additional doctors. In our previous paragraph the city crossed the line from bodily sustenance to culture of the mind—the arts—for the first time. In this one it crosses the line from peace to violence. The first addition, hunters, is a transition between appetite and spiritedness: hunters employ violence for the sake of appetite. In the healthy city meat was not part of the diet (372b), and cattle were used only for work and clothing (370d–e), and so could die a natural death. Now animals will be slaughtered for food, both in the wild by hunters, and domestically by herdsmen. The shepherds now display the characteristic that Thrasymachus emphasized in them, intending their flocks for food, in addition to the regard for the welfare of their flocks that Socrates emphasized (see 343b, 345c–d).

3) (373d–376c). Socrates makes explicit for the first time that there can be no end to this expansion of appetite, which always finds new desires as its previous ones are satisfied: once the boundaries of necessity have been left behind, the people will be caught up in limitless acquisition. They will eventually need more land and will be led into war with one of their neighbors. The final profession that will be added to this fevered city, then, is that of spirited soldiers or guardians,[16] who are also the city's first rulers, and the city has passed from appetitive to spirited. The kind of spiritedness that we look for in soldiers must combine gentleness to their own people with harshness to their enemies, and so, in passing from appetitive to spirited, the city also moves from Cephalus' ethic of honesty in exchanges to Polemarchus' ethic of helping friends and harming enemies. The soldiers represent more than an additional profession within the city. They represent a different character—spiritedness rather than appetite—and so the city has moved from a classless society to one in which the ruling class is motivated by a different value than the subject class.

In Book 4 Socrates gives the impression that the three classes, and three parts of the soul (appetite, spiritedness, and rationality), represent three completely distinct tendencies alongside one another. But at the same time he suggests that this view of things may be an oversimplification: "You should know, Glaucon, that in my opinion, we will never get an accurate answer using our present methods of argument" (435c); they continue with those methods, however, because Glaucon is satisfied with their present results. Similar suspicions arise when Socrates subsequently speaks of the three parts of the soul together with "any others there may happen to be between them" (443e). If there are additional parts between them, perhaps the number of intermediates is indefinite so that they form a continuum, in which case appetite, spiritedness, and rationality would be more like three parts of a line than discontinuous and independent qualities. From what we have just seen, appetite and spiritedness, at least, do form a continuum rather than being entirely discrete. The transition from the healthy appetitive city to the spirited city went through eight stages, with only minimal differences at each level, just as Polemarchus' spirited concept of justice developed out of a defense of Cephalus' appetitive concept. Although there is a definite moment at which the city ruled by appetite became a city ruled by spirited guardians, Socrates could have introduced that change at almost any time. The process that led from the healthy city through the fevered city to the spirited city was completely continuous, and the need for more land, which led to war and the ascendancy of warriors, could have been asserted at any point in its expansion. Spiritedness did not come from somewhere else to take its place alongside appetitiveness, but was an intensification of something that was present in appetite all along. Something implicit in the insatiability of appetite led to the inexorable transformation into spiritedness. The fact that the very earliest city kept expanding to accommodate new appetites—even if Socrates classified them as necessary rather than unnecessary appetites, a distinction that admits many borderline cases—shows that the temperature was already beginning to rise toward fever pitch from the outset. The transition from the spirited city to the rational one will be no less gradual.

Socrates is concerned that finding suitable guardians may prove to be impossible, for the two qualities required in them, gentleness (to their own people) and harshness (to enemies), seem to be incompatible, and yet neither can be dispensed with. Without a harsh spiritedness the guardians will be unable to prevent others from destroying the city, while without gentleness they will destroy it themselves; but spiritedness and gentleness are opposites (375a–c).[17] Now, for the first time, we are not only given hints that justice is some sort of mean, but we are also given some suggestion of what sort of mean it may turn out to be, and between what kind of extremes.

To demonstrate that the qualities of gentleness to friends and harshness to enemies are not incompatible after all, and that their combination is possible in nature, Socrates points to the example of the noble dog, which is "as gentle as can be with those who are familiar to it and whom it knows, and the opposite toward those it doesn't know" (375d–e). "Then does it seem to you", Socrates asks unexpectedly, "that the guardian will need, in addition to spiritedness, also to be a philosopher by nature?" (375e). He explains that the dog has a philosophical nature: "When it sees someone it doesn't know it treats him harshly even though nothing bad came to it from him, while when it sees someone it knows it welcomes him even though nothing good came to it from him" (376a). Since the dog judges friends and enemies on the basis on whether it knows them or not, Socrates concludes, it is a lover of learning, which is the same as love of wisdom or philosophy. Accordingly, "philosophy, spiritedness, speed, and strength must characterize for us the nature of anyone who is to be a noble and good guardian of the city" (376c).

Before we look at this argument more closely, let us note that philosophy and rationality are already implicit in the beginning of the spirited city, as spiritedness had already been implicit in the insatiability of the appetitive city; and just as the spirited city developed out of the healthy one through minute increments, by the end of Book 3 the rational city will have emerged seamlessly out of the spirited one by an almost imperceptible evolution. It is impossible to say precisely where one begins and the other ends, except that at 414b it is clear that the change has already occurred. Socrates says that it would "be most truly proper to call these people guardians . . . and to call the youths who we just now called guardians, auxiliaries and helpers for the guardians' beliefs". Instead of comparing the guardians to dogs as he did at 375a–376a, he will compare the auxiliaries to dogs and the true guardians to shepherds (416a). What started out as a guardian class of soldiers (374a–e) will by imperceptible degrees turn into a guardian class of philosophers whose decisions are enforced by soldiers. Moreover, although philosophy was not spoken of in the appetitive city, the third part of the soul, rationality, showed itself at the very beginning, when people reasoned that they could benefit by sharing: "When one person shares with another, if he shares, or takes from the other, he believes it to be better for himself" (369c). The seamless evolution of the city through these three stages shows that the three types of character, and the three parts of the soul, do not originate independently of one another, but are emergent qualities on a single continuum.[18]

The argument that dogs are philosophers is obviously a playful way of making the transition from spiritedness to philosophy, but Plato's playfulness has a serious side. When we come to Socrates' proposal in Book 5 that philosophers rule the city, we will see that one of the reasons the proposal is received with such outrage is that philosophers are perceived to be interested in a kind of knowledge for its own sake that has nothing to do with goodness.[19] Not until the last part of Book 6 is philosophy identified with a knowledge that is inseparable from goodness. It may be to allude to this inadequate conception of philosophy that governs the early part of the dialogue, that Socrates does not merely say here that a dog loves people it knows, and hates people it does not know, but emphasizes that it loves knowledge independently of goodness: it loves someone it knows "even though nothing good came to it from him", and hates someone it does not know "even though nothing bad came to it from him". In another way the comparison illustrates something positive, that when we do love the good and the beautiful we recognize them as something that is by nature familiar to us.[20] Looked at in that way it can be regarded, like the image of the large and small letters, as an allusion to the doctrine of Recollection.

We saw how in Book 1 Socrates' argument progressed through reversals of direction: when Polemarchus defended Cephalus' peace-centered ethic it became transformed into a war-centered one, and Cephalus' view that justice is beneficial to us became transformed into a view that justice is beneficial only to others. Something similar takes place here. The city is portrayed as growing and developing by its own internal logic, in accordance with appetite's demand for ever more variety, but as it continues to develop according to its own internal logic Socrates will eventually announce: "by the dog,[21] without noticing, we have been purifying the city that we just said was luxurious" (399e). The words, "without noticing", suggest that the argument seemed to continue in the same direction but inconspicuously reversed direction. As the appetitive ethic becomes transformed into the spirited one, the city's profuse self-indulgence turns surreptitiously into puritanical self-discipline.[22]

Notes

1. Nails puts the year of Adeimantus' birth at 432, Glaucon's at 429, and Plato's at 424/3 (2002, 2, 256, 246). She puts the dramatic date of Books 2–10 of the *Republic* at 408/7 (324–25).

2. A similar conclusion is reached by G. W. F. Ferrari in his comparison of the brothers: *City and Soul in Plato's* Republic (Sankt Augustin: Academia Verlag, 2003), 13–22. After a lengthy comparison Blondell concludes that "the brothers are marked less as intrinsically different than as variations on the same character type, with Glaukon serving as a superior and more fully developed example of that type" (2002, 199–220; 241). For a different view see Leo Strauss, *The City and Man* (Chicago: Rand McNally, 1964), 90–95, followed by Bloom (1968, 342–46). They point out Adeimantus' argument that most people say that justice is hard and onerous while injustice is sweet and easy (36e–364a), and they take Adeimantus to be asking Socrates to prove that justice, rather than injustice, is sweet and easy. But Adeimantus' point is that even when people claim to favor justice because it is "finer" than injustice, they secretly prefer injustice because they think it is sweeter and easier. He

himself never endorses those criteria, and he never asks Socrates to show that justice is sweet and easy. Instead, like his brother, he asks Socrates to show only that justice is good in itself, as well as for its consequences, and that it is beneficial to its possessor while injustice is harmful (367c–d). Strauss suggests that Glaucon is characterized by manliness while Adeimantus is characterized by moderation (90), but later he points out that just as Glaucon objected to the first city because it did not offer enough to the appetites, Adeimantus objects to the third city because the guardians are denied wealth (104). By those criteria both brothers would stand for appetitive values. Brumbaugh (1989) believes that Glaucon is more technical and abstract, while Adeimantus represents the ordinary man. Rudebusch too, regards Glaucon as a higher type than Adeimantus, but instead of identifying Glaucon with courage and Adeimantus with moderation, he identifies Glaucon with reason and Adeimantus with spiritedness (2002, 78). If Plato intended his readers to recognize differences of type between his two brothers, he has given no clear indication of what those differences might be.

3. Cf. Hobbes' "state of nature".

4. A form of the same term, πλεονεξίαν, was used by Socrates to characterize Thrasymachus' position in the first refutation at 349a–351a.

5. *Nicomachean Ethics* 1.8.1099a31–b2, 10.7.1177a28–30.

6. Although he does make it polemically against Thrasymachus (353e–354a). Also see Irwin 1995, 192–93 & n20, 199.

7. Thus there is no contradiction when R. E. Allen ("The Speech of Glaucon in Plato's *Republic*", *Journal of the History of Philosophy* 25 [1987]: 3–11) says, "our own good is in fundamental respects identical with the common good . . . [so] the egoist fails because he is not egoistic enough" (11); and when D. Z. Phillips ("Glaucon's Challenges", *Philosophical Investigations* 17 [1994]: 536–51) says, "if self-interest is introduced as a motivational force, it either falsifies or vulgarizes these acts" (541). Allen is speaking of intrinsic self-interest and Phillips of extrinsic self-interest. Some writers believe that the issue is problematic, however. For further discussion see Cross and Woozley 1964, 66–68; Nicholas White, *A Companion to Plato's* Republic (Indianapolis: Hackett, 1979), 78–9; and Irwin 1995, 190–91, 201–2.

8. Cf. Annas 1981, 66–8.

9. For a different explanation see Seth Benardete, *Socrates' Second Sailing: On Plato's Republic* (Chicago: University of Chicago Press, 1989), 45–6.

10. See below, 335–36, 340.

11. In a comparable way Kimon Lykos suggests that in Book 1 "Socrates' *elenchos*, the examination of the beliefs of his interlocutors, corresponds to the forcible 'turning around' of the soul of the prisoner" (*Plato on Justice and Power: Reading Book 1 of Plato's Republic* [Albany, N.Y.: SUNY Press, 1987], 6). I would add only that it is not the elenchus itself that achieves this, since Socrates' audience believes that Socrates has only tricked rather than refuted Thrasymachus; but rather the resulting dissatisfaction with this entire way of arguing, that turns them away from *eikasia*.

12. In full Adeimantus says, "I do not know, Socrates, unless it is in some need that these people themselves have of one another", followed by Socrates' reply, "Perhaps

what you say is right" (372a). Daniel Devereaux describes Adeimantus' response as a "vague answer . . . [which] Socrates in effect ignores" (37). He points out that when Glaucon demands a more luxurious city Socrates says, "by examining such a city . . . we might see the origin of justice and injustice in cities" (372e), and takes this to mean "that justice and injustice had not yet come into being in the first city" ("Socrates' First City in the *Republic*", *Apeiron* 13 [1979]: 36–40). What Devereaux says is true of injustice but not of justice, and that is the point: the first city does not show "the origin of *both* justice and injustice" (τε δικαιοσύνην καὶ ἀδικίαν). But Adeimantus' answer and Socrates' reply suggest that it does at least contain justice, although it is difficult to discern without the contrasting presence of injustice (had Plato wished to indicate that justice is not present it would be misleading for Socrates to tell Adeimantus that he may be right). Accordingly, in Book 4 Socrates will say, "it seems to me that although we have been speaking and hearing about [justice] for a long time, we did not understand ourselves, namely that we were talking about it in a sense" (432e). Strauss (1965) suggests, "The healthy city may be just in a sense but it surely lacks virtue or excellence" (95). Also see N. White 1979, 88, and John Cooper, "Two Theories of Justice" (*Proceedings and Address of the American Philosophical Association* 74 [2000] 5–27): 10–15.

13. 478e–479a, 484c, 507b, 540a, 596a; cf. *Phaedo* 80a.

14. At the end of Book 9 Socrates will say that people look down on manual labor (which would include all the occupations of the healthy city) because it is devoted to serving the needs of appetite rather than what is best in us (590a–c). A little later he says that a person of understanding does not look to health or prioritize it unless it contributes to self-control, and will always tune the harmony of the body for the sake of consonance in the soul (591c–d).

15. When Socrates explains the theory of forms to Glaucon in Book 10 these two, κλῖναι (couches or beds) and τράπεζαι (tables), will be his two examples (596a–b).

16. Since slaves are first acquired as spoils of war, they only come into the city at some point after the soldiers. There was no mention of slaves in the healthy city (see Bernard Bosanquet, *A Companion to Plato's Republic* [London: Rivingtons, 1906], 84) but by 395e they have become a fact of life.

17. Similarly in the *Statesman* the ruler must weave together the two opposite natures of moderation and spiritedness, for the moderate type "lacks drive and a certain sharp and active quickness", and may even be simple-minded; while the courageous spirited type "is lacking in justice and caution" and "inclines towards brutality" (309e–311b). Cf. *Gorgias* 492a–b.

18. As I have argued elsewhere, "There is a mutual dependence among the three, for not only are our rationality and appetite permeated with spiritedness to the extent that they exhibit their specific motivation and ambition, but spiritedness in turn requires our rational and corporeal nature as the instruments of its assertiveness: our attainments must be in terms of intellectual or physical goals. . . . The three are thus interpenetrating and inseparable. This can be expressed by conceiving soul generally as the agency of reason in corporeality" (*Plato's* Phaedo: *An Interpretation* [Toronto: University of Toronto Press, 1982], 190, slightly modified).

19. Compare 473d–474a with 487d–e.

20. Cf. Nettleship 1901: "The real meaning of the passage . . . [is] an anticipation of what he says more intelligibly later on. In Book III he speaks of the love of beauty as a sort of recognition by the soul of what is akin to it in the world about it; the soul welcomes (ἀσπάζεται) what is beautiful from a sense of kinship. In Book VI the desire of knowledge and truth is represented as the desire of the soul to unite itself to what is akin to it in the world" (75).

21. When Socrates swears by the dog in the Gorgias (428b) he identifies it as "the god of the Egyptians", i.e., Anubis, the god of the dead, but here the oath is more likely a playful reference to the "philosopher dogs" who govern this city.

22. Diskin Clay makes the related observation that the Republic shows how the prior existence of injustice is a necessary condition for the existence of justice ("Reading the Republic", in Platonic Writings, Platonic Readings, ed. Charles Grisold (New York: Routledge, 1988; reprinted University Park: Pennsylvania State University Press, 2002, 1–33), 24–29.

CHAPTER THREE

~

Education of the Guardians (Book 2.376c–Book 3.412b)

The Extent of Education

The discussion of education in the spirited city focuses on the education of the guardians, so it is not clear whether the appetitive class is also included in the educational process, and there is considerable controversy about the question. When the subject of self-control is introduced it seems that both the ruling class and the subject class are included since obedience to rulers is emphasized: "Won't our young people need self-control? . . . And aren't these the most important things about self-control for most people: to be obedient to the rulers, and to be rulers themselves over the pleasures of drink, sex, and food" (389d–e). Later, however, when Socrates says that "the rulers must be older and the subjects younger" (412c), he is obviously referring to a distinction within the guardian class, for he would scarcely mean that guardians are always older than farmers. So in the earlier passage, too, it is conceivable that the people who are trained to be obedient to the rulers are not the appetitive class but only the younger guardians. Nevertheless, if this kind of education can produce obedience in the citizens, we would expect Socrates to want to extend it to the whole populace. In Book 4 he points out that training the children's character in the way described will obviate the need for many laws, since the correct inclinations will already have been inculcated into them by their education (425a–c).[1] It would be strange if he did not extend this prin ciple throughout the population, given his constant emphasis on creating a unified city.

Again, since children are not always like their parents, the principle that people should do the work for which they are suited by nature requires that children will sometimes deserve to be moved into a different class (415a–c), and unless children of the appetitive class are educated alongside those of the guardian class—and later the auxiliary class—there would be no opportunity to recognize and promote those who deserve it (also see below, 144–47). Certain goals of the curriculum, such as the inculcation of courage in warfare, will be of use only to the guardians, but that does not mean that children of the appetitive class would not receive the same education until their vocation is ascertained.[2]

The guardians' education will take the traditional form of "physical exercise for the body and the arts for the soul" (376e).[3] Later, however, Socrates says that the common belief is mistaken that regards the value of physical exercise to be primarily for the sake of the body. Its primary importance, he insists, is for the soul as well, because the arts without physical exercise make us soft and too gentle, while physical exercise without the arts make us savage and too hard (410c–d, cf. 441e–442a). Just as in the guardians' nature spiritedness and gentleness needed to balance each other to produce a mean rather than an extreme, so too in their education exercise and arts need to balance each other for the same reason.

The Content of Poetry (376c–392c)

When Adeimantus supported Glaucon in challenging Socrates to combat the common belief in the superiority of injustice, he pointed out that the common view is supported by texts from Hesiod and Homer, among others (364b–e). Socrates' first step in establishing a poetic educational curriculum, therefore, will be to take Adeimantus as his partner in the purging of such texts.[4] "There are two forms of speech, one true and the other false . . . and education must be in both, but first in the false. . . . We first tell the children myths, and myths are on the whole false, although there is also truth in them (376e–377a).[5] We must begin with myths because young children are at their most impressionable and malleable, and therefore cannot be neglected, but they will not be ready for literal accounts until they are older. The criterion for excellence cannot be whether the myths are literally true, since they are by nature literally false, or even whether they are allegorically true because young people cannot always distinguish between allegorical and literal meanings (378d–e).[6] Instead it will be whether they are made beautifully (377c), which turns out to mean whether they are conducive to virtue. Consequently even if stories like Hesiod's account of the castration by Kronos of his father

Ouranos are true, they should not be taught to thoughtless young people, but should either be left in silence or communicated only to a select few (377e–378a). The myths will be tailored to encourage in the children all four of the cardinal virtues—wisdom, courage, self-control, and justice—except that since the children are not ready for the literal truth, piety will take the place of wisdom. That the first part of the discussion is aimed at piety is not made explicit until three pages after it begins (380c), but courage (386a), self-control (389d), and justice (392a–b) are identified at the outset.

Piety (377c–386a)

Later, when the philosopher-rulers are educated to philosophical wisdom, they will study the forms, not the gods. At this pre-conceptual age, however, they will hear about gods instead, but the two characteristics of the gods that will be emphasized for the sake of piety are especially characteristic of the forms: goodness (379a–380c) and self-sameness (380d–383a). Accordingly, the first law and pattern that Socrates and Adeimantus will impose on the poets is that "the god isn't the cause of all things but only of the good ones" (380c); while the second is that the gods neither become nor appear to be different from what they are in truth: "the god is simple and true, both in deed and word, and neither alters himself nor deceives others" (382e–383a). Here, as later with regard to the other virtues, Socrates cites a number of passages from the poets that violate these principles, and serve as examples of the kind of stories that would be excluded from the children's education.

Just as the *Timaeus* explains evil by an independent causal factor that limits the power of the rational and good creator god (48a), here too, since the god is good and can therefore be the cause only of good things, "we must seek the cause of evil in other things, and not in the god" (379b–c). The *Republic*, unlike the *Timaeus*, does not specify the nature of this cause, but the principle of dualism is firmly established. There is no argument for the principle that gods must be good, which, although certainly not apparent in Homer and Hesiod, seems to have been intuitively acceptable to a certain kind of intellectually sophisticated person of Plato's day, as in ours.[7] The principle that gods are changeless and always appear as they truly are is less so—Adeimantus hesitates before accepting it (380d, 381b, 382a)—and Socrates establishes it by arguing that a god can neither a) be changed by something else, nor b) by himself, nor c) have any reason to appear other than he is.

Socrates does not argue the first point (a) in the most obvious way, by pointing out that nothing is stronger than a god and therefore nothing can compel a god to change. Instead he argues more abstractly that: "Things that are in the best condition are least altered or moved by something else. . . . The god and all that pertains to the god is in every way in the best condition. . . . Therefore the god would be least likely to have many shapes" (380e–381b). The argument is not unreasonable, for things that are in good condition are more stable than those that are not, but why does Socrates go to the trouble of establishing the gods' strength indirectly, through the middle term of "good condition", rather than by appealing to the self-evidence of the claim that nothing is stronger than a god? If it is self-evident that gods are in the best condition, it is no less so that they have the most strength. This more abstract line of argument anticipates the later demythologization of gods into forms. It would make no sense to say that forms are supremely strong, since they are not active in the motive sense, but they are in the best possible condition, the supreme "form" of the quality they embody.

The second question (b) was whether, if the gods cannot be changed by something else, they might change themselves (381b–e). If so, "does the god change himself for the better and more beautiful, or for the worse and more ugly?" Conceived according to these alternatives the answer is obvious: gods cannot change for the better because they are already the best possible, and cannot change for the worse because no one would wish to become worse. There is a third possibility, that a god could change into something different that is neither better nor worse, namely another god; but none of myths depict gods as turning into other gods, the way they show them taking human or animal forms.

The remaining possibility (c) is that gods make us think that they change even though they do not (381e–383c). Socrates distinguishes two kinds of falsity: "true falsity" and falsity in words. The first kind produces ignorance and error in our highest faculty and is accordingly hated by all gods and humans, but the second kind is useful in various ways: 1) we can employ falsehood effectively against our enemies (in accordance with Polemarchus' contention that it is just to harm our enemies); 2) we can employ it as a medicine when our so-called friends are bent on evil because of madness or foolishness (a case in which even Cephalus agreed that telling the truth would not be just); 3) it is useful in mythology when we do not know the truth about the ancient events. As we saw, the myths were called false accounts that have some truth in them, such as allegorical truth. Although falsehood can be useful to us in all these ways, none of these reasons for employing it would apply to the gods: they are not ignorant of the past, they have nothing to fear from enemies, and no one who is foolish or mad is a friend of the gods. The emphasis on friendship in this passage is worth noting because of the implied incompatibility between friendship and falsehood. In the second example people who are mad or foolish were not our true friends but only our so-called friends (τῶν καλουμένων φίλων), and in what follows we are told that no one who is foolish or mad is a friend of the gods. To be a friend of the gods we must be reasonable and wise. It seems, then, that, among both gods and humans, to be a true friend and not a friend in name only means being reasonable and wise. To be a true friend is to be a friend of truth.

Courage (386a–389d)

The discussion of the role of myths in promoting courage forms the opening of Book 3. In order to inculcate courage, the fear of death must be discouraged with the help of the mythmaking poets (386a–388e). There is no suggestion that the fear of death can be simply eliminated; the goal is rather to make death less terrible to contemplate than defeat and the likely result of defeat, slavery. First of all, therefore, the afterlife in Hades must be praised rather than disparaged, and Plato has no trouble citing a multitude of passages about the repugnance of Hades as examples of what would have to be suppressed.[8] Second, as a corollary, pejorative synonyms for Hades would have to be avoided, such as Cocytus ("River of Wailing") and Styx ("Hateful River"). Third, poets must not make too much of lamentations of the dead, both because "a good man will not think that for his friend, who is a good man, death is a terrible thing" (387d), and also because a good person is as self-sufficient as possible, least in need of others, and therefore most able to bear it when he loses someone close to him (387e). Again Socrates quotes offending passages and remarks that it would be dangerous for children to listen to such stories without laughing at them as not worth hearing (388d).

Two other things must be also discouraged—love of laughter (388e–389a) and dishonesty (389b–d)—but whether they are connected with courage or are independent factors is difficult to determine.[9] They may be separate considerations unrelated to courage, since no explicit connection is established, but the warning about laughter follows naturally from Socrates' remark that the children ought to laugh at the emotional lamentations of the stories that have just been excluded (388d). Almost immediately afterward he adds: "And again they must not be lovers of laughter either, for when someone abandons himself to violent laughter a violent change is apt to follow" (388e). If a violent change follows violent laughter, that change is presumably something like violent grief; another example of the principle of reversal that permeates the dialogue. Abandoning ourselves to one form of emotion makes us vulnerable to the others as well, so if we want to avoid extremes of lamentation we must also avoid extremes of gaiety. The virtue of courage requires a kind of mental steadfastness that is not compatible with extreme emotions.

If the restriction on violent laughter is part of the discussion of courage, the next passage, which like the previous one is introduced with "moreover" (ἀλλὰ μήν), seems to stand on the same footing. If so, a fifth and final restriction in the education of the children to courage would be a prohibition of falsehood. We saw earlier that the rulers are permitted to use efficacious falsehood such as myths, and now we are told:

> All others cannot touch it, but we shall say that for private people to lie to rulers of that kind is as great a lapse—and even greater—as for a patient not to tell his doctor, or an athlete his trainer, the truth about his bodily condition, or for someone not to tell the facts to a ship's pilot about the ship and sailors, and how he and any of the others are faring. [389b–c]

Why is this point raised here, rather than ten pages earlier at the beginning of the discussion when the subject of truth and falsehood was originally introduced? What connection, if any, does it have with courage? In Book 4 Socrates says that courage in a city is the power to preserve through pain and pleasure, desire and fear, the belief inculcated in it by the ruler about what is to be feared (429b–c). Courage, then, is not just 1) fearlessness;[10] it also involves 2) an ability to resist the destabilizing effects of pleasure and pain, and 3) directions about what are the right things to fear. With regard to the second component, the restrictions against extremes of laughter or lamentation were meant to inculcate precisely that resistance in us. The third component tells us that in order to be truly courageous, we must receive correct instructions about what to fear. These instructions cannot be limited to general rules, for as we saw in the cases of Cephalus and Polemarchus, no rules are without exceptions, so rulers will not be able to give the right orders unless they grasp the individuating details of any situation as accurately as possible. Socrates compares them to other kinds of people who have knowledge of the relevant principles but cannot apply those principles without a full knowledge of the particulars: if the rulers must rely on false information, the course of action that they set for us will be no more reliable than the orders that doctors would give to patients who have lied about their condition, or trainers to athletes, or pilots to sailors. Courage, then, requires the ability to see things as they are, which will not be possible if the rulers are not told the truth.

Self-control (389d–392a)

As was the case with the passage on courage, the passage on self-control too begins unproblematically but then moves in unexpected directions. The poets are to be prevented from showing in a favorable light anyone who is overly devoted to the pleasures of wine (389e–390b), food (390b), sex (390b–c), and money (390d–391a). But the final examples no longer make obvious reference to appetitive pleasures, but instead to arrogance (ὑπερηφανίαν: 391c) and impiety (ἀσεβῆ: 391d). The reference to arrogance is understandable because Socrates had introduced the topic of self-control by saying that it included obedience to the rulers (389d). In context that was not surprising, because there it means obedience by the appetitive class to the guardians, and thus conforms with the sense of self-control as control over appetite. Now, however, the concept is extended to respect for the gods, regardless of whether appetite is involved. The connection seems to be that stories that cause us to lose respect for the gods may "produce in our young people a strong inclination to behave badly" (392d–e), i.e., without self-control; our respect for the gods is one of the most important checks on our appetites.

Once again a theme that had previously been treated under one virtue has returned under another. In the case of courage it was truthfulness, which had already been discussed under piety, while here it is piety itself that returns, and the return is explicit: "As we said earlier . . ." (391e). The implication is that the virtues are not independent of one another, but overlap and interpenetrate—and are perhaps ultimately indistinguishable—in accordance with the doctrine of the unity of the virtues that Socrates defended in the *Protagoras*, and which will be implicit again in Book 4.

Justice (392a–c)

The discussion of justice is brief but intriguing:

> What form of story still remains for our classification of what ought and ought not to be told? We've spoken about what ought to be said about gods, daimons, heroes, and those in Hades.
> Absolutely.
> Wouldn't speech about human beings be what is left?
> Clearly.
> It's impossible, my friend, for us to treat this at present.
> Why?
> Because I think we will say that poets and prose writers speak badly about the most important human matters. They say that there are unjust people who are nevertheless happy, many of them, and just people who are miserable, and that injustice is profitable if it is undetected, while justice is other people's good but one's own loss. And we shall forbid them to say such things, and direct them to sing and make myths about the opposite. Or don't you think so?
> On the contrary I know it well.
> Then if you agree that I'm right, I'll say that you agree to what we have been seeking all along?
> Your reply would be correct.

> Won't we agree that it's necessary to speak this way about human beings
> when we discover what justice is, and how it by nature profits the one who pos-
> sesses it, whether he appears to be just or not? [392a–c]

The description of justice as what is left over after the discussions of the other
virtues prefigures the way it will be approached when it is comes to be defined
in Book 4 (432b).

Socrates' prediction that they will "agree that it's necessary to speak this
way about human beings when we discover what justice is" implies that they
are not able to agree to this now because they have not yet said what justice is.
However, he has not hesitated to make such statements about the other
virtues even though he has not yet defined them. Thrasymachus, for one,
would be no more likely to accept the things that Socrates and Adeimantus
have said about piety and self-control than what they would be likely to say
about justice at this point—although he might approve of what they said
about courage. How were Socrates and Adeimantus able to make such claims
before defining the respective virtues? More radically, how can Socrates know,
before they have discovered what justice is, what they will want to say about it
after they have discovered what it is? We saw the same problem at the end of
Book 1, when Socrates claimed that until he has discovered what justice is he
cannot yet know whether it is a virtue and whether it makes us happy—a
claim that must have involved some irony since he obviously thought he knew
the answer to both those questions. Both of these passages carry resonances of
Meno's paradox: In order to search for something we must already have some
idea what it is (*Meno* 80d). The solution given there is "recollection", that we
have by nature a preconscious knowledge that guides our conscious search.[11]
The doctrine of recollection is never explicitly stated in the *Republic* but it
seems to be alluded to in the Myth of Er (below, 340), and in the reference in
Book 6 to "divining" (ἀπομαντευομένη) the Idea of the good (505e), as well
as the passages pointed to in chapter 2. It is perhaps being hinted at here as
well; otherwise the point of Socrates' paradoxical remark is hard to understand. The absence of any clear reference to the doctrine of recollection in the
Republic is perhaps because of the dialogue's emphasis on education by those
who already know, rather than on independent inquiry.

Why does Socrates say that the stories about justice are stories about
human beings, while the others were about gods, daimons, heroes, and those
in Hades? Almost any quotation from Homer or the other poets will be about
gods and heroes rather than ordinary human beings, and the preceding discussion of the other virtues focused on gods and heroes because it happened
to be focused on Homer, rather than because it was primarily concerned with

gods and heroes. The discussion of piety naturally had to concern itself with stories about the behavior of gods and daimons (382), and the discussion of courage would naturally center on heroes and Hades, but it did, in fact, turn to human beings when it moved to truth-telling: the rulers will punish any citizen they catch lying, "any one of the craftsmen, 'Whether a prophet or healer of illness or joiner of timbers'" (389d). The quotation is from the *Odyssey* (17.384–5), and the speaker is the swineherd Eumaeus, addressing the suitor Antinous, so the subject, speaker, and addressee are ordinary humans rather than gods, daimons, heroes, or shades. Socrates' statement, then, was not accurate. Not only were human beings exemplified in the discussion of the other virtues, but the discussion of justice could have employed examples of divinities, since there is no lack of stories about justice and injustice among gods and heroes in Homer and the tragedians. In Book 8 of the *Odyssey*, for example, there is a discussion of what the just penalty would be for Ares to pay Hephaestus to compensate him for having slept with his wife Aphrodite (266–358). Socrates could easily have said that we will not allow our poets to say that the gods could behave unjustly. Why then does Socrates say that the other virtues apply to gods, daimons, heroes, and those in Hades, while justice applies to human beings?

Piety, and even self-control when it deals with hubristic qualities (391c–d), must refer to gods and daimons; and courage not only makes reference to heroes, but ultimately to death and therefore Hades. Justice, on the other hand, has no direct reference to anything supernatural, and that may be why Socrates describes the discussion of justice as a discussion of human beings. Justice, then, is conceived of at this point as the one virtue that is directed only toward other human beings, and makes no reference to gods or daemons—either in our representation of them (piety) or respect for them (self-control) or our fear of death (courage). But if all the virtues are in some sense variants of one another, then what is said here about justice will apply to the others as well. In that case the transition from the divinely conceived virtues of piety, self-control, and courage, to the humanly conceived virtue of justice, is also a transition from a mythological conception of virtue generally, to a philosophical conception that makes no reference to mythology, and in which piety will be replaced by wisdom.

The Form of Poetry (392c–398b)

Socrates distinguishes between two kinds of poetic voice—narrative voice, in which events are described but not enacted, and imitative voice, in which the poet puts speeches into the mouth of his characters, acting out the events rather than merely describing them. This distinction is reflected in the differences among three kinds of poetry: epics, which use both voices; tragedy and comedy, which are entirely imitative; and dithyrambs, which are entirely narrative (392c–394c). Most people prefer the imitative style because it is more pleasant (presumably because it is livelier) and provides more variety: the voices of the different speakers are represented by different kinds of melody or mode, and rhythm, while in the case of narration the voice remains the same (397a–d). The pleasure of variety is outweighed by two disadvantages, Socrates argues: departure from specialization and the influence on emotions.

The city was founded on the principle that people will be able to do their work better if they specialize in the one thing that they are suited for by nature, and leave the others alone. It follows that the imitative poet too would be more successful at imitating one voice (narration) than at imitating many. Socrates' proof is that playwrights and actors who excel at either tragedy or comedy do not excel at the other, and if playwrights cannot compass this difference they will hardly compass the more extensive differences among the types of people represented in each one (395a). The strongest arguments to the effect that artists cannot have true knowledge of all the things that they imitate are reserved for the beginning of Book 10; at this point there has not yet been an investigation into what constitutes true knowledge.

Not only is the present argument more general than the later ones, but Socrates' denial that the same people excel at both tragedy and comedy was apparently contradicted by his own words in the *Symposium*, when he obtained the agreement of the tragic poet Agathon and the comic poet Aristophanes that "the same man would know how to write comedy and tragedy, and the one who is by *techne* a tragic poet would also be a comic poet" (223d).[12] We do not hear the details of that argument which Aristodemus, the reporter of the events, was too drowsy to follow, but we can guess from Socrates' use of the word *techne* that it was probably along the same lines as his argument in, for example, the *Ion*, that someone who possesses a certain *techne* will have knowledge of the whole field to which that *techne* applies rather than selective knowledge within that field (532d–533c). In that case Socrates would have been arguing that if Agathon and Aristophanes create their works by means of *techne*, there is no relevant difference between the *techne* that produces tragedy and the one that produces comedy, and each must have the skill to create the other kind of drama as well. But in the *Ion* the argument functions as a reductio ad absurdem: on the assumption that Ion achieved his results by means of *techne* he would have to be versatile, but he is not versatile, so the assumption is false and what he does cannot be the result of *techne* (533c, cf. 542a–b). We saw a related reductio in the Book 1 when Socrates argued that if justice is the *techne* of holding onto money it must equally be the *techne* of stealing it (334a). Given Socrates' consistent denial that that arts are forms of *techne*, it seems likely that in the *Symposium* too the argument was meant to function as a reductio: if dramatic poets did what they did by means of *techne*, then the same ones would be skilled at both comedy and tragedy, but they are not. Socrates had gotten as far as to establish the major premise ("the one who is by *techne* a tragic poet would also be a comic poet") while Aristophanes and Agathon were still barely awake, but they fell asleep before the argument could progress any further (223d). Otherwise it seems likely that Socrates would have gone on to point out that Aristophanes and Agathon are themselves proof against this claim, so it must not be by *techne* that they create their work. In that case the inconsistency between the *Symposium* and *Republic* is only apparent, and the implications of the *Symposium*, like the *Republic*, are that dramatists are not good at both tragedy and comedy. When Socrates argues here that this is true even though the two kinds of imitation are closely akin, the argument prefigures the critiques of poetry in Book 10 that deny it the status of *techne* or knowledge.

Regardless of whether poets can adequately understand the many different kinds of individuals that they imitate, the very act of imitation, according to Socrates, produces an emotional susceptibility in the audience that can undermine the goals of education: "Haven't you perceived that imitations, practiced continuously from youth, settle into habits and nature in the body, voice, and thought?" (395d). Consequently, children who inwardly imitate unworthy models may become corrupted by them over time.[13] Because of these dangers, imitation is to be permitted only of virtuous people, and imitations are to be prohibited of women who are acting intemperately, of slaves behaving slavishly, of men who are not virtuous or who are mad, of craftspeople of the appetitive class (since the character of the guardians is what is aimed at), of animals, or the noises of inanimate nature (395d–396b).

Music (398c–403c)

When we use the term "absolute music" today we mean instrumental music —music with words is seen as a subsequent mixture of poetry and music—but until the end of the eighteenth century the usual form of music, not only in the West, was song, and purely instrumental music was the exception rather than the rule. Accordingly, when Socrates discusses music he distinguishes it into words, harmonic mode (ἁρμονία), and rhythm. The composer's words, he says, will be subject to the same restrictions as the poet's words, which have already been itemized, "and the mode and rhythm must follow the words" (398d). The view that there is an intrinsic connection between psychological states (such as virtues and vices, and emotions generally) is as old as thinking about music. Plato takes it as the received view, Aristotle also endorses it, and in China the roughly contemporaneous Confucian classic, *The Record of Music*, takes it for granted as well.[14]

The kinds of subtle but significant distinction that Plato has in mind are no longer as evident to our ears because of the homogenization of our tonal sources. The original eight (or twelve) basic harmonic modes[15] have been reduced to two, the major (Lydian) and minor (based on the Hypodorian), and even these have had their distinctiveness compromised by well-tempered tuning, which averages out the different values for tones within different keys. We are still capable of noticing that, other things being equal, the minor mode sounds "sadder" than the major mode, and to ears accustomed to the full range of natural (as opposed to well-tempered) modes many more such distinctions would have been audible. The modes were developed not with the intention of imitating the tones of voice that accompany specific states of mind or moods, but rather because they represent the various possibilities offered by the Pythagorean relationships of tones; however, just as our major and minor modes turned out to suggest comparative cheerfulness and sadness, each of the complete set of modes was suggestive of, and associated with, a particular emotional condition.

After eliminating those that are associated with emotional conditions that are not conducive to virtue—lamentation, drunkenness, softness, and laziness (the Lydian, for example, is "slack")—Socrates, now partnered by Glaucon, who has taken over from his brother, retains only the two that reflect the virtues of the two classes that comprise the city at this point: the Dorian which reflects the temper of self-control in peacetime, and the Phrygian which reflects courage in wartime (398e–399c). The choice of musical instruments follows suit: the "multi-harmonic" and multi-stringed instruments of Marsyas (harp and flute) will be excluded, while the instruments of Apollo (lyre, cithara, and syrinx) will be allowed (399c–e). The consideration of the arts is then succinctly extended to the visual arts: painting, weaving, embroidery, architecture, and household furnishings are to follow the same general principles (400e–401a).

The correlation between musical form and emotion turns out to have been as imprecise in Plato's day as in our own, for Aristotle thinks Socrates is mistaken to employ the Phrygian mode, although he agrees with the choice of the Dorian. He associates the Phrygian not with courage in war but with Bacchic frenzy. Besides the Dorian, he recommends, instead of the Phrygian, the Lydian, as especially beneficial to children and conducive to the orderliness required for their education.[16] So where Plato heard courage Aristotle hears frenzy, and where Aristotle hears orderliness Plato heard slackness. Their agreement on the Dorian suggests that the associations were not hopelessly relative (courage in war is not unrelated to frenzy either), but obviously a good deal of subjectivity is involved.

"By the dog!" Socrates announces after they have formulated the restrictions, "without noticing, we have been purifying the city that we just said was luxurious" (399e). In Book 8, at a point in his account of the city's decline that corresponds to this point in its evolution, Socrates will formulate the general principle that accounts for what has just happened: "Anything that is done to excess is wont to produce a correspondingly great opposite reaction: in the seasons, as well as in plants, and in bodies, and not least in political constitutions" (563e–564a). In the present instance the excessive luxury of the city leads to an ascetic reaction of purification.

As we saw at the end of chapter 2, this point marks another reversal in the direction of the unfolding of the dialogue, another point whereby apparently going straight ahead Socrates and his partners suddenly find themselves going the opposite way. With the feverish city the emphasis was on variety, the natural effect of the principle of specialization on which the city was built. But that principle had a paradoxical consequence. In itself it embodied the virtue of simplicity, one person one job; but as an agent of appetite (370c) it made possible an increasing variety of products in response to the insatiability of appetite. The purification of the feverish city is an attempt to purify the principle of simplicity by keeping the appetites in check. Accordingly the simplicity of the gods (an image of the simplicity of the forms) is insisted on (380d, 381c, 382e), as is a simple narrative style for poetry (392d, 393d, 394a), and simplicity in music, physical training, and medicine (404b, 410a–b). Socrates is aiming at the kind of simplicity of character that gives rise to appetites that are healthy, so that we will be just by natural inclination without the need of external coercion. Cephalus exemplified one kind of need for external coercion insofar as he pursued justice only because of his fear of punishment after death; but fear of death and of Hades are among the attitudes that the restrictions on the stories of the poets are intended to eliminate,[17] because they work against courage. In his case appetitive greed was defeated only by appetitive fear of punishment, and so his just behavior was achieved through turbulent complexity rather than by desires that are simple and reasonable to begin with. The distinction is analogous to the difference in Aristotle between temperance, in which we have only virtuous desires, and continence, in which we also have vicious desires but are able to keep them under control.[18]

Socrates follows the discussion of the musical modes with a parallel dis-cussion of types of rhythm that distinguishes the metrical rhythms associated with healthy states of mind from those associated with unhealthy ones (399e–400c). Between them, the healthy modes (*harmoniai*) and rhythms produce harmony and eurhythmia[19] in the soul, but there is a difference between the otherwise parallel concepts of harmony and rhythm. Although bad rhythm and bad harmony are given the parallel names of "non-rhythm" and "non-harmony" (ἀρρυθμία, ἀναρμοστία), the parallel breaks down in the positive forms of the words, where good rhythm is *eurhythmia* but good harmony is not *euharmonia* but simply *harmonia*. In other words, *harmonia* is always good. If it ceases to be good it ceases to be harmony. The same thing is implicitly true of rhythm, since the rejected rhythms are not called "bad rhythm" but non-rhythm, but the point is more emphatic in the case of har-mony because an inept rhythm can still be said to have a kind of rhythm, in a way that is not true of an inept harmony. Harmony, like the virtues, is both a mean and an extreme: a mean between going too far and not going far enough, but an extreme of goodness. That is why the study of *harmonia* will be the highest propaedeutic for the study of dialectic that takes us to the Idea of the good (530d–531c).

It turns out, then, that the rejected modes or "harmonies" (*harmoniai*) are in another sense non-harmonies. A musical mode is a *harmonia* in two senses: insofar as the modes (*harmoniai*) are distinguished from one another they have different affective characters that are associated with specific human emotions, some good and some bad; but insofar as they all are *harmoniai* they all reflect the principles of rational order as identified by the Pythagoreans,[20] and are good. A particular mode is thus polarized between human emotion on one side and divine rationality on the other, and those *harmoniai* are called non-harmonies which emphasize the irrational species of emotion. Even though they are also species of rational proportion, their emotive nature undermines their rational nature. The Pythagorean principles will be felt in that case not as rationally ele-vating but as a pleasant penumbra around the emotion, which enhances the emotion's appeal. A good mode, a *harmonia* in the full sense of the word, dis-plays an emotional effect that encourages our appreciation of its rational basis, while a bad mode uses the rational basis (the pleasing proportions of vibrations) to make irrational emotions more pleasant. As the *Timaeus* puts it,

> However much of music in sound is useful for hearing is given for the sake of harmony. And harmony, which has motions akin to the revolutions within us of our soul, was given by the Muses to him who makes use of it with intelli-gence, *not for irrational pleasures*, such as now appears to be its use, but as a co-

fighter against the disharmoniousness of the revolution of the soul which has come about in us, to bring it into order and concordance with itself. [47c7–d7; emphasis added]

This distinction was implicit in the dual sense of *harmonia* as in one sense necessarily in tune with rationality, but in another sense as also including the irrational modes (*harmoniai*). Not until Book 10, however, is that danger spelled out more generally:

When [the poet] speaks in meter, rhythm, and harmony, he seems to speak very well, . . . so great a fascination do these by nature possess. However, when the statements of the poets are stripped of the colors of music, and are spoken by themselves, I think you know how they appear (601a–b).

In the limitations that are placed on the artists, Book 3 shows itself to be as much concerned with the dangers of the arts as is Book 10, but unlike Book 10 it is equally concerned with the positive value of the arts for education, and emphasizes the interconnection among harmony, rhythm, beauty, rationality, and goodness:

We must seek those craftsmen who are favored by nature and are able to track down the nature of beauty and grace (εὐσχήμονος) so that our young people, dwelling as it were in a healthy place, will be benefited by all things. There something coming from beautiful works will strike their eyes or their ears like a breeze bringing health from good places, and will guide them unawares (λαν-θάνη) to likeness and friendship and consonance with beautiful rationality.
   That would be by far the best education for them.
   Isn't it because of these things that education in music is most sovereign, namely because rhythm and harmony more than anything else enter the inmost part of the soul, taking hold of it most strongly, bringing it gracefulness and making it graceful if it is rightly trained—but if not, the opposite. Again, because someone who was properly educated in that way would most sharply perceive what is missing, and what is not beautifully made by a craft or in nature, and, having the right distastes he would praise beautiful things and wel-come them and receive them into his soul, and be nourished by them and become beautiful and good. As for what is ugly, the one who was educated in this way would rightly disdain it and hate it while still young, before he was able to employ rationality, but when rationality came he especially would welcome it, recognizing it because of its kinship with himself. [401c–402a]

This kind of emotional training when rational training is not yet possible has two advantages. First, it gives the children a kind of moral compass before they are able to make moral decisions in a fully rational way. Second, when rational understanding does come, there will be the least possible conflict between our rational decisions and our emotional inclinations; our good intentions will, as far as possible, not be undermined by irrational desires or dislikes.[21]

The next step is to move from these unconscious (λανθάνῃ) emotional affinities and distastes to a conscious awareness of what is involved in them. It is not enough to feel that one thing is good and something else is bad, but we must understand the elements that make us react to each of them the way we do. Just as we learn reading by learning the basic letters that all words are composed of, here our education in the arts will not be complete until we have learned the basic "forms" of self-control, courage, freedom, high-mindedness, and the like, together with their opposites, wherever they go, and perceive them in whatever they are in, both themselves and their images (402a–c).[22] We must learn to identify the good or bad components of the things we intuitively praise or blame. The term Socrates uses for the "forms" of the virtues and vices is *eide*, the word for the metaphysical forms, and it is perhaps an allusion to where the guardians' education must eventually lead if it is to be complete, but it does not mean that these pre-philosophical warriors are to learn the theory of forms. The forms spoken of here are not contemplated in themselves; we only "perceive them in whatever they are in" (ἐνόντα ἐν οἷς ἔνεστιν αἰσθανώμεθα). They correspond to what Socrates in the *Phaedo* calls "the bigness in us" as opposed to the form of "bigness itself" (102d). Similarly, the *Timaeus* says that when the receptacle, the substrate of becoming, manifests itself in particular forms like fire, white, gold, or any of the opposites, we should refer to these not as "this" (τόδε, τοῦτο) but "such" (τοιοῦτον) since they are always changing (*Timaeus*, 49c–50a). The implication is that what we perceive of changing things are the forms they participate in, but the forms only in their instantiations, not in themselves.[23] The latter can be known only by those who have learned to discern intelligible reality, but the former are at the level of perceptual knowledge—the courage that we see in particular individuals and their behavior, for example. In the early dialogues, when Socrates asks, "What is X?" his interlocutor typically replies with a list of examples instead of a univocal definition. In those cases, too, the speaker does not perceive the forms in themselves, but only "in whatever they are in". That is the only kind of knowledge available to the rulers at this stage; it is the most that they can perceive of the forms. In perceiving the forms of virtue at this level, what we actually perceive is virtuous people, and also images of their virtue in their virtuous actions, and so Socrates speaks of perceiving in individual cases both the virtues themselves and their images.

As if to emphasize the casual sense attached to the word *eidē* (forms) in the present context, in Socrates' next speech it is used as a synonym for the body: "When there is a coincidence of a beautiful character in the soul and a corresponding and consonant beauty in the body (εἴδη) that partakes (μετέχοντα) of the same type, is this not the most beautiful sight for one who can behold it?" (402c–d). Socrates proceeds to establish that what is most beautiful is also most lovable, and he thereby leads into one of the dialogue's recurring passages about eros, a puritanical critique:

> The lover may kiss, be with, and touch his beloved, as though he were his son, for the sake of what is fine and beautiful, if he can persuade him. But as for the rest, he must associate with the one he cares about in such a way that there is never any appearance of going further than this.[24] [403b]

Although the treatment of eros in the *Republic* is more severe than in the dialogues specifically devoted to eros, the difference is one of emphasis. Just as the *Symposium* and *Phaedrus* laud eros for its ability to take us beyond ourselves and to lead us to the highest contemplation of beauty and goodness, the *Republic* mentions eros as one way that those who are now called kings and rulers can become philosophers (499b–c); and the *Symposium* (199e–203b, 209a–212a) and *Phaedrus* (250d, 255e–256b) agree with the *Republic* that in its highest form eros leads us not toward sexual consummation but toward the forms of beauty and goodness. The reason that the issue is put more strongly in the *Republic* is that the *Republic* is an attempt to give a model of perfect justice, which requires the assumption or even fiction that we are capable of perfect wisdom, while the other dialogues take us in our imperfect finitude and they therefore need to invoke a power that can take us beyond ourselves.[25] The problem with eros is that excessive pleasure, as well as excessive pain, make us irrational (ἔκφρονα) and are thus incompatible with the virtues; and sexual pleasures (τὰ ἀφροδίσια) are the most intense of all. In other words, the virtues involve a kind of mean between the most extreme forms of pleasure and pain, while eros leads us to an extreme.

To regard something as a mean is to identify it not by itself but by contrast with the extremes. If we say that courage is a mean between cowardice and foolhardiness, that does not tell us in a positive way what courage is, but tells us that we can find it by making sure we have not shown too little boldness (cowardice) or too much boldness (foolhardiness); it is defined in reference to the extremes. In the passage quoted above at 401c–402a Socrates illustrates the psychology of this kind of indirect recognition when he says, "the one who was properly educated in that way would most sharply perceive what is missing, and what is not made beautifully by a craft or in nature, and, having the right distastes he would praise beautiful things" (401e). This is not an example of the mean, because only one the two extremes—the deficiency ("when something is left out")—is clearly specified, and it is paired not with its opposite, excess, but with a more general reference to "not being made beautifully".[26] Nevertheless, as with the mean, the children recognize when something is left out and when the object is not beautiful, without having a prescriptive rational concept of beauty that they can use to identify what is beautiful or not—in fact, they are explicitly said to be at a pre-rational age (402a). They do not know what something should contain in order to be beautiful, but they are sensitive to the presence of beauty and its absence because of the gracefulness that their training instilled in their soul. They perceive the beautiful and good not directly and positively in accordance with a pre-given concept or description, but the way we perceive a note as in tune because it does not sound sharp or flat. That is why their ability manifests itself as something negative: "the right distastes".

Physical Training, Doctors, and Judges (403c–412b)

The virtue of a good body does not necessarily make the soul good, so it would not have been enough to give a detailed account of physical training and trust the excellent body that results, to shape its soul virtuously. On the other hand, the virtue of a good soul does make the body as good as possible, so now that we have been given a detailed account of the soul's education in the arts we can trust the virtuous soul that results, to shape the body in the best possible way. Therefore the discussion of physical training need be no more than an outline, the details of which will be discovered by the guardians themselves (403c–e). There are five basic principles:

1. Drink (403e). Drunkenness[27] is prohibited, since a guardian is the last person who should require supervision.

2. Food (403e–404e). The guardians must avoid the highly specialized regimen of athletes, which makes them fit only for athletic contests and leaves them sluggish and drowsy the rest of the time, and liable to illness if they depart from it even slightly.[28] The guardians must aim instead at a simple and appropriate training along the same lines as the principles that governed the arts. Accordingly guardians must avoid sweets, prostitutes, and pastries—a quasi-echo of the growth of the fevered city, which is now being pruned back, where prostitutes were introduced between perfumes and pastries (373a).

3. Doctors (404e–408c). As its name implies, the feverish city produces a dissolute populace that is prone to illness, and because of its licentiousness it is also prone to frivolous litigation. Consequently the medical and legal pro-

fessions thrive at the expense of more productive activity. But to submit one's fate to judges is to lose control over it, and something of the kind is true also of those who, because of an undisciplined lifestyle, need to put themselves into the hands of physicians to reverse the damage to their health. The purified city cannot afford to cater to chronic invalids, but must expect the citizens to behave like people who cannot afford not to work. When such people are sick they want doctors to get them back on their feet as soon as possible so they can return to work. The idle rich, by contrast, can easily become self-indulgent and excessively solicitous of their bodily health. Today we ask whether someone in a coma should be kept alive by medical technology even if they are not viable without the machines; but we are a fevered society. Socrates' standard for the purified city is tougher: if some people cannot be made healthy enough by medical means to perform their work in the city, and the best that medicine can do is keep them alive indefinitely as invalids, then they should be denied treatment, and nature be allowed to take its course. Doctors cannot allow themselves to be seduced from this principle by the wealth of rich hypochondriacs or even invalids.

4. Judges (408c–410b). The principles of training for the soul and the body have been parallel. Training of the soul aims at the virtue of justice, and training of the body at the virtue of health. Accordingly, the role of the judge for the soul is parallel to that of the doctor for the body, and just as the doctor must be willing to allow the incurably ill to die, the judge must be willing to impose death on the incurably evil. These conclusions are subject to the assumption that a competent doctor and a competent judge will be capable of making those determinations. Just as the best doctors have a wealth of experience to guide them in the application of their *techne*,[29] judges too must be chosen from those with great experience, but the experience must be combined with a kind of innocence. Unlike a doctor, a judge must be uncontaminated by any internal experience of injustice, and must learn of it only by observing it in other people. Such a person will probably seem (and be) naïve when young, so judges must be chosen from among the old, who have attained the necessary experience of injustice by observing it in others. Glaucon accepts surprisingly easily the principle that "a soul that has been or is evil does not admit of treating anything well" (408e). The point seems to be that even reformed wrongdoers have a kind of stain that makes it impossible to see moral issues with perfect innocence and neutrality, perhaps because they may feel an inappropriate sympathy with or indulgence toward someone who has committed crimes similar to their own, or conversely because they may be excessively punitive in the way that people who have overcome a weakness in themselves are sometimes least tolerant of it in others. We may

wonder whether that standard of purity can actually exist in someone until they reach the advanced age at which judges will be appointed, but Socrates' model of the city is always guided by the question of what perfect justice is, regardless of whether it is possible as such.

5. Harmony (410b–412b). Physical training and training in the arts must balance each other to create a kind of harmony or mean, as we saw near the beginning of this chapter, for the arts without physical exercise make us too soft and gentle, while exercise without the arts makes us too savage and hard. "Savagery is produced by the spirited part of our nature which, if rightly trained, becomes courageous, but if it is strained more than it should be it becomes hard and harsh"; while "gentleness is possessed by the philosophical nature, and if it is relaxed too much it becomes softer than it should, but if it is well trained it becomes gentle and orderly". The guardians must possess both natures, and harmonize them within themselves, in which case they will be self-controlled and courageous; but if not they will be cowardly and coarse (410c–411a). We must keep in mind that at this point the guardians have not yet been separated into spirited auxiliaries and rational guardians; everything that Socrates says here refers to the original spirited guardians, who were called philosophical at 375e.

Unlike Aristotle, who would treat courage and self-control as independent virtues,[30] Socrates treats them here as products of a single harmony. The two components of the guardians' nature—the spiritedness that made them harsh to their enemies and the philosophical nature that made them gentle to their friends—produce opposite tendencies: savagery and gentleness respectively. These are only excesses; there is no need to specify deficiencies, as Aristotle does, because the excess of one is the deficiency of the other. Virtue occurs when they are harmonized; when they are not harmonized one is stronger than the other, and that produces the excess/deficiency. Courage is the virtue of the spirited part, and self-control the virtue of the philosophical part (410e)—not for another page and a half does Socrates introduce into the city the third class that makes possible a more adequate conception of philosophy (412b)—but they stand or fall together (presaging the unity of the virtues that emerges in Book 4) because each keeps the other in balance: without philosophy spiritedness leads to harshness instead of courage, and without spiritedness philosophy leads to softness instead of self-control. The complete picture, then, is that the philosophical part of the spirited guardians' nature provides them with gentleness, and the spirited part provides them with savageness, and the two can be brought into harmony with each other though education in the arts and physical training, because physical training promotes the savagery and the arts promote the gentleness (411a–412a). Education is a matter of fine-tuning the balance by using the arts and physical education to bring different natures from one of the extremes to the mean.

It is a little surprising that the arts are said to produce gentleness, with the implication that they are not capable also of producing savagery,[31] but when Socrates endorsed the Dorian and Phrygian modes, the other modes were rejected only because they encouraged various kinds of softness—lamentations, drunkenness, softness, and laziness. There was no suggestion that any of the modes could err on the side of savagery, and the survey was said to be exhaustive (398e–399a). It seems unlikely that if Greek music was capable of expressing courage in battle (Dorian), it was not also capable of expressing savageness in battle; certainly epic poetry was capable of doing so.[32] Plato seems to be oversimplifying for the sake of symmetry: the arts are to gentleness as physical training is to harshness.

The oversimplification means, however, that the philosophical side of the spirited guardians' nature, which is the source of the arts, is one-sided and, if not held in check by their spirited nature, responsible for a vice—softness instead of self-control. This is the first appearance of the tension that will reach its peak with the problem of the philosopher-rulers. Although they are chosen from among the most courageous natures (535a), and those who are most dedicated to the well-being of the city (412d–e), by the end of the *dianoetic* training described in Book 7 they will have come to discover the bliss of dwelling in contemplation of the intelligible being that underlies the material world of becoming, and will take no interest in the welfare of the city until they are reminded of their duty (520b–e). Seen in terms of the original guardians, it is no exaggeration to say that philosophy has made these people too soft. Consequently they will require fifteen years of additional training, experience, and testing in matters of war and governing before they will be fit to rule (539e–540a). Since virtue is relative to the function that one is performing (353b), a virtue in one context may be a vice in another. What is virtuous in pure philosophers may not be so in philosophers who are also rulers.

Because the requirements of philosophy and ruling are so different, and even antithetical, some readers have felt that their coalescence in a single person, the philosopher-ruler, violates the founding principle of one person–one job.[33] But matters are not so straightforward, because that principle is reinterpreted as the city changes in size and character. By the time the rationally governed city of the complete guardians is described, Socrates reformulates the principle as "having and doing one's own and what belongs to one", which means in context only that members of the productive, auxiliary, and guardian classes should not do one another's work, not that no one should combine two distinguishable functions within one of those groups (433e–434a). As Socrates points out:

> If a carpenter attempts to do the work of a cobbler, or a cobbler that of a carpenter, or they exchange their tools or honors with each other, or even if the same person attempts to do both jobs, and all the rest of the exchanges are made, would this seem to you to greatly harm the city?
> Not very much.
> But I think that if someone who is an artisan or some other kind of money-maker by nature . . . tries to enter into the class of soldiers, or one of the soldiers into the class of judges and guardians without being worthy of it, and these exchange their tools and honors with each other, or when the same person tries to do all these at once, then I think it would seem to you too that this kind of exchange and meddling is destructive to the city. [434a–b]

Now that the city has grown much larger it is no longer so important that each person be confined to one specific job, but only that everyone do the type of work for which they are naturally suited. Thus when the philosopher-rulers come on the scene in the next city, who combine in themselves the functions of philosophical contemplation and practical ruling, they do not violate the rule in its reformulation because both philosophy and ruling pertain to the rational class. Nor do they perform both jobs together, for they must interrupt their philosophical vocation in order to perform their service as guardians (540a–b).

This is not to dismiss the tension between philosophy and ruling that we have already glimpsed here—the fact that philosophy alone makes us too soft for ruling, and must be counterbalanced into an appropriate mean by the savaging qualities of physical training. We will explore this tension further in chapter 7.

Notes

1. Cf. Hoerber 1944, 9, 58.

2. Shorey commenting on 421e writes that one is "not justified in fearing that Plato would not educate the masses. . . . It might as well be argued that the high schools of the United States are not intended for the masses because some people sometimes emphasize their function of 'fitting for college'" (1935, 319). Similarly, Gregory Vlastos writes, "That [the curriculum] is directed at all the citizens, not only at the philosophers-to-be is certain: it is explicitly designed to inculcate *sōphrosynē* [self-control], a virtue required of all three classes". Vlastos points to the references to *sōphrosynē* at 389d ff; 399b–c; 402c; 410a ("Justice and Happiness in the *Republic*", in *Plato* 2 [Garden City, N.Y.: Anchor, 1971], 93). Others who agree that the appetitive

class will receive a similar education to that of the guardians include Taylor (1956 [1926], 280; and Klosko (1986, 120, 129). On the other hand, Guthrie believes that since the students are always referred to as guardians, the education is for them alone (1975, 455–57), although he does agree that the rest of the populace will at least get some of the same education, to prevent them from receiving "false and harmful notions about gods and heroes" (456). But if the groups have not yet been separated (the guardians will not be separated from the auxiliaries until the age of seventeen or eighteen: 537a–b) they would all have to receive the education appropriate for the guardians. Cognizant of that objection, Guthrie is forced to conclude that "Plato seems confused about this" (457). Reeve, too, concludes that children of the productive class will not receive the same education, on the assumption that children who are unlike their parents will be identified and relocated before they are educated rather than after (1988, 186–90). The question cannot be decided with confidence since we are not told at which point the natures of the children will be identified.

3. "The arts" translates *mousike*, "what pertains to the province of the Muses". The common translation of *mousike* as the cognate "music" is too narrow, since what Socrates has in mind goes well beyond what we call music, and includes not only poetry but painting and other visual arts (400e–401a, cf. 378c).

4. Cf. Friedländer 1969, 79.

5. The term for "form" of speech is εἶδος, but there is no reason to believe that any of its uses before Book 5 are meant to refer to the Platonic forms, although they may of course be intended to foreshadow the later use. It was already used in a colloquial way in Book 2, where clearly the theory of forms was not yet intended (e.g., 357c, 363e–364a, 369a), and is periodically used in a non-technical way throughout the dialogue. Also see Adam (1963 [1902], 168 on 402c.16); and Guthrie (1975, 459–60).

6. The power of the "noble lie", the Myth of the Metals, will consist precisely in the young audience's taking an allegorical truth for a literal truth (414b–415c).

7. Cf. *Phaedo* 62d–63a.

8. Gomperz (1905) believes that the presence of terrors in the Myth of Er shows a change of mind on Plato's part (67), but those terrors are punishments for those who were not virtuous, and therefore would not apply to those who took their education seriously.

9. Both are introduced with the words ἀλλὰ μήν ("moreover"), which can be used either to continue a previous thought or to introduce a new one. Also see Adam (1963 [1902], 201–2).

10. Cf. *Protagoras* 359b–360d.

11. Cf. *Meno* 81d–86c, *Phaedo* 74a–75c, *Phaedrus* 247c–250d.

12. It was noted above (ch. 1 n. 4) that there are a number of correspondences between the *Republic* and *Symposium*: 1) the two are the only dialogues that go through the night; 2) the reference here to comedy and tragedy clearly recalls the *Symposium*; 3) they are the only dialogues that attempt to give a non-mythic description of the vision of the good, and in virtually the same terms (cp. 490b with *Symposium*

212a); 4) Both present a six-part series leading to the vision of the good, in both of which the third item is belatedly moved to the fourth place (cp. 527d–528e with *Symposium* 185c–d).

13. Plato's claim receives some corroboration (to the effect that imitation can affect us more deeply than we recognize) from a study which showed that people who are asked to assume the facial expressions associated with certain emotions undergo the physiological changes associated with those emotions (R. Levenson, P. Ekman, and W. Friesen, "Voluntary facial action generates emotion-specific autonomic nervous system activity", *Psychophysiology* 27 [1990]: 363–83). Blondell (2002) remarks, "The possibility that the dialogues were performed by Academy members for their own benefit would therefore make *Republic*'s discussion of the influence of performance on the performer self-referential in a tantalizing way" (26). In another context she writes: "the construction and development of the guardians' characters takes place by *performing* appropriate behaviors in both senses of that word: by 'doing' as well as 'imitating' them" (238; emphasis in original).

14. See Plato, *Laws* 668b–c, Aristotle, *Politics* 8.7, and the Chinese *Record of Music* 1.4 and 3.2: "When the feelings are moved within, they are manifested in the sounds of the voice; and when these sounds are combined so as to form compositions, we have what are called airs". "To go to the very root (of our feelings) and know the changes (which they undergo) is the province of music" (*Yo Ki* or *Record of Music*, in *The Sacred Books of the East*, Vol. 28 [Delhi: Motilal Banarsidass, 1964], 93, 114, parenthetic material in original). The extent to which music without words can be expressive of definite emotions has been much debated in more recent times. In 1854 the influential German music critic Eduard Hanslick published a book-length attack on the belief that music is an expression of emotion (*The Beautiful in Music* [Indianapolis: Bobbs-Merrill], 1957), but a generation later Carl Stumpf, a student of Brentano and teacher of Husserl, acting on the opposite hypothesis, inaugurated a program of mapping a correspondence between musical elements and the emotions they evoke (*Tonpsychologie*, 2 Vols. [Leipzig: Weigel], 1883–90). Susanne Langer gives a balanced and creative discussion of this issue in *Feeling and Form* (New York: Scribner's, 1953). For a consideration of related issues see Roberto Assagioli, "Music as a Cause of Disease and as a Means of Cure" (chapter 7 of his book *Psychosynthesis* [New York: Viking, 1965]), and more recently the essays by Peter Kivy, Jenefer Robinson, Philip Alperson, and Joseph Margolis in Philip Alperson (ed.), *What is Music?: An Introduction to the Philosophy of Music* (University Park: Penn State Press, 1994), 147–236.

15. See Willi Apel, *Harvard Dictionary of Music* (Cambridge, Mass.: Harvard University Press, 1944), "church modes" par. IV.

16. Aristotle, *Politics* 8.7.1342a33–b34.

17. Cf. Bloom 1968, 353–54.

18. Cf. *Nicomachean Ethics* 7.1–10.

19. εὐρυθμία. I have reserved the more usual translation of "grace" for εὐσχημοσύνη.

20. Some recent support for the Pythagorean correlation between rationality and music comes out of experiments conducted by Frances Rauscher, Gordon Shaw, *et al.*, who conclude that a "high proportion of children . . . evidenced . . . dramatic improvement in spatial-temporal reasoning as a result of music training". See "Music training causes long-term enhancement of preschool children's spatial-temporal reasoning" (*Neurological Research* 19 [1997]: 2–8) 7.

21. Cf. Annas 1981, 84.

22. Reeve (1988) translates the phrase "wherever they go" (πανταχοῦ περιφερό-μενα) more literally as "moving around everywhere", and takes it to refer to a lower kind of form that is visible to the eyes and is in motion (52). It is difficult to conceive of an entity of that kind, and most translators interpret περιφερόμενα as a metaphorical way of saying "becomes present in". See the translations of Shorey (1930), Lindsay (1935), Cornford (1941), Bloom (1968), Grube (1974), Sterling and Scott (1985), and Griffith (2000).

23. For a survey of some of the controversy surrounding this passage, see John Sallis, *Chorology: On Beginning in Plato's* Timaeus (Bloomington: Indiana University Press, 1999), 101–5.

24. Since Socrates says there must be no appearance (δόξει) of going further, rather than simply no going further, Jacob Howland suggests that Socrates may be advocating hypocrisy if eros proves too powerful to be controlled in this way: *The Republic: The Odyssey of Philosophy* (New York: Twayne, 1993), 105. We can interpret it more charitably, however, to mean that not only does the lover not go further than this, but he behaves in such a way that not even the suspicion of impropriety can arise.

25. Stanley Rosen suggests that the *Republic* and *Symposium* balance each other insofar as the former emphasizes eros at the expense of justice and the latter emphasizes justice at the expense of eros ("The Role of Eros in Plato's *Republic*" and "Socrates as Concealed Lover", both reprinted in Rosen, *The Quarrel Between Philosophy and Poetry* [New York: Routledge, 1988]).

26. Perhaps this is because the mean applies primarily to activity (including *techne*) rather than perception. A perceiver may notice that there is something missing or something wrong with certain things, without being able to say it is because the producers worked either too quickly and carelessly or too slowly and indecisively, or because they aimed at a standard that was either too high or too low.

27. μέθης. The term can also mean nothing more than intoxicating beverages, but is unlikely to mean that here since even in the healthy city wine was permitted (372b). Also see Guthrie 1975, 454n3.

28. Cf. 410b. "Xenophanes, Euripides, Aristotle, and the medical writers, like Plato, protest against the exaggerated honour paid to athletes and the heavy sluggishness induced by overfeeding and overtraining" (Shorey 1930, 266 note b).

29. Cf. Aristotle, *Metaphysics* 1.1.981a13–24.

30. *Nicomachean Ethics* 3.6–12.

31. Martial music has always been encouraged on the assumption that music can produce the opposite of gentleness. Cf. Hanslick: "It is well known that the action of

music is most powerful of all in the case of savages. . . . [Even] Ericus Bonus, king of Denmark, in order to convince himself of the famous power of music, summoned a renowned musician to play before him, but not until every kind of weapon was put out of reach. By the choice of his modulation, the minstrel first cast on all around him a gloom, which he presently changed into hilarity. This hilarity he gradually worked up into a feeling of frenzy. 'Even the king rushed out of the room, seized his sword, and slew four of the bystanders'. (Albert Krantzius; dan. lib. v., cap. 3.) And that, be it noted, was 'Eric the Good'" (1957 [1854], 94).

32. E.g., *Iliad* 24.14–54, *Odyssey* 8.39–43.

33. For example, Bloom 1968, 407; Annas 1981, 262, and "Plato, *Republic* V-VII", in R. Bambrough, ed., *Philosophers Ancient and Modern. Philosophy* Supplementary Vol. 20 (1986), 3–18, esp. 17–18. Cf. Nichols 1984, 256.

CHAPTER FOUR

~

The Rationally Self-Controlled City (Book 3.412b–Book 4)

Complete Guardians (412b–417b)

The criterion for the future rulers is no longer spiritedness alone, now that the children have been educated; their ability to profit from their education must also be taken into account. This criterion will separate the guardians into complete guardians, who have the intellectual and temperamental capacity to rule as well as the spiritedness to fight, and the rest of the guardians who will now be called auxiliaries (414b). Those who will make the best guardians must not only be intelligent and capable, as well as spirited, but they must also care about the city. Accordingly, since we care most about what we love, they must love the city and regard their own interests as inseparable from those of the city (412c–d).[1] This quality of intelligence coupled with care for the city is the seed of what will later be called the wisdom of the guardians, their knowledge of and commitment to what is good for the city (428b–c). Until Book 5, however, knowledge is not distinguished from opinion, and no intellectual component is added to the guardians' education in physical training and the arts. According to the Divided Line, the kind of thinking called *pistis*, of which Books 2–4 are an illustration, is a species of opinion (*doxa*), so the guardians' knowledge is called opinion throughout this passage (412e–414b).

In additional to this proto-wisdom we must test the potential guardians' ability not to discard that attitude unwillingly. If they discard it *willingly* it will be because they discover that their previous opinion was false, so they will have grown in knowledge. But they may also discard it unwillingly, either through compulsion or bewitchment. Compulsion occurs when we change our mind because of pain or suffering, and bewitchment when our judgement is overcome by the spell of pleasure or fear (413a–c). The ability to resist compulsion is recognizably the seed of the later description of courage (429a–430b), while the ability to resist bewitchment is that of self-control or moderation (430e–431b). The future rulers will be chosen, then, by testing them for the tendencies from which these virtues grow. The fourth virtue, justice, will eventually reveal itself to be implicit in the other three.

The previous education of the children focused on the virtues of piety, courage, self-control, and justice. Wisdom, understood in the present context as the virtue by which the guardians will be able to rule the city in the best possible way, has not been part of their education, and must now be supplied as far as the city's present stage of development allows. Its components were intelligence, capability, and loving the city as they love themselves—the belief that what is good for the city is inseparable from what is good for themselves. The first two are native capacities, and the knowledge of what is good for the city will be supplied by apprenticeship, but the quality of loving the city as they do themselves must be implanted in young children in the same way as the previous virtues— by story telling. At the end of Book 2, in discussing the children's education to piety, Socrates remarked that the gods would have no reason to lie, although we ourselves can employ certain kinds of falsehood as long as the purpose is to achieve something good and not to introduce ignorance into the soul (382c–e). Here at the end of Book 3 the storytelling that Socrates recommends in order to inculcate the children's love of the city will be the kind of beneficial falsehood that he referred to then: "telling one noble falsehood to persuade in the best case even the rulers themselves, but if not them at least the rest of the city" (414b–c). The story, which Socrates calls "a Phoenician story",[2] is better known as the Myth of the Metals, or the Noble Lie; it has two components. First,

> we will try to persuade the rulers themselves, and the soldiers, and then the rest of the city, that the nurturing and training that we gave them were all things that they only seemed to experience and that only seemed to happen to them, like a dream, whereas in truth they were being formed and nurtured together with their weapons and other tools within the earth. And when they were finished being made, the earth as their mother gave birth to them. [414d–e]

The land where they live, then, is their mother, and they must defend it as they would their mother; and the other citizens, being born of the same mother, are their brothers. The myth then, like its Asian contemporary Confucianism, uses love of the family to open self-love out into altruism.[3]

The second part of the myth is that the god who made us mixed gold into some natures, silver into others, and iron and bronze into the rest. Those with gold natures are qualified to rule because they are the most valuable, the silver natures will be the auxiliaries, and the iron and bronze natures farmers and other craftsworkers.

> Since you are all akin, although for the most part you will beget children similar to yourselves, sometimes from a golden parent a silver child may be born, and from a silver parent a golden child may be born, and similarly all the others from one another. The first and most important injunction that the god lays upon the rulers, then, is that there is nothing that they should be better guardians of, nor anything that they should guard more fervently, than the mixture of the metals in the souls of their offspring. . . . There is an oracle that the city will be destroyed if an iron or bronze person becomes its guardian. [415a–c]

If golden parents produce children who have silver, iron, or bronze natures, the children must be relocated into the group for which they are suited by nature, however difficult this may be for their parents; by the same token those with golden natures who are born to the other classes must be elevated to that of the rulers, and so on. Socrates asks Glaucon whether he can think of any way that the people can be persuaded of the truth of this story, and Glaucon replies, "Not at all, as far as these people themselves are concerned, but I see a way for their sons and their successors, and the rest of the people who come later" (415d). Socrates says he thinks he understands, but does not say what he thinks he understands. Presumably we are to infer that only the first generation will be told that they were born this way. Subsequent generations will be told not that they were formed within the earth but only that their original ancestors were. It is not easy to persuade people that they themselves witnessed the objective presence of the divine, but to persuade them that something of the kind happened in an earlier age is much easier.[4]

Socrates' debate with Thrasymachus turned largely on whether, if rulers are like shepherds, shepherds insofar as they are shepherds tend their flocks with a view to their own welfare or that of the sheep. The present rulers are being trained to be Socratic shepherds rather than Thrasymachean ones, to care for the welfare of their charges like sheepdogs, rather than exploiting them like wolves (416a, cf. 375a–376a). But although the guardians have been reared with the appropriate stories, and have been screened to have moderate natures that can withstand the bewitchment of pleasures better than most, constant temptation can exert pressure against even the strongest natures, so the guardians must also be delivered from temptation as far as possible. Five rules will be imposed on them to that end: 1) they cannot possess private property beyond the necessary minimum; 2) their houses and store-rooms must be open to public inspection at all times; 3) they will be given the same level of sustenance as is given to the soldier-athletes; 4) they will live together and have common meals like soldiers on campaign; 5) they alone will not be allowed to touch gold or silver, or even be under the same roof with it. "Thus they would both be saved and would save the city", but if they acquire property they would soon be divided against the citizens and would bring the city to ruin (416d–417b).

The Rational City (419a–427c)

When Socrates' discussion with Polemarchus led to the conclusion that it is characteristic of the just person to help others, Thrasymachus broke in with the objection that since justice is the good of another, the key to one's own happiness is to be unjust rather than just. Now that Socrates has reaffirmed that the rulers are to be like altruistic sheepdogs rather than self-gratifying wolves, the antithesis previously supplied by Thrasymachus is now supplied by Adeimantus, who breaks in with the objection that "you are not making these men very happy, and it's due to themselves". The city really belongs to them but they derive no good from it, living like mercenaries while others enrich themselves and live in luxury (419a). Socrates adds to this list of deprivations, and replies that their aim was to make the city as a whole as happy as possible, and not one class in particular, although he adds that it would not be surprising if the guardians were happiest just as they are (420b). We thought, Socrates says, that we were most likely to discover justice in a city that is as happy as possible (420b).

In fact, when they proposed to construct a just city in order to discover what justice was, no reference was made to happiness at all (369a), so Socrates is here anticipating what he hopes later to prove, that true justice and true happiness coincide. He is not begging the question, however, since the happiness of the city and its guardians has not been an element in his argument, and is introduced only by Adeimantus. Nor does Socrates assume their happiness in his reply, which is only a defense (ἀπολογησόμεθα) against the objection, and introduces no further assumptions. He says only that it would not be surprising if these men were happiest just so—a conclusion that he affirms more confidently at 465d–466b—and follows with a simile to show that even if the rulers were not as happy as possible, this would not preclude the city from being as happy as possible: in painting a statue we would not paint the eyes the most beautiful color possible just because they are the most beautiful part of the body; rather we must paint all the parts in the colors most suitable to them if the statue is going to be beautiful as a whole (420c–d). If the city as a whole is to be happy, people within it must obviously be happy, so in Socrates' simile we must assume that the colors of the individual parts have some beauty, even if they are not supremely beautiful taken by themselves. In the same way, the classes within the city will have some happiness even if they might conceivably have had more. The appetitive people, for example, would have found more pleasures in a less puritanical city, the auxiliaries would have enjoyed more unfettered opportunities for power, and the lovers of truth might be happier if they did not have to rule. But any of these changes would destabilize the city, robbing it of its happiness as a whole and consequently diminishing the happiness of its parts.[5]

Socrates had replied with three arguments to Thrasymachus' imputation of inferiority to the just person: 1) just people are more knowledgeable because they do not aim at extremes but know where to draw the line (349a–350c); 2) justice makes a group more successful because its members work together in harmony (351c–352a); and 3) justice makes us happy by fulfilling the function for which we are suited by nature (352d–354a). It is not surprising that these three considerations—knowledge, harmony, and natural function—return in Book 4, where they will provide the elements of its definition of justice. The three principles of Socrates' defense against Thrasymachus now provide the basis for his defense against Adeimantus, although in reverse order. a) The reason that it would not be surprising if the guardians were happiest just as they are is that only in their present state do they fulfill the function for which they are suited by nature. And b) the reason the happiness of the city as a whole may be compared with the integrity of a painted statue is that the city achieved happiness by virtue of the harmonious relations of its parts. Here the argument is couched in terms of the city's happiness, whereas against Thrasymachus it spoke of the city's strength, but the resonance of the earlier argument becomes unmistakable later when Socrates remarks that the city will also be strong far beyond its size because it will be the only one not divided against itself (422e–423a). Finally, c) Socrates goes on to point out that each of the classes could be made independently happy by giving them as much luxury and liberty as possible, but then they would cease to be what they are and would destroy the city, whereas the rulers by contrast possess the due measure (καιρόν) to bring a good life and happiness to the city (420e–421a).

At this point the rational city is more or less complete. There is no point in legislating all the details of the citizens' lives, because if their education makes the rulers reasonable (μέτριοι) they will discover the rest by themselves (423e, 425a–d), whereas if the rulers do not become reasonable the additional injunctions would not be heeded in any case (425e–427a). But scattered throughout this section are some final rules to be enforced: 1) in another anticipation of the importance that will later be ascribed to the mean (619a) it is stipulated that the city be neither rich nor poor but intermediate (422a); 2) nor can the city be either too small or too big, it must be limited to a size that will support approximately 1,000 soldiers (423a–b);[6] 3) innovation in the arts and play must be prohibited in order to protect the forms of nurture and education decided on earlier (424b–425a); finally 4) religious practices are to be based on the Delphic traditions (427b–c).

Civic Virtue (427e–434c)

The discussion of the city's virtues begins with two questionable assumptions. First, Socrates says that if the city is correctly founded it will be completely good and thus will be wise, courageous, self-controlled, and just. But whether justice rather than injustice is good was precisely the point at issue in Book 1 and the beginning of Book 2, so Socrates is once again anticipating what he hopes later to prove, as when he assumed that the greatest justice and the greatest happiness coincide (420b). In neither case, however, is he begging the question since both assumptions function heuristically rather than deductively—they orient the discussion in the direction of the goal but do not function as premises in the final demonstration. The second questionable assumption lies in Socrates' statement that if they find any three of the above-mentioned virtues, whatever is left will be the fourth (427e–428a). Glaucon sees nothing wrong with this strategy, although Socrates had never argued that there are precisely four virtues, and earlier referred to a fifth—piety (380c)—which he counts as a virtue elsewhere,[7] and which is one of the aims of the guardians' education.[8] Socrates has prepared the ground in advance by constructing a city with three classes that are distinguished by their natural function, and had argued in Book 1 that each natural function has its own virtue (353b), so it would follow that there is a virtue for each of the three classes, as well as one that corresponds to the unity of the city itself.[9] The subsequent discussion will show to what extent these assumptions are justified.

Wisdom (428a–429a)
The first virtue that Socrates discerns is wisdom (σοφία), but the city's wisdom seems strange, he says, because it is good judgement (εὐβουλία) and is based on *episteme*, but all the craftsworkers in the city are possessed of good judgement and *episteme*, and we do not call the city wise because of them. The city's wisdom, then, must be the *episteme* and good judgement that the

smallest class, the guardians, employ about what is best for the city in itself and in its relations with other cities (428b–429a). We should note in passing that since wisdom is understood here only as good judgement, and *episteme* is ascribed to the craftsworkers, neither wisdom nor *episteme* is connected with the intelligible forms, as they will be in Books 5–7, but only with practical knowledge. Similarly, the word for the rational element represented by the rulers is not *nous*, which has connotations of the intelligible realm, but the *logistikon*, the calculative element, which does not, and its function is described only as calculation (ᾧ λογίζεται: 439d). At this point the argument is still at the level of *pistis*, investigation of the visible world in itself no longer (as in *eikasia*) merely in images, but not yet at the level of the intelligible forms.[10]

Courage (429a–430c)

The courage of the city is to be found "in that part which fights and wages war. . . . A city is courageous through a certain part of itself, because of the power that part has to preserve through everything the belief that what is to be feared are the things and the kinds of things that the lawgiver laid down in their education" (429b–c). "Through everything", Socrates says, refers to pains, pleasures, appetites, and fears. He explains that just as when people want to dye wool purple they first select the whitest wool, next prepare the wool in certain ways to accept the dye, and only then apply the purple, so too Socrates and the brothers first selected the right sort of children, and then they prepared them through the arts and physical training to be receptive to virtue in the form of the laws enacted by the guardians. And just as a properly dyed fabric will not easily be washed out of its color, properly cultivated auxiliaries will not easily have their virtue washed away by the powerful solvents of pleasure, pain, fear, and appetite (429d–430b). The auxiliaries will be resistant against both temptation and threats.

When we give a casual definition of courage we tend to think of it as not being deterred by fear, but that does not distinguish courage from mere boldness, and Plato had already pointed out in the *Protagoras* (349e–350c) and *Meno* (88b) that to be bold is not necessarily to be courageous, since it may lead to foolhardiness, which is not a virtue. Courage is a mean between boldness and cowardice because cowardly people fear too many things (not only what they ought to fear) while the foolhardy fear too few (not even what they ought to fear). Courage, then, requires knowledge of what it is right to fear (*Protagoras* 359b–360d). That is, so far, the same as the account in the *Republic*, but there is also a significant difference. In the *Protagoras* Socrates argues against the popular view that it is possible for knowledge to be "dragged around like a slave" by appetite, pleasure, pain, love, and fear (352b–c). But here courage is defined in terms of "the power . . . to preserve" the belief inculcated by the lawgiver, in the face of pleasure, pain, fear, and appetite— as if in the absence of courage pleasure, pain, fear, and appetite could indeed drag one's convictions around like slaves. Thus where the *Protagoras* defined courage in terms of knowledge or wisdom alone (361b), the present account does so in terms of correct belief together with an additional power of preservation. We cannot escape the tension by noting that the auxiliaries are said only to have opinion (δόξα), while the *Protagoras* is speaking about *episteme*, because a subsequent passage of the *Protagoras* extends the claim beyond *episteme* to belief (οἰόμενος, οἴεται: 358b–d). We will see, however, that this is not the *Republic's* last word on the subject.

Two ambiguities emerge from what Socrates says about courage. First, when he says that courage resides in only one part of the city, does that refer to the auxiliaries alone or the auxiliaries together with the guardians? The singular term, "that part" (τοῦτο τὸ μέρος), appears to indicate a single class, the warriors, but in other passages the guardians too share in the courage of the city. When they were said to be guardians against external enemies as well as internal friends (414b), it meant that they will participate in the fighting, as is later made explicit (457a), just as the philosopher-rulers at the age of thirty-five will be expected to hold command in war (539e). They are "complete" guardians because they retain their former responsibilities while adding new ones. In fact, when Socrates describes in detail how the guardians should behave in war, he moves from speaking about the guardians in particular (φύλαξι: 467a) to speaking about soldiers in general (στρατιώτας: 468a) in a way that collapses the distinction between guardians and auxiliaries (466–b). We will return to this ambiguity in the discussion of self-control.

The second ambiguity stems from the fact that the usual way of understanding courage concerns the ability to resist fear and pain, while the ability to resist appetite and pleasure belongs to self-control. Courage and self-control are usually contrasted insofar as the former urges us forward despite something that impedes us, while self-control holds us back despite something that attracts us. Consequently in both the *Gorgias* (492a–b) and *Statesman* (306b) the two are regarded as opposed to each other. In neither case is the speaker Socrates, but it is not clear why he would want to collapse this widely recognized distinction by defining courage in terms of resisting the attraction of appetites and pleasures as well as the repulsion of fears and pains. In fact, he has it both ways: insofar as his definition involves only a belief about what is to be feared, and not also a belief about what is to be desired, it is consistent with the usual view of courage, but insofar as that belief is to be preserved not only in the face of pains and fears, but also in the face of pleasures and appetites, the distinction between courage and self-control is blurred.[11] In the *Protagoras* (361a–b) Socrates argued for the unity of the virtues, the view that the various virtues were at bottom different names for the same thing. The view that emerges from Book 4 will entail the same result. In that case Socrates' tactic here of blurring the distinction between courage and self-control can be read as an anticipation of that eventual conclusion.

Self-control (430d–432a)

Socrates introduces the subject in a way that is doubly odd. First, he says, "Two things still remain to be discerned in our city, self-control and that which our entire inquiry aims at, justice. . . . How then might we find justice without having to bother any more about self-control?" (430d). Socrates seems to be suggesting that there is a preferable way to talk about justice that does not require reference to self-control. As we have seen, the *Protagoras* claimed that knowledge alone is sufficient for virtue, and there is no need for an additional measure of self-control to keep the emotions from overwhelming our knowledge because it is not possible that something as noble as knowledge could be ordered around by its inferiors. In fact, Socrates disparaged the contrasting view as the opinion of "the many":

> The many think something like this about knowledge, that it is not strong nor guiding nor ruling; . . . but that although knowledge often exists in a person, the person's knowledge is not what rules, but something else does—sometimes spiritedness, sometimes pleasure, sometimes pain, at times eros, often fear. They think about knowledge absolutely the same thing that they think about a slave, that it is dragged around by everything else. Is that how these things seem to you too, or do you think knowledge is noble and able to rule a person, and whoever learns what is good and what is bad will never be swayed by anything to act otherwise than as knowledge bids? [*Protagoras* 352b–c]

Socrates endorsed the latter alternative, but the view that he puts forward in Book 4 of the *Republic* is more like the view of the many. If the *Protagoras* is referring not just to any kind of knowledge but to knowledge in a very specific sense, and if the guardians of the *Republic* are able to achieve that knowledge which is sufficient for virtue, then there would be no independent need for self-control, and we could indeed find justice without first discovering self-control. Glaucon replies, however, that he wants Socrates to talk about self-control in any case; so if Socrates did have something else in mind it is left aside for now. But he continues to remind Glaucon (and Plato us) that the present approach is not entirely satisfactory:

> But you should know, Glaucon, that in my opinion, we will never get an accurate answer using our present methods of argument—although there is another longer and fuller road that does lead to such an answer. But perhaps we can get an answer that's up to the standard of our previous statements and inquiries.
>
> Isn't that satisfactory? It would be enough for me at present.[12] [435c–d]

Earlier Socrates remarked that the place in which they are seeking justice is hidden in shadows and darkness (432c). If this is an anticipation of the allegory of the cave, then it too alludes to the inadequacy of the present approach which is still at the level of the visible world of the city, i.e., within the cave. Later, when Socrates sums up their conclusions he does so with a caution commensurate with those earlier warnings: "Well then, if we said that we discovered the just person, and the courageous one, and the city, and what justice happens to be in them, I think we would in some way not completely seem to be lying" (444a); and in Book 6 he disparages the earlier treatment of the virtues as a mere sketch (ὑπογραθήν: 504d). Socrates' suggestion that there may be a preferable way to discern justice independently of self-control was his first hint of the inadequacy of this way of looking at matters.

In Book 7, after Socrates has left this approach behind in favor of one which does not have the same limitations, he will describe a kind of knowledge that is like turning from darkness to light. With respect to this,

> the instrument by which everyone understands is like an eye that cannot be turned to light from darkness except together with the whole body. Thus that instrument must be turned from the realm of becoming together with the whole soul until it becomes able to contemplate that which is, and what is brightest of that which is; and we say that this is the good. [518c–d]

If the whole soul turns to it together, then there can be no discord in the soul and no need for self-control, and to the extent that all the virtues turn out to be convertible with self-control, then they too will be superseded. As in the *Protagoras*, this sovereign knowledge is knowledge of the good. The knowledge referred to in Book 7 is *noesis*, and involves the intelligible forms; but here in Book 4 we are still within the realm of *pistis*, knowledge of the visible world, and the wisdom of the rulers is only "good judgement" about what is best for the city in itself and in its relations with other cities (438c–d). The limitations of this kind of knowledge will not apply to the later one. As we saw in the Introduction, it is typical of Plato to begin with a less adequate account and work toward a more adequate one, a strategy that enables him to begin with an examination of the received view and gradually move from it to a view that overcomes the limitations of the earlier one. It also enables him to offer us relatively clear and simple models which give us a preliminary understanding of difficult matters, and which act as intermediate steps by which we can advance to a more adequate understanding that is also more elusive. In the *Republic* this strategy is evident especially in the way the stages of the argument lead us up along the levels of the Divided Line. Those who never experience the kind of knowledge that Socrates describes in Book 7 will never have the opportunity to go beyond the present model of virtue; by calling attention to the limitations of that model only in a general way, Socrates avoids discrediting this account for those who are not able to replace it with something more adequate.

The resemblance between the view put forward in Book 4, and the one ascribed to the many in the *Protagoras* is evident from the beginning of the discussion:

> Self-control is surely some kind of order, the mastering (ἐγκράτεια) of certain pleasures and appetites, as they say, using the phrase "master of oneself" (κρείττω αὐτοῦ)—I don't know how—and other such phrases that are like traces that it has left behind. . . . Yet isn't the expression "master of oneself" ridiculous? He who is master of himself would also be subject to himself, and he who is subject master. The same person is referred to in all these statements. . . . But the saying seems to me to want to say that in the same person there is something in the soul that is better and something that is worse, and when the part that is better by nature is master of the worse, this is what is meant by speaking of being master of oneself. . . . But when, on the other hand, because of bad upbringing or bad company the better part which is smaller is mastered by the multitude of the larger, we blame this as something shameful, and call it being subject to oneself and licentious. [430e–431b][13]

In the present city "the appetites of the inferior many[14] are dominated by the appetites and wisdom of the superior few", so the city shows self-mastery and is self-controlled (431c–d).

If the first oddity in Socrates' account was his suggestion that it might be better to bypass the question of self-control in the search for justice, the second is his claim that, whereas wisdom and courage resided in individual parts (ἐν μέρει τινὶ ἑκατέρα), self-control runs throughout the city as a whole, as a kind of harmony among the three classes (430e, 431e–432a). This lack of symmetry is surprising. We have already seen that the city's courage was ascribed only to the auxiliaries even though the rulers too have a share in it. To be consistent Socrates should have done one of two things: either treat each of the virtues as the distinguishing excellence of a particular class, so that wisdom would be the distinctive virtue of the rulers, courage that of the auxiliaries, and self-control that of the appetitive class; or else treat them cumulatively, so that while only the ruling class has wisdom, both it and the auxiliaries have courage, and all three have self-control. But instead Socrates employs the first approach with regard to courage and the second with regard to self-control. By moving from the exclusive model in courage to the inclusive model in self-control, the progressive tendency is, once again, to break down the rigid boundaries between the virtues.

Justice (432b–435b)

Recalling his questionable assumption that whatever is left after they have found the other three virtues will be justice (427e–428a), Socrates concludes that justice must be a version of the principle that made the other three possible, namely the requirement on which the first city was founded, that everyone do only the one job for which they are suited by nature. They have come a long way since the original formulation of that principle (369b–370b), however, so the original version is now acceptable only in a certain sense (κινδυνεύει τρόπον τινά: 433b): it is reconceived as "having and doing one's own and what belongs to one" (433e–434a). Where earlier the principle was meant to ensure that the craftsworkers did not do one another's work, now that the city has grown to such an extent in size and complexity, that kind of interchange is relatively harmless. What is important at this point is only that the members of the productive, auxiliary, and guardian classes not do one another's work.[15] If someone who is by nature a craftsworker tries to become a soldier, or a soldier a ruler, or someone attempts to do all three, the city will come to ruin (434a–b).

Just as there is no difficulty about an interchange of jobs among the craftsworkers in this larger, more layered city, now that only the integrity of the *classes* matters and not of the more specialized professions within them, so too there is also no difficulty about the same people acting as both rulers and judges. When the rulers act as judges their guiding principle will be that no one have what belongs to others nor be deprived of what belongs to themselves, so here again justice means having and doing one's own and what belongs to one (433e–434a). We noticed that the principle of exchange on which the original city was founded was a version of Cephalus' conception of justice as "pay each other what you owe". In this revision of that principle the connection to Cephalus is still evident, although "what we are owed" now has more to do with what we are entitled to by nature than with the exchange of items or services.

If justice in the city is a transformed version of Cephalus' conception, the conceptions of justice by Polemarchus and even Thrasymachus have a place in it as well, although not in their original forms. When the complete guardians were first described they were said to be guardians "against external enemies and internal friends, so that the latter will not wish to, and the former are not able to, do harm" (414b). The friends/enemies dichotomy recalls Polemarchus' formulation, but with the corrections that Socrates had urged upon him: that friends do not always benefit us (334b), and a just person does not think in terms of harming others (335b). Now, instead of the rulers simply helping friends and harming enemies, they seek to make their friends good and to prevent their enemies from doing harm—it may be that the latter goal cannot be achieved without their doing harm themselves, but the goal is to prevent rather than inflict harm. As for Thrasymachus, the conception of justice here formally resembles his expanded definition of justice as obedience to the one whose superior knowledge makes him a ruler in the strict sense of the term (340d–341a). In Socrates' present account, however, knowledge means something quite different from what it meant for Thrasymachus. In all three cases the original definition is reconceived in a more adequate way, which means on one hand that none of the previous versions was satisfactory, as Socrates had already shown, but on the other hand that they were included in the first place because all of them contained an element of truth which could evolve into something more instructive.

The Tripartite Soul (434d–445b)

Socrates reminds Glaucon that the search for definitions of the virtues written in the large letters of the city was conducted for the purpose of seeing whether they would provide models by which to recognize the same definitions in the fine print of the soul.

> What has come to light for us there let us apply to the individual, and if there is agreement that will be fine. But if something different manifests itself in the individual we will return again to the city to test it, and perhaps by examining them alongside each other and rubbing them together like fire sticks we may make justice blaze forth, and when it has come to light confirm it for ourselves. [434e–435a]

The first sentence is what we would expect, but the second sentence comes as a surprise. Since the original purpose of the inquiry was to discover what justice is in the individual, if something different manifests itself in the individual, that would still seem to be enough to fulfill the quest. If the search for justice in the city was only for the purpose of discerning it in the soul, what is to be gained by reversing direction and using what we discover about the soul to revisit our conclusions about the city? In fact, that is not quite how Socrates puts it. The reconsideration will not be for the sake of getting matters right about the city, but for the sake of discovering something about justice itself that will be revealed through a tension between the city and the soul: "rubbing them together like fire sticks we may make justice blaze forth". That is, in fact, what will happen.

Since all the virtues in the city were conceived in terms of the three classes, if those definitions are to apply to the soul, the soul would have to be tripartite as well (435b–c). Before proceeding to his demonstration Socrates utters the warning that we have already noted: "But you should know, Glaucon, that in my opinion, we will never get an accurate answer using our present methods of argument" (435c). We saw that one explanation was that the highest virtue will turn out to be grounded in a knowledge which converts the soul as a whole—the whole soul turns to it together—so that any distinctions within the soul become irrelevant (518c–d). Another explanation will emerge only at the conclusion of the dialogue, when Socrates remarks that we have still not seen the true nature of justice, or the truth about whether the soul has distinct parts:

> We must see it as it is in truth, not maimed by communion with the body and other evils, as we now see it, but discern it adequately with reason when it has become pure. And then one will find it much more beautiful and will more clearly distinguish justice and injustice and everything that we have now gone through. Now, however, we told the truth about the soul as it appears at present. . . . But we must, Glaucon, look elsewhere, . . . [namely] to its love of wisdom (*philosophia*), and we must understand what it touches upon, and what kind of things it yearns to associate with, as being akin to the divine, and to the immortal, and to what always is. . . . And then one might see whether in its true nature it has many forms or one form, or in what way it is and how. [611c–612a]

In accordance with the *Republic*'s procedure of using less adequate formulations as stepping-stones to more adequate ones, Socrates (at the behest of Glaucon) sees his present approach through to its conclusion, despite his misgivings.

His first inference is that "the same forms and characteristics are in each of us that are in the city. For they could not come from anywhere else" (435d–e). This has the form of an Argument from Division, but it is not the fallacious variety, for Socrates' subsequent examples show that a city cannot have characteristics like rationality, spiritedness, and appetite if its inhabitants do not have them. But that does not yet prove that all three characteristics are in each of us. If some of us were only appetitive, and others only spirited, and others only rational, the city would still have all three qualities, but individuals would not. That is only a logical possibility, however, for we never actually encounter people who are entirely lacking in appetite, spiritedness, or rationality; it does seem that everyone who is fully human must have all three. In fact, Socrates' preceding warning, and the two passages that we adduced to explain it (518c–d, 611c–612a), reflect the fact that the three parts of the soul will turn out not to be completely separable from one another. That may be why he ignores the logical possibility that all three may be in the population without being in each citizen.

Even if we agree that each of us has all three, we do not yet know that our souls are tripartite. It may be that our soul acts as a unity when it learns, gets angry, and desires, rather than doing each of these with a different part of itself (436a). The subsequent argument that the soul is tripartite rather than behaving in all three ways as a unity, is an impressive one,[16] based on the ontological equivalent of the principle of contradiction. But it is also the subject of much controversy, if only because it is difficult to accept literally the conclusion that our soul or self can be neatly divided into separate pieces the way the body can be divided into different limbs.[17] For all these reasons it is important to take a careful look at the argument to see what it does and does not actually prove. Let us first look at it in summary form, reserving comment until the end.

1. "The same thing will not be willing to do or undergo opposites in the same respect (κατὰ ταὐτόν), in relation to the same thing, at the same time. So, if we ever find this happening in the soul, we'll know that we aren't dealing with one thing but with many" (436b).

2. It is not possible for the same thing to be at rest and in motion at the same time and in the same respect (c).

3. If a person were standing still but moving his arms and head, this would not violate the above principle because the person is not standing still and moving in the same respect: "something in him is at rest and something else is moving" (c–d).

4. For the same reason, neither would a spinning top that stays in one place violate it: "it has an axis and a periphery within it, and is standing still with respect to its axis . . . and moving in a circle with respect to its periphery" (d–e).

5. Rather than examine all such objections let us proceed on the hypothesis that the principle is correct, and agree that if matters ever seem to us to be otherwise everything that followed from it will be invalidated (437a).

6. Among the things that are opposite to each other are assent/dissent, pursuing/rejecting, embracing/repelling, desiring/not-desiring (b–c).

7. We say that there is a species (εἶδος) of appetites or desires, the clearest of them being what we call thirst and hunger (d).

8. Thirst is an appetitive relation to drinking, and additional qualities such as whether the drink is good or not are irrelevant to appetite as such: it wants nothing else than to drink (437d–439b).

9. Sometimes we are thirsty but decide not to drink, so there is something in us that tells us to drink, namely appetite, and something else that tells us not to, namely rationality, the two of which must then be different species (εἴδη) in our soul (c–e).

10. Sometimes we get angry at ourselves because of our appetites, in which case our spiritedness fights against our appetite as one thing against another, and it never sides with appetite against rationality (439e–440d).

11. Although our spiritedness never allies itself with appetite against rationality, it sometimes opposes rationality on its own if it has been corrupted by a bad upbringing, and so there are three not two species (εἴδη) within our soul,[18] just as in the city there were three kinds (γένη) of people. There are then the same kinds (γένη) in the soul as in the city (440e–441c).

Step 1 is analytically true as stated, but if κατὰ ταὐτόν is translated as "in the same part of itself" instead of "in the same respect", as it often is, the claim becomes questionable with respect to step 4, for the axis and circumference of a top are not really parts.[19] In fact, the term "part" is never used in the argument, only "species" and "kind", so it would be better not to inject it into the translation here. Not until Socrates redefines the virtues in terms of the individual, and compares them to the way they were defined in terms of the parts of the city, does he use the word "parts" (μέρη: 442b–c).

Steps 3 and 4 provide examples that are provocatively different. In step 3 Socrates is talking about separable parts, each of which could be physically removed from the others: the legs that are standing still and the arms and head that are moving could be entirely detached from the rest of the body. In the case of the top, however, the axis and circumference cannot be separated. If we cut off the circumference there will always be a new, narrower circumference, and even if we reduce the whole top to a one-dimensional line we can still distinguish in thought the axis (the aspect that is stationary with respect to the ground) from the circumference (the aspect that moves with respect to the surrounding space) even though they are physically one and the same. If, on the other hand, we tried to remove the axis by drilling a hole through the center of the pin, the top would continue to have an axis but the axis would be hollow. Circumference and axis aren't separable parts like arms and legs, but are abstractions that stand to each other as relations. If we apply this model the tripartite soul will look quite different. If appetite, spiritedness, and rationality are related to one another like the axis and circumference of a top, then they too are abstractions and relative to one another. They are more like locations on a continuum than discrete parts. We have two models, one of which is composed of real (physically separable) parts and another which is composed of virtual parts (separable only in thought). We will have to see which provides a better model for the soul.[20]

Step 5 is intriguing for Socrates' suggestion that there may be objections which would force us to overturn the original principle. One such objection might be that if κατὰ ταὐτόν means "in the same respect", then the proof will only demonstrate that soul does things in different respects, not different parts, and the parallel with the city has not been proven; while if it means "in different parts of itself" then the example of the top is problematic.[21] Whatever Plato may have had in mind, we are reminded that Socrates warned us about the accuracy of his method before the proof began, and later says that whether the soul has parts has not been satisfactorily resolved (611c–612a).

In steps 7, 9, and 11 there is no reason to think that εἶδος (species) is used in the technical sense of a metaphysical form—although it may be meant to foreshadow the appearance of the forms in Books 6 and 7—but only in the more colloquial sense that has been used since Book 2.[22] It is, however, an unusual term to use for "part", and, like the other steps that we have discussed, it makes Socrates' account less straightforward than at first it appears. In step 11 the term is used synonymously with "kinds" (or "classes"), and so the conclusion of the argument is not the simple but dubious claim that the soul contains three different parts, but the more complex and difficult claim that the soul contains three different kinds of motivations.

Step 8, like steps 3 and 4, adduces two kinds of examples that are strikingly different in their implications. To illustrate the way that appetite stands only in relation to the object of desire—thirst, for example, in relation to drinking—and not to broader concerns such as whether the object of desire is good, Socrates points first to the way that comparative quantities are related to their counterparts, and then to the way particular instances of knowledge are related to what they are knowledge of. In the first set of examples, greater is in relation to less, double to half, heavier to lighter, etc. (438b–c). In the second case knowledge of building stands in relation to building, while knowledge of medicine stands in relation to healing (438c–d). These two sets of examples are instances of quite different kinds of relation. The first set shows the relation between different degrees or quantities, while the second shows the relation between knowledge and its object, in other words between two quite different realms. It is hard to see how both types of example can serve as models of the relation between thirst and drinking. The second model is a useful illustration of that relation: it is reasonable to say that thirst is the species of appetite that is related to drinking, as medicine is the species of knowledge that is related to healing. But the first model makes no sense. How can we say that thirst is related to drinking the way the double is related to the half?[23] Either Socrates lost track of what he was talking about or the example serves a less obvious purpose. But he must have thought it was important because he gave us nine versions of it. Since the relation between knowledge and its object provided Socrates with a perfectly good example of what he meant, what was the point of confusing matters with a misleading example? Insofar as the relation of comparatives is an illustration of opposition (greater-less), even if it is not relevant to the relation between a desire and its object, it may have something to tell us about the opposition between the different forms of the soul. We will return to this question.

Not only is it unclear whether the soul is here depicted as composed of different parts or only of different kinds of motivation, and whether the differences are to be understood on the model of the extremities of the human body or the axis and circumference of a top, but eventually the ambiguity extends from what the three are to whether they can even be reduced to three, or whether they constitute a seamless continuum that begins with appetite and culminates with rationality.[24] At the end of the discussion of the individual virtues Socrates makes a remark in passing that points in that direction. He refers to the three parts of the soul together with "any others that may happen to be in between them" (443e). It is not hard to imagine borderline cases between the frustration of unfulfilled appetite and the anger of spiritedness, or between the striving of spiritedness and the striving of philosophy. In addition to what may be in between the three, further divisions can be made within each one. At the end of Book 6, for example, Socrates will subdivide rationality into *eikasia*, *pistis*, *dianoia*, and *noesis*, and in Books 8 and 9 he will divide appetite into necessary, unnecessary, and lawless species.[25] In the argument for the tripartite soul itself, Socrates changed his example of appetite from drinking (step 9) to looking at corpses (step 10), and it is hard to believe that he would consider these two to exemplify the same quality. Later he explicitly says that there is no common quality to all the ways of being and behaving that have been called appetite: "because of its multiple forms, we could not designate [appetite] with one appropriate name, but we named it by what was biggest and strongest in it" (580d–e). Again, spiritedness has various associations, from anger to competition to honor (436a, 581b, 586c–d). All these passages point to what he says here, that further subdivisions might be made in addition to the three parts that have been identified. We should not forget that the principle of opposition on which it was based was called only a hypothesis (437a), and that in the demonstration itself Socrates does not call the subdivisions parts but uses the less rigid term "species".[26]

The suggestion that there may be further divisions between and within each of the three parts of the soul corresponds to what we noticed in chapter 2 about the three classes of the city—that they developed seamlessly out of one another rather than being absolutely discontinuous. There may have been a reminder of this in the Myth of Metals when Socrates, instead of speaking unambiguously about three different classes, seemed to speak of four: the god mixed gold into the nature of the guardians, silver into that of the auxiliaries, and "iron and bronze into both the farmers and (τε . . . καί) other craftsworkers" (415a). The strong conjunction suggests that no explicit division is being made here between the farmers and other craftsworkers, but the choice of two metals instead of one, coupled with the verbal distinction between "farmers" and "other craftsworkers," pairings which continue to be used, may remind us that what is called the appetitive class is hardly homogenous—like the class of appetites itself according to Socrates' remark at 580d–e, quoted above—and could easily be subdivided. Farmers, merchants, courtesans, artists, and hunters, for example, are not the same kind of people (Socrates can hardly have failed to notice that his classification of painters and other artists as lovers of profit suggests that they have not chosen their professions very wisely). When Socrates returns to these matters in Book 8, he now says that there are *five* kinds of constitution, both in the case of cities and individuals (544a–e), with intermediate cases even among these (544d), and in Book 9 he calls lovers of wisdom, lovers of victory, and lovers of profit only "the primary (πρῶτα) three classes" (581c).

If there is no limit to the "others that may happen to be in between them", appetite, spiritedness, and rationality are more like three segments on a line (although a line does not do justice to the complexity of the relationships) than three distinct entities. If that is so, and if we can say that in a line which ends with rationality, the beginning of the line is in some sense "for the sake of" what is at the end of it, then rationality would, in fact, be shown to be the natural ruler of the three. The lack of complete independence among the three is apparent from the fact that each of them turns out to be present in each of the others. Rationality, for example, which here means only calculation (439d), can be seen to be present in appetite and spiritedness as well, when Socrates speaks of them as "sharing the belief" (ὁμοδοξῶσι) that rationality should rule the soul (442d).[27] Appetite and rationality, in turn, must both contain spiritedness as well as their own distinctive quality, for not only do they strive against one another, but their strife is intense enough to be called a waging of civil war.[28] Finally, some form of appetite or desire (ἐπιθυμία) must belong to rationality insofar as rationality is the *love* of learning (435e), and to spiritedness insofar as spiritedness is love of honor (581b); later, in fact, Socrates explicitly ascribes appetites to rationality and spiritedness (580d).[29]

In Book 6 Socrates will offer a description of our soul's striving that confirms these hints that the tripartite division of the soul can be reduced to something much more continuous. In a passage that could have been taken from Freud's discussion of the libido, Socrates says,

> We surely know that when the appetites strongly incline toward some one thing they are thereby weakened toward others, like a stream from which there is a diversion into another channel.
>
> Of course.
>
> So when they flow toward learning and all such things, they will be concerned, I suppose, with the pleasures of the soul itself by itself, while those that come through the body it will abandon, if someone is not a contrived but a true philosopher. [485d–e]

Here again the distinction between appetite and rationality is collapsed since we can have appetites for learning. Moreover, just as in chapter 2 we saw spiritedness and rationality emerge from appetite in the course of the city's evolution, here all three parts of the soul may be considered channels through which eros (to use the word that Socrates employs in leading up to the above quotation) flows toward different kinds of gratification (485b1, b8, c7).[30]

We saw that step 8 of the demonstration of the division of the soul used the example of "knowledge of something" to illustrate that thirst too stands in relation to something, namely drinking; but that Socrates also used examples of comparative relations like greater and less, even though the relationship between comparative quantities or degrees does not exemplify the kind of relation that he is talking about. It was puzzling that he not only offered such a misleading example, but did so in considerable detail and with a series of nine illustrations: the relations of greater to less, much greater to much less, formerly greater to formerly less, about-to-be greater to about-to-be less, more to fewer, double to half, heavier to lighter, faster to slower, hot to cold, "and all similar cases" (438b–c). We noted that while this set of examples makes no sense as an illustration of the relation between desire and its object, it provides us with examples of opposition and may therefore shed some light instead on the opposition between the different forms of the soul. The examples show that differences in degree or quantity may produce fundamental oppositions; accordingly, if the different forms of the soul are indeed more like locations on a line than like the discrete parts of the human body—differences of degree or quantity rather than quality—we now have a model of how it is possible for two things to be in opposition to each other without actually being separable. Quantitative differences can produce opposition as well as qualitative differences can. When rationality and appetite are in conflict, for example, we can say that the opposition is between, on one hand, greater rationality and less appetite, and, on the other hand, greater appetite and less rationality, or between short-term gratification ("about-to-be less") and long-term gratification ("about-to-be greater").

What the doctrine of the tripartite soul is meant to show is that the self can be divided against itself, and that the ways it can be divided can be classed conveniently into three broad categories; but this tripartite division turns out to be anything but definitive. The reason the soul can be divided against itself without having discrete parts is that, as Socrates says later, the soul as we see it now is "maimed by communion with the body and other evils" (611c). The *Republic*, like other dialogues, sees the function of the soul as living and bringing life to corporeality, and the fulfillment or virtue of the soul as the achievement of divine rationality to which its nature is akin.[31] Its function of bringing life immerses it in corporeality while its fulfillment in pure intelligibility aims at the transcendence of the body, and it is this tension that is the ultimate source of the soul's division against itself. In its corporeal immersion the soul functions in terms of a living body with appetites for the things that enhance corporeal thriving and enjoyment, and aversions to those that do not, whereas in its aspiration to fulfillment it seeks to turn away from the corporeal to the intelligible.[32] That tension produces the opposition of appetite and rationality.

But there is an intermediate state between that opposition: it is possible to reject the attractions of appetite without yet appreciating the attractions of the rational. We may feel contempt for the self-indulgence of appetite without feeling drawn to the life of the mind. We may find satisfaction in our freedom from the tyranny of pleasure and pain, and delight in our toughness and our ability to overcome obstacles, the consciousness of our own power, independently of any concrete rewards that our power may bring us; this stage is called the "honor-loving" form because honors are recognition of our prowess, but they do not provide any intrinsic satisfaction like pleasure or truth; power itself is only a means to an end. Beyond the positive rewards of appetite and before the positive rewards of rationality are the merely notional rewards of indominability or spiritedness, and so, while the appetitive and rational parts of the soul are designated by positive goal-directed activities ("the desiring part" and "the rational part"), the spirited part is characterized by a merely negative designation as "the part by which we get angry" (436a); it is the intermediate rebelliousness through which one positive regime (appetite) may become transformed into another (rationality). Accordingly, in the development of the city the appetitive stage (the first city) was characterized by the positive value of physical fulfillment, and the rational stage (the third city) will be characterized by the positive value of rational fulfillment, but the spirited stage (the second city) was characterized by the privative value of self-discipline (399e), and it was by a further development of that class that the rational class arose. Similarly, when the spirited form of the soul was distinguished from the appetitive, it was distinguished by its contemptuous rejection of the body's appetites (439e–440a).

The same point may be seen in another way. We know how difficult it is to control our appetites simply by reasoning with ourselves. If our soul were composed only of rationality and appetite, rationality would have very little power over the appetites. The intensity of the appetites would make them less likely to obey rationality than to turn rationality against itself in the form of rationalization in order to achieve the appetites' own goals. There is an image of this at the beginning of the *Philebus*. Philebus maintains that the good in life is pleasure, and Socrates claims that the good is the life of the mind, including such activities as true rationality (λογίσμος). When Socrates suggests that they try to give an account (λόγος) to determine who is right, Philebus declines, saying, "I regard and I will continue to regard pleasure as the absolute winner" (12a). In other words, to a hedonist the proper judge of what is better is not rationality (λόγος) but enjoyment: why should appetite submit to an alien set of values? But if reasoning with our emotions does little to change them, setting one emotion against another can be very effective. Thus, when our appetites master us against what rationality tells us, we revile ourselves and become angry with ourselves (*Republic*, 440a–b), and our sense of shame is much more likely to bring our emotions under control than simply reasoning with ourselves alone.[33] Spiritedness is rationality's enforcer—the mediating principle between rationality and irrational appetite—as the auxiliaries enforced the decrees of the guardians.[34]

In spite of the presence of all three characteristics in each part of the soul, Socrates' argument shows that as far as a basic understanding of virtue is concerned, it is more helpful not to say that our soul acts as a unity when it learns, gets angry, and desires, but that it does each of these with a different form of itself (436a)—nevertheless the different forms of itself look more like the difference between axis and circumference in step 4, than between arms and legs in step 3. Socrates uses the term "parts" only after the demonstration, when he wants to assimilate the model of the soul to the discrete classes of the city. But we have seen that even the discreteness of those classes, too, was ambiguous. In Book 2 the three temperaments (appetitive, spirited, and rational) and the classes that represent them were not presented as coming from three different sources, but as a progressive evolution of the original principles—the drive of appetite and the principle of specialization. The soldiers emerged by imperceptible degrees from the evolution of the workers, and the philosophers emerged by imperceptible degrees from the evolution of the soldiers. In the present passage the same result has appeared within the soul itself. What appeared to be absolute distinctions between the parts of the soul now seem to be merely differences of emphasis or degree.

In the context of the virtues, Socrates speaks of appetite and spiritedness as if they are capable of reasoning (442d).[35] But when he first distinguished those two "irrational" elements from rationality, in the context of the division of the soul, he portrayed them as utterly excluding reasoning. Appetite, for example, was nothing but the desire to drink—a simple response to corporeal stimuli, which did not even reason far enough to care whether the drink is good or not (437c–438a, 439a–b).[36] Although the difference between these two descriptions is sometimes taken to be an incoherence in Socrates' account, we can see it instead as implying a distinction that resolves a further problem. In the city each of the three classes of people have tripartite souls (they all can reason, be competitive, and have appetites),[37] but since the individual soul is treated throughout the *Republic* as being perfectly parallel to the city, each of the three parts of the soul ought to have a tripartite structure as well. So it looks as though either the analogy between city and soul breaks down, or there will be an infinite regress in which each part of the soul has all three parts, and each of those parts three further parts ad infinitum.[38] What enables us to pass between the horns of the dilemma is precisely the distinction we just looked at, where the three parts of the soul absolutely excluded one another when Socrates was distinguishing them, but partially included one another when he began to speak of how they function in the context of virtue. In their essential nature the three parts of the soul are mutually exclusive, but in their activity they are interdependent and mutually inclusive: we saw above that they each have appetites, spiritedness, and rationality. We can say that *abstractly* the three parts are mutually exclusive, but *concretely* they make use of each other as part of their essential activity. In the city the individual classes are distinguished not by what parts their soul has, since each has all three, but by the relative strengths of those parts: appetite predominates in the commercial classes, spiritedness in the auxiliaries, and rationality in the guardians. The same now turns out to be true of the parts of the soul themselves, for each of the three concrete parts must involve all three abstract parts, but in different proportions—one in which appetite predominates, another in which spiritedness predominates, and a third in which rationality predominates. There is a regress, to be sure, since the concrete elements of the soul are composed of primitive abstract elements, but not an infinite regress since the abstract elements themselves are no longer complex. Socrates does not make this distinction explicit, but he does speak of the elements in both ways, and it is entailed by the parallel between the city and the soul. Significantly, it fulfills Socrates' prediction that "if something different manifests itself in the individual we will return again to the city to test it, and perhaps by examining them alongside each other and rubbing them together like fire sticks we may make justice blaze forth" (434e–435a). When we rubbed them together just now, a more sophisticated conception of the three parts of the soul blazed forth; but what blazes forth about justice? To anticipate: the justice that is here said to be what marks forms of the soul off from one another and keeps them apart (noninterference)—and which is therefore also responsible for the distinctions among the other virtues, each of which is related to a different form of soul (appetite, spiritedness, rationality) or different combinations of them—will later turn out to be what unifies and harmonizes them, submerging those very distinctions.

The progression from the pure abstract type of appetite as a simple response to corporeal stimuli, to the mixed concrete type that includes a spirited drive and reasoning processes, is almost as gradual and continuous as was that from the appetitive city to the rational one. The first example of appetite was devised in order to distinguish it from rationality, namely the desire to drink even when rationality disapproves (439c–d). We would expect Socrates next to differentiate appetite from spiritedness by extending the same example—we get angry at ourselves for drinking when we know that we should not—but he introduces instead the new, bizarre example of someone who gets angry at himself for indulging in his appetite for looking at corpses (439e–440a). Whatever else we may think of this example, it is no longer a corporeal response to corporeal stimuli, but now involves a cognitive component. The cognitive component is not yet at a level we would normally call reasoning, but we saw that when appetite is considered again, in the context of virtue, some kind of reasoning is now involved that enables appetite to "share the belief" of rationality (442c). This progression in which appetite becomes increasingly rational reaches its culmination in Book 8, where appetite—as distinct from rationality and spiritedness—can even have philosophy as its object (ἐπιθυμία . . . ἐν φιλοσοφίᾳ διατρίβων: 561c–d).[39] There is thus a continuity among the three parts of the soul in their concrete forms, despite the discontinuity of their abstract forms, and that is presumably what Socrates alludes to when he speaks of the three parts together with "any others there may happen to be between them" (443e). The two models of opposition that Socrates gave us in steps 3 and 4—the extremities of the body, and the periphery and axis of a top—illustrate the difference between the abstract and concrete conceptions of the forms of the soul.

Individual Virtue (441c–445e)

In view of the parallel between the three classes of the city and the three parts of the soul, Socrates and Glaucon agree that the virtues within us will have the same structure as those in the city:

> Doesn't it follow necessarily that as the city was wise in a certain way and in a certain part, the individual will be wise in the same way and the same part?
> Of course.
> And the part and way in which the individual is courageous is the same as the part and way in which the city was courageous; and both have all the other things relevant to virtue in the same way.
> Necessarily.
> And so, Glaucon, I think we will say that a man is just in the same way the city was just. [441c–d]

Socrates explicitly mentions every virtue except self-control. After referring to wisdom and courage individually by name, he alludes to self-control only with the words, "all the other things relevant to virtue", but then goes on to specifically speak of justice as he did with the first two. We may remember that something of the kind happened in the discussion of the virtues in the city: after talking about wisdom and courage, Socrates had said, "How then might we find justice without having to bother any more about self-control?" (430d). Here again he seems to want to find justice without bothering about self-control, and once again the temporary bypassing of it seems to be a fore-shadowing of the fact that when we pass from the realm of *doxa*, the visible world, to that of *noesis*, the intelligible world, a kind of knowledge will become accessible that cannot be overpowered by the emotions (518c–d), and so justice, and virtue generally, in the deepest sense has no need of self-control.

After ignoring self-control in his preliminary remarks, Socrates gives an expanded account of all four virtues, self-control included, in which the definitions offered in the examination of the city are closely imitated for the individual. Justice is once again saved for last. The just person regulates well what is really his own and governs himself. He sets himself in order and is a friend to himself, and he harmonizes the three parts of himself like the three limits of a musical scale—literally, the low, the high, and the middle—and any others that there may be in between. He binds all these together and becomes completely one from many; self-controlled and harmonious. Only then does he act, and if he does something, whether in order to obtain money, or to take care of his body, or in politics or commerce, the action that he believes to be just and beautiful, and that he calls just and beautiful, is the one that preserves this condition and helps produce it; and wisdom the knowledge that supervises this activity. [443d–444a]

Justice, understood in this way as each part doing its proper work, so that rationality rules over the whole without being challenged by the appetites and spiritedness, is compatible with the way it is ordinarily conceived. People motivated by rationality rather than appetite could be trusted not to embezzle gold or silver that has been entrusted to them (442e),[40] nor would they have any reason to rob temples, steal money, betray their friends and cities, or to engage in adultery or disrespect for their parents or gods (443a); for each of these could only be motivated either by a failure of wisdom, or by an appetite or spiritedness that failed to heed the wise counsel of rationality, and thus failed in self-control or courage.[41]

As justice in the city was the noninterference by the three classes with what pertains to each class by nature, justice in the individual is the noninterference by the three parts of the soul with what pertains to each part by nature (i.e., refraining from usurping one another's natural function) (443c–d). It seems clear what it means for appetite and spiritedness not to interfere with rationality: we should not follow our emotions and passions when rationality counsels against doing so. But it is not clear 1) how rationality could possibly do the work of appetite, or 2) the work of spiritedness, and 3) how spiritedness could do the work of appetite, or 4) appetite the work of spiritedness.

In the first case, the prohibition against rationality's doing the work of appetite means that (contrary to the usual perception of him) Socrates believes it is possible to be too rational. It is the counterpart of the earlier statement that the city should not favor the guardians (or any one class) above the other citizens (420b). Subsequently, he insisted that the city should be neither rich nor poor but intermediate (422a), which, in view of the correspondence between city and soul, means that individually too we should be neither voluptuary nor overly ascetic. We can imagine rationalistic people who are so contemptuous of the body that they would despise even the necessary appetites and starve themselves, or embrace a level of poverty that prevents them from flourishing. In the second case, if rationality completely overrides spiritedness and results in an extreme of passivity, Hamlet-like, this too would miss the mean in favor of one of the extremes. Some readers are uncomfortable with the extent of the military aspect of the proposed city, but Socrates would reply that this response is symptomatic of an excessive repression of spiritedness by rationality. As we saw near the end of Book 3, a harmonious soul must balance its philosophical nature by its spirited nature if it is not to become too soft (410d–411e). The third case, spiritedness doing the work of appetite, can be exemplified, like the first, by extreme asceticism, but in this case an asceticism born not of rationality but of competitiveness: the challenge of resisting appetites and enduring pain. Finally, an obvious example of appetite doing the work of spiritedness is cowardice, where our avoidance of pain overrides our fighting spirit.

Although it seemed at first that for appetite and spiritedness not to interfere with rationality simply meant that we should not follow our emotions and passions when they conflict with the counsel of rationality, it now turns out that matters are not so simple. If it is possible not only for appetite and spiritedness to overreach themselves, but for rationality as well, then justice cannot be determined simply by following the dictates of rationality against the promptings of the other two. We would first have to be sure that rationality itself was acting within its proper limits. Justice requires not only self-mastery but wisdom, which includes knowledge of what is fitting for each of the parts, as well as the whole soul (442c). In that case we cannot be fully just until we have achieved adequate knowledge of the good. We cannot reduce justice to a rule even when that rule is merely formal, such as "always follow rationality", any more than we could when the rule was concrete, like "tell the truth and pay what you owe", or "help your friends and harm your enemies".

When Socrates turns from the definition of justice to that of injustice, however, something different happens. Justice was defined as each (ἕκαστον) of the three parts doing only its own work and not meddling with the function of the others (443c–d), which meant that rationality too might overstep its bounds. But injustice is now defined only as a rebellion by the two lower parts against the rule of rationality (444b), in which case the possibility of rationality overstepping its bounds does not enter into it. If Socrates has chosen his words carefully, it seems that although the overly rationalistic people we spoke of before, who have excessive contempt for appetite and spiritedness, are not perfectly just, neither should we go so far as to call them unjust. A person who is not just according to the definition of justice (an extreme ascetic, for example) is not necessarily unjust according to the definition of injustice. Justice and injustice would then be contraries, both of which can be false, rather than contradictories, which have opposite truth values. Someone may be not quite just and not quite unjust. As Socrates will put it in Book 6, it is possible to become not good without becoming bad (491d).

There are two further surprises in the above quotation from 443d–444a. For one thing, as we anticipated earlier, although justice started out as the principle of keeping things distinct from one another, it has now become that principle that makes one from many. The other surprise is that justice is said to be the virtue that produces friendship and harmony within us, whereas earlier that was how self-control was identified (430e, 431e–432a, 442d). In fact, justice is here described not only as harmonious but also as self-controlled; whatever distinction there had been between self-control and justice has now collapsed. Again, the description of justice as that which preserves the condition of the soul as ruled by rationality, is virtually identical to the way courage was previously described (429b–c, 442b–c). And when wisdom is here described as the knowledge that supervises the activity that preserves and produces that condition, it seems to be nothing more than yet another way of saying the same thing. There no longer seems to be any clear distinction among the four virtues; in their case, too, from many comes one. Every virtue now turns out to be a way of expressing the harmonious relationship among appetite, spiritedness, and rationality.

The central question of the *Protagoras* was whether the virtues are different names for the same thing or whether they essentially differ from one another (349b), and the dialogue concluded in favor of the first alternative: all are different names for knowledge. The discussion here in the *Republic* began as if the virtues were different from one another, so that the people in whom wisdom resided were in no cases the same as the people in whom courage resided, but it has now shifted so that all four virtues are nothing more than the proper ordering of our soul—in which case it turns out that the first alternative of the *Protagoras* is closer to the truth. But it may go too far to say that the *Republic* shows all four virtues to be different names for the same thing, since at least the emphasis is different in each case. They may not be identical to one another but they mutually imply one another.[42]

After giving us the clear and simple model of the tripartite soul and the subsequent picture of the four virtues as following from the division of the soul, Plato introduces complicating factors that lead to more sophisticated but less neatly structured models of both the soul and the virtues.[43] He begins by treating the virtues as discrete from one another, in accordance both with our usual beliefs and with the rigidly separated classes of the soul writ large, but then deconstructs that model by putting increasing evidence before us that they cannot be isolated from one another after all. That evidence first appeared as indications, in the form of puzzles or anomalies, in his original treatment of the virtues. Although initially the definitions of wisdom and courage in the city seemed to accord with the conventional view that the virtues were entirely different, we saw warning signs that threatened to erase the boundaries that mark off courage from rationality, on one side, and self-control on the other. In the first instance, Socrates insisted that the city's courage resided only in the auxiliaries, when in other places it was clear that the guardians too were warriors and equally in need of courage—an anomaly that was intensified when Socrates went on to locate self-control in all three classes. If Socrates seemed arbitrary in denying civic courage to the guardians, and it seemed that the guardians must have both wisdom and courage, the distinction between the two virtues begins to erode, and the simple model begins to develop into something more complex. By his exclusion of the guardians from the civically courageous, Socrates preserves the simple model; but by the conspicuous impropriety of that exclusion he points beyond that model. We noted as well that when he defined courage in terms of resisting not only pain and fear, but also pleasure and appetite, he threatened to collapse the distinction between courage and self-control. In retrospect, what seemed arbitrary at the time now seems to be a foreshadowing of the unity of the virtues. Again, when he turned from courage to self-control Socrates said that, whereas the first two virtues each resided in a single class, self-control extends throughout the city as a whole. We saw that this divergence from his treatment of the previous two virtues could easily have been avoided, either by being consistently exclusive and treating each of the virtues as the distinguishing excellence of a particular class, with self-control that of the money-making class; or by being consistently inclusive and treating them cumulatively, so that while only the ruling class has wisdom, both it and the auxiliaries have courage, and all three have self-control. When Socrates took the first approach with courage and the second with self-control it seemed to be an inconsistency of method, but in retrospect it too now looks different. The result of saying that self-control extends throughout the city as a whole is that the rulers and auxiliaries now each have two virtues which can hardly be distinguished from each other.

Wisdom is the proper relationship of the three parts to one another and to the whole, expressed cognitively; courage is that same optimum relation expressed as stability; and self-control is again the same relation expressed as a harmony. The unity of the virtues becomes even clearer in the discussion of *injustice* that follows, when Socrates says that the rebellion of the lower parts of the soul against rationality "is injustice, licentiousness, cowardice, and ignorance, and in a word the whole of vice" (444b). If all the vices correspond to the same definition, as rebellion against rationality, then presumably all the virtues too correspond to the same definition. This inference soon becomes explicit, when the pairs justice/injustice and virtue/vice are treated interchangeably. Socrates says that as health is the proper ordering of the elements of the body, and disease is the reverse, so justice is the proper ordering of the elements of the soul, and injustice the reverse; consequently virtue corresponds to the health of the soul while vice corresponds to its disease (444d–e). What is true of one virtue turns out to be true of virtue generally.

We have seen a number of passages that foreshadow the claim, not made explicit until almost the final page of the dialogue (619a), that justice is a kind of mean. The present passage carries the same implication, for if justice is the harmony or proper balance of its elements, and a harmony is destroyed when one of the elements is taken too far or not far enough, it follows that a life of justice requires us to avoid the extremes and pursue the mean. That is not to say that when Socrates claims in Book 10 that justice is a kind of mean, he has in mind the harmony of the parts of the soul, any more than he has in mind the senses of "mean" that arose in the first three books, but rather that the *Republic* constantly keeps before us the idea that what is good may be conceived as a mean between extremes. But we are not yet in a position to see the most important implications of that idea.

In Book 1 the discussion of justice focused on justice and injustice as actions, whereas here they are considered as inner states. The relationship between those two aspects is now made explicit in a way that Aristotle subsequently takes up in his ethics: just actions produce just characters (justice in the soul) while unjust actions produce unjust ones (444c–d), and the same is true for virtue generally (444e). Were it not for the warnings that their present approach will not lead to accurate answers, Socrates' task would seem to have been accomplished,[44] for Glaucon thinks that the question of whether justice or injustice is superior now looks ridiculous: just as an abundance of possessions is worthless if one's health is ruined, so too whatever advantages can be had by injustice are worthless if one's soul or self—that by which we live—is ruined (445a–b). Book 4 ends with Socrates about to enumerate five different kinds of political constitutions and the corresponding types of soul. They have found the one just type, but there are an unlimited number of unjust ones, four of which Socrates now proposes to discuss.

Notes

1. This passage confutes the view of Plato's Socrates as a cold rationalist who divorces himself from all human feelings (cf. Gregory Vlastos, "The Individual as an Object of Love in Plato's Dialogues" in Vlastos, *Platonic Studies* [Princeton: Princeton

University Press, 2nd ed., 1981], 1–34; and Martha Nussbaum, *The Fragility of Goodness* [Cambridge: Cambridge University Press], 195).

2. See Shorey 1930, 302 note *a*.

3. Bosanquet (1906) takes this to be "a legend which more or less caricatures the current Athenian belief (the word rendered 'children of the soil', literally, 'earthborn', below, was an epithet of Erechtheus, the mythical ancestor of the Athenians)" (122). Whether a caricature or not, it is generally recognized to be based on myths of autochthony in Athens and elsewhere.

4. Cf. Hume "Of Miracles": "When we peruse the first histories of all nations, we are apt to imagine ourselves transported into some new world; where the whole frame of nature is disjointed, and every element performs its operations in a different manner, from what it does at present. . . . Prodigies, omens, oracles, judgements, quite obscure the few natural events, that are intermingled with them. But as the former grow thinner every page, in proportion as we advance nearer the enlightened ages, we soon learn, that there is nothing mysterious or supernatural in the case, but that all proceeds from the usual propensity of mankind towards the marvelous, and that, though this inclination may at intervals receive a check from sense and learning, it can never be thoroughly extirpated from human nature. It is strange, a judicious reader is apt to say, upon the perusal of these wonderful historians, that such prodigious events never happen in our days. But it is nothing strange, I hope, that men should lie in all ages". *An Inquiry Concerning Human Understanding*, Section X, Part II (Indianapolis: Bobbs-Merrill, 1955), 126–27.

5. Cf. N. White: "rather than saying that if we provide sufficient happiness for the various groups of people in the city we shall make the city as a whole happy, he moves in quite the opposite direction, and says that if we secure the greatest possible happiness for the city, by making the citizens perform their tasks, then we may expect the citizens to have the appropriate amount of happiness" (1979, 108). Whether non-philosophers can ever be fully happy is problematic, since happiness depends on being internally virtuous, i.e., being governed by reason rather than by appetite or spiritedness (442c–444a) as the non-philosophers are. For an extended discussion see Christopher Bobonich, *Plato's Utopia Recast: His Later Ethics and Politics* (Oxford: Clarendon Press, 2002), 51–88.

6. How large a population that points to is not specified, but at *Laws* 740d the ideal number of households is said to be 5040, a figure that would be compatible with an army of 1,000.

7. *Protagoras* 324e–325a, 349b, *Meno* 78d–e. Also see Guthrie 1975, 471n3.

8. See above, 75–77.

9. Did he decide on those three classes because he already had conceived of a tripartite soul, or was the latter modeled on the former? It is usually supposed that his psychology came first, but Cornford argues that rather than reading his psychology back into the structure of the society, Plato extrapolated from the natural structure of a society to the structure of the soul ("Psychology and Social Structure in the *Republic* of Plato", *Classical Quarterly* 6 [1912]: 246–65; 247). The natural structure is that

self-control is the virtue of children, courage that of young adult men, and wisdom the virtue of old men (254).

10. As Gomperz points out with reference to the development of the city from Books 2 to 4, "*In the whole of this section* (as also in that part of the fifth book which several critics also assign to this 'stratum') *there is not a single word on the subject of intellectual culture*" (1905, 70; emphasis in original).

11. Cf. Nettleship 1901: "Starting, then, from a narrow conception of courage, Plato widens it to include everything that we should call moral courage" (149). In the *Laches* (191c–e) and *Laws* (1.633c–d) too he extends the meaning of courage to include self-control against appetites and pleasures, but only after courage is first conceived narrowly with reference only to fear and pain.

12. Accordingly when Irwin (1995) writes that "*Republic* IV, by contrast [with the Socratic dialogues], presents accounts of the virtues, and they are not accompanied by any of the usual Socratic disavowals or expressions of puzzlement" (262), this is correct only in the sense that Socrates' disavowal here is not of the "usual" kind.

13. Lloyd Gerson ("Platonic Dualism", *Monist* 69 [1986]: 352–69, 359) and Glenn Lesses ("Weakness, Reason, and the Divided Soul in Plato's *Republic*", *History of Philosophy Quarterly* 4 [1987]: 147–61, 148) both take Plato to be talking about *akrasia* there, the view rejected in the *Protagoras* that knowledge can be dragged around by its inferiors; as I have. W. K. C. Guthrie (1975), on the other hand, thinks that throughout the *Republic* "the Socratic Virtue as knowledge was still [Plato's] guide" (435–36). G. R. F. Ferrari points out that this is the one case where the nature of the virtue in an individual is described before, and in order to explicate, the civic virtue, in exception to Socrates' strategy of first defining the civic virtue in order to use that definition to discern the individual virtue. Socrates does this to convey "the suggestion that it is because such individuals rule it that the city comes to be self-disciplined" (*City and Soul in Plato's* Republic [Sankt Augustin: Academia Verlag, 2003], 91–92). There was a partial exception to this when Glaucon had difficulty in understanding Socrates' definition of courage, and Socrates had appealed there too to a preliminary description of individual courage (429d–430c); although in that case the preliminary description of the individual virtue came immediately after, rather than immediately before, the initial definition of the civic virtue.

14. Bernard Williams argues that passages like this imply the absurdity that for Plato "cobblers are characteristically men of powerful passions" ("The Analogy of City and Soul in Plato's *Republic*, in E. N. Lee, A. P. D. Mourelatos, R. M. Rorty, eds., *Exegesis and Argument* [New York: Humanities Press, 1973], 196–206; 204). But all that is meant is that those who are by nature most suited to being cobblers are by nature more inclined to value pleasures than honors or the search for truth, and so their appetites, although not necessarily powerful, are more likely to be so than those of the other classes. Socrates classes with the artisans in this context not only children and slaves but also women (431b–c). Commentators have been at pains to reconcile passages like this with Socrates' later claim in Book 5 that women are or can be the equals of the most accomplished men and should rule equally with them. But

the passages that speak of women in a derogatory way reflect the status of women in the existing paternalistic Greek cultures, while the egalitarian passages reflect what their potential would be in a different kind of society. Also see Susan Moller Okin, "Philosopher Queens and Private Wives: Plato on Women and the Family" in Carole Pateman and Mary L. Shanley, *Feminist Interpretations of Political Thought* (Oxford: Blackwell, 1991 [orig. 1977]), 11–31; and Gregory Vlastos, "Was Plato a Feminist?" in Kraut 1997 [orig. 1989], 115–28, 121–22. The issue will be discussed more extensively in the next chapter.

15. Williams (1973) claims that justice can be present in the city only by virtue of being present individually in the citizens, and that this leads to problems of coherence in Plato's treatment of the city-soul parallel generally. He argues that justice can be present only if either the citizenry in general are just (the "whole-part" argument) or if at least "the leading, most influential, or predominant citizens" are just (the "predominant section" argument), and he points out difficulties that follow from both alternatives (197–201). But we see from the present passage that justice is present in the city neither because the citizens generally are individually just (in the sense that will be identified at 443c–444a), nor because the ruling class is just, but simply because all three classes make their distinctive contribution without interfering with one another. In other words, justice is a harmony among the parts of the whole (443d)—in the city the three classes, in the individual the three parts of the soul—and as long as the three classes do their proper work without interfering with one another the city will be just, even if none of the citizenry were individually just (i.e., were internally harmonious). Williams bases his argument on the fact that Socrates uses the whole-part argument to establish that if the city has appetitiveness, spiritedness, and rationality, it must follow that these characteristics are present in the individuals comprising the city, "for they could not come from anywhere else" (435e). But that is as far as it goes: the whole-part argument explains how the three characteristics (appetitiveness, spiritedness, and rationality) get into the city, but the presence of the four virtues and the five constitutions (see Williams 200–201) is explained by the internal relationship of the three characteristics (parallel accounts for the city and individual), not by additional whole-part arguments. For extended replies to Williams see Jonathan Lear, "Inside and Outside *The Republic*", *Phronesis* 37 (1992): 184–215, 194–208, and Ferrari 2003, 42–50 *et passim*. Also see Gerasimos Santas, "Plato's Criticism of the 'Democratic Man' in the *Republic*, *Journal of Ethics* 5 (2001): 57–71, 58–61.

16. John Cooper points out that Aristotle appears to accept it despite the dualistic psychology that appears in the *Nicomachean Ethics*: "Aristotle does in fact preserve the distinctions that led Plato to regard the human soul as having three parts. He regularly divides ὄρεχεις (desire) into three sub-kinds, βούλησις, θυμός and ἐπιθυμία (see *de An.* II 3, 414b2, III 9, 432b3–7; *de Motu* 6, 700b22; *EE* II 7, 1223a26–7, 10, 1225b25–6; *MM* I 12, 1187b36–7), and he assigns the first to reason itself (*de An.* 432b5, 433a23–25; *Top.* IV 5, 126a13)" ("Plato's Theory of Human Motivation", *History of Philosophy Quarterly* 1 [1984]: 3–22, 17 n.2). Readers have taken issue with various principles on which the argument is constructed, but the objections are not fatal.

For a discussion of such objections and how they may be answered, see Reeve 1988, 123–31. For an earlier survey of attitudes that have been taken toward the tripartite soul doctrine, see T. M. Robinson 1970, 39–41.

17. In which case we would have to take it as part of the *Timaeus'* mythical (or at least metaphorical) dimension when Timaeus says that the rational part of the soul is located in the brain, the spirited element between the neck and the midriff, and appetite to the lower thorax between the midriff and the navel (44d, 70a).

18. Terry Penner argues that Plato's arguments justify only a bipartition of the soul: "The fact that *thumos always* takes reason's part when there is a conflict with appetite suggests that Plato doesn't really have an argument for *thumos* and reason being different parts. . . . Plato's arguments for the existence of *thumos* as a third part of the soul are singularly few and weak" ("Thought and Desire in Plato", in Vlastos, *Plato*, Vol. II [Garden City, N.Y.: Anchor, 1971], 96–118, esp. 111–13). But the present passage shows that the fact that *thumos* may never side with appetite against reason does not imply that it never opposes reason at all. Socrates illustrates the independence of spiritedness from reason in terms of Odysseus' conflict between his reason and his anger. I am not sure why Penner regards this as a singularly weak illustration, but a more familiar instance is the conflict that Plato occasionally points to between our love of truth and our love of winning arguments. Plato is clearly concerned that the spiritedness of our love of victory may conflict with reason's pursuit of truth—see, for example, 539a–b, 547d–548a, 548d–549b; cf. *Phaedo* 91a. Also see T. M. Robinson 1970 44–46, N. White 1979, 126, and Irwin 1995, 212.

19. See R. F Stalley, "Plato's Argument for the Division of the Reasoning and Appetitive Elements within the Soul", *Phronesis* 20 (1975): 110–28, and Reeve 1988, 118–40. For a detailed analysis of the argument as a whole see Bobonich 2002, 219–35.

20. This may be another instance of Plato's providing us initially with a simple model by which to grasp a thesis in its most elementary form, but then leading us to a more subtle model—as in the *Phaedo* Socrates at first presents a theory of forms that is "safe" but also simplistic, artless, foolish, and ignorant (100d, 105c), and subsequently replaces it with a more sophisticated one that is "not safe and ignorant . . . but [safe and] subtle" (105b).

21. Cf. Stalley 1975, 112–14.

22. E.g., 357c, 363e–364a, 369a.

23. Something that is double in relation to its half, is half in relation to its own double; but thirst is appetite in relation to drinking without being drinking in relation to something else.

24. Glaucon sharply differentiates them, saying that children "are full of spirit as soon as they are born, while in the case of rationality some seem to me never to partake of it, while the majority do so very late" (441a–b). But this is rationality only in its most refined sense; in a more ordinary sense children make use of reasoning all the time. Penner rightly calls Glaucon's remark a "gross equivocation" (1971, 104n6).

25. Cornford (1912) suggests another reason why "it is not a complete psychology: faculties such as sensation and perception are not even mentioned" (262). Julius Moravscik mentions "perception, and . . . purely instrumental reasoning" ("Inner Har-

mony and the Human Ideal in *Republic* IV and IX", *Journal of Ethics* 5 [2001]: 39–56, 42). But perception and instrumental reasoning may be regarded as powers of the soul without being distinguishable parts. Only if they can be shown to conflict with something else in the soul would they count as parts or species in the required sense.

26. Adam (1963 [1902]) writes, "It is doubtless true (as Archer-Hind holds [*Journal of Philosophy* X 120–31]) that 'parts' of the soul can only be different modes of its operation" (1.243).

27. Cf. Penner 1971, 101–3; R. C. Cross and A. D. Woozley, *Plato's Republic: A Philosophical Commentary* (London: Macmillan, 1964), 124; N. White 1979, 129; Glenn Lesses, "Weakness, Reason, and the Divided Soul in Plato's *Republic*", *History of Philosophy Quarterly* 4 (1987), 147–61, esp. 149; Leon Craig, *The War Lover: A Study of Plato's* Republic (Toronto: University of Toronto Press, 1994), 101; Terence Irwin points out that for Plato appetite must at least be capable of something very much like reasoning "since he takes the desire for wealth to be an appetitive desire" although it is only a means to an end (*Plato's Ethics* [Oxford: Oxford University Press, 1995], 219).

28. στασιαζόντοιν and its cognates appear at 440b, 440e, 442d, 444b.

29. Cf. Richard Lewis Nettleship: "In every desire there is an element of rational activity, and in the most reasonable direction of our activities there is an element of desire. So we may say that the real conflict is . . . between different kinds of desires, and accordingly in Book IX we find that each of the three forms of soul has its own special ἐπιθυμία" (Richard Lewis Nettleship, *Lectures on the Republic of Plato* [London: Macmillan, 1964 (1901)], 158. Also Guthrie 1975, 475–76. For a discussion of this issue see Julia Annas, *An Introduction to Plato's* Republic (Oxford: Clarendon Press, 1981), 139–51. For a different view see Moravscik (2001) who argues that each form of the soul has the other two characteristics only in a metaphorical sense.

30. For a detailed discussion of these same themes of eros, Freud, and the tripartite soul, which reaches similar conclusions by a different route, see Charles Kahn, "Plato's Theory of Desire", *Review of Metaphysics* 41 (1987): 77–103.

31. *Republic* 353d & 611e respectively, cf. *Phaedo* 105c–d & 80a–81a, *Phaedrus* 245c & 247c–e, *Timaeus* 30b & 47a–e.

32. This is the basis of the *Phaedo's* paradox that death, the soul's separation from the body, is good for the soul but that we have a duty to continue our corporeal existence (62a–b), and also of the *Timaeus'* definition of time as "the moving image of eternity" (37d), for eternity refers to reason (29a), the motive principle is soul (36e), and what is moved is body (30b).

33. In one way Aristotle agrees with this, in another way not. He posits two parts of the irrational soul—vegetative and appetitive—the former of which is indifferent to reason, but the latter, although in itself irrational, may listen to reason as a child listens to its father, and in that case it may be better to say that the appetitive soul is a species of the rational soul (*Nicomachean Ethics* 1.13.1102b28–1103a3). On this account there is no need for an intermediary to impose rational conceptions onto irrational appetite. However, Aristotle illustrates the ability of reason to persuade our irrational side by pointing to our practice of influencing people to right behavior by means of warning, rebuking, and exhortation. The term for "rebuking" is *epitimesis*,

from the word *timē*, honor, which in Plato is associated with the spirited rather than appetitive part, so when Aristotle refers here to the appetitive part of the soul as "appetitive and desiring as a whole" he is already including the spirited element without distinguishing it from appetite in the narrower sense as Plato does.

34. Cf. Iris Murdoch: Freud's "reasons for preferring a trio are the same as Plato's: an unmediated fight does not present a realistic picture of human personality" (*The Fire and the Sun: Why Plato Banished the Artists* [Oxford: Clarendon Press, 1977], 37).

35. This corresponds to the point that he had recently made about the classes of the city—that the appetitive citizens are no less possessed of their proper knowledge and judgement than the guardian class (428b–c).

36. For a discussion of the controversy surrounding this passage, see Gabriela Roxana Carone, "*Akrasia* in the *Republic*: Does Plato Change His Mind?" in D. Sedley, *Oxford Studies in Ancient Philosophy* XX (Oxford: Clarendon Press, 2001), 107–148, esp. 117–29.

37. The craftsworkers and auxiliaries both have rational knowledge in their activities and share beliefs of the rulers (428e, 433c), the guardians and the auxiliaries both have appetites (429d, 431d), and both the guardians and craftsworkers are spirited (414b, 434a–b).

38. Cf. Annas 1981, 149–51.

39. Cf. Cooper 1984, 9.

40. In accordance with Cephalus' understanding of justice as returning what we owe, and Polemarchus' understanding of it as keeping money safe for friends.

41. David Sachs misses this point when he argues that wisdom, courage, and self-control are, on the contrary, "*prima facie* compatible with a variety of [conventionally understood] injustices and evil-doing", including the ones mentioned above ("A Fallacy in Plato's *Republic*", reprinted in Vlastos [ed.] 1971, 35–51, 37, 47–48). On the *Republic*'s account we do wrong either because we lack wisdom and do not know what is really good, or because we lack self-control and allow our appetites to override our knowledge of the good, or because we lack courage and allow our fears to override our knowledge of the good (442b–d). Therefore if we possess all four virtues there can be no possibility for wrongdoing, and the above kinds of behavior are not even prima facie compatible with it. Also see Raphael Demos' refutation of Sachs: "A Fallacy in Plato's *Republic*?" *Philosophical Review* 73 (1964): 390–95, reprinted in Vlastos 1971, 52–56; Gregory Vlastos, "The Argument in the *Republic* that Justice Pays", *Journal of Philosophy* 65 (1968): 665–74, "Justice and Psychic Harmony in the *Republic*", *Journal of Philosophy* 66 (1969): 505–21, and "Justice and Happiness in the *Republic*", in Vlastos 1971(1), 67–95; Charles Kahn, "The Meaning of Justice and the Theory of Forms", *Journal of Philosophy* 69 (1972): 567–79; Leon Galis, "The State-Soul Analogy in Plato's Argument that Justice Pays", *Journal of the History of Philosophy* 12 (1974): 285–93; Mitchell Miller, "Platonic Provocations: Reflections on the Soul and the Good in the *Republic*", in *Platonic Investigations*, ed. D. O'Meara (Washington, D.C.: Catholic University of America Press, 1985), 163–93, 171–92; F. C. White, "Justice and the Good of Others in Plato's *Republic*", *History of Philosophy Quarterly* 5 (1988):

395–410; Timothy Mahoney, "Do Plato's Philosopher-Rulers Sacrifice Self-Interest to Justice?" *Phronesis* 37 (1992): 265–82, 275; Irwin 1995, chapter 18; Richard Kraut, "Plato's Comparison of Just and Unjust Lives", in Ottfried Höffe, ed., *Platon Politeia* (Berlin: Akademie Verlag, 1997), 275n8; David Roochnik, *Beautiful City: The Dialectical Character of Plato's "Republic"* (Ithaca: Cornell University Press, 2003), 7–8.

42. Irwin reaches a similar conclusion after a lengthy discussion (1995, 224–39).

43. In this sense I would agree with Roochnik that the tripartite soul doctrine is a provisional one that will be reversed in Books 5–7 (2003, 2–5).

44. For a different view see N. White 1979, 137.

~

CHAPTER FIVE

The Three Waves
(Book 5)

A New Beginning (449a–451b)

As Socrates prepares to list the four unjust types of constitution and soul, he notices Polemarchus and Adeimantus agreeing not to "let it go", and he asks them what they mean. They think Socrates was being evasive when he said that "with regard to women and children it is clear to everyone that the possessions of friends are held in common" (449c, cf. 423e–424a), and they have been waiting for him to elaborate. Now that he is about to move on to other subjects they can no longer remain silent, and accuse him of trying to cheat them out of a crucial section of the argument, for they believe that the details of how the sharing of women and children is to be accomplished "makes a big difference, and even the whole difference, to whether the regime is right or not right" (449d). Since Socrates himself had warned of the inadequacy of his treatment it is not surprising that he admits the seriousness of his omissions: "You don't know what a swarm of arguments you're stirring up by your demand, which I saw at the time and bypassed to avoid creating a lot of trouble" (450b).

Eventually Socrates' reply will introduce the theory of forms and thus raise the discussion to a new level, but the transition, like those from the appetitive to the spirited and spirited to rational cities, is very gradual. For now there is the merest hint of what is coming: when Adeimantus complained that Socrates cheated them out of a whole section of the argument, the word that Plato has him use for "section" is *eidos* or "form" (449c),[1] which will, in fact, turn out to be what was missing from the earlier argument. Although the transition to the theory of forms will be gradual, the transition from Book 4 to Book 5 is remarkably abrupt, as if to emphasize that the discussion is about to proceed on a different level. The transitions between Books 2 and 3 and Books 3 and 4 were so seamless that they did not even provide me with natural dividing places for my chapters, but the break between Book 5 and 6 is made even more conspicuous than it needed to be. As we saw in the Introduction, Books 5–7 sit within their neighbors so awkwardly that some readers have supposed them to be a later addition clumsily grafted onto the rest of the dialogue.

When Polemarchus and Adeimantus force the insertion of Books 5–7 between Books 4 and 8, Socrates complains that they are forcing him to re-examine the issues "as if from the beginning" (450a). The idea that in some sense this is a new beginning is reinforced by the dramatic byplay that accompanies this exchange. The beginning of the dialogue saw Socrates, accompanied by Glaucon, prevented from leaving by Polemarchus and Adeimantus. Socrates was inclined to persevere but Glaucon took the side of the others and Socrates bowed to the united front of the opposition who say they will not let him go. The incident began when Polemarchus' slave grabbed Socrates' cloak from behind to get his attention. The present incident begins when Polemarchus himself grabs Adeimantus' cloak from behind to get his attention, and they inform Socrates, who is being accompanied in the discussion by Glaucon, that they will not let him go.[2] Socrates resists but Glaucon takes the side of Polemarchus and Adeimantus (as does Thrasymachus, speaking for the first time since Book 1), and Socrates bows to the unanimity of the opposition. The resonances are unmistakable, and signal that a new beginning is indeed taking place, one that will be seen to remedy the short-comings of the previous approach that Socrates had warned us about. They are, in fact, about to cross from the realm of *doxa*, the examination of visible reality, to *episteme*, the examination of intelligible reality.

Socrates expresses considerable misgivings about pursuing the matter, because much about it lacks confidence (ἀπιστίας), and there is no confidence (ἀπιστοῖτ') even that it is possible, and not even confidence (ἀπιστήσεται) that it is best. Glaucon encourages Socrates by saying that his audience does not lack confidence (ἄπιστοι) in him, and Socrates replies that that would have been encouraging if he were confident (πιστεύοντος), but since he is not confident (ἀπιστοῦντα) he fears misleading his friends about beautiful, good, and just institutions (450c–451a). At the beginning of Book 2, when the discussion was about to move from the *eikasia* (images of visible things) of Book 1 to *pistis* (visible things themselves) the shift was signaled by Glaucon's challenge, "Socrates, do you want to seem to have con-vinced (πεπεικέναι) us or to truly convince (πεῖσαι) us that it is in every way better to be just than unjust?" (357a–b)—Do you want to seem to have given us *pistis* or to truly give us *pistis*? Now that the dialogue is about to move beyond *pistis* to *dianoia* we are given a cluster of references to *pistis* in its priv-ative form, absence of *pistis*. On one level Socrates is merely disclaiming con-fidence, but on another level the passage can be read as saying that we are moving to an area that outstrips *pistis*, namely the intelligible realm rather than the visible.

First Wave: Equality of Women (451c–457c)

Socrates is worried not only about his ability to do justice to the subject, but also about the reception that his ideas are likely to receive. The vehemence of the opposition which he expects his proposals to meet leads him to com-pare the challenge to that of someone who falls into water and must swim to save himself from drowning (453d). In the course of his swimming, three waves of protest of increasing size threaten to overwhelm him: the first results from the claim that qualified women must rule equally with men (457b–c),[3] the second from the claim that instead of families there must be communities of men, women, and children (457c–d), and the third in response to the claim that the rulers of the city must be philosophers (473c–e).

When Socrates, returning to the metaphor of the guardians as dogs, asks Glaucon whether the female guard dogs should guard and hunt with the males or whether they will be "unable to do so because of the bearing and rearing of pups", Glaucon replies that "everything should be done in common except that we regard one as stronger and the other as weaker" (451d–e). We should not attach too much importance to the fact that it is Glaucon, not Socrates, who makes this decision, for Socrates explicitly supports the con-clusion and presents rebuttals to the kinds of objection that might be antici-pated. Even the form of his question assumes a general equality between men and women, insofar as the only reason he permits for the possible incapacity of women to share the guardian duties is their maternal responsibilities; he never suggests any unsuitability of nature. Moreover, by posing the question in terms of the metaphor of the dogs Socrates encourages a positive answer, since female dogs do share the hunting and fighting with the males. This makes it more difficult to claim that to a Greek of Plato's time it will be so obvious that women should not be the equals of men, that Plato's audience will recognize that this whole passage is a reductio ad absurdum designed to convince us not to take the new proposals seriously.[4] Plato did, after all, admit female students to the Academy,[5] and he has Socrates express indebtedness to the teachings of Aspasia and Diotima. Aspasia, he says, was not only his teacher of oratory but also the teacher of Athens' greatest orator, Pericles (*Menexenus* 235e), while Diotima was his teacher of eros and was wise about many other things as well (*Symposium* 201d). It is possible, of course, to dismiss all such passages in the same way as this one, as reductios ad absurdum of the context in which they occur, but when evidence for a conclusion is dismissed precisely because it is evidence for that conclusion there is a danger of begging the question.

On the other hand there are numerous passages in which Plato himself writes dismissively of women, including passages of the *Republic* itself; but at least in the *Republic*, as I suggested in the previous chapter, those passages refer to women who have been formed by the paternalistic Greek culture, while Plato is here speaking of their potential in a society that gives them equal opportunities for growth and fulfillment. This is clearly the implication when, in response to Glaucon's egalitarian reply, Socrates asks whether it "is possible to use any animal for the same purpose if you don't give it the same upbringing and education" (451e). The Athenian women who are spoken of disparagingly in the dialogues have certainly not been given the same upbringing and education as men. They were treated and regarded as possessions, first of their fathers then of their husbands, were denied the education given to males, and were kept in the confinement of their homes, unable to attend the theater or even go shopping.[6] What Socrates concludes, then, is that "What we have legislated is not impossible or naïve since we established the law according to nature. It seems, rather, that the way things are done now goes against nature" (456c).

Nevertheless, even in the present context women on the whole are not regarded as completely equal in potential to men. At Socrates' prompting Glaucon acknowledges that "one sex is much better at everything than the other. Many women are better than many men at many things, but on the whole it is as you say" (455d). In the final analysis, then, the position seems to be that women in general are less capable than men in general, but the best women may be the equals of the best men; so if we are talking about genders as a whole, men are superior, but if we are talking about individuals we cannot say that a particular man is necessarily superior to a particular woman. To put it differently, exceptional women are considered to be comparable to exceptional men, but the average woman is not considered to be comparable to the average man; a lower proportion of women than men have exceptional natures, but those who do are approximate equals of exceptional men.[7] It is not clear from the text whether Socrates is saying that the best women are fully the equals of the best men—in some cases conceivably even better than the best men[8]—and inferior only in numbers, or only that the best women are "close enough" to equality with the best men.[9] If the latter, it could explain why Plato's recommendation that women rule jointly with men is not carried over into the paternalistic *Laws*: if Plato considered women to be on average only almost the equals of men, then in different contexts he might sometimes emphasize the implication that they are virtually equal, and at other times emphasize the implication that they are not quite equal. Another possibility is that because the *Laws*, unlike the *Republic*, is concerned with the feasibility of its proposals and does not abolish families, women can no longer be liberated from their traditional role within the family.[10] On either explanation, Plato's view of the equality of women is revolutionary for the culture in which he lived, although from our own cultural perspective it is not revolutionary enough. His position, limited though it may be, seems, however, to have been even more audacious than he realized, for although Socrates expected each proposal to meet with more a violent wave of opposition than the last, it is the first one, the proposed equality of women, that appears to have met with the greatest opposition from antiquity until some thirty years ago.[11] Since then it has met with a different kind of objection: that Plato is making women the equals of men only by assimilating women to the male model.[12] It is not clear that this is the case, however, since on one hand Socrates appeals to examples of female behavior in the animal kingdom, and on the other hand the way of life that he proposes for male and female guardians is arguably no more male than female. Certainly no men lived like philosopher-rulers in Plato's day, and the way of life proposed for them, while comparable to that of Sparta in some ways, is vastly different in others. The goal of their philosophical life, the contemplation of an eternal goodness that lies at the basis of reality, does not depend on a male model of rationality, and has been practiced by female mystics in all eras; and if the goal of their *practical* life, wise governance of the city, has not been associated with women as much as with men, it is only because women have rarely been given the opportunity to govern.

Socrates anticipates that the proposal may be objected to on two main grounds: propriety and natural ability. People will object on grounds of propriety that it would be unseemly and ridiculous for women to exercise naked alongside the men (452a–b), and on grounds of natural ability that the nature of women is different from the nature of men, so having them both rule would violate the principle of having people do only what they are fitted for by nature (453b–c). Socrates replies to the first objection by pointing out that propriety depends on what we are accustomed to, and there was a time when it was considered improper even for men to exercise naked, so there is no reason to suppose that the new proposal will continue to seem improper once people become used to it. We should not think that anything is ridiculous except what is bad, or that anything is noble or beautiful except what is good (452a–e).

As for the second objection, to argue that because men and women are different with regard to their sex they must be different with regard to their ability to rule makes no more sense than to say that since a bald person differs from a long-haired one, if bald people can be shoemakers then long-haired people cannot. In both cases the argument is merely eristic rather than part of a serious dialogue, for what counts is not just any difference but only a relevant difference (454a–c). It is in this context that Socrates and Glaucon agree that men tend to be better at everything than women (455c–d). The assertion seems odd in a discussion devoted to proving that women have an equal claim to rule, but the point is that if women were better than men in certain areas—that is, if they could learn those skills more readily and their bodies were better suited to carry them out—then those would be the ones for which they were suited by nature. When Socrates suggests that men excel over women even at weaving, baking, and cooking,[13] this is meant not to attack women (although it is hardly flattering) but to deny that there is by nature any such thing as "women's work". Apart from giving birth, women's range of activities is the same as men's, and if it is not, on average, quite at the same level of excellence it is at least at the level of competence, even where ruling is concerned (455b–456b). Since it is possible for women to receive the same education as men and carry out the same duties, and since there is nothing better for the city than to be ruled by the best men and women, this strategy is not only possible but also what is best (456c–457a).

But Socrates' argument is a non sequitur when he says that since it is better for the city if the best men rule, it is also better for the best women to rule. That is true if women are to be rulers at all, but that is just what needs to be shown. Glaucon might have asked: if men are even slightly better at things than women, would it not be better for the city to be ruled only by the best men? There are three answers to this. We have already noted the first, that men may be on average better than women while the best women are still as good as the best men. The second answer, which is already implicit in the argument, is that since the principle of justice requires that we do the job for which we are best suited by nature, justice demands that women who are by nature rational should act as guardians; to deny this to women on the grounds that they might not be quite as good as men would be no more just than to prevent a man from doing what he is naturally suited for because other men might be even better at it. The third answer leads to the next issue, the raising of children. We can best prepare for the next generation of potential rulers by pairing the best men with the best women, but in order to do so the women must be selected in the same way as the men and therefore receive the same education. Moreover, in order to prevent the guardians from favoring their own children they will not be allowed to live as families, so the women will do the work for which they have been educated rather than raising their children.

Second Wave: Communities of Men, Women, and Children (457b–471e)

Having just escaped drowning in the first wave of opposition, Socrates and Glaucon must now cope with an even bigger one: the law that "all these women shall be in common to all the men, and none shall live together privately. And again the children will be in common so that no parent will know its own child nor any child its parent" (457c–d). The references to "these" women and "these" men means that at this point Socrates is speaking only of the guardians. He says he is surprised that Glaucon thinks there is any doubt that this is a good proposal, and that he himself thinks the only point at issue is whether it is possible. Allowing for Socratic irony, we will see that the proposal follows from what they have previously agreed upon, so it is not entirely unreasonable that Socrates might expect Glaucon to agree with its desirability, apart from questions of its feasibility.[14]

As Glaucon must know from his breeding of hunting dogs and pedigree birds, Socrates says, the best offspring are produced by mating the best parents in their prime. But eros will draw the male and female guardians to each other in unpredictable ways, so the natural drive of eros will have to be constrained in the city by a combination of sanctified marriage and "drugs", the drugs being the therapeutic falsehoods spoken of at 382c, which in this case will consist of devices such as rigged lotteries sanctified by hymns and ceremonies (458d–460a). The chief goals of these machinations will be to ensure optimum quality and quantity—in the first instance that the best men have sex with the best women as often as possible, and the opposite for their opposites (459d), and in the second that the total number of males remain at the optimum size (460a). The children of the best parents will be raised in a common enclosure, while those of inferior parents or defective birth will be hidden away. This is usually taken to be a euphemism for the then common practice of infanticide by exposure, but according to 415c inferior children will simply be relocated among the craftsmen and farmers, and when the argument of the *Republic* is recapitulated in the *Timaeus* Socrates says that "we said that the children of the good would be raised, but that those of the bad were to be sent out secretly into the rest of the city" (19a), presumably meaning the lower classes.[15] "All these things must come about without being noticed by anyone but these rulers, if again the herd of guardians is to be without dissension as far as possible" (*Republic*, 459e). This is not in principle difficult to achieve since the guardians would not become rulers until they are past the stipulated age for having children. The prime procreative age for women ends at 40, and for men at 55—after which they are free to have sex as often as they like and with whomever they like within the same generation, as long as the fetus does not see the light of day (460e–461c)—and according to what is said later, guardians will not be considered suited to rule until they reach the age of 55 (539a–540b).

If Socrates expects the greatest wave of opposition to be the third wave of the philosopher rulers (473c), and the one that has traditionally met with the greatest opposition is the first wave of the equality of women, it is the eugenics proposal of the second wave that seems hardest to accept today after the excesses of the twentieth century.[16] Had Socrates predicated it on the hypothesis that the rulers would be infallible in making their decisions, the proposal might be considered worth entertaining at a purely theoretically level, although worrisome in practice. But since he explicitly says that even the wise rulers will not be infallible in these matters because of the uncertainties of sensory knowledge (546a–b), the proposal is unsettling even in theory. On the most charitable interpretation the underlying argument would run as follows: A city of this kind can perpetuate itself only if a sufficient number of the guardians' children (or those of other classes) have golden natures,[17] but given that the children of good people are not necessarily good themselves,[18] if we want to minimize the risk that the next generation will fail to provide a sufficient number of potential rulers we will have to exercise as much control as possible over the reproductive process. The recommendation, then, would be a hypothetical imperative subject to the goal of ensuring as much as possible the continuation of the city.

The above proposals speak explicitly only about the guardian class, but if one of the goals of the selective breeding is to maintain the optimum population level, it seems that these practices will have to extend to the other classes as well. We would expect that by definition the appetitive class would be the ones most likely to overproduce offspring and to become too large for the established number of guardians to govern effectively. Moreover, if their children are to be upwardly mobile, as Socrates had said (415a–c), then they would need to be raised side by side with the children of the guardians in the children's compound. Again, if women are included among the rulers because justice requires that everyone do the job for which they are suited by nature, and some women are by nature governed by rationality, then it also follows that women who are more suited by nature to be farmers than to raise children should, as a matter of simple justice, be allowed to pursue that way of life; in that case we cannot take it for granted that the women of the appetitive classes would necessarily raise families, and so the communal lifestyle might have to include them as well. Socrates never denies that these policies apply to the other classes, although neither does he explicitly include them in the policy, and Aristotle concludes that he leaves the question undetermined.[19] Why does Socrates speak only of the guardians in that way, and not the others? One possibility, of course, is that the provisions do not apply to the lower classes, but another may be that, difficult as it is to imagine the guardians being willing to give up their children in this way, it would be impossible to imagine the appetitive class doing so, and so the question of the very possibility of such a city would become even more vexed.

The communities of men, women, and children accomplish more than facilitating the practice of surreptitious eugenics. Socrates had said earlier that the city will function properly only if the guardians love the city and regard their own interests as inseparable from those of the city (412c–d). Ownership of property was identified at that time as a particular obstacle to the guardians' identification of their own interests with those of the city (416d–417b), and now the same point is extended to the possession of families. As confirmation of their correctness in establishing communities of women and children instead of families, Socrates points out that a city will most attain unity when all the citizens feel pleasure and pain in the same events, and that this is possible only if they all say "mine" and "not mine" in unison about the same things in the same way (461e–462c). It follows, then, that private families will tear the city apart, whereas communities of men, women, and children will unify it, for everyone will address all members of the older generations as father, mother, grandfather, or grandmother, and all members of the younger generations as son, daughter, grandson, or granddaughter, as well as calling their contemporaries brother or sister (461a). After itemizing in some detail the benefits that will accrue to the city and its rulers as a result of these policies, Socrates believes that he has confirmed his earlier suggestion to Adeimantus that the rulers are indeed happier in this city than anywhere else, and that only an uncritical conception of happiness might lead one to conclude otherwise (465d–466b, cf. 419a–420b). He then extends the conception of identifying our self, not with our body but with our city, to an identification with all of Greece, although not with all of humanity: "the Greek race is familial to itself and akin, but to the barbarians foreign and alien" (470c), so wars with other Greek cities should be regarded only as civil wars, and enslavement of enemy combatants should only be allowed when the enemy are barbarians.

Socrates' reference at 462b (above) to "all the citizens" once again suggests that the communities might extend to all three classes, but that suggestion is once again rendered ambiguous in what follows:

> These citizens most of all will have the same thing in common which they call "mine" and from this commonality they most of all will feel pain and pleasure in common.
>
> Certainly.
>
> Then is the cause of these things, in addition to the other institutions, the communities of women and children of the guardians [phulaxin]?
>
> It is certainly the most important.
>
> But we agreed that this is the greatest good for the city, and we compared a well-governed city to a body, in respect to the pleasure and pain of its parts.
>
> And we agreed correctly.
>
> Then the cause of the greatest good for the city has appeared to us to be the auxiliaries' [epikourois] communities of women and children. [464a–b]

Schematically represented the argument runs as follows:

1. If we call the same thing "mine" we will share the same pleasures and pains.

2. The cause of calling the same thing "mine" in this case is the communities of women and children of the guardians.

3. Therefore the cause of sharing the same pleasures and pains is the communities of women and children of the auxiliaries.

In drawing this conclusion about the auxiliaries rather than about the guardians as step 2 requires, Socrates seems to be using the terms interchangeably despite the fact that the two classes have been rigorously distinguished from each other since the end of Book 3. The terminological distinction had been collapsed three pages earlier when Socrates asked Glaucon what people in this city will call their rulers, and Glaucon replied, "preservers and epikourous" (363b). Epikourous, which had previously been translated as "auxiliaries", here means "helpers", as it will again at 466a. It would be strange if Plato simply forgot his distinction in these three passages, but it is also strange that he would deliberately confuse terms that have been so consistently and fundamentally distinguished, and none of the explanations that have been proposed completely dispel this strangeness.[20]

Earlier Socrates seemed to collapse the distinctions among the classes when he spoke as if the practicing of eugenics for the guardians would be able to control the population of the whole city (460a), and when he suggested that by eliminating the family in the case of the guardians, "all the citizens" would feel pleasure and pain in the same events. One possible explanation for all these apparent confusions is that he is hinting at difficulties that have been suppressed in order to minimize the size of the second wave. He speaks explicitly only of instituting the communities of men, women, and children in the case of the guardians, but he justifies himself by pointing to benefits for the city as a whole—benefits that do not seem possible unless the communities extend to all three classes. His account seems to be haunted by the dilemma that if the communities of men, women, and children do not extend to all three classes, then the measure will not be able to accomplish all of its goals; but if it does extend to all three classes it is hard to believe that the artisans, and perhaps even the auxiliaries, can ever be prevailed upon to accept it. The problematic ways that Socrates speaks of the three classes in these passages is perhaps meant to alert us to the possibility that the city may be even less capable of actual existence than he acknowledges. In fact, when Socrates continues by presenting a surprisingly extended discussion of matters related to the conduct of war, Glaucon interrupts him to express the fear that no time will be left for this further question of whether such a city can actually come into being, and Socrates admits that he has been temporizing because of his reluctance to face the biggest wave of all (471c–e).

Third Wave: Philosopher-Rulers (472a–474e)

Before exposing himself to the biggest wave of all, Socrates spends a page and a half reminding Glaucon that the question of whether such a city is possible was always secondary to the question of what a good city would be like. Their purpose was to provide a model of justice in relation to which the justice in an individual might be recognized; and if such a model has been constructed, its value will not be diminished if they cannot prove that it can actually come into being, any more than the value of a painted paradigm of a perfectly beautiful human being would be diminished if such a person could not be proven to be capable of actually existing (472b). For the first time Socrates' words contain clear allusions to the theory of forms. He says that if they find what justice is they should not expect the just man to be identical with it, but to participate (μετέχη) in it more than others do. What they are seeking is a pattern (παραδείγματος) of justice itself (αὐτό . . . δικαιοσύνη) in which we can see how it is related to happiness. Just as the pattern of the good city that they made in words is no less good if it cannot be brought into existence, the pattern of the just man is no less valid if a perfectly just man cannot actually exist (472b–e).

It would hardly be surprising if no actual city could do justice to their model because, as Socrates asks rhetorically, "Is it possible for something to be put into practice just as it is in theory (ὡς λέγεται), or is it the nature of practice to attain to truth less than theory does?" (472e–473a). Socrates suggests that instead of trying to prove that the city they described can actually exist they pursue a more modest goal: to find the smallest alteration in the present way of governing cities that might bring into being a city as much like theirs as possible (473a–b). He is referring to the institution of the philosopher-rulers; but later it seems that even in that case a further condition of the possibility of such a city would be the willingness of parents to leave their young children behind and allow themselves to be sent into exile (540e–541a). It is hardly surprising that in the end it is very much in doubt whether the city that Socrates is about to describe could actually come into being (592a–b).

Socrates says,

> Unless either the philosophers govern as rulers in the cities, or those who are now called kings and rulers practice philosophy genuinely and satisfactorily, and these two, political power and philosophy, coincide in the same one— while the many natures who at present pursue either one separately are prevented by compulsion [ἐξ ἀνάγκης] from doing so—there will be no rest from evils in the cities nor, I think, for the human race. . . . But this is what made me shrink so long from saying so—that I saw how very paradoxical it would be. [473c–e]

Socrates was not worried unnecessarily that this would be the hardest wave to surmount. Glaucon agrees with Socrates' expectation that it will provoke not only derision but outrage (473c, 473e–474a). We need only recall the Athenians' judgement that a philosopher like Socrates did not even deserve to live, to imagine how they would respond to the suggestion that someone like Socrates ought to be their king. The very way that Socrates expressed his proposal shows how paradoxical it is: if philosophy and ruling are so different that practitioners of one must be *compelled* to practice the other, then their unification in a single person may be simply unfeasible. Philosophy is contemplation directed toward intelligible being, while ruling is practical activity directed toward visible becoming; so each pursuit appears to undermine the conditions necessary for the other. By compelling people to do what goes against their inclinations, we may ensure only that the city will have unhappy or incompetent rulers. So the proposal is problematic, not only with regard to its possibility, but even with regard to its desirability. It does not, however, violate the definition of justice, since, as we saw in the previous chapter, the definition of 'each person doing a single job' pertained only to the classless first city (369b–370b), and evolved into 'having and doing what is appropriate to one's natural class' in the tripartite third city (433e–434a). Justice is now violated only if we try to do the work of a different class, not if we combine different jobs within the same class. Since philosophy and ruling both belong to the rational class there is no injustice in combining the two. We are still left with the problem of how the two jobs can be combined without undermining each other, to which we shall return in the context of Book 7, where Socrates turns from the philosophical component of the philosopher-rulers' function to the ruling component.

Socrates proposes to begin the defense of his proposal by defining what a philosopher is, and since "philosopher" means "lover of wisdom" he first examines the nature of love. In accordance with the root of the term that he is seeking to define, he speaks of *philia* rather than eros, but to shed light on the nature of *philia* he includes examples of eros in such a way that the only distinction between them seems to be the objects that they are directed to (474c–e). Any doubts that eros lies at the heart of philosophy, even in the *Republic,* are erased later when Socrates says that philosopher-rulers may come about in two ways: if philosophers become rulers or if rulers become inspired by "a true eros for true philosophy" (499b–c).[21]

Dianoia (474c-480a)

Socrates' claim is that when we love something or someone—regardless of whether we call the love *philia* or eros—we love it as a whole, and we love the parts because they belong to the whole. So if we love someone with a snub nose we find the snub nose lovable and call it cute, even if in other cases a snub nose is not considered a perfection, and the same is true of all the other attributes of our beloved: what might seem a deviation from perfection in someone we are indifferent to becomes something lovable in someone we love (474d–475a). Glaucon is not impressed with this argument: at the beginning he does not at all understand what Socrates is talking about (474c–d), and even after Socrates' examples he says only that he is willing to agree "for the sake of the argument" (475a). We can understand his misgivings: we may say that "love is blind"—blind to the imperfections of the beloved—but at the same time we know that this is hyperbole, and that people often find fault with those whom they love. Socrates' next example seems even more open to that objection: lovers of wine love every kind of wine. How can we reconcile that claim with the fact, which must have been true in Plato's day as well, that wine lovers are notoriously discriminating about the wines that they love? We have to distinguish, however, between loving wine per se and loving good wine,[22] in the way that Socrates earlier distinguished between having an appetite for drink and having an appetite for good drink (437d–438a). Someone who loves wine as such loves it because it is wine and not necessarily because it is good. This explanation is suggested by Socrates' final example: "And I think you have observed that lovers of honor, if they can't become generals become captains, and if they are not honored by the great and important they like to be honored by the lowly and inferior" (475a–b). Even though true lovers love the whole of what they love, they need not love every aspect of it equally. Lovers of honor prefer prestigious honors to minor ones, but enjoy minor ones when only those are available; and true lovers of wine prefer fine wines to plonk, but would rather have any wine than none; so the wine lover that Socrates has in mind seems to be less a wine connoisseur than a wino.

With these considerations in mind, Socrates' remarks about loving all the attributes of a beloved person are easier to understand. If we truly love individuals we do not love them less because of their lapses, and we can even be said to love their lapses, not per se but as expressions of the distinctiveness of the beloved. If their lapses are so severe as to seem no longer to be endearing foibles but something more serious, then we might say that we do not really love the person but only certain qualities of the person. It is not a natural way of speaking, however, and like Glaucon we may be willing to agree with Socrates—if at all—only for the sake of the argument; in any case the sequel of the argument will not depend on our acceptance of that example. Socrates concludes that if we desire something, we desire the whole form of it (475a–b). The appearance of the word "form" (εἴδους), like the language of the forms at 472b–e, is significant, for this part-whole concept of oneness is an anticipation of the member-class oneness of forms.

In accordance with the above examples, a philosopher desires all of wisdom and learning, and no one who desires only certain kinds of learning is a philosopher. Are then people philosophers, Glaucon asks, who love looking at things or listening to things generally, even though they never willingly participate in serious arguments? The question is surprising, since their lack of love for argument is an absence of love for the whole, but Socrates merely replies that they resemble philosophers without being philosophers (475d–e).[23] Who then are true philosophers? Glaucon wants to know, and Socrates ominously replies, "It would not at all be easy to tell someone else, but you I think will agree to this" (475e). I say "ominously" because the argument that follows will eventually be able to establish its key premises only by depending on Glaucon's sympathetic and uncritical responses, an extension of his present willingness to agree for the sake of the argument.

In Book 10 Socrates says, "We are accustomed to posit some one form for every multiplicity to which we give the same name" (596a). In that context a form is the referent of the meaning of words,[24] and just as the same word applies to innumerable cases, the same form extends over innumerable individuals. There are two ways of trying to discern the nature of a universal form, namely the methods that the *Phaedrus, Sophist,* and *Statesman* later call collection and division. Collection gathers together various instances that are called by the same name and tries to discern what they have in common. Division is based on the principle that the meaning of a word may be thrown into relief by distinguishing it from its contrasting species within the same genus. The early dialogues employed the method of collection, but without obvious success, since it proved difficult to say just what it was that the instances all had in common. Perhaps for that reason, Socrates here employs a simplified version of what in its multi-step form will be called in later dialogues the method of division. He does not attempt to say what the beautiful, the just, and the good are, except that the beautiful is the opposite of the ugly, the just of the unjust, the good of the bad, and all other forms may be described in the same way (475e–476a). If these oppositions are meant to be perfect dichotomies—contradictories rather than contraries—we must assume that here "ugly" means "not beautiful" (as at 479a) lest there be a third intermediate category of what is neither beautiful nor ugly; and the same with the other two pairs.[25] Since each pair is two, each member of the pair is one, but they appear to be many, Socrates says, because of their association with action, with bodies, and with each other: there are many beautiful faces, for example, even though beauty itself is one, and many just actions even though justice is one; and we may even say that many of the forms are good even though the good itself is one.

Socrates did not call the distinctions between beautiful and ugly, just and unjust, and good and bad, divisions, but he now uses that term to distinguish those who are capable of discerning the forms from those who are not: "I divide as one separate group those who we just called lovers of sights, lovers of crafts, people of action; and again as another separate group those with whom our argument is concerned, those who alone would appropriately be called philosophers" (476a–b).[26] The former, who perceive things but not forms, are like dreamers who cannot see waking reality; while the philosophers, who perceive both forms and things, and can distinguish between them, are awake. Their thought (*dianoia*) therefore is knowledge (*gnōmēn*), while that of the others is opinion (*doxan*) (476a–d). This rigid division between knowledge and opinion corresponds to the main division of the Divided Line, and it is with this passage that the new beginning spoken of at the start of Book 5 becomes manifest. For the first time the dialogue passes from the realm of visible reality to that of the purely intelligible forms, and the discussion of justice moves from *pistis* to *dianoia*. The highest level to which the complete guardians attained was still in the realm of opinion, *doxa* (412e–414b), but that is now left behind. At the end of Book 6, when Glaucon fails to understand Socrates' explanation of *dianoia*, the examples that Socrates introduces are instances of the method of hypothesis used by mathematicians, and consequently it is often concluded that *dianoia* is concerned only with mathematics. But we should not forget that in the *Meno* (86e–87c) and *Phaedo* (100a–101e) Socrates has shown how the mathematical method of hypothesis is employed by philosophy as well, so the things that are said about *dianoia* would apply to the corresponding kind of philosophical as well as mathematical methodology. This will be discussed in detail when we come to the Divided Line.

We have seen that simple models in Plato are often precursors of more complex ones, and that the rigid distinctions among the three divisions of the soul became more subtle in the further course of the discussion. Something of the kind will turn out to be true of the Divided Line as well. The very image of a line suggests something continuous rather than discontinuous, and it is not surprising, therefore, that there is a transitional moment between *pistis* and *dianoia* at the end of Book 4.[27] The argument of Books 2–4 began with Socrates' suggestion that they search for justice in the soul by first searching for it in the city and then looking to see whether justice in the soul is the same, the way one might use larger letters in one place as a way of recognizing what smaller letters at a distance say, if we can see that they are the same (368d–e). Since the nature of *dianoia* is to use visible images as a way of thinking about intelligible objects (510b–d), Socrates' investigation of the visible city as a way to recognize what is in the non-visible soul is a foreshadowing of *dianoia*. It is only a foreshadowing, however, because the soul does not belong to the intelligible realm, but is intermediate between the physical and the intelligible, bringing intelligible form to the corporeal world (as evident throughout the *Timaeus*). The most we can say is that its nature is closer to that of the forms than to corporeality, but it is active while the forms are motionless (*Phaedo*, 80a–b, 105c–d). Accordingly, at the end of Book 4 when Socrates began to use their conclusions about the city for the intended purpose of learning about the soul (beginning at 435b), we were in a realm that was no longer quite the visible realm and not yet quite the intelligible one.[28]

The distinguishing features of *dianoia* are its use of visible models to think about intelligible reality and its hypothetical nature. Like *noesis* it begins with a hypothesis, but whereas *noesis* ascends from the original hypothesis to higher hypotheses, culminating in an unhypothetical principle, *dianoia* never questions the original hypothesis but proceeds downward only, affirming the consequences that follow from it (510b–d). Both of these features of *dianoia* are clearly present here in Socrates' presentation of the theory of forms. The use of visible models to illustrate the nature of the intelligible was evident in his examples of the love of visible things—boys, wine, honors—to illustrate the love of truth; and the hypothetical, provisional nature of his presentation became clear when he said, "It would not at all be easy to tell someone else, but you I think will agree to this" (475e), and introduces what the *Phaedo* calls the hypothesis of forms (100a–b) and the *Republic* calls a thesis (596a): the belief that beauty, justice, goodness, and the rest are each a unity even though they manifest themselves as multiplicities (475e–476a).

When Socrates says, "What if someone who we say has opinion but not knowledge [someone at the level of *eikasia* or *pistis*] becomes angry with us and disputes that what we say is true?" (476d), he seems to be envisioning the possibility described in the *Phaedo*'s discussion of the method of hypothesis: "But if someone takes issue with your hypothesis" (101d). At this point in the *Republic*, Socrates does not yet follow the *Phaedo*'s procedure of meeting that contingency by seeking a higher hypothesis. That cannot be because the present formulation is already at the highest level, for ultimately the forms must be seen as offsprings of the Idea of the good (509b), but here they include not only the beautiful, the just, and the good, but also the ugly, the unjust, and the bad (475e–476a). Not only does Socrates not try to derive the present thesis from something higher; he does not even claim to demonstrate the truth of his claim to the imagined objector at all, but only to "soothe and gently persuade him" (476e). We shall see that in valuing his argument so humbly Socrates is not being modest. What he offers is a strangely repetitive and problematic argument in defense of the claim that knowledge is directed to the forms, and that we can have only opinion about physical things. The lines of inference are not always clear, but the argument can be construed as follows.

1. To know (γιγνώσκει) is to know something that is (476e) (premise).

2. Therefore what completely is, is completely knowable, and what is not at all, is completely unknowable (477a) (from 1).

3. If anything is in between what completely is and what is not at all, it must be directed to something between knowledge and ignorance (477a) (2).

4. Opinion and knowledge (ἐπιστήμης) are different powers (477b) (p).

5. Therefore they are directed to different things according to their distinctive power (477b) (4).

6. Knowledge is directed to what is (477b) (1).

7. Powers differ from one another if they are directed to different things and accomplish something different (477c–d) (p).

8. Opinion accomplishes something uncertain while knowledge accomplishes something certain (477e) (p).

9. Therefore opinion and knowledge are different (478a) (8).

10. Therefore they are directed to different things (478a) (9, 7).

11. Knowledge is directed to what is (478a) (1).

12. Therefore opinion cannot be directed to what is (478b) (11, 10).

13. Neither can it be directed to what is not, since ignorance is directed to that (478c) (2).

14. Opinion is between knowledge and ignorance (478d) (p).

15. Because visible things are equivocal they are between what completely is and what is not at all (478e–479c) (p).

16. Therefore opinion is of physical things (479d) (12–15).

Step 15 has been discussed extensively because Socrates never fully explains what he has in mind. By the equivocity (ἐπαμφοτερίζειν) of visible things he means that nothing is so beautiful as never to appear ugly (i.e., not beautiful), or so just or pious as never to seem unjust or impious. But he does not defend or clearly explain those claims. In the *Phaedo* he similarly argues that equal things are deficient in their equality compared to equality itself (74a–75a), but there too Socrates' precise meaning is left for his audience to work out. In the present case perhaps no further specification is made because any number of explanations are possible and all of them will serve the purpose of the argument. Something that seems beautiful to me 1) may not seem beautiful to you, whereas the beautiful itself always seems beautiful; or something that seems beautiful to me at one time may not seem beautiful at another because 2) I have changed or 3) it has changed or 4) what is present for comparison has changed, although the beautiful itself always seems beautiful to me. Any of these cases would establish Socrates' point that things have a kind of essential ambiguity that is unlike the univocity of the form.[29] The same kind of equivocity applies to his example of justice. We saw, for example, both in the context of Socrates' reply to Cephalus, and in his doctrine of the therapeutic lie, that not telling the truth can be an instance of justice even though in most circumstances the failure to be truthful would be an instance of injustice. The equivocity of Socrates' other example, piety, can be seen in a similar way: in general, lying is impious because is it hated by the gods (382a), but it becomes an instrument of piety when the noble lie teaches us piety toward the earth, who is our ancestral mother.

If step 15 is defensible despite its lack of specificity, other steps are deeply problematic. The initial inference (step 2) is clearly fallacious: from the fact that all knowledge implies being, we cannot infer that all being implies knowability, let alone that complete being implies complete knowability. The false conversion slips past Glaucon only because he already accepts the assumption that it is meant to justify—that the forms represent the convergence of what is and what is knowable. Hence Socrates' opening remark that Glaucon will probably agree with what follows where others would not (475e).[30] In the demonstration of the tripartite soul Glaucon had pronounced himself satisfied even after Socrates cautioned that the way they were proceeding was inadequate (435c–d). As I suggested in the introduction, we can accordingly interpret the present remark to imply: 'In our discussion of the tripartite soul you were willing to accept avowedly oversimplified analyses, so I think you will accept this one where someone else would not'.

One source of perplexity has been that the argument as a whole is pervaded by a fundamental ambiguity about the meaning of "is". The Greek term admits of a number of interpretations and the context does not enable us to be certain which one is intended here. "What is" has a veridical sense ("what is true"), an existential sense ("what exists"), and a predicative sense ("what is F"), all three of which have been proposed at one time or another as the sense intended here.[31] Rather than posing the question in terms of contemporary distinctions that may not quite correspond to Plato's way of conceptualizing the term,[32] let us look at Plato's own way of distinguishing between "what is" and a sense of "what is in between what is and what is not". In Book 9 Socrates distinguishes between "what is always the same, and immortal" and "what is never the same, and mortal" (585b–c). And in the *Phaedo* he makes a similar distinction between "the divine and immortal and intelligible and uniform and indissoluble and what is always related to itself in the same way about the same things" and "the human and mortal and multiform and unintelligible and dissoluble and what is never related to itself in the same way about the same things" (80a10–b5). The first half of each of these pairs ("what is always the same", "what is always related to itself in the same way") corresponds to "what is" in the present passage. While the second half of each pair ("what is never the same", "what is never related to itself in the same way") corresponds to "what is in between what is and what is not", the concept of equivocity in step 15. It refers to what is in a constant state of becoming, in contrast to complete being or absolute nonexistence. The contrast then is between the unchanging (being) and the changing (becoming).

What are the implications of this way of looking at it for the predicative, existential, and veridical interpretations? The phrase "related to itself in the same way" clearly implies predication; it refers to properties and thus to the possibility of saying that something is F. A form is purely what it is (it is purely

F), whereas a thing is only equivocally what it is (in some sense it is F but in another sense it is non-F), and "what is not" is in no sense F. But that does not rule out the veridical interpretation,[33] for we can also say that truth in the fullest sense applies only to the form because only it admits of unambiguous affirmation, whereas truth applies to things only in a provisional and qualified way because of their equivocal nature, and does not apply at all to what is not. The existential interpretation applies as well: the form alone fully exists because it is unchanging, while individual things are always in a process of becoming other than what they were, and therefore not fully existent. The argument is defensible, then, on any of the ways of interpreting its use of the term "is".

Apart from the ambiguity of some of its terms, the argument is confusing also for structural reasons: it appears that steps 4–7 could be dropped without affecting the logical sequence. Step 3 says that if anything is between what is and is not, it must be directed to something between knowledge and ignorance; step 8 begins the demonstration that opinion is between knowledge and ignorance;[34] and step 15 shows that physical things are between what is and what is not. Steps 4–7 only seem to make the argument more confusing by introducing steps that are either repetitive or redundant. Their value in soothing and persuading the objector appears to be that they reinforce a fundamental feature of the claim which has been challenged, namely that knowledge is reserved for the forms, and about physical things there can be only opinion. But despite its appearance of defending that claim, the passage merely begs the question, as step 2 had already done in a different way. The question-begging premise is step 7:

> In the case of abilities [like seeing and hearing] I do not see any color or shape or any other such quality . . . to which I can look in order to distinguish them for myself from one another. . . . The only thing I can look to is what it is directed to and what it accomplishes. . . . That which is (1) directed to the same things and accomplishes the same thing I call the same, while that which is (2) directed to different things and accomplishes something different I call different.

The question-begging character of this passage has been widely noted in more recent literature, although it is also not without defenders.[35] Socrates presents these two possibilities as if they were the only alternatives, but obviously we also call things the same when they are (1a) directed to different things but accomplish the same result, as when we know different things through the power of knowledge. And we also call things different when they are (2a) directed to the same things but accomplish something different, as when perception and action are directed to the same things and result in perceiving and doing. In other words, a difference in what the abilities are directed to *or* what they accomplish would be enough to distinguish them, and Socrates is not justified in saying that a difference in *both* is required. By limiting Glaucon's choices to (1) and (2) Socrates prevents him from separating "what it is directed to" from "what it accomplishes", and forces him to conclude that if knowledge and opinion accomplish something different they must be directed to different things. But this is part of what the argument was supposed to demonstrate, so the question is begged. Glaucon fails to notice the false dichotomy because it follows from the opposition between the intelligible and the visible which he already accepts.

This passage reveals the limitations of *dianoia*, hypothetical thinking about intelligible forms, namely that it does not derive its first principles from something higher, but takes them for granted (510b). It can never justify them when challenged, therefore, except on the basis of its original assumptions, and so it cannot avoid begging the question. Like *eikasia*—which is to *pistis* as *dianoia* is to *noesis* (509d)—it is capable of making perfectly valid inferences from its assumptions, but it perceives only images of the highest reality rather than that reality itself, and can never rise above its words to justify its assumptions. When it must do so it can only try to soothe and persuade; it cannot justify its own principles until it passes from *dianoia* to *noesis*.

The resultant model, whereby knowledge is of what is (the forms), opinion of what is intermediate (physical things), and ignorance of what is not, is one of the best known doctrines in Plato but, like all such clear-cut models that we have seen, it will be found to be an oversimplification, a vivid way of making a point that requires a subtler and more complex account to do it justice. In the next book, Socrates, who professes to have no knowledge of the Idea of the good, finally, though reluctantly, agrees to state his "opinions" about that form (variants of δόξα and δοκεῖν appear eight times from 506b–e). But he can only claim to have opinions about the forms if he has moved beyond Book 5's insistence that there can be only knowledge of being, while opinion must only be of becoming. Conversely, in Book 7 he proposes telling the guardians that when they return to the Cave they will know (γνώσεσθε) the images there because they have seen the realities (520c). If that were not the case, if knowledge and physical things were absolutely divorced as the argument of Book 5 insists, how could philosophy make us more knowledgeable as rulers in the physical world?

There is no question that for Plato it is of fundamental importance to distinguish between knowledge and opinion, and between being and becoming; consequently in Book 5 he contrasts them as strongly as possible to establish the distinctions. But he softens the edges in Books 6 and 7 to avoid the problems that result from distinguishing the members of these pairs too rigidly—the problems that Aristotle clearly identified in his criticisms of Plato's theory of forms. If being is separated too strictly from becoming, it can never function as the cause and essential nature of transient things; and if knowledge is separated too strictly from opinion, how can we use the fallible as a starting point to aim at the infallible? Socrates had good reasons for his apparent slips when he spoke in Book 6 of having "opinions" of the Idea of the good and in Book 7 of having "knowledge" of visible things. None of this means that the distinction between intelligible forms and visible things is vitiated, but only that no simple way of expressing it can do it justice. That is the point of Parmenides' critique of the theory of forms in the dialogue named after him.

Notes

1. At 454a there is, perhaps, an anticipation of the subject of dialectic in the word διαλέγεσθαι.

2. Forms of ἀφεῖναι are used both at 327c5 and 449b6,8.

3. For the resemblance between this section and Aristophanes' *Ecclesiazusae*, see Adam 1963 (1902), 1.345–55; Thesleff 1982, 103–5; S. Halliwell, *Plato Republic 5* (Warminster: Aris & Phillips, 1993), 9–16, 224–25; and Myles Burnyeat, "Utopia and Fantasy: The Practicability of Plato's Ideally Just City", in Fine 1999, 297–308, esp. 305. There is a division of opinion as to whether Plato is alluding to Aristophanes, or Aristophanes to Plato (or Socrates), or both are drawing on common sources.

4. For example, Hoerber regards the requirement that women rule equally with men as a reductio ad absurdum to show that the political dimension is not to be taken seriously (1944, 34–45). In a similar vein, although in the service of a different view of the *Republic* as a whole, Bloom writes that "Book V is preposterous, and Socrates expects it to be ridiculed. . . . [W]hat he appears to teach seriously is impossible" (1968, 380–81). Bloom's interpretation is an elaboration of that of Strauss: "The just city then is impossible . . . because the equality of the sexes and absolute communism are against nature" (1964, 127). Comparable views are defended by Seth Benardete (*Socrates' Second Sailing: On Plato's Republic* [Chicago: University of Chicago Press, 1989], 113–17, esp. 125–26); Zdravko Planinc (*Plato's Political Philosophy: Prudence in the Republic and the Laws* [Columbia: University of Missouri Press, 1991], 32, 280–81); and Leon Craig (*The War Lover* [Toronto: University of Toronto Press, 1994], 183–244). Whereas Hoerber takes the proposed equality of women to be a way of discrediting the political aspect of the *Republic* as a whole, the latter scholars regard it as discrediting only the *Republic's* apparent utopianism: "At the beginning of the dialogue Glaucon and Adeimantus set the severest standards for political justice. In order to try to meet those standards, they would have to establish a terrible tyranny and would fail nevertheless" (Bloom 1968, 410). Hyland (1990), while agreeing that the second and third waves

are meant to be fatal to the proposals, does not believe that that is true of the proposal of equality for women. Gadamer questions the seriousness of the proposals on different grounds: "*Per se*, the institutions of this model city are not meant to embody ideas for reform. Rather, they should make truly bad conditions and the dangers for the continued existence of a city visible *e contrario*. For example, the total elimination of the family is intended to display the ruinous role of family politics, nepotism, and the idea of dynastic power in the so-called democracy of Athens" (*The Idea of the Good in Platonic-Aristotelian Philosophy* [New Haven: Yale University Press, 1986], 71).

5. Diogenes Laertius lists among Plato's disciples "two women, Lastheneia of Mantinea and Axiothea of Phlius" (III.46).

6. In fact, "a citizen could give his sister or daughter into concubinage, from which she could be sent to a brothel without any reproach to her owner" (Okin 1991 [1977], 17 & n32). Another way that the image of women as weaker was maintained is that "women were traditionally responsible for lamentation of the dead[,] . . . a performance as ritualized as it was excessive involving wailing, loud and public dirges, self-laceration, breast-beating, and tearing of hair, face, and clothes. Such excessive displays, in fact, contrasted sharply with the restrained, formal one of male grievers" (Ramona Naddaff, *Exiling the Poets* [Chicago: University of Chicago Press, 2002], 44–45). Ironically, in terms of equality within their class, working-class women were better off than wealthy women because they often were forced to supplement the family income. Socrates' mother Phaenarete is an illustration of this in her work as a midwife. Kenneth Dover writes that "below a certain point in the social scale, in families which owned few or no slaves, it simply cannot have been practicable to segregate the women-folk. They would have to go on errands, work in the fields, or sell in the market-place; the bread-woman of Ar. *Wasps* 1396–8 is unquestionably of citizen status" (*Greek Popular Morality in the Time of Plato and Aristotle* [Berkeley: University of California Press, 1974], 98).

7. Also see Brian Calvert, "Plato and the Equality of Women", *Phoenix* 29 (1975): 23, 1–43.

8. Natalie Harris Bluestone points out by way of analogy that it is possible to say both that male mammals are larger than females, and also that the largest mammal of all is female, namely the female blue whale (*Women and the Ideal Society: Plato's Republic and Modern Myths of Gender* [Oxford: Berg, 1987], 154.

9. Or, as Gomperz (1905) puts it, that women differ quantitatively from men even if not qualitatively (78). Cf. Calvert 1975, 238–39.

10. See Okin 1991 (1977), 22–27.

11. For a detailed account of this opposition and its history see Bluestone 1987, esp. 3–63. She writes, for example, that "not until the 1970s has there been a single commentator who wholeheartedly agreed with the Platonic suggestion of identical leadership roles for both genders. In fact, throughout the centuries, Plato's passage on sexual equality has suffered a singular fate; it has been largely dismissed, deplored, or ignored. . . . Before Ficino [reintroduced Plato in the fifteenth century], Leonardo Bruni had translated several of the *Dialogues* and the *Letters*, but declined to translate

the *Republic*. He feared that its radical ideas, particularly those on women, would upset his readers" (2–3).

12. E.g., Arlene Saxonhouse, "The Philosopher and the Female", in Kraut 1997 [orig. 1976], 95–113, esp. 111; Annas 1981, 329; and Bruce Rosenstock, "Athena's Cloak: Plato's Critique of the Democratic City in the *Republic*", *Political Theory* 22 (1994): 363–90, esp. 372.

13. Socrates asks, aren't these the tasks "in which women appear (δοκεῖ) to distinguish themselves and in which it is (ἔστι) most ridiculous of all for them to be inferior?" (455c7–d1). His point is one that is sometimes still claimed today (ignoring differences in opportunity) by those who insist that although cooking, for example, is considered to be the province of women, the best chefs are men. Saxonhouse (1997 [1976]) takes Socrates instead to be saying "that there is no area except such ridiculous ones as weaving or cooking in which the male is not superior" (99). In that case, however, we would expect Socrates to say that it is ridiculous that women are superior in these areas, not that it is ridiculous for them to be inferior (καταγελαστότατόν ἐστι πάντων ἡττώμενον). Moreover, the fact that women are said only to "appear" to distinguish themselves, and that it "is" (not "would be") ridiculous for them to be inferior, makes it unlikely that the remark is intended as contrary to fact, in the sense: "It would be ridiculous to say that women are inferior in these areas, but these (minor) areas are the only ones in which they aren't inferior". Neither of these readings fits the Greek as naturally as the one suggested above, and Glaucon's reply, too, takes Socrates' point to be that there are no areas in which women in general excel: "It is true that one sex is, in general [ὡς ἔπος εἰπεῖν], much better than the other in everything, although many women are better than many men in many things" (455d2–4).

14. We should also bear in mind that family life in the modern sense was not characteristic of ancient Greek culture, so the abolition of the family would not be quite as shocking to them as it is to us. See Okin 1991 (1977), 15.

15. Also see F. M. Cornford, *The Republic of Plato* (New York: Oxford University Press, 1945), 159n1. On the common practice of infanticide see Adam 1902, 1.357–60. Since infanticide was not an uncommon practice, even if this passage were interpreted as a reference to it by Plato's contemporaries (as Adam believes it would be) the policy might not add to the size of the wave that Socrates is swimming against. But another policy certainly will: because the citizens have no way of knowing who their biological family members are, incest will be unavoidable. By preventing copulation between members of different generations incest can be avoided between parent and child, but not between brother and sister (461b–e).

16. See, for example, Halliwell 1993, 16–18.

17. Plato never suggests an optimum number of guardians, as he did with the figure of 1,000 auxiliaries (423a–b), but comparisons with other dialogues invite speculation. Here are three possibilities based on different combinations of extrapolation and hypothesis. 1) At *Laws* 740d the ideal number of households is said to be 5,040. If we extrapolate that number to the *Republic* there will be approximately 10,080 adult men

and women, and the ratio of auxiliaries (1,000) to the number of adult citizens will be approximately 1:10. If we assume that the ratio of guardians to auxiliaries is the same as the ratio of auxiliaries to the number of adult citizens, there will be about 100 guardians. 2) Halliwell (1993) points to the remark in the *Statesman* (292e) and Seventh Letter (337c) "that not even 50 out of 1,000 people can attain to true political wisdom", and suggests that since the auxiliaries are already an elite perhaps there will be 1,000 guardians as well (19, 157); but the guardians are a smaller class than the auxiliaries (428e). Suppose, however, that we take the ratio from the *Statesman* (50 guardians for every 1,000 adult citizens) to mean 50 guardians for every 1,000 adult members of the appetitive class, and combine this with the previous hypothesis that the ratio of guardians to auxiliaries is the same as the ratio of auxiliaries to appetitive people; then, given that there are 1,000 auxiliaries, the number of guardians would be about 224 and the total size of the city would be about 4,464 adult citizens or 2,232 households, less than half the size of the city in the *Laws*, and probably too small to support 1,000 soldiers and 224 rulers. 3) If we extrapolate the figures from both of the other dialogues such that (according to the *Laws*) there will be a total of about 10,080 people and (according to the *Statesman*) about 50 in every 1,000 will be guardians, then there will be some 500 guardians together with 1,000 auxiliaries—the latter number being the only one in all three calculations that is not entirely speculative as applied to the *Republic*.

18. Cf. *Protagoras* 326e–328a, *Meno* 93c–94e.

19. *Politics* 1264a13–17.

20. See, for example, Adam 1902, 309.

21. For a discussion of the relation between the *Republic*'s references to eros and Plato's doctrine of eros generally, see Irwin 1995, chapter 18. This positive sense of eros in the *Republic* should be kept in mind together with the negative sense that has sometimes been called attention to. See Strauss 1964, 111; Stanley Rosen ("The Role of Eros in Plato's *Republic*", *Review of Metaphysics* 18 [1965], 452–75); and Jacob Howland ("The Republic's Third Wave and the Paradox of Political Philosophy", *Review of Metaphysics* 51 [1998]: 633–57, esp. 646–55.

22. Cf. N. White 1979, 154.

23. Cf. Aristotle, *Metaphysics* A.1.

24. In other contexts it is seen as a paradigm, a cause, or a manifestation of goodness. See below, chapter 6, 199–202.

25. Alternatively, the divisions here may resemble those of the *Statesman* (from 287c on), where divisions may contain any number of species, rather than the *Sophist* where the divisions are binary.

26. Friedländer suggests that Socrates' use of the word "divide" introduces the method of division here. He says it introduces "a set of divisions (διαιρῶ, 496a9) distinguishing between 'philosophy', on one side, and the 'love of sounds and sights and of the arts', on the other, between 'beauty itself', on one side, and its embodiment in images single and dimmed, on the other, between waking and dreaming, between knowledge and opinion" (1969, 3.105). It is somewhat misleading to call this a set of divisions, since that phrase leads one think of a series of progressive bisections that

gradually narrow the definition of something until we reach its exact species, whereas the set of divisions that Friedländer points to is a single division followed by several ways that the opposed realms may be characterized. It is less problematic to think of the present passage, and its predecessor, as proceeding by single-step contrasts in a way that resembles but does not exemplify the multi-step method of division.

27. Nor would it be hard to imagine borderline cases between the kind of disputation characteristic of *eikasia* in Book 1 and the investigation of cities characteristic of *pistis* in Books 2–4; disputation and investigation can easily shade into one another.

28. Smith classifies Book 4 as the beginning of genuine *dianoia* rather than the culmination of *pistis* (or a transition between them). He points to Plato's use of the word *eidos* or "form" at 435b and 445c (1999, 200), but we should not read too much into the simple appearance of the word *eidos*, since often it has nothing to do with the theory of forms. The word was already used in a colloquial way in Book 2, where clearly the theory of forms was not yet intended (e.g., 357c, 363e–364a, 369a), and is periodically used in a non-technical way throughout the dialogue. The word "form" often occurs before Book 5, but the theory of forms—intelligible reality—is not thematized until then. Further to this point see Adam 1902, 168, and Guthrie 1975, 459–60.

29. Cf. *Symposium* 211a. Thus Annas (1981) points out that in the *Symposium* "Diotima talks of all the ways that particular beautiful things can also be said to be the opposite of beautiful": they may be beautiful and ugly in different ways, at different times, in different relations, or in different contexts (205). For a different interpretation see Irwin 1995, who suggests that what Socrates is referring to is not the things themselves but their properties: a bright color looks beautiful in some contexts but not others (269–70). However, Socrates' words—"Is there one among the many beautifuls that does not seem ugly"—seem to refer to things rather than properties.

30. Michael Stokes suggests that even though as an inference step 2 is fallacious, it nevertheless would be acceptable to the sightlovers as a premise because they believe that whatever exists is material, visible, and/or audible, so one can know it ("Plato and the Sightlovers of the *Republic*", *Apeiron* 25 [1992]: 103–32, esp. 112–13).

31. The predicative interpretation has the most support among recent commentators. For example: N. White 1979, 160; Annas 1981, 195–99, 208 (although she acknowledges some difficulties: 211–12); Reeve 1988, 63–71; Nicholas Smith, "Plato on Knowledge as a Power", *Journal of the History of Philosophy* 38 (2000): 145–68, esp. 151–52. But the existential interpretation has had defenders in N. R. Murphy, *The Interpretation of Plato's Republic* (Oxford: Clarendon Press, 1951), 126–29; Guthrie 1975, 490–98; Stokes 1992, 129; and Francisco Gonzalez, "Propositions or Objects?: A Critique of Gail Fine on Knowledge and Belief in *Republic* V", *Phronesis* 41 (1996): 245–75, esp. 258–62. The veridical interpretation has been defended by Charles Kahn, "Some Philosophical Uses of 'to be' in Plato", *Phronesis* 26 (1981): 105–134, esp. 112–13; and more recently by Chase Wren, "Being and Knowledge: A Connoisseur's Guide to Republic V.476e ff", *Apeiron* 33 (2000): 87–108.

32. See Charles Kahn, "The Greek Verb 'to be' and the Concept of Being", *Foundations of Language* 2 (1966): 245–65, esp. 262.

33. Kahn, who argues that the present passage moves from a veridical sense to a predicative one, writes: "the shift from absolute (veridical) to predicative εἶναι need not be fallacious, since the veridical value of τὸ ὄν ("what is so") is an operator on an arbitrary sentence. A particular F participates both in being-so and not-being-so (with ὄν absolute) just because it both is and is not F, in other words, just because it is both true and false to say that it is F, whereas for a Form such a predication is true without qualification" (1981, 114).

34. Cf. *Symposium* 202a.

35. Stokes (1992) seems justified when he writes that the passage "has attracted perhaps more furious criticism than any other major argument in Plato" (117). Its most prominent defender has been Gail Fine, who reinterprets the argument, and especially step 7, in a way that avoids the appearance of begging the question ("Knowledge and Belief in *Republic* V", *Archiv fur Geschichte der Philosophie* 60 [1978], 121–39; and "Knowledge and Belief in *Republic* V-VII" in S. Everson, ed., *Epistemology* [Cambridge: Cambridge University Press, 1990], 85–115). Fine takes the referent of step 7's "different things" to be not different objects but different thought contents (1978, 129; the term "thing" does not appear in the Greek), which gives the argument a different cast and does not beg any questions. She believes this reading is superior also because the sightlovers would accept it as a premise, but not the other, in which case the usual reading saddles Plato not only with a *petitio* but also with inappropriate premises (1978, 125). However, since Socrates began by saying, "It would not at all be easy to tell someone else, but you I think will agree to this" (475e), the premises are directed to Glaucon as proxy for the sightlovers, and there is no suggestion that they themselves would find this argument convincing—if anything the opposite is suggested. Moreover, Fine's emendation makes the argument less obviously relevant to its context of the distinction between the intelligible and visible realms, and her attempts to resolve these difficulties are problematic; for a reply to Fine's interpretation, see Gonzalez 1996. Stokes also rejects Fine's interpretation (123) and offers a different kind of defense of the argument: from the sightlovers' point of view there is no real difference between what something is directed to and what it accomplishes: "sight, hearing and the other senses are capacities each distinguished from the others by both province [what they are directed to] and effect [what they accomplish]. Notoriously you cannot see sounds, smell colours, hear tastes, touch smells. . . . Of course their effects are different too: to see is not the same as to hear, and so on. Once we set Socrates' point in its original context of an argument against the sightlovers, it becomes clear". At the same time, Stokes acknowledges that although understood in this way the argument may be more reasonable by the standards of the sightlovers, it is still not satisfactory by our standards (120–21).

CHAPTER SIX

~

The Sun, Line, and Cave
(Books 6 and 7 to 519b)

The Paradox of Philosopher-Rulers (484a–485a)

The comparison at the end of Book 5 between lovers of wisdom and lovers of
sight led to the conclusion that philosophers alone have knowledge because
they apprehend what is always the same, while lovers of sight have only opinion because they apprehend only what is always changing. Which of the two,
Socrates now asks, should be the rulers? Glaucon does not know how to
answer, and Socrates proposes that it will be whichever group appears to be
capable of guarding the laws and conventions of the city. For guardians to be
able to keep watch over the city they must have clear sight, but those who are
really deprived of knowledge of the real being of each thing (τῷ ὄντι τοῦ
ὄντος ἑκάστου) are like the blind. Lacking a clear paradigm in their soul,
they cannot do what painters do and base their work on a model, contemplating what is most true in order to establish here the laws of the beautiful,
the just, and the good.[1] Which then would make better rulers, those who do
have such knowledge or those who are blind to it, assuming that the former
do not fall short of the blind in experience or any other part of virtue? "It
would be strange to choose the others *if these do not fall short of them in other
ways*" (484d; emphasis added), Glaucon replies, and we can see now why he
hesitated at first to answer Socrates' leading question about which should
rule: if it came down to a choice between practical experience on one hand,
and rational knowledge of the being of things, without practical experience,
on the other, it is not obvious which would be the more important asset to

rulers. As Aristotle says, "With regard to practical matters . . . those with experience are more successful than those who have rational knowledge without experience. The reason is that experience is a knowledge of individuals while *techne* [i.e., rational knowledge] is one of universals, and all practical matters and processes are concerned with individuals".[2]

Socrates concludes that they must now say how it is possible for the same people to have both rational knowledge and experience. The task does not appear at first to pose a serious problem since there seems to be no reason why we cannot simply take philosophers and give them experience. That is, in fact, what will be proposed in Book 7, but not before we are faced with a serious difficulty that threatens to undermine the possibility of the conjunction. According to the allegory of the cave, there are two kinds of blindness, each of which is the antithesis of the other, such that being able to see the forms renders us blind to individuals, and the ability to see individuals entails blindness to the forms (518a). In that case, the endeavor to create rulers by giving philosophers experience in the world of individuals may be inherently self-contradictory. Perhaps Glaucon was right to think that the choice between philosophers and non-philosophers as the city's guardians was by no means clear, and perhaps Socrates' audience was right to think that the concept of philosopher-rulers is absurd after all.

The Nature of the Philosopher (485a–487e)

Socrates begins by reminding Glaucon that the philosophical nature is the love (ἐρῶσιν) of learning, and eros always loves the whole of what it loves. It follows, then, that the philosopher will hate all falsity and love (στέργειν) the truth, for truth is most akin to wisdom, and the real lover of learning will strive for truth from childhood on. It is at this point that Socrates presents us with the image that we looked ahead to in chapter 4, that the erotic appetites are like a stream that can be diverted into different channels, so that if they incline more strongly to one thing their force is weakened toward others. In this way someone who loves the truth "will be concerned with the pleasures of the soul itself by itself, while those that come through the body it will abandon" (485e). However, this image intensifies rather than resolves the problem of combining the philosophers' love of intelligible forms with experience's requirement of attentiveness to individual things, for if the philosophers' erotic stream requires them to abandon concern with what is experienced through the body, then philosophy does indeed prevent the acquisition of experience. Although the philosophers are said to love the whole of learning, it now seems that this means only the whole of knowledge (learning directed toward being) and not also opinion (learning directed toward becoming). In Book 4 one of the requirements for those who are worthy to rule was that they love the city as they love themselves (412c–d), but now it seems that the philosophers' love is so entirely directed away from anything having to do with the corporeal realm that love for the city is inconceivable, and nothing can flow through that channel. Why does Socrates construct such a self-defeating argument?

Effective rulers must be concerned above all with what is good for the city, and that kind of altruism is possible only if the rulers are morally good (i.e., just) rather than unjust on the Thrasymachean model. If Socrates can show that moral goodness in the fullest sense is ultimately inseparable from the philosophical love of truth, he will have vindicated the proposition that the good city can come into being only if philosophers and rulers are one and the same. Although the argument seems to have begun unpromisingly, the next step will be to draw the connection between the love of truth and moral goodness (485e–487a). Whether it will be enough to dispel the present misgivings remains to be seen.

The nature of true philosophers whose erotic flow toward truth is not diverted by the body, Socrates says, will be self-controlled rather than greedy, for it does not attach importance to money or the things money can buy; nor will it be stingy, for such pettiness is incompatible with a soul that is always reaching for the whole and the totality of the divine and human. In fact, a mind that is characterized by high-mindedness and the contemplation of all time and all being will not even think human life is very important, and will therefore not fear death or be vulnerable to cowardice (although the question arises once again of how people who do not value human life could make good rulers). Since such people could never be unjust, we can select the appropriate natures by noticing whether they are just and gentle or unfriendly and savage. The passage is reminiscent of Socrates' argument in the *Phaedo* that not only are philosophers virtuous for these reasons, but *only* philosophers are virtuous: those who love the body rather than wisdom are virtuous only by resisting one fear or pleasure in favor of another—resisting the fear of death from a greater fear of being a coward, or resisting a pleasure in order to avoid pain—so that their courage is a kind of cowardice and their self-control is a kind of self-indulgence (68d–69a). The present argument does not make this further claim, that not only are lovers of truth moral but that they alone are truly moral; however, it was already implicit in the conclusions of Book 4. If the virtues all are variants of a soul that is governed by wisdom, then indeed we can be truly moral only to the extent that we are truly wise, thus only to the extent that we are successful lovers of learning and truth.

To character must be added talent: the nature appropriate to philosophy must learn easily, for no one can love an activity that gives them more trouble than rewards; and the nature appropriate to philosophy must have a good memory. Moreover—in a passage reminiscent of the children's education in beauty (401c–402a)—the philosophical soul cannot be unmusical or without grace, for then it would be unmeasured, and truth is akin to measure. They must seek a mind that is by nature measured and graceful, so that it can be easily guided to the idea of the being of each thing. The nature they are seeking, then, is one with a good memory, quick to learn, high-minded, graceful, a friend and kin to truth, just, courageous, and self-controlled (487a). The last three are three of the four virtues; the fourth, wisdom, is no longer merely good judgement (εὐβουλία: 428b), but now seems to correspond to having a good memory, being quick to learn, high-minded, graceful, and a friend and kin to truth. It is a matter of character as well as judgement.

"Not even Momus could find fault with this", Glaucon responds, and Socrates asks, "When such people are perfected by education and maturity wouldn't you turn the city over to them alone?" (487a). Before Glaucon can tell us whether or not the god of blame would find fault with that last conclusion, Adeimantus steps in and assumes the mantle of Momus:

> No one, Socrates, could contradict the things you say, but on each occasion that you say them your hearers are affected in some such way as this: they think that because of their inexperience in asking and answering questions they are led astray by the argument, a little at each of your questions, and when all their small concessions are added together at the end of the discussion, a great fallacy appears which contradicts what they said at first. Just as inexperienced checkers players are in the end trapped by the experts and can't make a move, so they too are trapped in the end and have nothing they can say in this different kind of checkers which is played not with counters but with words; yet they don't believe the conclusion to be in any way more true for that. [487b–c]

It may seem a relatively innocuous place for Adeimantus to break in, after he let the argument at 476e–479d go without protest, where Socrates' sleight of hand established that there is knowledge only of the unchanging forms, and only opinion of changing things. But, in fact, he has caught Socrates trying to make a crucial connection as if it were a mere afterthought.

We noted earlier that in order to establish the philosopher's claim to be the best ruler, Socrates would have to establish that philosophy is inseparable from moral goodness, and that the philosophers' moral goodness entails their worthiness to rule. The first of these claims he established by an argument, but the second he dropped in as if it followed self-evidently from the first. But we saw that not only does it not follow self-evidently from the first, it even seems to be antithetical to it, for the moral goodness of the philosophers is established on the grounds of their indifference to all things in the corporeal realm, in which case they could be argued to be the ones least, not most, to be trusted with the welfare of the city. The argument for the first premise resembled that of the *Phaedo*, and there it was used partly to establish that philosophy is the practicing of death (64a). Here too the philosophers are indifferent to life (486a–b) and will seek to withdraw from the land of the living (the political life of the city) to the Isles of the Blessed (519c), a metaphorical equivalent of the abode of the dead, unwilling to rule until they are compelled to do so. As we saw, when Socrates first proposed the philosopher-rulers, he conceded that they would have to be compelled to rule (473d4–5), a conclusion that was required by his absolute distinction between the intelligible world beloved of philosophers and the visible world where the city lies. How can someone whose heart is elsewhere be the best of rulers? Not until Book 7 will we be in a position to see whether Socrates is successful in overcoming this objection. At this point it is certainly not enough simply to ask, "Wouldn't you turn the city over to them alone?"

Adeimantus' objection does not take the form of pointing out the logical flaw in Socrates' argument—in fact, he concedes that Socrates has been able to outwit them logically—but rather of insisting that Socrates' conclusions, however he arrived at them, are absurd—not only the claim that philosophers' moral virtue qualifies them to rule, but even that philosophers possess such virtue at all. Socrates had anticipated that the proposal for philosophers to rule would call down upon him the greatest wave of opposition of all, so great was the contempt that the ordinary Athenian felt for philosophers. All readers of the *Republic* know what verdict the Athenians will pass on Socrates' virtue. However difficult it may be to see how to refute Socrates' argument, "in fact", Adeimantus says, "one sees that of those who take up philosophy . . . and pursue it at length, most of them become completely strange, not to say entirely vicious, while those who seem perfectly decent become useless to cities as a result of the pursuit that you recommend" (487c–d).

Socrates can respond to Adeimantus' criticism only by justifying the controversial assumptions that underlie his proposal that the city be ruled by philosophers. It is not controversial to say that philosophers are concerned with truth, nor to say that rulers ought to be concerned with the good of the city that they rule (it was Thrasymachus' denial of that principle that was controversial). What is controversial is the claim that there is an essential connection between philosophical truth and moral goodness, and that those who most clearly discern such truth are most competent to rule. The claimed connection between truth and goodness was controversial then and it remains controversial today, as we see from the common insistence on an absolute distinction between facts and values, or between the is and the ought, or from those who reject the possibility of truth but not that of goodness. In his attempt to soothe and persuade the objector, Socrates rejected the distinction between truth and goodness by saying that the love of truth draws our erotic stream from the visible to the intelligible, and leaves us without the attachments (to material things and to life itself) that corrupt our character. The devotee of truth is thus virtuous if only by default. A clever argument, Adeimantus is willing to concede, except that we know the conclusion is not true: philosophers are useless at best, and vicious at worst. It order to defend his hypothesis against the objection, Socrates must do more than soothe and persuade. He will have to justify it by establishing some higher principle by which to vindicate his hypothesis that a love of truth leaves no room for a love of personal gain. He will gradually have to leave *dianoia* for *noesis*.

The Notoriety of Philosophy (487e–497c)

The next stage begins still within the confines of *dianoia*, however. One of the characteristics of *dianoia* is that it represents the intelligible realm by means of images drawn from the visible realm (510b–e). Adeimantus asks how Socrates can maintain that cities will not be free from evils until philosophers rule, "who we agree are useless to them", and Socrates replies that his question will have to be answered by means of an image. The image must be an artificial one, because what the most decent people experience in relation to their city is so hard to bear that there is no other single experience that compares with it (488a). Socrates will have to construct the image from a number of things the way painters do when they paint goat-stags and similar things. He paints the image of a ship whose owner is bigger and stronger than anyone else aboard, but with poor eyesight and hearing, and little knowledge of navigation. All the sailors want to be captain but they too have no knowledge of navigation and insist that in any case it is not teachable, and they are not only ready to kill anyone who disagrees, but they kill anyone else who persuades the owner to turn the operation of the ship over to them. They drug the noble ship owner, take over the ship, and consume its stores. They call "navigator" or "captain" whoever is best at persuading or forcing the owner to turn the ship over to him, and regard anyone else as useless. Since they have no conception of the importance of the seasons, the sky, the winds, and the rest of what belongs to navigation, they consider the true captain to be a stargazer, a babbler, and useless (487e–488e).

Adeimantus agrees that the image does not need to be explained. It is, in fact, an elaboration of remarks that Socrates had made in Book 4 about badly governed cities (426b–d), before philosophy came onto the scene. The one point worth calling attention to is that the ship owner, an image of the populace of the city, not only has weak sight and hearing, and an absence of knowledge, but is also called noble (488c). Whatever contempt Socrates may have for the politicians of his day, and despite his derogatory references to "the many", there is respect for the populace as well.

In the allegory, the true captain appears only indirectly, in the contempt in which he is held by the self-styled captains. He himself never competes with them for control over the ship, for it is not natural for a captain to beg sailors to let him pilot the ship, nor for the wise to petition the rich (489b). Rather those who are in need should seek out the one who has the skill with which to help them, as the sick seek out doctors. Socrates rejects the claim, attributed to Simonides, that it is better to be rich than wise because the wise go to the doors of the rich;[3] on the contrary, people in need go to the doors of those with the knowledge to help them. If the wise are truly self-reliant, they will not seek to impose themselves on others.[4] That does not mean that the wise hold back out of self-importance, wanting to be courted for their help; the allegory makes clear that the politically ambitious do not scruple to have their rivals for power (including the wise) put to death—a danger that would hardly seem hyperbolic to Plato's readers. It is a double point: the wise are perfectly satisfied with the rewards of wisdom and do not need to knock on anyone's door or seek the rewards of office (which in their case consists of not having to be ruled by their inferiors: 347a–c); but even to the extent that they would like to put their wisdom into practice for the sake of the city, they recognize that any attempt to take the initiative themselves would make a wise person seem to be no more than another seeker of power.

A crucial factor is left out of the allegory's equation, however. The allegory shows that it is possible for someone to have useful knowledge and yet not be perceived to have it, but it does not address the problem that emerged earlier: how can the kind of knowledge that philosophers attain be useful for ruling if it makes them care only about the unchanging ground of the world, and not about the living world itself (486a–b)? To make the allegory more completely resemble the things he will say about philosophy, Socrates might have added that the true captain, when he looks to the stars for guidance, becomes so fascinated by the order that they display that he regards the ship and all that concerns it to be of little importance; for that is precisely what will happen with the education of the philosophers in Book 7. They will begin by studying the mathematical sciences for their usefulness (522c–e), and end by using them "to rise out of becoming and grasp being" (525b). By the time they reach astronomy the preponderance of the emphasis has swung so far away from practical utility to theoretical contemplation that Socrates will ridicule Glaucon for trying to justify the study of astronomy by any appeal to its practical utility (527d). But in the present allegory the true captain does not become enthralled by the stars and indifferent to transient things, so the issue is never dealt with. The allegory only partly justifies the claim that people are wrong to see philosophers as useless. It may be, as with the true captain, that people misunderstand philosophers because they are incapable of understanding them, but it is still not clear how, by studying the realm of being, philosophers are able to govern well in the realm of becoming.

The allegory showed how it is possible for people to be perceived to be useless when they are not, and that goes some way to defend the best philosophers against the accusation of uselessness, but it still leaves Adeimantus' other complaint unaddressed—that not only are the best philosophers thought to be useless, the rest of them are vicious. Socrates turns now to showing why that viciousness is not the fault of philosophy; but the first part of his defense only reinforces the difficulty that we observed in the previous paragraph:

> It is the nature of the real lover of learning to strive for what is, and not to remain with the many individual things that are believed to be, but to go forward and not be blunted or decline in his eros until he touches upon the being and nature of each thing with that part of his soul which is fit to touch upon it because it is akin to it. Being near to and having intercourse with true being he would give birth to reason and truth, would know, truly live and be nourished, and cease from travail, but not before. [490a–b]

As a defense against the claim that philosophy can make us bad, Socrates urges even more eloquently than he did with his image of eros as flowing through competing channels, that the philosophers' love of truth and being makes them indifferent to the realm of becoming: those who are indifferent to the things of this world have no motive to be vicious (490b–c). But here again we are left with the corollary, not addressed until Book 7, that they also have no motive to govern cities conscientiously, if at all.

The bad behavior of many of its students is not the fault of philosophy itself, but of additional factors by which their natures are corrupted. The surprising thing, says Socrates—in a passage which echoes his doctrine that no one pursues what is bad, and which prefigures the medieval doctrine that evil is nothing but the preference of a lesser good to a greater—is that these corrupting factors are either things which are good in themselves, or things which are at least thought to be good. The first group, which are good in themselves, are the virtues: "courage, self-control, and all the ones that we went through" (491b). The second group, comprising only so-called goods (λεγόμενα ἀγαθά), include beauty, wealth, bodily health, and powerful relatives. That we can be corrupted by things which only seem to be good is not surprising, but how can we be corrupted by actual goods?

"With every natural thing, the more vigorous it is the more it will fall short of its optimal state if it does not have its proper food, season, and location" (491d). The statement is puzzling, for we might suppose that to be more vigorous (ἐρρωμενέστερον) means to be more capable of coping with adversity—that survival belongs to the fittest. Socrates defends it by saying, "the bad is presumably more opposed to the good than to the not-good . . . so the best nature unsuitably nourished will fare worse than a paltry one" (491d). The premise implies only that if both the best things and lesser things end up in the same bad condition, the best will have fallen further than the others relative to their potential. But Socrates takes it to prove that in adversity the most vigorous things will become worse than ordinary things not only relative to their potential, but in their capacity for evil: "then should we not similarly say with regard to souls, too, that those best endowed by nature, if they receive a bad upbringing, become exceptionally bad?" (491e). The fallacious inference depends on equivocal senses of "bad", which in the premise means to *fare* worse than lesser natures (κάκιον ἀπαλλάττειν: 491d8), but in the conclusion means to *become* worse (διαφερόντως κακὰς γίγνεσθαι: e3).

It is not clear why Socrates derived this conclusion invalidly from the premise that badness is more opposed to good than to mediocrity (not-good), when he is about to derive it validly from a different premise, namely that the exceptional nature that is necessary for achieving the greatest good is also capable of achieving exceptional evil. He introduces it in the very next line almost as an afterthought: "Or do you think that great injustices and unadulterated evils originate in a paltry nature rather than a vigorous (νεανικῆς) one corrupted by its upbringing, or that a weak nature will ever be the cause of anything great, whether for good or evil?" (491e, cf. 518e–519a). From this premise, though not from the earlier one, it follows that the very qualities that enable the philosophical nature to excel—its forcefulness and erotic drive—enable it to be as formidable in its pursuit of the so-called goods as the true goods: just as the philosophers have here been characterized in terms of their eros, so will the tyrant in Book 9 (572e–573c). Moreover, we will see that such natures are targets of the most determined attempts at corruption (494b). How then are they corrupted?

Those who blame the moral corruption of the youth on the educational practices of the sophists must be the greatest sophists of all, Socrates says, for they themselves exercise the greatest influence on people's beliefs, young and old alike. In assemblies, courtrooms, theatres, army camps, and other public gatherings, they loudly and excessively object to the things they disagree with and approve those that they agree with, which has the effect of sweeping the convictions of young people along with the torrent. If that does not work, they employ an even stronger kind of compulsion, chastisement in the form of deprivation of civil rights, fines, or death. Such an education never has and never can produce any kind of character or virtue that goes against it. If such a character or virtue comes about it at all, it can only be due to divine dispensation (492a–493a). A few pages later Socrates will remind us that he himself has been the beneficiary of such dispensation in the form of his "divine sign" (496c).

The actual sophists (as distinct from this multitude who are the "greatest sophists") are so far from being responsible for the values that corrupt the youth that they teach nothing but the views of the multitude. Since their goal is to manipulate the multitude, they study its moods and acquire the ability to handle it the way one might learn to handle a large and strong beast, and this knack they call wisdom and believe to be a *techne* that they can teach.[5] They do not know which of the beast's opinions and desires is noble or ignoble, good or bad, just or unjust. They simply call whatever pleases the beast good, whatever displeases it bad, and whatever is necessary they call just and good, having no conception of how different the good is from the necessary (493a–c). The distinction between the good and the necessary corresponds to Glaucon's distinction at the beginning of Book 2 between what we value for its own sake and what we value for its consequences (357b–c). In this case the sought-after consequence is the approval of the multitude (493d).

There are striking differences between this simile of the beast and the earlier one of the ship owner. When the citizens were represented as the ship owner they were seen as noble (488c), whereas here there is no suggestion of nobility but only of size and power, and no suggestion that their desires are noble rather than ignoble. Moreover, in the earlier simile the sailors dominated the weak-eyed, hard-of-hearing owner, who seemed to be an all-but-defenseless victim of their predations, while here sophists are subservient to the moods and opinions of the large and powerful beast. The difference in emphasis results from the different purposes of the two similes. The first was designed to show why philosophers appear to be useless, so it emphasizes the ways that the politically ambitious (including but not only the sophists) disparage the qualifications of their rivals (including philosophers). Where the philosophers' reputation for *uselessness* is concerned, it is not the citizens themselves but the aspirants to power who are to blame, who want to minimize the importance of their own lack of knowledge of what is essential to the flourishing of the city, by denigrating the importance of that knowledge among philosophers. But where the philosophers' reputation for *immorality* is concerned, the culprit is not primarily the sophists and other politicians, who are not the authors of the conception of morality by which the philosophers are unfavorably judged; the author is the citizenry themselves, and there is nothing noble about their intimidation of everyone who might disagree with them.

The very virtues of the philosophical nature make it vulnerable to being corrupted. The ease of learning, good memory, courage, and high-mindedness that characterize it are likely to set such children apart from the others, and people will seek to influence and ingratiate themselves with them in anticipation of their future power (494a–c). In a passage generally taken as a reference to Alcibiades, Socrates remarks that if someone like that comes from a great city, and has beauty, birth, and wealth as well, his successes and the attendant flattery are liable to fill him with vain and empty confidence, and those who seek to use him for their own ends will do anything possible to keep him from self-knowledge and philosophy. And so, as Socrates and Adeimantus said before, it is, in a way, precisely the good qualities of the philosophical nature, and the so-called goods like wealth, that contribute to its falling away from philosophy. Moreover, when philosophy is thus abandoned by its rightful consorts, it appears to less gifted natures as an unclaimed prize of greater repute than their own craft, and they give themselves the pretence of being philosophers. They are like men who are able to marry above themselves because the bride is poor and abandoned; but where the true philosopher, "having intercourse with true being would give birth to reason and truth" (490b), this other marriage will produce children who are illegitimate and undistinguished. In other words, these pretenders to philosophy produce sophisms rather than true wisdom (494a–496a). It is for such reasons that philosophy comes to be regarded with suspicion and hostility, without deserving such repute on the basis of its own nature.

Once we eliminate the philosophically gifted natures that have been corrupted, and those who are philosophers in name alone, only a small group remains who are genuine philosophers. Socrates said earlier that the philosophically gifted nature can be saved from corruption only by divine dispensation (493a), and presumably the species of this small genus are amplifications of that phrase. There are five types of people who are worthy consorts of philosophy both in nature and attainment, and in each case an insulating factor protects them from the conditions that corrupted the likes of Alcibiades. These insulating factors can only be what Socrates meant by divine dispensation:

[1] Maybe someone of noble and well brought up character who is held down by exile,[6] in the absence of corrupting influences remains with philosophy in accordance with his nature. Or [2] when in a small city a great soul is born and has contempt for the city's affairs and looks down on them. And [3] maybe a few who have good natures might come to it from other crafts for which they justly have contempt. And [4] the bridle that holds back our friend Theages may act as a restraint; for in the case of Theages all the other preconditions were present for dropping out of philosophy, but his sickly physical constitution restrains him from taking part in politics. [5] My own case is not worth mentioning, the divine sign, for it must have happened to only a few or none before me. [496a–c]

In the first case the solitude of exile removes people from corrupting influences, in the second the provinciality of the city, in the third humility of station, in the fourth feebleness of the body, and in the fifth curtailment by the warning voice. The list goes from being rejected by the bad, at the beginning, to being chosen by the source of goodness, at the end, and passes through a descending order of limiting factors: city, livelihood, body. Four of the five cases, then, are negative, and would hardly seem like divine dispensation to those who struggle with exile, provincialism, unrewarding work, and a sickly constitution; divine dispensation is not always easy to recognize. These examples illustrate something that Socrates says later, in a passage that is the counterpart of his present claim that the very things that are good about the philosophical nature may lead to its downfall: "if a just man falls into poverty or disease or any other of the apparent evils, for him these things will eventually be something good" (613a).

In all these cases philosophy is possible only because the person in question has been kept apart from the political life of the city—this is true even of Socrates and his divine sign, which kept him out of Athenian politics (*Apology* 31c–d). The life of the philosopher would be better still, Socrates says, if it could be at one with its city rather than living within the city like an outsider; and so we return to the persistent question of how philosophy and political life can be brought together (497a–c).

Transition to *Noesis* (497c–505a)

The two previous defenses of philosophy in Book 6 conformed to the later description of *dianoia*: they made use of visible images (the ship, the beast) to enable us to think about the intelligible; and they did not attempt to justify philosophy as a consequence of something higher, but only showed that the consequences of the claim that had previously been made about philosophers (that only they would make satisfactory rulers) were not refuted by Adeimantus' objection that the public perceives philosophy as useless or insidious. This kind of argument is no longer adequate, however. According to Adeimantus, the rest of the audience was as little persuaded by this defense of philosophy as he was: "I think most of your audience will oppose you even more eagerly and will not at all be convinced, beginning with Thrasymachus" (498c). Socrates replies that he will spare no effort to persuade them, or at least to make them more receptive when they are reborn into another life. This is the dialogue's first reference to reincarnation, anticipating the doctrine of the myth of Er—that only a life lived according to rationality and philosophy is lived in accordance with the divine (618b–619b).

The reason that people have not been convinced of the virtue of philosophy, Socrates says, is that they have never seen true philosophers as rulers, those who increasingly immersed themselves in philosophy over the course of their lives rather than giving it up just when it becomes challenging (497e–498c)—it is the latter, who become argumentative and abusive, that give philosophy a bad name (500b). Socrates cannot remedy his audience's lack of experience of true philosophers, but perhaps he can remedy another deficiency: "Nor have they sufficiently listened, blessed one, to discourses that are beautiful and free, which strain in every way to seek the truth for the sake of knowledge" (498d–499a).

The discourse up to now did not yet strain in every way to seek the truth. It only attempted to mollify criticism and made no attempt to show philosophy's origins in the divine. Accordingly, Socrates will now call what follows a demonstration (ἀπόδειξιν: 497d), whereas he called the earlier attempts only a defense (ἀπολογησόμεθα: 490a), and rather than straining in every way to seek the truth, they were content to be merely adequate, metriōs (490a).[7] That was how Socrates introduced his remarks at 490a–b (quoted above), and Adeimantus agreed then that the defense was metriōtata, as adequate as possible. The significance of both speakers' use of metriōs in the earlier passage emerges now, when Socrates is no longer satisfied with the previous level of argumentation: Adeimantus says that the investigation of Books 2–4 was adequate, metriōs, to him, and Socrates replies:

> But, my friend, a measure (metron) of such things that falls short to any extent of what is, is not at all a measure (metriōs); for nothing incomplete is a measure (metron). However, it seems to some people that they have already done enough and there is no need to search further. [504c]

In other words, the things that we call metriōs or adequate in the colloquial sense are not really adequate, because we should not rest satisfied with anything less than what is completely good. Their previous defenses of true philosophers—the ship and beast analogies—against the notoriety attached to them from the behavior of false pretenders were called *metriōs* in the colloquial sense of "adequate", because they were incomplete. They did not yet demonstrate that these seekers of truth are not only plausible but indispensable rulers of the city.

Prior to Book 6, philosophy was not justified in terms of what is highest. Although it was connected with what is unchanging rather than what is changing, there was no mention of the divine in relation to philosophy. The connection between philosophy and the divine was first made at 486a, when Socrates described the philosophical soul as "always reaching for the whole and the totality of the divine and human", and the connection was reinforced at least verbally by Socrates' claim that philosophy cannot survive except by a divine dispensation (492a, 493a, 496c), but there was no indication yet that philosophy itself derives from the divine, or that philosophers are in some sense divine. Now, in response to the question of how philosophers can be other than strangers in their city, Socrates says that although none of the present political constitutions are worthy of the philosophical nature, if that nature "finds the best constitution, as it too is the best, then it will be clear that this was in reality divine while the others were human, both in their natures and practices" (497b–c). Not only the constitution but also the corresponding philosophical nature is divine. After explaining why so few aspirants become true philosophers, Socrates finally turns to the demonstration of the need for, and not just the possibility of, the philosophical regime. Now something new is added to his previous characterization of philosophers. The philosopher

> looks upon and contemplates what are organized and eternally the same, which neither commit injustice nor are treated unjustly by one another, but which all are orderly in accordance with rationality, and he imitates them and assimilates himself to them as far as possible. . . . Associating with the divine and orderly, the philosopher becomes orderly and divine as far as is possible for a human being. . . . Do you think he would be a poor crafter of moderation, justice, and all of popular virtue? [500c–d]

In his earlier defense Socrates spoke of philosophers only in terms of reason and truth, which would not convince the objector in whose experience all too many seekers after truth are scoundrels, while the rest are useless. Nothing in the former characterization of the philosopher as a seeker after truth (490a–b) refuted those concerns by connecting truth with goodness, but in the new characterization the realm of truth and reason that philosophy is concerned with is not only of intellectual interest but of moral, political, and spiritual value. It promotes a thinking and being that is free from injustice and disorder, and that promotes virtue and godliness in others. It became evident in chapter 4 (124–28) that wisdom is inseparable from virtue as a whole, so only a virtuous person can possess wisdom—only in such a person is rationality liberated from the distorting influence of appetite and spiritedness. The relation between the two is reciprocal: we saw then that only a morally virtuous person can be wise, and see now that wisdom in turn conduces to virtue. When Socrates later distinguishes between *dianoia* and *noesis*, *dianoia* follows the implications of hypotheses about intelligible reality that make no necessary reference to value—to virtue or the good. *Noesis*, on the other hand, rises above those hypotheses and demonstrates them by derivation from something higher, ultimately the good itself. The present passage illustrates how the proposal of a philosopher-ruler can be demonstrated to an objector by showing how it alone follows from the demands of goodness and divinity: "This regime is divine and the others are human" (497c).

Until now Socrates' defense did not meet with success, as we saw from Adeimantus' prediction that "most of your audience will oppose you even more eagerly and will not at all be convinced" (498c). Now, however, that Socrates has presented philosophy as an emulation not merely of truth but of goodness, when he asks whether, "if the multitude perceive that what we are saying about the philosopher is true, they will still be harsh with philosophers and unconvinced by what we say?" Adeimantus replies, "They will not be harsh if indeed they perceive that" (500e).

Socrates proceeds to elaborate how, if these philosophers were rulers, they would seek to extend the fruits of their contemplation and emulation to the rest of the city:

> As they work they would frequently look both ways, both toward the just, the beautiful, the wise, and all such things in nature, and again to that which they are producing in human beings . . . until they had made the characters of human beings as dear to god as they are capable of being. [501b–c]

When he asks again, "Will they still be angry with us when we say that until the philosophical class take control of a city there will be no rest from evils for the city or its citizens?" Adeimantus replies only, "Perhaps less so"—although at Socrates' behest he is willing to say that they will be completely convinced "in order to make them agree out of shame if for no other reason" (501e–502a). Socrates is under no illusions about what can be demonstrated to the multitude. At this point he seems to feel that he has demonstrated his claims to the objector, if not to the objector's satisfaction, at least to his own satisfaction, and that he is entitled to say that anyone who still does not agree is intellectually at fault.

Socrates now turns to the problem that has been shadowing the proceedings since his original announcement of the need for the hybrid of philosopher and ruler: how it is possible for such natures to exist, which combine the antithetical drives toward contemplating the intelligible and governing the visible? He begins with a negative argument (502a–b):

1. It is not impossible for philosophical natures to be born to kings and rulers.

2. It is not impossible that at least one of them could escape becoming corrupted.

3. One such person could bring the city into being if people obey him.

4. It is not impossible that people would agree to the laws and practices that have been described.

5. It is not impossible for others to arrive at the same beliefs that Socrates and the brothers have.

The negative form of the argument merely puts the burden of proof on the objector to show that their conclusions are impossible. The next step is to give their proposals positive content by describing the character of the rulers so as to show not only that they do not seem to be impossible, and should therefore be regarded as possible, but also how they are possible. Here for the first time the seemingly contradictory nature of the philosopher-ruler is explicitly addressed, although only in a preliminary way.

The requisite nature will be rare not only because of the tension we noted between the direction of contemplation and the direction of ruling, but also because it comprises two nearly antithetical characteristics. When they were discussing the character necessary for the first guardians, the warriors, Socrates said that without spiritedness the guardians would be unable to prevent others from destroying the city, while without gentleness they would destroy it themselves, but that spiritedness and gentleness are opposites (375a–c). Now that the guardians are philosophers, the requirements have changed, but not the need to combine opposite qualities. One of those qualities is the cluster that Socrates pointed to at 485e–487a, such as ease of learning, memory, readiness of mind, quickness, youthful contention, and high-mindedness. However, these traits, he says,

> do not want to grow together with the desire for a life that is orderly, quiet, and completely stable. But such people are carried by their quickness wherever chance takes them, and all stability leaves them.
>
> What you say is true.
>
> And again, those who have stable characters and don't change easily, whom one would employ with greater confidence, who in war are not easily moved in

the face of fear, are the same way in the face of learning. They are not easy to move, and learn with difficulty as if they were numb, and are filled with sleep and yawning when they have to work through anything of the kind. [503c–d]

Although the coexistence of such attributes would be rare, Socrates never doubts that it is possible, presumably because he has known examples of it.[8]

After reviewing the efforts that will be made to identify such natures among the city's children, Socrates reminds Adeimantus of his earlier warning (435c–d) that the discussion in Book 4 was not at an adequate level, and reiterates that it is necessary for them to take a longer road (504b). But just as Glaucon had said at the time that the previous approach was good enough for him, Adeimantus now says that he considered it to be adequate too, and Socrates replies with the speech that was quoted above to the effect that what is merely adequate (*metriōs*) is not truly adequate, for we should not stop short of the best that can be accomplished (504c), i.e., we should not stop short of an account of the nature of the good, the unhypothetical principle at the apex of *noesis* (509a, 511b).[9] Unless we take the longer road, Socrates says, we will never reach the goal of the study that is most important and most appropriate. Adeimantus does not understand how anything can be more important than the study of the virtues, but Socrates assures him that not only is there a more important study, but that without it their previous account of the virtues remains a mere sketch.

This greatest study, as Socrates insists that Adeimantus must already know, is of the Idea of the good.[10] The "defense" (490a–b) was still at the level of *dianoia*, since it was only adequate, *metriōs*, but the "demonstration" (497d–501c) transcends such limitations (504c), and now introduces a study that goes even beyond the form of justice and the other forms, the study of the Idea of the good (504d–505a). In the progress of the investigation philosophy is first seen in terms of its relation to being, then in terms of its relation to the kind of being that is divine and productive of human excellence, and finally to what lies beyond being altogether (509b) and is the source of all that is valuable (505a–b) and divine—that is the upward movement of *noesis*.

The Image of the Sun (505a–509c)

The reason that the Idea of the good is an even more important study than that of the virtues is that the virtues are useful and beneficial only in relation to it:

You have often heard that the Idea of the good is the greatest study, and it's by the use they make use of it that what is just, and the others (τἆλλα), become useful and beneficial. Now, you pretty well knew that I would say that, and further that we do not know it adequately. But if we do not know it, then without this, even if we knew the others (τἆλλα) as thoroughly as possible, you know that that knowledge would not benefit us. Just as if we possessed anything (κεκτήμεθά τι) without the good—or do you think there is anything gained by owning every possession (κτῆσιν), without, however, what is good? Or to know all the others (πάντα τἆλλα) without the good, and not to know what is beautiful or good? [505a–b]

When Socrates speaks of the "the others" at 505a6, and "all the others" at b2, the references go back to "the others" at a3 (i.e., the other virtues). In that case he is not saying that *no* knowledge is any good to us unless we study the Idea of the good (as it is interpreted when τἆλλα is translated as "other things", and πάντα τἆλλα as "all other things"), but only that knowledge of the *virtues* is of no ultimate benefit to us without it. It is a restatement of what he has already said in Book 4—that discussion of the virtues in isolation from the intelligible realm is necessarily inadequate.

But what does he mean by saying that nothing is gained by owning every possession "without what is good"? If this meant only that if there is nothing good about our possessions we will get no benefit from them, it would merely be a tautology. Socrates must mean that nothing is gained by owning every possession without *knowledge* of what is good, which also makes it more relevant to the context. It is a long standing Socratic principle that our actions always aim at the good and no one deliberately does evil.[11] If we are to get the use and benefit of anything whatever, then, our aim must be correct, and the more we understand what goodness really is, the more the anticipated benefit will really follow from our course of action. If we aim at the good but we are mistaken about what is good, then the good that we hoped to achieve may escape us, and we will indeed lose the potential benefit of anything we have, whether conventional virtues or possessions. If we are courageous in a misguided cause, the goodness that courage has the power to achieve will elude us—which was why wisdom was built into the definition of true courage in Book 4. Money, too, has the power to achieve good, but only if the supposed good that it is used for is genuinely good. Book 9 will show how an uninformed pursuit of the good can result in its exact opposite.[12]

Having just said that we do not know the good adequately, Socrates must address the claims of those who believe that they do know it. In a passage that anticipates the *Philebus* and Book 10 of Aristotle's *Nicomachean Ethics*, Socrates distinguishes between the multitude who believe that the good is pleasure and the more sophisticated who believe it is knowledge.[13] The latter, however, cannot explain what kind of knowledge they mean, and are reduced to saying that it is knowledge of the good, which leaves the original question

- the good   vs   the other   virtues.
- knowledge of the virtues vs K of the good.
    no ultimate benefit without K of G.

unanswered; while those who say the good is pleasure are forced to admit that
there are bad pleasures, and thus to concede that the same thing can be both
good and bad (505b–c). Socrates does not give any examples here of bad
pleasures, but will provide numerous examples in Book 9's discussion of the
nature of the tyrant (573c–580a). In the *Gorgias* he gave the examples of
scratching of an itch for a lifetime (cf. *Philebus* 46a), or enjoying being
sodomized (i.e., being a catamite) (494c–e).

When Socrates spoke of the importance of knowing the good he treated
the terms "good" and "beautiful" synonymously (505b3), but now he argues
that the beautiful is no more equivalent to the good than the virtues were.
Many people choose things that appear to be just or beautiful even if they are
not really so, but no one is satisfied with what only appears to be good, and
they seek the things that are really so (505d). People might, for example,
approve of a contract even if they discovered that it only seemed to be just, if
it was advantageous to them or if it remedied past injustices. Or they might
like something that may seem beautiful but which they knew was really only
gaudy, if they liked gaudy things. In both cases people are satisfied with
merely apparent justice or beauty if it is thought to be really good in some
way. But the good itself is different: if we get something that appears to us to
be good, but which turns out not really to be good, we will suffer as a result.

> The good, then, is what every soul pursues, and does everything for its sake.
> The soul divines that it exists, but is at a loss about it and unable to grasp ade-
> quately whatever it is, or to employ the kind of firm convictions that it has
> about the other things. It thus loses even the benefit that the others may have.
> [505d–e]

– good is K.

Until we pass through all the stages of the Divided Line and are able to perceive the Idea of the good in itself, we can have no true knowledge of it; but
in a metaphor that echoes the doctrine of recollection, we can nevertheless
divine (ἀπομαντευομένη) *that* it is, even though we are at an impasse as to
what it is.[14] There is thus a sense in which we have a precognitive awareness
of the good without which we would not know how to recognize and benefit
from what is good in anything else.

– precognitive awareness of the good

No one could be a worthy guardian, then, who does not understand in
what way just and beautiful things are good, Socrates says. "I divine that no
one will know them adequately until then". "You divine well (καλῶς)",
replies Adeimantus (506a). In spite of Socrates' explanation why the good
cannot be identified either with knowledge or pleasure (or virtue or beauty),
Adeimantus now asks him whether he thinks the good is knowledge, pleasure, or something else. Socrates points out that Adeimantus has made it

abundantly (καλῶς) clear that he won't accept other people's opinions (δοκοῦν) on these matters, but Adeimantus objects that it does not seem just (δίκαιον) of Socrates to discuss the opinions (δόγματα) of others without being willing to express his own. Socrates asks whether it would appear (δοκεῖ) to him to be just (δίκαιον) for Socrates to speak as if he knew what he does not know, and Adeimantus points out that he can at least say that he believes what he believes (οἰόμενον . . . οἴεται). Opinions (δόξας) without knowledge are ugly (αἰσχραί), Socrates replies, and the most beautiful (βέλτισται) of them are blind. Does it appear (δοκοῦσι) to Adeimantus that those who have true opinion (ἀληθές . . . δοξάζοντες) without reason are any different than blind people who take the right road,[15] and does Adeimantus want to contemplate what is ugly (αἰσχρά), blind, and crooked, when from others he can hear what is luminous and beautiful (καλά) (506a–d)? It is surprising that immediately after having Socrates assure Adeimantus that what appears to be (or "opinions about") the just or beautiful is not a sure guide to what is good, Plato repeatedly uses the terms "appear/opinion" (δοκοῦν, etc.), "just" (δίκαιον), and "beautiful/ugly" (καλά, αἰσχρά, etc.) to determine what is correct or incorrect. The verbal incongruity may be meant to flag a more serious incongruity that accompanies it.

In Book 5 Socrates made use of a questionable argument to draw a rigid distinction between knowledge, which can only be of unchanging forms, and opinion, which can only be of changing things. But now, instead of saying that it is impossible for him to have an opinion of the Idea of the good, because it is an unchanging form and therefore accessible only to knowledge, he only says that he is reluctant to express his opinion about the Idea of the good (508e2–3) because opinions are such poor substitutes for knowledge. It seems that one can have opinions of unchanging forms after all,[16] and the ostinato repetition of terms for opinion eight times in this brief passage makes it unlikely that we will fail to notice. Just as here Socrates implicitly rescinds his denial that there can be opinions about the forms, in the next book he will rescind the denial that there can be knowledge of the sensible world (520c). Moreover, a page after collapsing the absolute epistemological distinction of Book 5, between knowledge and opinion, Socrates will collapse its ontological counterpart, the rigid distinction between being and becoming. In Book 5 he said that only unchanging forms *are*, while changing things are between what is and what is not. Here when he speaks of the forms he says unproblematically that we posit (τιθέντες) a single Idea for each multiplicity that we posited (ἐτίθεμεν) (507b5–7), but in the preceding speech, instead of saying only that we posit individual things, he put it more strongly: "We claim there to be (εἶναι) many beautiful things, and many good ones, and all such things" (507b2–3).[17] Coming so soon after the misdirected use of "opinion" this misdirected use of "being" cannot be easily dismissed.

In response to Socrates' reluctance to declare his mere opinion, Glaucon enters the conversation to assure him that he would be satisfied if Socrates discussed the good in the same way that he earlier discussed the virtues (506d)—as little deterred now by Socrates' dismissal of that approach as inadequate as he was then. It now seems that just as that earlier discussion of virtue was instructive but not adequate, in the same way Socrates' absolute distinction in Book 5 between opinion as only applicable to things, and knowledge as only applicable to forms, is useful but not definitive. Both are simplified models that help us proceed with the inquiry, but that are eventually meant to be superseded. The tripartite model of the virtues was useful at the level of *pistis* but not at the level of *dianoia*, because it interpreted the virtues in terms of the moving soul rather than in terms of intelligible forms; and now the two-world theory of Book 5, as well, seems to have been only provisionally adequate. Since *dianoia* uses the visible world as a model by which to understand the intelligible world, the rigid bifurcation of the two is one of its hypotheses, but when we rise above its hypotheses to the unhypothetical principle contemplated by *noesis*, we may also need to rise above the rigidity of the previous distinction.[18]

As we have seen, the soul itself is an exception to the rigid two-world bifurcation since it belongs neither to the world of becoming nor that of being, but mediates between them. It does not belong to the world of becoming because it cannot be perceived by the senses (*Phaedo*, 79a–b), and because something in it is akin to the divine (*Republic*, 490a–b), nor to the world of being because it is inseparable from motion. Just as within the soul itself the rigid distinctions between the three parts are dissolved by the fact that there may be any number of intermediate elements (443d), so too the rigid and exclusionary distinction between being and becoming is dissolved by the existence of a transitional nature that mediates between them, and indeed one that may be subdivided into innumerable degrees between its corporeal (appetite) and intelligible (rationality) poles. Thus in the myth of Er, depending on which elements of the soul are most strongly expressed, the same soul may range, in its incarnations, from the corporeal life-forms of the lowest beasts (620a–d) to the philosopher's nearly divine life of the mean (618b–619b). The soul is a kind of continuum that binds the corporeal realm to the intelligible.

The entire discussion since the third wave has been shadowed by the problem of how a discipline that turns us toward the intelligible realm can help us become rulers, if the realms of being and becoming, knowledge and opinion, have no common basis. The softening of the boundary between them that is implied here and at 520c is the first indication that Socrates may have in mind a solution to that problem when the time comes—or, to put it differently, that what appears to be a contradiction at the level of *dianoia* may resolve itself at the level of *noesis*.

Socrates' disclaimer of knowledge of the good has an ironic aspect since he is able to give illustrations of its nature, but his later claim that such knowledge cannot adequately be put into words (533a) seems to be in earnest.[19] It is not surprising then that even here at the highest level of the discussion Socrates must resort to the *dianoetic* technique of using visible images to conceive the intelligible, whereas pure *noesis* would be beyond all imaging (511b–c). In place of an account of the good, Socrates offers to speak of the offspring of the good (i.e., the sun as a visible image of the good). In that way, even though he will not be able to discharge his debt, he will be able to pay the interest on it (506e–507a).[20] After warning Glaucon to be on guard lest Socrates unintentionally pay him false interest, he reminds him of the distinction between forms and things (in the passage cited earlier where he predicates "being" of individual things). The things are visible but not intelligible, while the Ideas are intelligible but not visible (507b–c).

With regard to visibility three things are necessary: vision (the sense of sight), something visible, and light which yokes together the first two so that what is in principle visible can, in fact, be seen;[21] the source of light is a god, the sun, and is the offspring of the good that Socrates referred to earlier. Sight is the most sunlike of the senses because it is the only one that is inseparable from light; it receives its power from the sun and so the sun is both the cause of sight and is seen by sight (508b). The good engendered the sun as an analogue of itself: what the good is in the intelligible (νοητῷ) realm with respect to reason (νοῦν) and the rational (τὰ νοούμενα), the sun is in the visible realm with regard to vision and the visible.

> When people turn their eyes to things whose colors are no longer within the light of day but the glimmer of night, they are dulled and appear to be nearly blind, as if pure sight were not in them.
>
> Very much so.
>
> But when they turn to things illuminated by the sun they see clearly and sight does appear to be in them.
>
> Of course.
>
> Think of (νόει) the soul in the same way. When it is turned to what is illuminated by truth and being (τὸ ὄν) it understands (ἐνόησε) and knows (ἔγνω) them and appears to have reason (νοῦν), but when it is turned toward what is mixed with darkness—what comes to be and passes away—it opines and is dulled, its opinions change back and forth, and it seems not to have reason.

That it how it seems.

That which provides truth to what is known, and the power of knowing to the knower, you must say is the Idea of the good, and since it is the cause of knowledge and truth you must conceive of it as something knowable. [508c–e]

The analogy is seemingly straightforward: just as the eye's ability to see visible things is actualized by light which comes from the sun, the sun itself being visible, so too the mind's ability to know knowable things (forms) is actualized by truth which comes from the good, the good itself being knowable. But whereas in Book 5 knowledge and opinion were two entirely distinct faculties—knowledge is of being and is blind to becoming, opinion is of becoming and is blind to being—here they are a single faculty which is capable both of knowing being and opining becoming, depending only on the direction in which it is turned: "When it is turned to what is illuminated by truth and being it understands . . . but when it is turned toward . . . what comes to be and passes away it opines". In order to present a model on which the two are no longer absolutely distinct, but more like opposite ends of a spectrum, Socrates no longer contrasts the two as seeing opposite realms and being blind to the other, but only as having brighter or dimmer vision of the same objects: "When people turn their eyes to things whose colors are no longer within the light of day but the glimmer of night, they are dulled. . . . But when they turn to things illuminated by the sun they see clearly". Here, for a third time, Socrates tacitly sets aside the simplified dichotomy of Book 5, after it served its purpose of calling our attention to the difference between being and becoming in the clearest (but not the most nuanced) possible way.

What does it mean to say that the Idea of the good provides truth to what is known and the power of knowing to the knower? Since the forms correspond to what can be known (rather than opined), what does the good contribute to the forms' knowability and to our ability to know them? In the case of the forms of virtue the answer is clear enough, since we cannot understand virtue without understanding goodness (the absence of that latter understanding was one of the reasons why the account in Book 4 was inadequate). But how does the Idea of the good provide truth to forms that have no moral dimension, forms like largeness, equality, or species of things? One aspect of the forms is that they are the possibilities of what can exist in accordance with the nature of reality. In saying that it is the Idea of the good that supplies truth and being to the forms, Socrates is saying that the nature of reality is a consequence of what is good, a suggestion that is defended in detail in the *Timaeus*, the sequel to the *Republic*. To fully understand even the forms of mathematics, therefore, it is not enough to understand the definitions of the terms, but we must also understand why such terms exist at all, and the path to that understanding does not stop until it reaches the Idea of the good and discerns the return path that leads from the good back to the particular form (510b–511c, cf. 523b–533b).

Now, just as the sun furnishes visible things not only with visibility but also with their genesis, growth, and nourishment, although the sun itself is not genesis, so too intelligible things receive not only their intelligibility from the good, but also their existence (εἶναι) and being (οὐσίαν) from it, although the good itself is not being but even beyond being, superior to it in dignity and power.[22] "And Glaucon very comically said, 'By Apollo! What daimonic excess'" (509c). Glaucon's reference to the sun god and the divine points to an ambiguity in the analogy.[23] When Socrates says that the sun provides genesis but is not itself genesis, that seems reasonable enough; but when he goes on to say that the good provides being but is beyond being (ἐπέκεινα τῆς οὐσίας), he is saying more than that the good is not identical with being, just as when he later says that the highest level of *noesis* is beyond what can be put into words (533a) he is saying more than that it is not identical with words. In Book 5 Socrates had spoken of the good, the beautiful, and the just as forms like all the other forms (476a5), but now that we are passing from *dianoia* to *noesis* we are told that the good is something more than that. At one level it is a form like others, because we call some things good rather than beautiful or just or large; but at another level it is the raison d'etre of all forms because being as a whole is good. So although Plato makes no consistent distinction between *eidos* (form) and *idea* (Idea), here he verbally distinguishes the *idea* of the good that is beyond being, from the *eidos* of the good that is a being by virtue of the Idea of the good.

Since the Idea of the good is beyond being, not merely in the sense of non-identical with being, the analogy between the sun and the Idea of the good will be complete only if the sun is not only not the same as genesis, but is altogether beyond genesis. However, in that case it would violate the principle that whatever is visible belongs to the realm of coming to be and passing away.[24] Earlier in Book 6, however, Socrates said that in the case of most people who study philosophy without sufficient dedication, toward old age their light is quenched even more thoroughly than Heracleitus' sun, insofar as it is not rekindled (498a–b). If for Heracleitus, like most pre-Socratic philosophers, the sun is subject to genesis, then the analogy breaks down: the good is beyond being but the sun is not beyond genesis. But there is another way of regarding the sun. The analogy holds if the sun is conceived in its aspect as an immortal deity, which was how Socrates introduced it (508a5, a9). The reference to Apollo, reminding us of the earlier references to the sun's divinity,

- virtues are

- the good is beyond being

may be a way of saying that if, at least for the sake of argument, we think of the sun as eternal, then the analogy is complete.[25]

It is possible to regard this passage as the origin of Western emanationism (Neoplatonists saw it as a forerunner of their cosmology). If intelligible things (the forms) receive not only their intelligibility but also their existence and being from the good, which is itself beyond being, then being (the forms) can be regarded as emanating from the good. And when Socrates goes on to say that when _noesis_ comes to know the good itself it then "descends again to a conclusion, . . . moving from forms themselves, through forms, to them, it concludes in forms" (511b–c), this suggests that the forms to which the good gives rise may be hierarchically ordered in the way that emanationism requires. Again, since the sun too is the offspring of the good (508b), and visible things receive not only their visibility but also their genesis, growth, and nourishment from the sun (509b), then we can regard first the intelligible realm, and then the visible one (beginning with the sun), as following from the good in an emanationistic way.

An emanationist interpretation would also explain the _Timaeus_'s puzzling description of the motivation of the demiurge or creator in creating the world. The demiurge is not a personification of the Idea of the good, although he is described as good, because he creates only the world of becoming that is known by _doxa_, not the realm of eternal being that is known by rationality; and, in fact, looks to the latter for patterns to follow in making mortal things (28a–29a).[26] As the creator of the world of becoming, the demiurge makes the sun (38c) and the soul as well, which is the principle of motion (34b–c). The demiurge represents the transition from unchanging being to the realm of change, beginning with soul, as he looks to the former to create the latter. In the _Timaeus_, as in the _Republic_, the Idea of the good is spoken of only by analogy with its "offspring". Although the demiurge is not a personification of the Idea of the good, he may be regarded as an "offspring" of it like the sun, but mediating between the two, and his creativity as an image of the creativity of the good. The demiurge's motivation in creating the world is that he "was good, and for one who is good no jealousy can ever arise about anything. And being free from jealousy he desired that everything should be as much like himself as possible" (29e). It is puzzling that the explanation is given only in privative terms: not that because the creator was good he was generous, and therefore wanted to share his goodness; but rather that he was "not jealous". The consequence of putting it privatively rather than positively, "not jealous" rather than "generous", is that what is attributed to the creator is not a positive reason for creating the world, but the absence of a negative reason for not creating it. The implication is that unless a restraining force like jealousy operated to prevent creation, creation would automatically follow from the nature of the creator. Even so, this could not be regarded as emanationism in the Neoplatonic sense because the *Timaeus*, like Greek cosmology generally, regards creation not as the bringing into existence of a world ex nihilo, but the bringing of order to a preexisting disorderly material. Unlike Neoplatonic emanationism, the emanationism implied by the *Republic* and *Timaeus* does not create that into which the rest of creation is received, the receptacle (*Timaeus*, 49a); it is a dualism rather than a monism.[27]

However comically Glaucon may have expressed himself, he appears to have been genuinely impressed by Socrates' words, and no longer says that he will be satisfied with inadequate explanations (as at 435d and 506d), but now insists over Socrates' protests that Socrates not leave out even a little (509c8). Socrates seems to have raised Glaucon up from *pistis* in Book 4, and *dianoia* in Book 5, to a genuinely *noetic* attitude here at the end of Book 6. The best that Socrates can offer is not to intentionally omit anything as far as possible, which nevertheless means omitting a great deal (509c9), and with that he introduces the Divided Line.

The Divided Line (509d–511e)

The previous section presented the sun as both an analogue and an offspring of the good (i.e., as parallel to and as derivative from the good) but did not integrate the two relationships into a single account. That integration is now supplied by the Divided Line, which makes the visible realm an analogue of the intelligible realm, and also an image of it at a lower ontological level. The good and the sun are sovereign over the intelligible and visible realms, respectively. Socrates calls the realm of the sun the visible realm rather than the realm of the heavens (*ouranou*) lest he seem to Glaucon to play the sophist (509d). *Ouranos* can refer either to the sky (i.e., the realm of the sun) (488d), or to the "heavenly" realm of the divine (i.e., of the forms) as when Socrates says that the rulers will look to the "divine paradigm" of the forms in fashioning the lives of the citizens (500e), and later speaks of a "paradigm in heaven" (592b).[28] To call the visible realm the realm of the heavens would therefore permit sophistical equivocations. Since Socrates had been speaking of the sun in terms of "the visible realm" throughout his analogy of the sun and the good, there seems no reason for him to now introduce the possibility of calling the realm "heavenly" only to reject it in favor of the term he has used all along, except perhaps that the ambiguity of the term suggests a common ground (if only metaphorically) between the divine and visible realms—

in other words that it reflects the recent softening of the rigid two-worlds model proposed at the end of Book 5.

Socrates illustrates his meaning with a line divided into two unequal segments, one representing the intelligible realm of knowledge and the other the visible realm of opinion; each segment is then subdivided in the same ratio as the original division (509d). The subdivision of the visible segment represents things and their likenesses, and since this further division was in the same proportion as the original division which represented knowledge and opinion, "as the opinable is to the knowable, so is the likeness to that of which it is a likeness" (510a). The line illustrates differences of clarity and lack of clarity (509d), and corresponding to its divisions are parallel conditions within the soul itself, to which Socrates gives the names *noesis*, *dianoia*, *pistis*, and *eikasia* (511d–e).[29] So much is clear, but the overall interpretation of the line is one of the most contentious and divisive issues in Platonic scholarship, and in more than one place.[30]

Eikasia

The lower subsection of the visible segment, *eikasia*, represents images. "By images (*eikones*) I mean first shadows, then reflections in water and in all compacted, smooth, and shiny materials, and all such things" (509d–510a). Readers are understandably puzzled by the nature of *eikasia*. People spend little or no time looking at shadows and reflections rather than the actual things, so the significance of this subsection is difficult to fathom, and it is sometimes supposed that Plato included it here only to fill out the symmetry of the proportions, or that both *eikasia* and *pistis* are meant to do nothing more than illustrate the relationship between an image and its original for the sake of understanding the relationship between *dianoia* and *noesis*, rather than having any intrinsic significance.[31] In order to see why *eikasia* is not trivial, we need to consider the words, "reflections in . . . *all such things*". In Book 10 Socrates says that a painter is like someone who carries a mirror and shows reflections of everything, and a poet does the same thing in words (596a–599a).[32] The poet's imitation of the visible world in words is also an example of *eikasia*; it cannot fit anywhere else on the line. Socrates could not give it as an example in the context of the metaphor of the Divided Line because words do not primarily belong to the visible world, which is what the lower segments of the line refer to, but it can hardly be doubted that imitative paintings belong to *eikasia*, in which case imitative words must belong to it as well.[33] At the beginning of Book 2, when Adeimantus says with reference to the inadequacy of the discussion in Book 1, "Don't only show us in

words that justice is stronger than injustice" (367e), that description of looking at things only in words (eristic arguments) rather than in themselves (by
actual investigation), refers to *eikasia*. Unless we take the "all such things" of
eikasia to extend to verbal images as well as other kinds of reflections, not
only will *eikasia* be trivial and its presence here hard to account for, but one
of the most common ways of looking at reality, one that focuses on what we
hear about it rather than observing it in itself, would not be accounted for on
the line at all.

Pistis

In the second subsection, *pistis*, "place the things of which these are
images—the animals around us, all the plants, and the whole class of artifacts"
(510a). Whereas the eristic arguments of Book 1 illustrated the way we sometimes investigate matters by looking only at what is said about them, rather
than at the phenomena themselves, Books 2–4 were an investigation of justice
by looking at physical entities, cities, in which it could be observed. When
Socrates says to place in this category the animals around us, plants, and artifacts, he does not say that these are the only things that belong in it. Rocks
would certainly belong as well, as would we ourselves insofar as we are visible
bodies, and so would our actions and communities. Otherwise, when Socrates
says that the lower division of the line is a visible image of the intelligible
realm, it could not include visible images of the most important forms, like justice and wisdom—the outward signs of virtuous character, as at 402c–d.

image of virtue ??

Dianoia

The lower subsection of the intelligible sector, *dianoia*, has two main characteristics. First, it uses as images those things (physical objects) which were
imitated (by reflections, shadows, etc.) in *eikasia* (510b, cf. 511b). Second, it
is compelled to investigate from hypotheses, and can only draw out the consequences of its hypotheses without being able to rise above them to a first
principle (510b). The examples that Socrates gives when Glaucon fails to
understand are geometry and calculation, where categories such as odd and
even, the various kinds of figure, and the three kinds of shape, are taken as
given—as hypotheses or assumptions—and the investigations lead downward
to what follows from these hypotheses, not upward to how they themselves
can be deduced from something higher, since they are taken to be self-evident
and in no need of justification. Although the practitioners of *dianoia* employ
visible models to assist them in their investigations, their interest is not in the
models but in the intelligible reality that the models illustrate. When we
draw a triangle to help us think through a demonstration in geometry, for

no visible images at all.
(4) physical images as bodies, hypothesis without
raising to higher pples; also intelligible
reality.

The Sun, Line, and Cave ~ 193

example, we are not interested in the particular physical triangle that we have drawn, but only in the universal intelligible triangle that all such diagrams point to. The diagrams and (especially) three dimensional models of solid geometry exist in physical space and are therefore capable of casting shadows and reflections, so we can see how the objects of *pistis*, which exist in physical space, are at the same time both images of something intelligible and things which themselves cast further images. As was mentioned in the previous chapter (above, 152), we should not forget that the *Meno* and *Phaedo* show how philosophy too makes use of the method of hypothesis, and that *dianoia* is not confined to mathematics.

Noesis

Both of the above-mentioned characteristics of *dianoia* find their complement in *noesis*. Where *dianoia* proceeds only downward, to the consequences rather than foundations of its assumptions (hypotheses), *noesis* proceeds to the beginning rather than the consequences, upward from the hypotheses to an unhypothetical first principle. And where *dianoia* employed particular things as images of the intelligible reality that it investigates, *noesis* makes no use of visible images at all, but using only forms it methodically proceeds through them (510b). Whereas mathematical thinking could function as an example of *dianoia*, *noesis* is more difficult to illustrate, not only because images are foreign to its nature, but also because of its rarity. Here rationality itself (that is, *logos* in its highest function rather than merely as calculation)

> takes hold of the power of dialectic, employing the hypotheses not as first principles but as literal hypotheses, things set under us—stepping-stones and springboards to reach the unhypothetical first principle of everything. Having grasped it, it once again hangs onto the things that depend from it, and proceeds downward to a conclusion, making use of nothing at all visible but only of forms themselves, from them to them, and concludes in forms. [511b–c]

In the *Statesman* the Eleatic visitor says that he cannot at present make his method of division entirely clear (262c), which is puzzling in context because there is no obvious way in which it is not made clear. If we look again at the passage quoted above we can see that, like the visitor's method of collection and division, it contains two stages, the first of which unifies classes by proceeding synoptically (537c) upward to a first principle, the other proceeding downward through forms alone. It is conceivable that the method of collection and division is Plato's attempt to say something more about the nature of *noesis*. Since the Idea of the good is the one source from which all things follow, one way that we can make progress in understanding it is by understanding the world as a unified series of relationships, which the method of collection and division helps us do. The upward path of *noesis* is not the same as the method of collection, however, since a higher hypothesis has more explanatory power while a higher genus may have less explanatory power.[34] For example, the education of the philosopher-rulers will take them through the *dianoiai* of arithmetic, plane geometry, solid geometry, astronomy, and harmony, which will finally bring them to dialectic (i.e., *noesis*); and we shall see in the next chapter that this progression corresponds to the upward path through hypotheses that is described here, since the hypotheses of each of these *dianoiai* are grounded in the next. Thus astronomy has more explanatory power than arithmetic because it combines the principles of arithmetic with principles related to bodies and to motion; since arithmetic is a part of astronomy it is lower in the hierarchy of *dianoiai*. But if we rank the studies in terms of class inclusion as the method of collection and division does, we would have to put arithmetic above astronomy because astronomy can be classed as a species of arithmetic, but arithmetic is not a species of astronomy.

Once the upward path reaches the synoptic point (537c) in which the unity of all things is evident, there is still another step that must be taken if we are to pass from an understanding of the unity of being to an apprehension of the source of this unity that is beyond being. Socrates made no attempt to give a demonstration or explanation of *noetic* dialectical thinking, and when Glaucon later asks for a more detailed account Socrates says, in a passage previously quoted:

> You will no longer be able, my dear Glaucon, to follow me, although for my part I would not willingly omit anything. But you would no longer see an image of what we are saying, but the truth itself. . . . And [we must insist that] the power of dialectic alone can reveal it to someone who is experienced in the things we just went through, and it is not possible in any other way. [533a]

The Eleatic tetralogy can be seen as an illustration of the stages of the Divided Line. 1) The *Parmenides* devotes itself to verbal refutations in the first part, followed by an apparent admission by Parmenides that his refutations were, in fact, inconclusive,[35] reminiscent of Socrates' comparable confession at the end of Book 1; while the second part of the dialogue is a demonstration of how arguments can be constructed to prove both sides' contradictory claims. Like *Republic*, Book 1, it is at the level of *eikasia*. 2) The *Theaetetus* (which is Eleatic only indirectly: 183c–184a) investigates the nature of knowledge, not in a merely elenctic or verbal way, but by examining the phenomenon of knowledge itself. Although refutations occur, something positive is continuously learned as well, but the dialogue never reaches a satisfactory conclusion because it never rises above *pistic* sense experience to the intelligible forms. 3) The *Sophist* does introduce abstract formal categories, as the starting points for divisions into species. Nevertheless, as with *dianoia*, it provides no justification of these starting points (or any argument that one is better than another) but takes them as first principles from which to descend. Moreover, it explicitly avoids concerning itself with the good (227a–b). 4) The *Statesman* begins with genus-species divisions like those of the *Sophist*; but then, in an attempt to justify them, it moves to an examination of the source of goodness (283e–284b), which eventually becomes the only relevant consideration in political constitutions (293b–d). The ideal ruler in the *Statesman* is not practicing *noesis*, however, because he is concerned not with forms but actions; he corresponds to the philosopher-rulers of the *Republic* only at the point when they have achieved *noesis* and return to apply it to the art of ruling.[36] No dialogue could be written on the final theme, the philosopher (cf. *Sophist* 217a), because it would correspond to *Republic* 533a (quoted in the previous paragraph). The one other place where Plato comes as close to this limit as he does here is in the *Symposium* (210e–212a).

There is an asymmetry in the way Socrates explains the two subsections of the visible side of the line and those of the intelligible side: his explanation of the visible pair talks about their objects (images of physical things, physical things themselves) but not about the kind of thinking that corresponds to them, while in his discussion of the intelligible pair he explains the nature of the thinking that they represent (inferential thinking with the help of images, pure dialectical thinking) but does not say what their objects are. Consequently, just as it was not easy to decide what kind of thinking was intended by *eikasia* and *pistis*, it is not easy to see what kind of objects are intended by *dianoia* and *noesis*. If the objects of *noesis* are forms (511b–c), then the objects of *dianoia* must be images of forms, but images of forms are physical things, and the objects of *dianoia* are intelligible. Conversely, if the objects of *dianoia* are forms, then what higher objects can there be for *noesis*, of which the forms of *dianoia* are images?[37]

It is sometimes suggested that the objects of *dianoia* are intermediate mathematical forms such as Aristotle ascribes to Plato, but in that case not only would mathematical intermediates (*dianoia*) be images of metaphysical forms (*noesis*), but physical things (*pistis*) must be images of mathematics—a quasi-Pythagorean view for which there is no evidence in Plato.[38] *Dianoia* is not limited to mathematical thinking, although mathematics is Plato's favorite example of it. His mathematical demonstrations of recollection in the *Meno* and *Phaedo*, and the mathematical studies used to awaken the prisoners in the cave to the intelligible world, refer to intelligible reality generally. Socrates does not refer to mathematics at all when he first describes *dianoia* (510b) but only as a subsequent example when Glaucon is puzzled (510b–c). Any thinking that posits and draws consequences from intelligible reality without inquiring into its foundation (as when Empedocles posits Love and Strife, and Anaximander Mind) is *dianoia*. To limit *dianoia* to mathematical thinking is to exclude one of the most fundamental forms of philosophical thinking from the Divided Line. The other main feature of *dianoia*, its use of the objects of *pistis*, physical things, to facilitate thinking about the intelligible realities of which the physical things are images (510b–d), is clearly not limited to mathematics, as we can see from the doctrine of recollection in the *Meno*, *Phaedo*, and *Phaedrus*, and the method of paradigms or examples in the *Statesman* (285e–286b). Similarly, it can be nothing else than *dianoia* when in the *Republic* Socrates utilized images of sexual intercourse, pregnancy, and birth (490b), and images of the sun, the line, and the cave, to help us think about the intelligible realm.

One reason for the vast variety of interpretations is an ambiguity in the way the line is described. It is explicit that the two lower parts of the line ("opinion") are an image of the two upper parts of the line ("knowledge"), and that the lower part of opinion (*eikasia*) is an image of the upper part (*pistis*) (510a). Since *dianoia* is related to *noesis* in the same ratio as opinion to knowledge, and *eikasia* to *pistis*, the objects of *dianoia* are usually inferred to be an image of the objects of *noesis*, even though that relationship is never explicitly stated. More problematic is the relation between *pistis* and *dianoia*. They are not related to each other in the same proportions as the other pairs, but turn out to be the same size (n. 37 above), so there is less reason to infer that they are intended to stand in the same relationship to each other as the other pairs. When Socrates says that in *dianoia* the soul is compelled to use (χρωμένη . . . ἀναγκάζεται) the objects of *pistis* as images of its own objects (510b), does this mean that the objects of *pistis* really are images of the objects of *dianoia* in the same way that the objects of *eikasia* are images of those of *pistis* (an intrinsic relationship), or does it mean only that *dianoia* necessarily treats them as such but that is not what they are in themselves (an extrinsic relationship)?

We can see how important this distinction is by considering the proposal that the objects of *dianoia* are verbal formulations or hypotheses.[39] If the objects of *pistis* are, *in fact*, images of the objects of *dianoia* (the intrinsic interpretation), then this proposal would be impossible because it would mean that physical things are simply images of verbal formulations—a view that might appeal to post-modern textualists but could not be defended in Plato. But if the objects of *pistis* are only *employed* as images of the objects of *dianoia* (the extrinsic interpretation), there would be nothing wrong with saying that practitioners of *dianoia* use physical things as examples (images) of their theses and definitions, even though such things are not in themselves images (imitations) of them. This view, however, seems impossible to reconcile with Socrates' statement that the practitioners of *dianoia* use visible objects (of *pistis*) as images to enable them to think about objects like "the square itself and the diagonal itself" (510d), for that means that the proper objects of *dianoia* are the forms themselves and not words or hypotheses about the forms.

Although there are problems with the *extrinsic* interpretation, we saw above (n. 37) that if the allegory of the cave is an elaboration of the Divided Line, as I believe it is, there is also a problem with the *intrinsic* interpretation, the view that the objects of *pistis* are in themselves imitations of the objects of *dianoia* and not merely treated as such by practitioners of *dianoia*. In the allegory the objects of *dianoia* are shadows and reflections of natural things outside the cave, while the objects of *pistis* are puppets or statues of these same things. How can we say that statues or puppets are imitations of reflections and shadows, rather than of actual things? To repeat the reply that was given above, a statue or puppet is at a further remove from the thing it imitates than the reflection or shadow is, because human artifice is added; accordingly, both paintings and sculpture were thought to have originated in the tracing of shadows. That a Greek painter could work from someone's shadow (as today painters and sculptors can work from photographs) shows that works of art are ontologically further from the original than are reflections and shadows (and photographs). There does not seem to have been any other way that Plato could have illustrated his point, since there is no additional level of reflection—images of images in the natural world—that he could have pointed to. Moreover, as we shall see when we come to the cave allegory, the human intervention that separates natural shadows and reflections from artificial puppets is a matter of importance.

We saw that *noesis* and *dianoia* begin at the same place—with hypotheses based on forms—but proceed in different directions. *Dianoia* and *noesis* thus have the same *initial* objects, intelligible forms that serve as the basis for hypotheses—not only mathematical forms like odd, even, and triangle, but also forms like virtue and beauty—but their ultimate objects are different. *Dianoia* is concerned with forms as causes (what follows from them), and *noesis* with forms as effects (how they follow from the unhypothetical principle of the good). *Dianoia* looks downward from particular forms (the being of things), and does not see all forms as related to one another. *Noesis* proceeds upward hierarchically and synoptically (537c) until it unifies all true beings (forms) in the Idea of the good, their common source beyond being (509b).

⟨6⟩ Thus the ultimate object of *noesis* is not the forms as such—which are the objects of *dianoia*—but the Idea of the good. As *dianoia* attends to visible things for the sake of understanding the forms of being (510d), *noesis* attends to the forms of being for the sake of understanding the good that is beyond being. The forms, as articulations of the rationality or goodness of the world, are not only effects of the good, but also images of it. Physical things, in turn, by participating in the forms are images of them; and reflections and shadows are images of things. Thus the object of attention at each level is the image of the one above.

Is there any significance to that fact that the two middle sections of the line, *pistis* and *dianoia*, are the same size (n. 37)? It has been doubted whether Plato could have intended this implication, since the subsections of the line represent differences in clarity and truth (509d, 511e), and a subsection of *doxa* (opinion) does not seem capable of as much clarity and truth as a sub-section of *episteme* (knowledge). But since *dianoia* is a kind of thinking that posits intelligible reality without inquiring into its foundation, it is lacking in transparency and clarity. When Socrates introduced the hypothesis of forms in the *Phaedo* without reference to their source, he gives the not very clear explanation that the only cause of beauty is the "presence or communion—however you call it—of the beautiful" (100d), and concedes that this kind of account is simplistic, artless, foolish, and ignorant (100d, 105c). The natura-listic explanations that pertain to *pistis* can, by contrast, be very sophisti-cated, as we saw in the case of the construction of the city in Books 2–4 (cf. *Phaedo* 100c), even though they are concerned only with the visible realm. Perhaps, then, *pistis* and *dianoia* do achieve comparable levels of clarity and truth, although their strengths and weaknesses are the opposite of each other—one giving genuinely informative accounts at the physical level, the other operating on the more adequate intelligible level but offering less informative accounts. In the *Timaeus* when Plato works out detailed and sophisticated explanations of corporeal phenomena in physicalist causal terms, it is not hard to believe that he regarded such explanations as having as much clarity and truth as the statement that things are beautiful because of beauty itself, or as the purely formal divisions of the *Sophist*, whose place on the Divided Line could not be anywhere but at the level of *dianoia*. In that case we can take Plato to be implying that the most sophisticated physicalist or anthropological (in the case of *Republic* 2–4) explanations do have as much truth and clarity as the least sophisticated formal explanations, although it is a clarity and truth of a different kind.[40]

Connected with this, there is another reason why *pistis* and *dianoia* may be of equal size. When Socrates recommends the mathematical studies that lead the prisoners from the visible world to the intelligible (523c–531c), each study will have two aspects, an empirical one that belongs to *pistis* and an abstract one that belongs to *dianoia*. The equality of size of *pistis* and *dianoia* may reflect the fact that they represent two aspects of every field of study in the physical world, depending on whether we turn our attention to its corporeal manifestation or its intelligible underpinnings.

The Theory of Forms

According to the usual chronological ordering of the dialogues, the theory of forms developed out of Socrates' concern in the early dialogues with definitions. In one dialogue after another he asks what courage is (*Laches*), or self-control (*Charmides*), virtue (*Protagoras, Meno*), beauty (*Hippias Major*), or friendship (*Lysis*); other dialogues contain similar questions even if not as centrally as these, and he regularly uses the words *idea* or *eidos* for the common character possessed by all instances called by that name. Although his inquiries focus on objects of value like the ones listed above, the principle of definition extends universally, and Socrates often prompts his partners with parallel illustrations that use clearer concepts drawn from mathematics, or physical qualities like heaviness or largeness.[41] There is no explicit evidence in those dialogues that Plato had taken the further step of inferring that if a form is what all instances that are called by the same name have in common, then the form is not reducible to any of its instances and is not only logically but also ontologically distinct from all of them. A common view is that the procedure of the early dialogues is Plato's legacy from Socrates, and that the further step represents the development of his own distinctive philosophical point of view, although it is also possible to argue that the early dialogues represent Plato's own contribution which he later extended ontologically, or that the ontological theory of forms is already implicit in the early dialogues and is progressively clarified in subsequent dialogues.[42] The *Republic*, in any case, presents the theory of forms in its maturity, so the question for us is less how it arose than how to understand it. Plato never gives a detailed presentation of it, but rather introduces the forms in particular contexts for particular purposes. In the *Republic* we are told that they are unities (476a), that things are what they are by participating in forms (476d), that forms are unchanging (479a), that they owe their existence and intelligibility to the good (509b), and that there is a form for every group of things that is called by the same name (596b).

It is helpful to look at the theory of forms in the context of pre-Socratic philosophy which, from Thales to Anaxagoras, posited an underlying substance that served as the substrate of changing things. Rather than things coming into being or passing away absolutely, the stuff of which they were made disintegrates and reforms into other things, according to what we now call the principle of conservation of matter. Plato's theory of forms recognizes that not only is matter conserved, but so, in a sense, are the forms that it takes. The reason that we use the same names over and over again to designate the things that are newly arising is that things resemble one another in relevant ways—they have the same look or form (*idea, eidos*). So when matter changes form, not only is the matter conserved, but so were the forms: matter repeatedly takes the same forms. To say that something is a form, then, is to say that things of that kind are possible; a form is in the broadest sense a possible configuration of material substance. Forms are universals (596a) because they represent repeatability.

Since the forms are the pure possibilities of what can be generated in accordance with the nature of reality, whatever is generated reflects that possibility: it imitates and is a likeness of particular forms. To say that something participates in a particular form is to say nothing more than that is manifests a particular possibility, and to say that the forms are causes of particular things is to say that it is a necessary condition for the existence of a thing that such things be possible and that the conditions of its possibility have been met (what the *Phaedo* calls "that without which the cause would never be a cause": 99b). Put in this way the theory of forms sounds somewhat trivial—it is not very informative to say that the cause of a thing is that such a thing is possible—and that was why Socrates described it in the passage cited earlier as seemingly simplistic, artless, foolish, and ignorant (*Phaedo*, 100d, 105c). But although the importance of formal causes is not as obvious as that of efficient causes, behind their apparent triviality are important consequences, as Aristotle's objections and the subsequent polemics over the problem of universals attest. To say that *x* is caused by participation in the form X may be deficient in obvious explanatory power, but it implies that individuals are not simply reducible to unique and transient configurations of a material substrate, although that is one aspect of them; they are also manifestations of an order and regularity that permeates the visible world. On that basis too they are, at least in part, knowable by reason. We cannot know an individual as such because it is always in the process of becoming other than it was, but we can know it as a particular kind of thing, and the kind has the self-sameness and stability that the individual lacks. What is unique in an individual can only be known through the senses, here and now, but in addition to its becoming (an ontological condition between what-is and what-is-not) it also possesses being or essence which, as universal and unchanging, is knowable by reason.

Thus far we are still at the level of *dianoia*, forms understood with reference to visible things. However, not only do formal causes imply order and regularity in the world, but the particular set of forms provides evidence of the underlying basis of that order, the Idea of the good.[43] That is why the forms that Plato focuses the most attention on are not species, as they are for Aristotle, but rather those which most obviously manifest value: goodness, beauty, virtue, justice, wisdom, piety, moderation, courage. The others must also be manifestations of goodness insofar as they manifest the goodness of reality, but the connection is no longer obvious. Because the forms are products of the good, the structure of reality as articulated by the regularities that the forms instantiate is not merely one among many possible worlds, but exists necessarily as the consequence of the rational goodness that is the creative principle. To say that the Idea of the good gives existence and knowability to the forms (509b) is to say that the actual set of forms that exists, rather than any other possible set of forms, exists by virtue of its rational goodness; and because goodness is rational the forms are knowable. That is the level of *noesis*.

Is it possible to justify these claims to skeptics? People at the level of *pistis* or *eikasia* do not admit any reality beyond the physical, and even people at the level of *dianoia*, who perceive an intelligible reality as well as the physical one, do not acknowledge that it has its source in the good. The only adequate way of perceiving the truth of Socrates' claims would be to reach the level of *noesis* ourselves, to which the whole of the dialogue has been endeavoring to bring us: "the power of dialectic alone can reveal it to someone who is experienced in the things we just went through, and it is not possible in any other way" (533a). Short of that, the only way to defend these claims against the objections of those who find nothing in their own experience to confirm them, is to show that they are at least compatible with our experience, however much they may at first seem to violate it. The arguments of Thrasymachus in Book 1, and Glaucon and Adeimantus in Book 2, showed how little most people see the world as the product of goodness. They see it rather as a battleground of opposing wills, in which justice exists only as an artifice against natural injustice, and justice itself is never rewarded in the nature of things, but rather the appearance of justice is rewarded by the artifact of the city. How can a world in which the unjust prosper and the just suffer be a consequence of goodness?

Some effort to justify the goodness of the world, in the light of the badness of so much of our experience of it, will be made in the Myth of Er, where our own responsibility for human evil is emphasized. But the attempt to show how the goodness of the world is also compatible with natural evil is not made until the *Republic*'s sequel, the *Timaeus*, where it is shown that structures that are good in themselves may allow suffering, partly because what is felt as suffering by individual parts may turn out to be rationally necessary for the whole, and partly because of the way contingency necessarily enters into individual existence. We should not suppose, however, that when Plato wrote the *Timaeus* he was rejecting Socrates' claim that it is impossible to give an account of the nature of the good and what follows from it. The tentative nature of the claims in the *Timaeus* is indicated by its presentation as a myth rather than a logos, by having the myth presented by someone other than Socrates, and by abridging the completeness of the account in crucial places for no apparent reason. For an explanation of this latter point see chapter 11.

The Allegory of the Cave (Book 7 to 519b)

"Next, then", Socrates says, "compare our nature with respect to education and lack of education to the following condition". After his initial presentation of the allegory of the cave he explains:

> This likeness, my dear Glaucon, should be applied to the things we said previously, likening the region that appears through sight to the prison dwelling, and the light of the fire in it to the power of the sun; and if you take the ascent to the upper region and contemplation of the things above to be the soul's road up to the intelligible realm, you'll not miss what I hope to convey. [517a–b]

Socrates' words show how the difference between the world within the cave and the world outside is to be taken as an image of the visible and intelligible realms represented by the two main segments of the Divided Line; and the allegory's distinction at each of these two levels between first looking at images, and then looking at the things from which the images are copied, completes the parallel with the Line. There is ample reason, then, to regard the allegory of the cave as an illustration of the principles of the Divided Line,[44] and the allegory is accordingly presented within the discussion of the Line, which is interrupted by it at 514a and resumes when the discussion of the cave concludes at 532d.

Each of Socrates' three images adds something to its predecessor. In the image of the sun, the sun and the visible world served as analogues to the good and the intelligible world, but aside from the unelaborated statement that the sun is an offspring of the Idea of the good, the two realms were not brought into relation with one another; one was an analogue of the other, but there was no continuity between them. The Divided Line provided that continuity by integrating the analogy into the proportional divisions of a single line. The entity that mediates between those two realms for Plato is soul, which as mind can discover the intelligible order of which the visible world is an image, and as the principle of motion brings form to materiality;[45] but so far it has not been incorporated into Socrates' models. The allegory of the cave, with its depiction of "the soul's road up to the intelligible realm" supplies what was missing. To put it differently, the allegory of the cave shows what is necessary for us to make the journey along the Divided Line. The cave allegory has political implications that were not present in the Divided Line, but even if that means that the Line is an epistemological model and the cave a political one,[46] it does not follow that they cannot be given a continuous interpretation, for what makes political manipulation possible are the ways that we hold things to be true, which are classified in the Divided Line. We can say without overt reference to politics that our most common way of holding something for true is through images of reality in words and other media (in accordance with the Line), and from that it follows that we can be influenced politically by the manipulation of these images (in accordance with the cave).

Eikasia (514a–515c)

We are, Socrates says, like people who have been chained within a subterranean cave their entire lives so that they can neither move nor turn, and must look directly forward at a wall. The cave is open to the light along its entire width, but the entrance is so high and so distant that the prisoners' only light comes from a fire burning far away above them. Between them and the fire is a wall behind which people walk like puppeteers behind a screen, some uttering sounds (which presumably correspond to the puppets they are holding) and some silent, holding up all kinds of artifacts: statues or puppets of people and other animals, made of stone, wood, and all other materials. The prisoners can see neither themselves nor anything else, but only the shadows that are cast on the wall, which is the only reality they know and the referents of all their words. Assuming that the cave has an echo, even the puppeteers' voices would seem to come from the shadows. The image seems less contrived if we remember that there are traditions of shadow-puppet theaters that function in very much this way.[47] The puppets in the cave are images of living things, as in the Divided Line the visible world is an image of the intelligible; and the shadows in turn are images of the puppets, as the shadows and reflections of *eikasia* too are images of images.[48]

In order to display all the levels visually the allegory represents the intelligible world as the visible sunlit world, and the visible world itself by puppets of it. Who are the puppeteers, and why are the prisoners in chains? Socrates could have attributed the prisoners' failure to turn around and see the puppets not to bondage, but simply to the fact that when they do turn they are dazzled by the light and think that the only reality is what is in front of them (515c–d). Earlier, Socrates pointed out that in assemblies, courtrooms, theatres, army camps, and other public gatherings, people aggressively object to the things they dislike and loudly approve of those they like, and if this is not enough to sweep the beliefs of young people along with the torrent, they resort to deprivation of civil rights, fines, or death (492a–d). This coercion of young people's perceptions of reality by their elders and by peer pressure is represented by the prisoners' enchainment. But the puppeteers do not represent the adult generation as a whole, for they are aware of the deception that they are practicing, whereas the older generation are usually themselves captive to the beliefs in which they indoctrinate the young. The puppeteers represent those who knowingly manipulate the beliefs of others: the ones who utter sounds represent poets, sophists, and rhetoricians, while those who are silent correspond to legislators, painters, and sculptors.[49] But if we are not to conclude that the puppeteers are depicted in a misleading way, they must represent only those who deliberately try to convince the public of what they themselves know to be only a charade: manipulative or paternalistic politicians, for example, as well as manipulative or paternalistic religious leaders including mythopoeic poets and sophists. Thus Plato puts into Protagoras' mouth the claim that sophists of old, fearing persecution, hid behind poetry and religion: specifically Homer, Hesiod, Simonides, Orpheus, and Musaeus (*Protagoras* 316c–e). What "Protagoras" means by "sophists" is no doubt something more favorable than what Plato means by it, but they agree that it practices deception with regard to its true beliefs. To the class of the puppeteers would belong all those who try to manipulate the public, whether for its own good or not, into believing what they themselves do not consider to be literally true, even if the falsehood is noble.[50]

Another aspect of *eikasia* is brought out by the depiction of the prisoners as competing for honors and prizes "for him who most sharply discerns [the shadows] that go by, and best remembers which of them customarily pass by earlier, later, or together, and who is most able to prophesy from these things what is about to happen" (516c–d). Their predictions are not based on any understanding of what they are looking at, but only on customary (εἰώθει) sequences, which may change at any time. Unable to see the physical causes of what they are experiencing, the prisoners must rely on the mere shadow of causality, the customary associations that give rise to superstition. Since the customary sequences can change, the memories on which the prisoners rely may well conflict with one another and produce contradictory principles on which to base their predictions.

Pistis (515c–e)

Suppose now, Socrates says, one of the prisoners came by nature to be released and healed from his bonds and ignorance. This happens "by nature" because the nature of the soul is to strive after truth, even if its embodied nature distracts it with appetite and spiritedness, and even if we easily mistake opinion for knowledge; until we are released from the bonds our nature is deformed, and so the release is also a healing (ἴασιν). What in our nature enables us to overcome such obstacles is the power to "divine" truth before we are capable of grasping it, that Socrates spoke of at 505e. When the freed prisoner turned around after staring at the shadows his whole life, Socrates continues, he would be dazzled by the light of the fire and be unable to see the objects themselves that had cast the shadows. Suppose someone now told him that what he saw before was insignificant, but now that he is closer to reality he is seeing things that are more real, and seeing more correctly. If that person pointed to each of the passing things and compelled him to answer questions about what each one is, the prisoner would be at a loss (ἀπορεῖν) and would think the shadows he saw earlier were truer than this. This is a vivid illustration of a phenomenon repeatedly portrayed in the Socratic dialogues:[51] Socrates tries to liberate someone from an uncritical acceptance of what he has been told, by forcing him to look to the subject at issue and answer questions about it, with the result that the person becomes utterly at a loss and unable to answer—at an impasse or *aporia*—and believes that Socrates has merely tricked him, and that the truth resides in his previous beliefs even if he is unable to defend them.[52] What is not mentioned here, but becomes explicit at the next stage, is that once the prisoner's eyes become accustomed to the light he will be able to discern the things at the new level. Eventually he will be able to see the puppets that were pointed out, and will realize that what he saw earlier is indeed less real. Next, in a transitional moment, the prisoner will eventually be able to look directly at the fire itself, whose light he had previously seen only as reflected against the wall. The fire is transitional between the lower and higher realms: on one hand it is made by us, like the puppets, but on the other hand it is a natural phenomenon that is "made" only in the sense that we can create the conditions in which is appears, but not in the sense that we make an artifact: we cannot design its form.

Dianoia (515e–516a)

If now the freed prisoner were dragged up to the entrance, which is rough and steep, he would find it painful and be annoyed, and when he came out he would be unable to see anything until his eyes became accustomed to the sunlight. Here, as before, he passes from shadows to realities: at first he would most easily see shadows, and then the reflections of people and the rest (τῶν ἄλλων) in water, including the sun itself (516b). And just as in the Divided Line's description of *eikasia* there was a progression from shadows to reflections (509d–510a), there is a similar progression here (516a).

Noesis (516a–c)

Whereas *dianoia* made use of images and unquestioned hypothetical starting points, *noesis* made no use of images and used the hypotheses as stepping-stones to an unhypothetical principle, the Idea of the good (511b–c). Accordingly, the freed prisoner now looks at things themselves rather than shadows or reflections, and ascends to brighter and brighter kinds of entities until he is able to see the sun itself: from physical things to the night sky and the things in it—the stars and the moon—and finally the daytime sky, and the sun and its light. The downward path of *noesis* discerned how the forms depended from the good (511b–c), and so here the one who has risen up to a vision of the sun reverses direction and perceives how the sun is the source of the seasons and the years, presiding over everything in the visible realm, and in a way the cause of everything that they have seen (516b–c).

Later Socrates concludes that people are wrong about the nature of education who say that they can put knowledge (*episteme*) into the soul of someone who lacks it, as if they were inserting vision into blind eyes (although Socrates does not say so, that model is closer to what the puppeteers do, a condition that Socrates calls a *lack* of education: 514a2). It would be more accurate to compare education to an eye that cannot be turned to the light from the darkness except by turning the whole body. In the same way rationality ("the instrument with which we learn") must be turned around together with the entire soul, from the realm of becoming, until it is able to endure the contemplation of what is, and what is brightest of what is, namely the good (518b–c). Since this kind of knowledge follows from the turning in unison of the entire soul, when it is achieved the soul cannot be divided against itself, and the need for self-control that figured so strongly in Book 4 evaporates.[53] That is why the analysis of virtue in Book 4 had only provisional value. At the level of *noesis* it is superseded, and Socratic claim that "virtue is knowledge" is vindicated when this kind of knowledge is achieved.

> The other so-called virtues of the soul, on one hand, are somewhat close to those of the body, for they were not really present beforehand, but are produced by habit and training. While intellectual virtue (ἡ δὲ τοῦ φρονῆσαι), on the other, seems to be more divine rather than anything else. Its power is never destroyed, but depending on which way it is turned it becomes useful and ben-

eficial or useless and harmful. Or have you never noticed about those who are said to be evil but wise, how keenly and sharply their petty soul perceives the things toward which it is turned, so there is nothing wrong with its vision except that they are forced to serve evil, and thus the more sharply it sees, the more it accomplishes evil. [518d–519a]

Here again we see why those natures which have the greatest potential for good also have the greatest potential for evil.

When the former prisoner who has come to understand the true nature of reality sees the prisoners priding themselves and honoring each other for their ability to conform to unexamined socially imposed conceptions of reality, he will no longer envy them but, on the contrary, would "go through any sufferings, rather than share their opinions and live as they do" (516d). Just as Socrates will. Socrates adds ominously that when someone returns to the cave from divine contemplation, whose eyes are not accustomed to the darkness, he will seem awkward and ridiculous if he must testify in court or anywhere else, about shadows and images of justice, in front of people who have never seen justice itself.[54] A reasonable person will distinguish between the blindness of those who cannot see the light because they are accustomed to the dark, and those who cannot see in the dark because they are accustomed to the light.

This brings us back to the paradox of the philosopher-ruler: if philosophers have difficulty seeing the socially constructed reality of the city clearly, how can they function effectively as rulers, and how can they love a city (412d) that they cannot really see? Socrates assures us that when their eyes are reaccustomed to the dark they will see immeasurably better than the cave dwellers (520c), but it is not clear how that is possible, or how in that case they would still be able to see the light of truth, given that each blinds us to the other.

Aristotle points out that since experience comprises many memories of individuals, while *episteme* knows only universals, "with regard to practical matters . . . those with experience are more successful than those who have a rational understanding without experience . . . [for] practical matters and processes are concerned with individuals".[55] What Aristotle means by experience (ἐμπείρια) is the kind of thinking exhibited by the residents of the cave, which sees reality in terms of individuals rather than forms. But Socrates' philosophers are weaned away from this kind of thinking rather than nurtured in it. How can they govern a world of particulars, when they aim to leave behind their practical skill in matters of particularity for an intellectual skill in an exclusively formal realm where even its downward path "makes use of nothing perceived by the senses" (511b–c)? Plato is not blind to this problem, for it proves to be the eventual undoing of the kallipolis, the beautiful or noble city. The city will inevitably decline, Socrates says, because "although they are wise, those who you have educated to be rulers in the city still won't, by using rationality *together with sense perception*, hit upon the [moments of] fertility and barrenness of your race" and so they will produce inferior rulers in the next generation (546a–b; emphasis added). The problem extends to all aspects of governing, for no matter how wise and rational the rulers are, they will always have to employ their rationality "together with sense perception". Since moving from the light to the darkness produces blindness, the bright light of their wisdom may blind them to the realm of sense perception more than anyone else in the city.

The difficulty arises not only for the philosophy of the *Republic*, but for the classical conception of philosophy generally. A similar tension can be found in Aristotle when he insists that philosophy at its most distinctive is also the most useless kind of knowledge, but nevertheless the one that is most capable of governing[56]—an echo of *Republic* 487e. Or when on the one hand he compares philosophy favorably with statesmanship precisely because it has no practical application, while on the other he claims that philosophy is what most enables us to become good legislators.[57] The common source of these paradoxes in Plato and Aristotle is the belief that metaphysical philosophy can somehow make us more effective in concrete life.[58] Consequently, the importance of our question is not limited to exegetical concerns, but it is ultimately the question of the relevance of philosophy to life.

Notes

1. Cf. 472b.

2. Aristotle, *Metaphysics* A. 1. 981a12–17. *Techne* is rational knowledge because, although it is concerned with practice rather than theory, it is based on universal teachable principles.

3. Aristotle, *Rhetoric* 1391a7–12.

4. On the self-reliance of wisdom see Aristotle, *Metaphysics* A.2, *Nicomachean Ethics* 10.7.

5. Cf. *Gorgias* 462b–c, *Phaedrus* 259e–260a.

6. Adam (1963 [1902]) suggests this may be a reference to Dion (30).

7. The literal meaning of *metriōs* is "moderate" or "measured"; the translation that would capture both its literal and idiomatic sense would be the archaic adjective "meet".

8. In the *Theaetetus* Theodorus praises Theaetetus' ability to unite these apparently opposite virtues in himself in a way that otherwise "I would not have supposed to exist, nor do I see it. Rather, those who are as sharp as he is, and quick and with reten-

tive memories, are also for the most part quick-tempered, . . . manic rather than courageous. Those, on the other hand, who are more sedate are also somewhat sluggish when they come up against their studies, and are forgetful" (144a–b).

9. Kenneth Sayre argues that the unhypothetical principle is not the Idea of the good but "the interconnected field of eternal Forms" (*Plato's Literary Garden: How to Read a Platonic Dialogue* [Notre Dame: University of Notre Dame Press], 1995, 178). The Divided Line has both an ontological side (509d–510a) and a psychological side (511d–e). Sayre's explanation can account for the psychological side—"nothing is left to the mind's surmise when the field of Forms is finally grasped in its full interconnectedness" (81)—but it does not explain the ontological sense of "unhypothetical", (i.e., the ground of the forms' necessary existence) (509b).

10. ἡ τοῦ ἀγαθοῦ ἰδέα, 505a. Although I translate *idea* and *eidos* as "Idea" and "form", respectively, I see no evidence in Plato of a consistent distinction between them. For example, when Socrates spoke of the Idea of the beautiful (479a), the Idea of the being of each thing (486d), or the Ideas generally (507c), the term seems interchangeable with "form". Plato was not one to formulate a precise technical terminology—we have already seen several appearances of *eidos* (form) in a non-technical sense (e.g., 357c, 363e–364a, 369a, 435e), and there are similar instances of *idea* (for example, 369a, 380d, 508a). In some places the two are used interchangeably, as at *Euthyphro* 6d–e. The choice of two different terms for forms/Ideas may even be meant to minimize any appearance of a systematic technical vocabulary.

11. For example, *Protagoras* 345e, *Meno* 77b–e. Cf. Aristotle: "Every *techne* and every inquiry, and similarly every action and decision seems to aim at some good" (*Nicomachean Ethics* 1.1.1094a1–2).

12. Also see Francisco Gonzalez's discussion in *Dialectic and Dialogue: Plato's Practice of Philosophical Inquiry* (Evanston, Ill.: Northwestern University Press, 1998), 209–17.

13. The noun φρόνησις is normally translated in Plato as "wisdom", but in the previous paragraph the verbal form φρονεῖν meant "know".

14. Forms of μαντεύομαι recur at 506a6 and a8. Also see Howland's discussion (1993, 125–27).

15. Cf. *Meno*, 97a–b.

16. Also see 509c.

17. In Shorey's translation, "We predicate 'to be' of many beautiful things and many good things, saying of them severally that they *are*" (1935, 97; emphasis in original).

18. In his discussion of the objects that correspond to the Divided Line, Nettleship (1901) writes, "we should divest ourselves of the notion that they represent four different classes of real objects; they only represent four different views of the world, or different aspects of the same objects. . . . The sensible triangle is the 'intelligible triangle' *plus* certain properties other than triangularity" (239 and 251). There are important differences between Plato and Aristotle, but important correspondences as well.

19. For a different view see Sprague 1976, who argues that knowledge of the good is a kind of *techne* (91).

20. The passage trades on the fact that *tokos* means both "child" and "interest" on a loan. The wordplay is itself an image of the relationship between an original (the literal meaning of *tokos* as "child") and an image (the parent-child relation as an image of the principal-interest relation).

21. Although here Socrates claims that no comparable third thing is necessary for hearing, in the *Timaeus* it is recognized that air functions in that way (67b).

22. This line has been interpreted in a variety of different ways. See, for example, Glenn Rawson, "Knowledge and Desire of the Good in Plato's *Republic*", *Southwest Philosophy Review* 12 (1966): 103–115, esp. 111; N. White 1979, 181; Gadamer 1986, 84–101; Gerasimos Santas, "Plato's Idea of the Good", in Giovanni Reale and Samuel Scolnikov, eds., *New Images of Plato: Dialogues on the Idea of the Good* (Sankt Augustin: Academia Verlag, 2002), 359–78; Lloyd Gerson, "The development of the doctrine of the Good and Plato's development", *ibid.* 379–91; Christopher Gill, "A critical response to the hermeneutic approach from an analytic perspective", *ibid.* 211–22.

23. The reference to Apollo may have further significance. "We know that 'Apollo' was the symbolic name by means of which the Pythagoreans referred to the One [Plotinus, *Enneads* V5, 6]. And, etymologically, when it is broken down into 'a' as the privative prefix and 'πολλόν', meaning the many, the whole would mean the 'not many'" (Giovanni Reale, "The One-Good as the load-bearing concept in Plato's protology", in Reale and Scolnicov 2002, 29–48, esp. 35).

24. When in the *Theaetetus* Socrates gives a definition of the sun (208d), that does not show the sun to belong to the realm of intelligible, knowable, realities, for the purported definition is nothing more than a description ("the brightest of the heavenly bodies that revolve around the earth"), as if we defined Theaetetus by saying that he is the tallest person in the room. The essential nature is never determined.

25. In the *Timaeus* the sun exists from the beginning of the world (39b), but both this claim and the claim that the world had a beginning are ambiguous, given the mythical presentation of the material. Plato does not seem to believe that anything visible can be ungenerated (e.g., *Republic*, 508d, *Phaedo*, 79a).

26. For an argument to the contrary see Josef Seifert, "The Idea of the Good as the sum total of pure perfections: A new personalist reading of *Republic* VI and VII", in Reale and Scolnicov 2002, 407–24, esp. 413–18.

27. This limited sense of emanationism requires nothing beyond the ontological implications of Nettleship's account: "The reality of things is what they mean; what they mean is determined by their place in the order of the world; what determines their place in the order of the world is the supreme good, the principle of that order. Thus their very being is determined by that order" (1901, 230–31).

28. Not everyone takes this latter passage to be a reference to the forms. We will consider that passage when we come to it, but for now all that needs to be noted is that since the forms are often called divine, the term "heaven" is ambiguous and could refer either to the visible realm of the sun or the intelligible realm of the good. The remark in the present passage about playing the sophist is usually taken to refer

to some sort of word play, although precisely what sort is a matter of dispute. See Reeve, 1992, 183n25.

29. *Noesis* can be translated as "intellection", *dianoia* as "thought", *pistis* as "conviction" or "belief", and *eikasia* as "image-thinking" or "surmise", but translators render them in different and sometimes incompatible ways (some translators, for example, use "understanding" for *noesis*, while others use it for *dianoia*). Since there is no consensus either about what the terms refer to or how to translate them, it seems better simply to transliterate the terms and allow their meanings to emerge from the discussion.

30. A good sense of the variety of interpretations, apart from what will emerge from our discussions below, may be seen in Nicholas Smith's comprehensive discussion: "Plato's Divided Line", *Ancient Philosophy* 16 (1996): 25–46.

31. Such views were already common a century ago, as J. L. Stocks witnesses in "The Divided Line of *Plato Rep. VI*", *Classical Quarterly* 6 (1912): 73–78, esp. 75. More recently they have been championed by Murphy 1951, 156–64, and Annas 1981, 248–49, 255. David Roochnik argues, following Jacob Klein (*A Commentary on Plato's Meno* [Chapel Hill: University of North Carolina Press], 1965), that since no one would ever confuse these things with reality, *eikasia* means seeing an image as an image—not being deceived by an image ("Images as Images: Commentary on Smith", in John Cleary and Gary Gurtler, eds., *Proceedings of the Boston Area Colloquium in Ancient Philosophy*, Vol. XIII [Leiden: Brill, 1999], 205–9, esp. 205–6; also see Howland 1993, 129–31). In that case we could not take the allegory of the cave to be an illustration of the Divided Line, since *eikasia* would be represented by prisoners who have no conception that the shadows they are seeing are images rather than realities. The relation between the Line and the cave is controversial and will be discussed below.

32. As does the sophist, according to the Eleatic visitor (*Sophist*, 234b–235d).

33. In the *Phaedo* Socrates similarly compares the investigation of reality by looking at words, to looking at the reflection of an eclipse in water (99d–e)—although since the reality he is referring to there is intelligible, what he has in mind is the relation between *dianoia* and *noesis*, rather than the analogous relationship between *eikasia* and *pistis*. Both of those relationships are in the same proportion as the relationship between knowledge (*dianoia* and *noesis*) and opinion (*eikasia* and *pistis*). Cross and Woozley (1964) point out that at 476c Socrates described

> the non-philosopher who believes in the existence of beautiful things, but not of Beauty itself and the other Forms . . . as leading a dreaming life. He there explains what he means by 'dreaming' as 'thinking what is like something not to be like it but to be the thing itself, which it is like', i.e. taking the likeness for the original. Next, at 533b the mathematician, in his attitude to his hypotheses or assumptions [i.e. *dianoia*], is described as 'dreaming about being'. . . . [It follows from the proportions of the Line that] the man in the state of *eikasia* does the same. [219]

Recognition of the significance of the dreaming metaphor goes back at least to W. F. R. Hardie (*A Study in Plato* [Oxford: Clarendon Press, 1936]); see J. L. Austin, "The Line and the Cave in Plato's *Republic*", *Philosophical Papers*, 3rd edition (Oxford: Oxford University Press, 1979). Austin himself takes *eikasia* to refer to sense-data (297–98). Reeve (1987) similarly takes *eikasia* to refer to the objects of "perceptual thought" or qualities (56); as does Desjardins (2004), who identifies them with the phenomenal images that we perceive before we posit external objects as their cause (56–68). This line of interpretation is plausible insofar as the Divided Line alone is concerned, but if the Divided Line is illustrated by the cave, that interpretation could not account for the role of the puppeteers, or the prisoners' resistance to being turned around.

34. Also see Robinson, who provides a useful survey and discussion of the various ways this passage has been interpreted (1953, 160–79, esp. 163). For a more recent survey see Gonzalez 1998, 220–34. In taking dialectic to mean moving to hypotheses that have greater explanatory power, I agree with the usual view that when Socrates subsequently describes this as "destroying the hypotheses" (533c) he means destroying their hypothetical character by deriving them from a higher principle. The fact that "for the mathematicians the 'hypotheses' do not have hypothetical character but are first principles", does not seem to me to be problematic as it does to Gonzalez (1998, 238) because they are hypothetical whether the mathematicians realize it or not.

35. "On the other hand if anyone . . . does not admit the existence of forms of things or mark off a form under which each individual thing is classed, he will not have anything on which to fix his thoughts . . . and in this way he will utterly destroy the power of discourse" (135b–c).

36. For a discussion of the relationship between the ruler in the *Statesman* and the *Republic* see my article, "Philosopher-Rulers: How Contemplation Becomes Action", *Ancient Philosophy* 21 (2001): 335–56, esp. 346–53.

37. One type of solution that has been proposed depends on the fact that the two segments turn out to be the same size (see the demonstrations in Adam 1963 [1902], 64; and Klein 1965, 119n27; Smith gives a detailed survey of the issue: 1996, 31, 40–42). Although some have suggested that this consequence was neither intended nor recognized by Plato (e.g., Anders Wedberg, *Plato's Philosophy of Mathematics* [Stockholm: Almqvist & Wiksell, 1955], 102–3), Desjardins points out that "on the two separate occasions [510a, 534a] on which he spells out the proportion, he switches the two central sections which he could do only if they were equal" (2004, 84). The equality of the middle segments, it is sometimes argued, may mean that the objects of *dianoia* are at the same ontological level as those of *pistis*. But even so, there is disagreement about what those objects are. Smith (1996) proposes that the objects both of *dianoia* and *pistis* are physical things, although *dianoia* takes them as images of abstract objects. This conflicts, however, with Socrates' statement that although *dianoia* makes use of visible images, its object is not those images but "that of which they are images; they produce an account for the sake of the square itself and the diagonal itself, rather than the ones

they draw" (510d). Smith acknowledges two further difficulties. First, his interpretation violates the stipulation that the objects of the lower level be images of the objects of the higher; in his view both are visible objects at the same level. He replies that the cave's portrayal of *pistis* as puppets or statues is not an image of its portrayal of *dianoia* as shadows and reflections; rather, statues and shadows are both images of physical things. Granted, a statue is not an image of a shadow but of the thing itself, but it is nevertheless at a further remove from the thing than the reflection is, because human intervention is added. In fact, painting and sculpture were thought to have had their origin in the tracing of shadows, a view that is documented as early as Pliny (see *Natural History* 35.15 and 35.43; and Victor I. Stoichita, *A Short History of the Shadow* [London: Reaktion, 1997], ch. 1). The other difficulty that Smith acknowledges is that his account leaves us with only three levels—forms, things, images of things—instead of the four that the Line and cave lead us to expect (Smith 1999, 203n16). J. S. Morrison similarly argues that the objects of *dianoia* and *pistis* are on the same level but seen in different ways; however for him the objects are "common characteristics" ("Two Unresolved Difficulties in the Line and the cave", *Phronesis* 22 [1977]: 212–31). But since common characteristics are recognized by the mind rather than the senses, they cannot be present on the visible side of the Divided Line. Vassilis Karasmanis suggests that "*pistis* and *dianoia* deal with mathematics. But while the objects of *pistis* are visible diagrams, etc., the objects of *dianoia* are intelligible (Forms)" ("Plato's *Republic*: The Line and the cave", *Apeiron* 21 [1988]: 147–71, esp. 164). On that view, however, physical things (which would be the objects of *eikasia*) would be images of visible diagrams.

38. Reeve gives a comparatively recent defense of "mathematicals" (called "figures": 1987, 55 & n.9 [287]), but rather than showing how they are images of forms or how the objects of *pistis* are images of them, he leaves "figures" (*dianoia*) out, when he writes: "The quality [*eikasia*] of F minimally resembles F, the mode [*pistis*] of F resembles F to a somewhat higher degree, and the form [*noesis*] of F completely resembles F itself" (64). Neil Cooper documents Plato's use generally of *dianoetic* thinking in non-mathematical contexts ("The Importance of *ΔIANOIA* in Plato's Theory of Forms", *Classical Quarterly* New Series 16 [1966]: 65–69). Also see Guthrie 1975.3 509 and n.2, and Smith's detailed survey of the "mathematicals" interpretation and other proposals (1996, 35–37).

39. See, for example, Austin 1979, 301; and David Gallop, "Image and Reality in Plato's *Republic*", *Archiv für Begriffsgeschichte* 47 (1965): 113–31. Although the Austin chapter was not published until 1979, it was reconstructed from material written in the 1930s and 1940s, and Gallop's 1965 paper was based on Austin's interpretation (Gallop n.1).

40. Gomperz writes that for Plato "all that is given in experience counts as a hindrance and a barrier to be broken through. . . . The highest abstractions possess for our sobered thought no more than the widest sphere of validity; Plato, with the fever of altitudes upon him, overlooks the poverty of their content, and invests them with supreme worth and supreme reality" (1905, 88–89). But the passages quoted above show that Plato was indeed aware of both the value of empirical explanations—which

214   Chapter Six

is not a hindrance and barrier but a stage on the way to something more adequate—and the apparent poverty of formal explanations when left at their simplest level. Cf. Taylor 1956 (1926): "because it is the source of all *reality*, every predicate which expresses a 'positive perfection' must, in its degree, characterize the source of all 'perfections'. . . . All we gain by knowledge of the 'detail' of the universe must add to and enrich our conception of the source of reality" (287–88; emphasis in original).

41. See, for example, *Euthyphro* 6d–7c.

42. Or even that Plato deliberately introduces it in stages: cf. Charles Kahn, *Plato and the Socratic Dialogue: The Philosophical Use of a Literary Form* (Cambridge: Cambridge University Press, 1996).

43. Cf. *Symposium* 205e–206a, *Phaedo* 99c, *Republic* 6.509b, *Phaedrus* 245e, *Philebus* 13e, 15a, *Timaeus* 29e.

44. Not everyone agrees. Richard Robinson, for example, points out that there are transitional moments in the allegory of the cave that are not mentioned in the Divided Line (1953, ch. 11). But we have seen that transitional stages between the categories of the Line have been illustrated throughout the dialogue. The choice of a continuous line would have been a strange metaphor for Socrates to choose if he did not want to suggest transitional stages. Thus Nettleship writes, "Plato, in choosing this symbol, may have wishes to express the continuity of the process which it represents" (1901, 238); and David Ross points out that they are ranged on a *continuum* of greater or lesser clarity (*Plato's Theory of Ideas* [Oxford: Clarendon Press, 1951], 48), followed by Annas (1981, 249–50). Irwin, after matching up the stages of the cave with those of the Line, writes: "The cave . . . sets out to show how someone can progress through the different stages it distinguishes, and so it ought to illustrate how someone can progress through the different stages of the Line" (1995, 275). For additional discussion see J. Malcolm, "The Line and the Cave", *Phronesis* 7 (1962): 38–45; Cross and Woozley 1964, 208–28. So vexed is the question of the relation of the cave to the Line that it is the one question on which Cross and Woozley could not reach an agreement with each other (227–28).

45. A function that is not treated thematically until the *Timaeus*, but insofar as soul is the principle of rational motion that makes possible the participation of corporeality in form, the conception seems to be implicit in the *Phaedrus* (245c–e) and *Phaedo* (69e–72e). On the latter, see Dorter 1982, 40–43.

46. As Miguel Lizano-Ordovás puts it, the Line is epistemological ("*erkenntnistheoretisch*") and the cave ethical-political ("'Eikasia' und 'Pistis' in Platons Höhlengleichnis", *Zeitschrift für philosophische Forschung* 49 [1995]: 378–97, esp. 379). Cf. Lachterman: "The image of the Sun pictures the *knowing* soul. . . . The image of the Divided Line pictures the *learning* soul. . . . The image of the cave pictures the *embodied* or *political* soul" (1989–1990, 155).

47. Perhaps the best known today is the Indonesian puppet theater tradition, but Guthrie writes, "It looks too as if Plato's Greece was familiar with puppet shadowshows like the modern Turkish Karagöz playlets, reintroduced into Greece under their Turkish name" (1975, vol. 3, 518).

48. Here the living things function as illustrations of *dianoia*, whereas in the Divided Line they were illustrations of *pistis*. Perhaps it is only a coincidence that this parallels the fact that in the Divided Line *dianoia* and *pistis* are the same size.

49. Commentators generally take the puppeteers to represent one or more of these groups. It is difficult to see what they would represent on the view that the shadows represent something like sense-data (assuming the shadows in the cave to correspond to those of the Divided Line). Cf. the end of n.33 above.

50. Unlike the prisoners, who are at the level of *eikasia*, the puppeteers are at that of *pistis*, the level that the dialogue had reached when the noble lie was introduced in Book 3.

51. Cf. Shorey 1935, 124n.a.

52. E.g., *Gorgias* 513c, *Republic* 487b–c.

53. For additional discussion of the unity of knowledge and will in Plato, see: Horace Fries, "Virtue is Knowledge", *Philosophy of Science* 8 (1940): 89–99, esp. 91 & n.5; Emile de Stryker, "The Unity of Knowledge and Love in Socrates's Conception of Virtue", *International Philosophical Quarterly* 6 (1966), 428–44, esp. 440–41; A. O. Rorty, "Plato and Aristotle on Belief, Habit, and *Akrasia*", *American Philosophical Quarterly* 7 (1970): 50–61, esp. 52, and "The Limits of Socratic Intellectualism: Did Socrates Teach Arete?", in Cleary 1987, 317–330, esp. 320; Samuel Scolnicov, "Reason and Passion in the Platonic Soul", *Dionysus* 2 (1978): 35–49, esp. 45, and *Plato's Metaphysics of Education* (London: Routledge, 1988), 102 and 112; Frederick Rosen, "Contemplation and Virtue in Plato", *Religious Studies* 16 (1980): 85–95, 933; Annas 1981, 237. Because for Plato knowing transforms us and is more than believing a proposition to be true, it cannot be the case that "he would accept the view that true belief . . . if it is a firm conviction, would be sufficient for acting justly" (Gerasimos Santas, "The Socratic Paradoxes", in Alexander Sesonske and Noel Fleming, eds., *Plato's Meno: Text and Criticism* [Belmont, Calif.: Wadsworth, 1965], 62). Also compare the arguments of Wang Yang-ming for the unity of knowledge and action (1963, 10, 82). Cf. *The Great Learning* § 6, on which Wang is commenting (in Wing-tsit Chan, *A Source Book in Chinese Philosophy* [Princeton: Princeton University Press, 1963], 89).

54. The point is put even more strongly at *Theaetetus* 174b–175b, which abounds in echoes of this passage.

55. *Metaphysics* 980b28–981a17.

56. *Metaphysics* A.1.981b13–25 and A.2.982a14–19.

57. *Nicomachean Ethics* 10.7.1177b1–25 and 10.9.1180b28–1181a23.

58. Also see Elizabeth Cooke, "The Moral and Intellectual Development of the Philosopher in Plato's *Republic*", *Ancient Philosophy* 1999 (19): 37–44. By contrast, George Klosko writes that practical wisdom "is not to be gained from studying metaphysics" (1986, 163).

CHAPTER SEVEN

~

Philosopher-Rulers
(Book 7 from 519b)

Compulsion to Rule (519b–521b)

We now come to the problem that has shadowed our investigation since the
unification of philosophy and ruling was first proposed in Book 5: how to reconcile the essential movement of philosophy away from the material world
with the need of ruling to engage with that world. Those who fail to escape
the cave and to apprehend the good would have only limited success as rulers
because they lack the single goal at which all that they do must aim; but those
who succeed would be unwilling to engage in practical activity, thinking that
they had reached the Isles of the Blessed while still alive (519b–c). Socrates
reiterates that they must compel the best natures to attain the highest knowledge, since the prisoners balk at each new level of ascent until their eyes
adjust to the brighter light, and now he adds that they must not be allowed to
remain in the Isles of the Blessed but must be compelled to serve as rulers
(519c–520a). The need for compulsion was mentioned when the concept of
philosopher-rulers was first introduced (those who pursue philosophy or ruling separately must be compelled to combine them: 473d), and was already
prefigured in Book 1 when Socrates said that the best natures will not want to
rule for money or power, but only under compulsion (347c3) in the fear of
being ruled by their inferiors.[1] When Glaucon objects, like many readers
since, that it would be unjust to require the philosophers to live a worse life,
Socrates replies that Glaucon has forgotten that the aim of the city is not to
make a single class outstandingly happy, but to make the city as a whole as

217

happy as possible (519e)—"forgotten" because Adeimantus had raised a similar objection in Book 4 and received a similar answer (419a–420d).

There are two antithetical criticisms of the *Republic*. One is that it is a proto-fascist state in which the general populace is forced to serve the interests of the ruling class;[2] the other is that the city unfairly exploits not the subjects but the rulers, and cannot have been a serious proposal by Plato.[3] In response to the former criticism, it should be clear from the present passage and its antecedent in Book 4 that there is no question of the rulers ruling for their own greatest advantage; the intention of the city is that everyone be able to pursue their natural proclivity with as much support and as little interference as possible, setting only such limitations on it are as necessary to make it compatible with the others. Those, on the other hand, who claim that the city is unjust to its rulers take justice to mean getting the greatest possible advantage, but nowhere in Plato is justice understood to mean getting as much for oneself as possible. In support of their charge they point out that if people who understand the good do not want to rule, and must be compelled to do so, then it cannot be a good thing. But it is important to notice that the compulsion does not take the form of force but only of reminding them of their indebtedness. It is the compulsion of reason:

> We will say, "You have received a better and more complete education than the others, and are more able to participate in both realms. You must take your turn at going down then to the common dwelling place of the others and accustom yourselves to see the things in the dark . . ." Do you think that those whom we have nurtured will disobey us and refuse to share in the labors of the city?
>
> Impossible, for we shall be imposing just behavior onto just people. [520b–e]

This is one instance when Cephalus' definition of justice (331b–c) does apply: it is just to repay one's debts.[4] The argument resembles the argument of the Laws in the *Crito* (50a–52d) that persuades Socrates that his duty to the city that nurtured him compels him to submit to the punishment it imposed on him. In neither case does compulsion mean forcing someone to do something against their will. In both cases it is a matter of making them aware of something that they may not have considered. Contemplation of the good is not in itself enough to get the philosophers to recognize their practical obligation because *noesis* is always at the level of forms, not individuals (511b–c), so the obligation to other people must be introduced to them from outside. But once it is pointed out to them they will not refuse because "we shall be imposing just behavior onto just people". There is no talk of coercion by threats or force but only of persuasion.[5]

Sacrifice or Completion?

Do the philosophers sacrifice, or even defer, their self-interest when they are compelled to rule, or is compulsion necessary here for the same reason that it was necessary at every stage of liberation from the cave, namely that we do not always recognize when changing our way of life will benefit us? We have certainly seen evidence in favor of the first alternative. If justice in Book 4 means "having and doing one's own and what belongs to one" (433e–434a), and the philosopher-rulers will be compelled to surrender the contemplative life that belongs to them, it is understandable that Glaucon fears that they are treated unjustly (519d).[6] In fact, in accordance with the principle of the "third kind of wage" (347c), if any of them were not reluctant to rule it would seem to be a sign that they cared too much about power or money.[7] But perhaps there is another side to the matter.

Before introducing the need to compel philosophers to return to the cave to govern (520c–d), Socrates reminded his audience that they had to be compelled to leave the cave in the first place (519c). How are the two compulsions related to each other? Of the two blindnesses, our blindness to the light as a result of dwelling in darkness is a bad condition, while our blindness to the dark as a result of dwelling in the light is a good one. Are the two compulsions related in the same way—the compulsion to leave the cave good for those who are compelled, and the compulsion to return bad for them? Or is it possible that with respect to the compulsions, unlike the blindnesses, in both cases our resistance turns out to be misguided, and that even though we may think that it is against our personal advantage to return to the cave, we may discover otherwise as we proceed, just as the reluctant prisoners did on the way up? The two kinds of compulsion on the prisoner to ascend and on the philosopher to rule are similar, at least insofar as force is prohibited in both cases: just as the compulsion on the philosophers to rule took the form of persuasion rather than force, so too in the case of the education that raises the prisoners up from the cave, "because a free person ought not to learn any study slavishly . . . turn the children to these studies not by force but by play" (536e). The oligarchs of Book 8, by contrast, are unreliable precisely "because they were educated not by persuasion but by force" (548b).[8] But whether the philosopher-rulers also resemble the prisoners in benefiting personally from the compulsion that is put on them (515c–e, 519c–d, 540a) remains to be seen.

It is often claimed that to have a vision of the highest truth is only the first stage of wisdom, and that wisdom can be consummated only by integrating that vision into the lived world. Bergson, for example, believed that the return from contemplation of a higher reality to the world of action is simply the completion of that contemplation, and that no one is a "complete mystic" who, like Plotinus, believes that "action is a weakening of contemplation".[9] This view has been attributed to Plato as well. It has been argued, for example, that "Plato is no champion of a mere *vita contemplativa* divorced from practical social activity. . . . [For] the Good is only seen by the man who *lives* it",[10] and that what counts as fulfillment is not whether we contemplate the forms but whether we imitate them, and the contemplative state is one kind of imitation, but ruling justly is another.[11] Algazali, on the other hand, like Plotinus, testified that his contemplative vocation and his familial duties were mutually inhibiting.[12] Every contemplative tradition divides into one school that supports Plotinus and Algazali's claims, and another that supports Bergson and Taylor's. In Hinduism it is the difference between *Dhyana* yoga and *Karma* yoga, in Buddhism between *Theravada* and *Mahayana*, and in Christianity between the anchorite tradition and the ministry tradition. Dov Baer, one the earliest Hassidic rabbis, remarks that "There are two kinds of righteous men. Some spend their time on mankind. They teach them and take trouble about them. Others concern themselves only with the teachings themselves. The first bear nourishing fruit, like the date-palm; the second are like the cedar: lofty and unfruitful".[13]

The problem of reconciling the apparently antithetical claims of contemplation and practice is a persistent one in Plato's dialogues. Already in the *Ion* Plato has the rhapsode admit that when he is performing Homer, on one hand he believes he is present in Homer's world (535b–c), but at the same time he is carefully watching the reactions of his present audience (535e). Like the philosopher-ruler, the rhapsode must combine the contemplation of one reality with a practical attention to a different reality and the need to minister to the public. The same tension lies behind the apparent disunity of the *Phaedrus*, the first half of which is devoted to the erotic ascent to a vision of truth, and the second to the techniques of rhetoric by which that vision can be communicated. The *Phaedo* too begins with a tension between our natural vocation toward the intelligible, according to which we ought to welcome an escape from corporeal life, and our responsibilities to the corporeal world (61b–63a). Does this pervasive tension mean that our duties to the practical world are simply distractions from our contemplative vocation, and that the philosopher-rulers not only follow Cephalus' justice of repaying our debts, but also Thrasymachus' justice of sacrificing our own good for the good of another?

On the other hand, Socrates says later that the person who most knows the value of a particular flute is neither the one who makes it nor the one who paints a picture of it, but the one who puts it to use (601c–602c). If we can have knowledge of the goodness of something only by putting it into practice, does it follow that the philosophers' contemplative knowledge of the good too remains incomplete if it is not translated into action? In the *Ion* passage above, the rhapsode was both intensely present at the imagined events he was contemplating through Homer, and also intensely aware of the performance he was giving himself. The intensity of his contemplation was not something he achieved in spite of distractions from the audience, but rather, as performers regularly find, the presence of the audience in some paradoxical way enhances the ability to contemplate the work being performed. Live performances of music tend to be more revelatory than studio productions because performers' consciousness of the audience can intensify their concentration on the music, at least as much as it may distract them in other respects. Teachers, too, know that the best way to understand a subject or author is to teach it, and that reading a book with an audience in mind focuses us on it more intently, rather than distracting us from the deepest elements of the work, because we are reading it with the practical end in view of how to present the material most clearly to others. The consciousness of these practical exigencies intensifies rather than distracts from our insight into the subject. It turns out not only that accustoming ourselves to the light of the intelligible ultimately enhances our ability to see in the darkness of the corporeal (520c), but that the return to the corporeal may also enhance our ability to discern the intelligible. It is conceivable, then, that although the philosophers' return to the cave may seem to be a sacrifice of their contemplative vocation, it may turn out instead to be a furthering of it. It may be that the compulsion that must be set upon them to rule is indeed like the compulsion that had to be set upon them to bring them out of the cave: an unwelcome but ultimately advantageous disruption.

Nevertheless, Socrates says "it is fitting that people like this who come about in other cities do not take part in the labors there, for they grow spontaneously, from no volition of the regimes in those cases" (520b). If their abstention from politics is fitting because the contemplative life is always preferable to the active life when there is no obligation to the contrary, it would imply that philosophers really do sacrifice their self-interest when they rule. But their abstention may be fitting only in the sense that in other cities it would not constitute an act of ingratitude, or even because in any other kind of city they could not participate in government without becoming involved in injustices.[14] It is not clear, then, that Plato is allied with Plotinus on this question, nor is it clear that he is not. We can only say that the compulsion on philosophers to rule need not be construed in merely negative terms, as a sacrifice without intrinsic benefit. If the practical application of their wisdom increases their access to one source of wisdom, even as it limits their access to another, the city would not be depriving the philosophers of their true vocation by making them rule. In other words, Plato may agree that there is intrinsic value in both the contemplative and the service traditions, and that even though those who lose themselves in contemplation may not lack completion the way Bergson claimed, those who combine their contemplation with practice may not lack a certain kind of completion of their own.

The Role of *Techne* in Escaping the Cave (521b–535a)

Since Socrates has shown himself to be aware of the problem of reconciling the opposition between the visible and intelligible realms, he must believe that his proposed educational system will help overcome the paradox at the heart of the third wave, the synthesis of philosophy and ruling. But the primary focus in the middle books is on the *attainment* of wisdom, rather than on its subsequent employment in the world of action, and the solution of that paradox is assumed without being explained. An explanation is, however, implied: *techne* is what creates the bridge between the intelligible and practical realms that enables us not only to move from the practical realm of visible entities to the contemplative realm of intelligible entities, but also to function subsequently within the practical realm without abandoning the intelligible one. Since the bridging character of *techne* is more evident in the transition from the practical to the intelligible—the education of the philosopher-rulers—let us begin by examining how it operates in that direction.

The previous educational curriculum is no longer adequate, since it comprised only physical training and the arts. Physical training is confined to the body and consequently cannot elevate us out of the cave of visible things that come into being and pass away; the arts, on the other hand, educated the children by inculcating habits rather than knowledge, so although they can make us harmonious, they do not arouse the intellect (521e–522a). *Techne* does not at first seem any more promising,

> for we thought that all the *technai* were vulgar[15]. . . . But if we are unable to take anything else outside of these, let's take something that applies to all of them.
>   What?
>   This thing in common that is employed by every *techne*, *dianoia*, and *episteme* . . . [is] the humble matter of distinguishing the one and the two and the three. I mean, in short, number and calculation. [522b–c]

Accordingly, the transition from the original warrior-guardians to the philosopher-rulers is effected by a series of mathematical *technai* designed to awaken the students to the intelligible foundation of visible reality. The mathematical character of these studies has both a purgative and a cognitive aspect. The purgative aspect is the ability of mathematical thinking to turn us away from the potentially corrupting world of appetite: whereas "all other kinds of *techne* are directed to human opinion and appetites, or generation and composition, or to serving things that grow and things that are put together" (533b), mathematical studies are directed to knowledge rather than opinion, and to what is incomposite and eternal. Since they are eternal, they cannot be objects of appetite.[16] When we focus on mathematical reality, we learn to recognize the insubstantiality of corporeal, composite, mutable things, and this limits our appetites for them.

The terms *techne* and *episteme* are sometimes used interchangeably because both refer to thinking that is based on concepts or rational principles,[17] but *techne* is a species of *episteme* which also includes practical utility.[18] Thus the *Republic* will shortly use "*techne*" especially for knowledge directed toward practical utility, and limit "*episteme*" to knowledge that is primarily intellectual (533e7–8). At this point, however, there is no distinction because "*techne*" is being employed in its maximum extension in order to bridge the division between the visible and intelligible realms. That can be accomplished only by a kind of thinking that comprises both *episteme* (not yet distinguished from *dianoia*) and sense perception, which is precisely what *techne* does. All five *technai* that Socrates recommends combine a practical employment in the visible world with a theoretical component in the intelligible realm; and one of the ways that they function as transitions between the two is that in the course of advancing from each *techne* to the next, the practical component is progressively disengaged while the intelligible component is increasingly emphasized.

Because the philosophers will be drawn from the ranks of the auxiliaries, the *technai* that are designed to effect their conversion and liberation from the cave (521b–c) by leading them from the visible to the intelligible must be useful to warriors so that they will take an interest in them, like arithmetic, which enables them to count and marshal troops (522c–e). But since these transitional studies must also lead the warriors beyond their present way of thinking, which in the case of the warriors is at the level of sense perception, we are looking for a kind of sense perception that reveals its own inadequacy and shows the need to go beyond the senses.[19] Socrates' reference to the propensity of the senses to lead to unsatisfactory results is interpreted by Glaucon as an allusion to the errors that result from seeing things at a distance and from shadow-painting, in which shading is used to produce an illusion of solidity. Socrates dismisses this reply, but it foreshadows Book 10, where these very examples will be employed in his criticism of visual art (602c–d).

His point now is that when a perception leads to an apparent contradiction it summons the intellect (*noesis*) to resolve the difficulty, and thus leads beyond itself (523a–c). If we look at three fingers, for example—the smallest, the second, and the middle finger—insofar as they are perceived simply as fingers there is nothing contradictory, and no reason to go beyond sense perception. But when we perceive the second finger to be both big (in relation to the smallest) and small (in relation to the middle) we are faced with an apparent contradiction. Since it is impossible for something to be opposite to itself, the fact that the finger is both big and small requires the calculative faculty to distinguish its bigness and smallness as two even though the sense of sight regarded the finger as one. And since the intellect and sense perception are thereby in opposition to each other, the visible and intelligible realms must also be two rather than one (524c). In Book 4 Socrates pointed out that "the same thing will not be willing to do or undergo opposites in the same part of itself, in relation to the same thing, at the same time. So, if we ever find this happening in the soul, we'll know that we aren't dealing with one thing but with many" (436b). Here the same principle is applied not to its motivations but to its cognitions. Similar reasoning applies to other senses than sight. The same thing, for example, can appear to the sense of touch as both hard and soft, or heavy and light, depending on what it is compared to (523e–524a), and Socrates had pointed to cases like these in Book 5 as evidence of the inadequacy of the sense-lovers' conception of reality (479b). One reason that Socrates does not pursue these other examples is that "we see the same thing *at the same time* as one and as an unlimited plurality" (525a; emphasis added), whereas when the sense of touch perceives the same thing as light and heavy, or hard and soft, it is more likely to be the result of consecutive perceptions rather than simultaneous ones. Perhaps another reason he does not pay as much attention to these cases is that the sense of sight is of more concern to warriors than the other senses.

The first study, then, arithmetical calculation, meets both criteria—usefulness to warriors and summoning of the intellect (as well as the additional criterion of testing the intellectual acuity of the students by virtue of its difficulty: 526b): "arithmetic is necessary for the warriors to learn because they have to order their troops, and necessary for the philosophers because they have to rise out of becoming and grasp being" (525b). As a *techne* it comprises both sense perception and *episteme*. Moreover, as the art of counting it determines whether what we are looking at is one thing or two, and thus is the repository of the law of opposition. When Socrates points out here how mathematics summons our higher thought, he says that things which produce oppositions of this kind summon *dianoia*, while those that do not, fail to arouse *noesis* (524d, cf. 523a1, b1). The two terms that here seem to be used interchangeably, *dianoia* and *noesis*, had just been given distinct meanings in the Divided Line, so the substitution of the latter for the former is perhaps a reminder that the ultimate goal is *noesis* even if the studies initially arouse *dianoia*.

One difference between *dianoia* and *noesis* is that *dianoia* takes its basic principles as given (the odd and the even, the different kinds of angles, etc.) and does not investigate their ontological status (510c), while *noesis* questions their provenance (511b). The *techne* of arithmetic "forcefully leads the soul upward and requires that the discussion be about numbers themselves, never permitting someone to propose for discussion numbers that are attached to visible and tangible bodies" (525d): arithmetic is not about a quantity of cows or sheep but about the intelligible numbers alone. This represents a transition from the sensible world to *dianoia*, but not further:

> What do you think would happen if someone were to ask them, "You surprising men, what kind of numbers are you talking about, in which the one is such as you postulate,[20] each and every one equal to all the others without the slightest difference, and without containing any parts within itself?" What do you think they would answer?
>
> This, I think: that they are speaking about numbers which can be accessed only in thought,[21] and it is not possible to deal with them in any other way. [526a]

What is surprising (θαυμάσιοι) about the people Socrates is addressing is that they have no interest in discovering the underlying basis of the claim that there are realities of this kind.

The bridging that we saw in arithmetic between the sense-directed thinking of the warrior and *episteme*-directed thinking of the philosopher is present in the other types of *techne* as well. Geometry helps the warrior plan maneuvers but would be of no use in the philosophers' education unless it also helped them to discern the Idea of the good, which it will do if "it forces the soul to turn around to that place in which dwells what is happiest of what is, that is in every way necessary for the soul to see" (526d–e). It achieves that because it is "knowledge of what always is, rather than what comes to be at one time and passes away" (527b). Astronomy helps the warriors by giving them a more precise awareness of the seasons (527d), and is conducive to philosophy because the heavenly movements are signs of the order underlying the cosmos (529c–530b). Finally, harmony helps the warrior by supplying music that instills courage (399a), and contributes to philosophy by providing an auditory sign of the same cosmic order of which the motions of heavenly bodies are visible signs (531c–d). But after plane geometry the situation became more complicated.

"Should we put astronomy third or do you think otherwise?" Socrates asks Glaucon, inviting an answer that turns out to be mistaken. "I agree indeed", Glaucon says, taking the bait, "for to have a better awareness of seasons, months, and years is fitting not only for agriculture and navigation, but just as much for a general" (527d). Before exposing the mistake in Glaucon's answer Socrates first criticizes him on another matter in which Glaucon had also simply followed Socrates' lead. After Socrates showed how arithmetic and geometry were useful to warriors as well as uplifting to philosophers, it is not surprising that Glaucon goes on to explain why astronomy too is useful to warriors, as well as farmers and pilots. What is surprising is that Socrates mocks him for doing so—"I'm amused that you seem to fear that the multitude might think you're proposing useless studies"—when he himself had done just that in the case of the previous two, and as recently as the previous paragraph (527c). Socrates asks whether Glaucon wants to address himself to that multitude, or to the few who are able to understand "that in these studies a certain instrument of learning in everyone's soul is purified and rekindled after having been destroyed and blinded by our other pursuits, an instrument whose salvation is more important than ten thousand eyes"; or else whether he is considering these matters primarily for his own sake, without begrudging others who may profit from it as well. Glaucon chooses the last of the three, and the implication is that in that case he needn't show that the studies are useful to warriors and the like (527d–528a).

The reference to purification and blindness in the above quotation bears on the question of how education in various kinds of *techne* can not only accustom philosophers to the light outside the cave that blinds them to the darkness within it, but also lead them to be able to see inside the cave, and indeed to see immeasurably better than the cave dwellers (520c). The purification that the philosophers will undergo as a result of these *technai* will turn out to enhance their power of sight.

Now Socrates reveals that they "did not rightly choose that study that follows geometry" because astronomy deals with the motion of solid bodies, and solid bodies at rest should be dealt with before solid bodies in motion; they should therefore have put solid geometry before astronomy (528a). When Glaucon objects that a science of solid geometry has not yet been formulated, Socrates replies that one reason for that is that it is not honored by any city because it is not seen to be useful. The implication, once again, is that its importance for the purposes of educating rulers no longer needs to make reference to practical utility (528c). Socrates' correction of the placement of astronomy reveals the principle on which the order of the studies is based, namely that each study includes the principles of its predecessor and adds something new. Geometry takes quantity and calculation from arithmetic and adds two-dimensional space, solid geometry adds depth, astronomy motion, and harmony the unity of parts and whole. Dialectic, the science to which all these were said to be preparatory (536c–d), incorporates them all in providing a synoptic overview of all the branches of study taken together: "Someone who can see synoptically is a dialectician; someone who cannot is not" (537c).[22]

The study of astronomy, then, at the midpoint of the series, provides us with two fundamental insights into the series of studies: not only the principle of their sequence, but also the point to which we looked ahead earlier, that as the series progresses the practical component that was intended to recommend the studies to the warriors drops away, while the intelligible component is increasingly emphasized. As the student proceeds upward from the cave and along the Divided Line, the component that links each study to the visible realm is gradually discarded. Not only does Socrates downplay the utility of solid geometry and astronomy, but the utility of the next study, harmony, is not even mentioned here; we must go back to Book 3 (399a) to find a reference to its practical use for warriors.

More than a turning away from utility is at stake. Even when Glaucon tries to redeem himself by attributing to astronomy the virtue of forcing the soul to look at the things above, and away from the things here, Socrates tells him that he has missed the point: "For I am not able to conceive of any study that makes the soul look upward except that which concerns itself with being and the invisible" (529b). The studies should ultimately turn us away not only from utility but the sensible world altogether. The heavenly bodies are the most beautiful and exact of visible things, but they fall far short of the true— of real quickness and slowness in true number (the earlier study of arithmetic) and in all the true shapes (the earlier study of geometry). "These can be apprehended by rationality and mind (διανοία) but not by sight" (529d). And since the things in the sky have bodies and are visible, it would be strange to think that the ratios of night to day, day to month, month to year, and so forth, remain exactly the same forever without any deviation. So it would be better to study astronomy by means of problems, the way geometry is studied, and dismiss the things in the sky (530a–c).

This passage has often and understandably been taken to indicate a lack of regard by Plato for empirical science,[23] but it is important to distinguish between the questions of whether the empirical studies have an intrinsic role to play in the proposed city, and whether they have any intrinsic value at all for Plato. The answer to the first question must be no, since the sole purpose of that city is to provide a model of perfect justice, and everything is subordinated to that end. From that perspective the empirical studies make no intrinsic contribution and therefore, like the arts, are given only an instrumental role to play. Their function here is only as stepping-stones to *noesis*, and so the series moves to ever more synoptic kinds of *dianoia* until we reach an absolute first principle. Focusing on the stars themselves or, in the next case, the performance of music, rather than their intelligible underpinnings, would not take us past astronomical and harmonic *dianoiai*, and so is of no importance. Instead they would most likely be a hindrance by setting up rival claimants to wisdom that would destroy the indispensable organic unity of the city.[24] But this does not mean that Plato fails to appreciate their intrinsic value in other contexts, for throughout the dialogues he shows that he has taken the trouble to acquaint himself in depth with the scientific theories of his day, and finds these matters of interest. And in the *Timaeus* his accounts of physical and biological causality are presented in detail and—allowing for the mythic context—in a serious way. Every *dianoia* provides a kind of knowledge at a certain level, and so is valuable at that level. The same may be said of *pistis*, the realm of empirical science, for if we did not become acquainted with matters of fact we could not discover their intelligible basis. That is made clear in dialogues like the *Phaedo* and *Phaedrus*, which emphasize the necessity of "recollecting" the intelligible by seeing it instantiated in something visible; and in the *Republic* too the present occupation with the intelligible could not have been achieved without first going through the *pistic* examination of what happens in physical cities. Learning at any level has its own value, but some levels are more valuable than others for achieving wisdom; only *eikasia* is devoid of any kind of meaningful learning. So we cannot extrapolate a general condemnation of empirical science from what Plato says in the context of a city that is conceived as nothing more than an embodiment of perfect justice.

As we have seen, when they turn to the fifth study, harmony, there is again no mention of its usefulness (although its usefulness was mentioned in Book 3 and elsewhere). Harmony is the counterpart of astronomy, and as the eyes are fixed on the motions of astronomy the ears are fixed on the motions of harmony, so that the two sciences are akin, as the Pythagoreans claim. The goal in studying harmony is the same as before (purification and turning from becoming to being), so the students must rise above the physical side of music—such as the stretching of strings and the attempt to discover the smallest discernable interval—and concern themselves with problems such as which numbers are in harmony, and which are not, and what is the reason in each case. "A superhuman task", Glaucon says, and Socrates, in another reminder that they have left the utilitarian world behind, replies that it is useful for searching out the beautiful and the good, but not for anything else (530d–531c). Plato approaches that superhuman task in the *Timaeus*, but with constant reminders that there too the investigation is incomplete, even apart from its mythological presentation (see below, chapter 11).

Harmony and its counterpart astronomy, as well as the preceding kinds of *techne*, are only preludes to the song that they must learn, dialectic. In dialectic we attempt by rationality, avoiding sense-perception, to see what each thing itself is, not resting until we grasp the good itself with *noesis* itself. Each of the studies is called not only *techne* (532c, 533d4) but also *dianoia* (533d6), so the previous account illustrates both subsections of the intelligible sector of the Divided Line. Each study taken by itself is an example of *dianoia*, and since *dianoia* uses images of the visible world in order to think about the intelligible world, each study begins with the visible world (the way that each study has practical applications) and proceeds to discover the intelligible basis of those phenomena. On the other hand, the process by which each study leads to the next, and eventually to the good itself, illustrates the upward path of *noesis*: arithmetic is included within plane geometry, plane geometry within solid geometry, solid geometry within astronomy, and the principles of astronomy are akin to those of harmony, leading to the synopsis of dialectic (537c) through which the limitless variety that flowed from the Idea of the good is followed back to the unity of its source.

In accordance with the original purpose of this curriculum, the students' progress through the five kinds *techne* is their liberation from the cave, in which what is best in the soul is led up to contemplation of what is best among that which is (532b–c). Glaucon understandably thinks the time has come for a detailed explanation of *noesis* (532d–e), which has been partially displayed in its upward path toward contemplation, but not in its contemplative mode or in its subsequent downward mode (511b–c). Socrates' reply has already been anticipated in the previous chapter:

> You will no longer be able, my dear Glaucon, to follow me, although for my part I would not willingly omit anything. But you would no longer see an image of what we are saying, but the truth itself. . . . And [we must insist that] the power of dialectic alone can reveal it to someone who is experienced in the things we just went through, and it is not possible in any other way. [533a]

In that case, even to say this much about it may be misleading, and Socrates accordingly adds: "So at least it seems to me, but whether it is so or not can no longer be appropriately insisted on" (533a3–5). What can be insisted upon is that "something of the kind is to be seen" (533a5) and that, whereas "all other kinds of *techne* are directed to human opinion and appetites, or generation and composition, or to serving things that grow and things that are put together" (533b), mathematical studies are directed to knowledge rather than opinion, and to what is incomposite and eternal. That explains why they have a purifying effect on those who study them: since they are eternal they cannot be objects of appetite. When we focus on mathematical reality we learn to recognize the insubstantiality of corporeal, composite, mutable things, and this limits our appetites for them.

Since the preparatory *technai* are also *dianoiai*, they are unable to give an account of their hypotheses (533c). Dialectic, on the other hand, as the upward movement of *noesis* which aims at the unhypothetical first principle (511b), overcomes the hypotheses of the *dianoiai* and progresses to the first principle itself in order to make itself secure (533c–d). Socrates' next words make it clear that at this point in the dialogue the transition from *dianoia* to *noesis* has finally been effected, at least as far as is possible in discourse:

> Dialectic gently draws the soul forth and leads it upward, using as assistants and helpers in this conversion the kinds of *techne* mentioned above. We often called them *episteme* out of habit, but they need a different name that is clearer than *doxa* but dimmer than *episteme*. *Dianoia* is how I think we designated them in the previous discussion, but we shouldn't dispute about names when matters of such magnitude lie before us to be investigated.
>
> No indeed.
>
> It will be sufficient then, as before, to call the first part *episteme*, the second *dianoia*, the third *pistis*, and the fourth *eikasia*; and to call the latter pair *doxa* and the former pair *noesis*. [533d–e]

Glaucon fails to notice that this is not, in fact, the same terminology "as before". Previously the highest part was called *noesis* (511d8) and the two highest parts jointly were called *noetic* (509d4 & *passim*). The change in the name of the upper pair from *noetic* to *noesis* does not seem significant, but the change in the name of the highest subsection from *noesis* to *episteme* can hardly be described as the same terminology as before. Again, what are we to make of Socrates' claim that he has been applying the term *episteme* to the various *dianoiai* only out of habit? Plato could have given him any habits that he liked. The fact that he waited until now means that at this point something has changed; something that seemed to be deserving of the name *episteme* now can be seen to be "dimmer than *episteme*". What has changed is the level at which the discussion is being conducted. In the earlier passage they were still at the level of *dianoia*, so *dianoia* appeared to be the most rigorous kind of knowledge (*episteme*), but now that they have moved from *dianoia* to what was formerly called *noesis*, and they directly experience a way of knowing that is higher than the previous one, *dianoia* no longer seems to be *episteme*, the most rigorous kind of knowledge. What this passage tells us, then, is that at this point the dialogue has finally reached its pinnacle at the top of the Divided Line.

Returning to the Cave

Socrates explained in detail how a transition from the world of action to the intelligible world can be accomplished, but says virtually nothing about the transition from the intelligible back to activity. We were hoping that the power of the educational curriculum to liberate the prisoners from the cave and convert them to philosophy would enable us to resolve the paradox of the philosopher-rulers; for if the rulers' education shows how a connection can be established between the world of the cave and that of the light, it might also show how our eyes can become re-accustomed to the darkness of the cave without ceasing to see the light. If it is *techne* that enables the citizens to make the transition from practical activity in the visible world to the intellectual activity of philosophers, then *techne* is a likely candidate to explain the philosophers' ability to return to the cave.

The reason that the propaedeutic studies could be called both *techne* and *dianoia* was that both terms refer to kinds of thinking that bridge the intelligible and the practical. *Techne* uses intelligible principles to provide guidance for working on the physical world, while *dianoia* uses the physical world as instances to enable us to conceive intelligible truths. In other words, *techne* uses the intelligible for the sake of the visible, while *dianoia* uses the visible for the sake of the intelligible. As we progressed through the studies from arithmetic to dialectic, the *dianoetic* aspect of the studies gradually superseded that of *techne* because we were leaving the physical world in the background. On that model, what would be needed for a return to the cave in which the intelligible is not wholly lost sight of would be a corresponding shift from a *dianoetic* way of looking at the world to a *techne*-governed one in which the highest intelligible reality is continually kept in view and employed in a *techne* of governing. As Socrates said earlier, the true philosopher, who can discern the divine and constant realities, could least of all become a poor craftsman (δημιουργόν) of self-control, justice, and the whole of civic virtue (500d, cf. 484d, 592b). Since ruling requires excellence "both in actions and *episteme*" (540a) it is, like the studies that drew the children upward, spoken of as a *techne*.[25]

Just as the *techne* of the warrior opened out into the mathematical studies that led to the intelligible, the path from the intelligible back to the cave begins by requiring the guardians "to hold command in war and other offices suitable for youth" (539e).[26] This takes place at the age of thirty-five, after they complete the mathematical studies that they began as children, devoting the final five years to a study of dialectics. They spend the next fifteen years gaining experience in various arts related to ruling, and then are led to contemplate the Idea of the good until it is time for them to take their turn at governing the city.

The study of mathematics purified the students by directing them away from the realm of appetite and opinion, toward that of intelligibility. When they now return to the cave, what is to stop them from becoming corrupted again by these arts that "are directed to human opinion and appetites" (533b)? The corruptibility of the arts and their practitioners was alluded to at the beginning of the dialogue, when Socrates secured Polemarchus' agreement that the same *techne* that enables us to do something beneficial will also enable us to do its harmful counterpart (332d–334b). Socrates subsequently insisted, however, that *techne* in the strict sense is not capable of doing harm, but only when combined with payment (341c–347c). If we apply this to the present context, the way to prevent corruption is to ensure that the philosophers practice ruling only as a *techne* in the strict sense, that is, one which is not combined with the positive forms of payment—money or personal power—but only with its negative form of not being ruled by their inferiors, and the retroactive form of regarding their prior education as payment already received for work that they are now expected to perform (520b–e). In order to prevent the insidious kinds of payment from having any influence, the rulers were already forbidden in Book 4 from possessing any private property beyond what is absolutely necessary (416d) and from touching gold or silver, or even being under the same roof with it (416e–417a). And in Book 5 the prohibition against private attachments extended also to spouses and children, so that the guardians will have the same relationship to all members of the opposite sex in common and to all children in common, and the rulers will apply the word "mine" in common (457b–c, 462c). If such strictures ensure that ruling will be practiced as a *techne* in the strict sense rather than the impure self-interested version, then the nature of *techne* can provide a downward bridge from *noesis* to practical activity—as previously it provided an upward bridge—while protecting its practitioners from the possibilities for corruption offered by the kind of *techne* that is concerned with "human opinion and appetites".[27]

The emotionally purifying character of philosophy explains why, after they are reacclimatized, the philosophers will see in the cave immeasurably better than the cave dwellers (520c), that is, be more adept in the practical virtues as well as intellectual virtue.[28] The blindness that they initially suffer cannot refer to an inability to see individual things in a literal sense—contemplation does not literally deprive us of our sense of sight. Knowing the good itself would not make us less able to see good things. Rather than an inability to *perceive* the cave dwellers' behavior, the philosophers' blindness is the inability to *understand* it, to understand how the prisoners can prefer pleasure and honors to virtue. The philosophers would "go through any sufferings rather than share their opinions and live as they do" (516d, cf. 583b–586e), for they "know what each of the images is and what it is an image of, since [they] have seen the truth about beautiful, just, and good things" (520c).[29] They remain blind in the sense that they no longer see *as* the cave dwellers see, or share the cave dwellers' opinions and way of life. Rather than an inability to see, it is a blindness to certain attitudes toward what is seen, just as earlier Socrates said that the guardians must know about base appetites and emotions, but should not actually have those attitudes within themselves (396a, cf. 409b–c).

If *techne* by nature seeks the good of its object rather than its practitioner (342b), it seems made to order for philosophers who are going to apply their knowledge of the good to their charges. But precisely how does it enable the philosophers to bring their knowledge of the good to bear on particular situations? Since every *techne* involves number and calculation (522c), we need to identify the kind of calculation that the *techne* of ruling makes use of. Socrates calls the soul's ruling capacity "calculation" (*logistikon*: 439c–441e, cf. 546b), which is also the term he used to describe the initial training in mathematics that leads from the cave (525a–526b), but that does not mean that the philosopher-rulers' *techne* of ruling could be precisely quantified like arithmetic, geometry, astronomy, and harmony.

The only context in which Socrates devises a precise formula of measurement for ruling is the "nuptial number" by which the guardians' procreation is arranged:

> It is the first number in which are found root and square increases, comprehending three lengths and four terms, of elements that make things like and unlike, that cause them to increase and decrease, and that render all things mutually agreeable and rational in their relations to one another. Of these elements, four and three, married with five, give two harmonies when thrice increased. One of them is a square, so many times a hundred. The other is of equal length one way but oblong. One of its sides is one hundred squares of the rational diameter of five diminished by one each or one hundred squares of the irrational diameter diminished by two each. The other side is a hundred cubes of three. This whole geometrical number controls better and worse births. [546b–c, Reeve trans.]

In fact, the nuptial number is introduced with reference not to the philosopher-rulers of the kallipolis but to the complete guardians of the rational city (544a–b), but it would have to be incorporated into kallipolis as well. There are two reasons why this cannot be considered a step in the development of a rigorously mathematical *techne* of ruling—a theoretical reason and a practical one. The theoretical reason is that the passage is irredeemably obscure both in its meaning and application,[30] so if it is meant to show us how to make the transition from *noesis* to the practical world it is a spectacular failure. The *practical* problem is that Socrates introduces the calculus by saying:

> since for everything that comes into being there is a destruction, not even a constitution like this will remain intact for all time, but it will be dissolved. And this is the way it will be dissolved. . . . Even though they are wise, those who were educated to be rulers of the city will not hit upon the fertility and barrenness of our race through calculation together with sense perception. [546a–b]

Even if we are able to achieve the calculation, our efforts to combine it with sense perception cannot be relied on. The calculus of the nuptial number, then, does not form a bridge between the realm of *noesis* and the realm of action. It is wholly within the *noetic* realm, and sense perception must be combined with it extrinsically and with no guarantee of success. We should not be surprised by this result if we remember that when Socrates described the downward path of *noesis* he said that it never leaves the realm of forms (511b–c). *Noesis* alone does not enable us to cross over into the realm of sense perception and action. That was why the philosophers' *noetic* contemplation of the good could not show them their duty to govern, and they had to be compelled to see it by an external argument. *Noetic* contemplation that stays within the realm of forms cannot translate automatically into an ability to promote the good in practical action.

The problem underlying the application the nuptial number extends beyond that one case, for as Socrates asks rhetorically in Book 5, "Is it possible for something to be put into practice just as it is in theory (ὡς λέγεται), or is it the nature of practice to attain to truth less than theory does?" (472e–473a). The difficulty in translating the intelligible back to the visible realm is that, as Socrates says in the *Phaedo*, "we never see or hear anything accurately" (65b)—a view that is reflected in the *Republic*'s doctrine that knowledge is possible only of intelligible forms, and in the case of sensible objects only opinion is possible (478a–479e). Accordingly, no rigorous calculations like the nuptial number can be applied infallibly. The problem for the philosopher-rulers (and for Plato) is to find some way of applying a knowledge of the good that is based on and concludes in the precision of the forms, to the imprecision of the sensible world.

It is just because ruling must apply its precise theoretical basis to the imprecision of the physical world that it is conceived as a *techne* rather than an *episteme*. Every *techne* brings a universal conceptual foundation to bear in relation to *kairos*, the demands of the moment. As Socrates said earlier, if someone who is working at a *techne* "lets the right moment (*kairos*) go by, the work is ruined" (370b). That is why the nuptial number could not be relied on: their project will fail because eventually the rulers will apply the number contrary to *kairos* (παρὰ καιρόν, 546d2) and their work will be ruined. The ability to recognize the *kairos* is not contained within the conceptual apparatus of the *techne* itself because it cannot be conceptualized at all; it depends on a sensitivity to the flow of particularity.[31] That sensitivity is what the philosopher-rulers achieve when they re-accustom themselves to the darkness of the cave (516c–d); it is what transforms the *episteme* of the philosopher into the *techne* of the ruler.

Recognizing the Mean

The *Republic* never makes explicit the precise nature of the thinking by which *techne* is able to achieve its downward mediation from the intelligible to the practical (i.e., to recognize the *kairos*), but there is such an account in the *Statesman*, explicitly related to *kairos*, which helps bring into focus some of the implications of what is said in the *Republic*. Even if Plato had not yet formulated this account at the time of the *Republic*, it can at least be regarded as a fulfillment of one of the elements of the *Republic*'s project, in which the implications of that project become clearer.[32]

The *Republic* had maintained that every *techne* makes use of number and calculation (i.e., measurement) (322c). The *Statesman* adds that the *techne* of measurement has two components:

> One is with respect to the shared largeness or smallness of things toward one another. The other is with respect to the necessary essence of coming into being. Doesn't it seem to you that, in the nature of it, we must say that the greater is greater than nothing other than the less, and, again, the less is less than the greater and nothing else? But what about this? With regard to what exceeds or what is exceeded by the nature of the mean, whether in words or actions, must we not also say that it really exists? And that in this lies the chief difference between those of us who are bad and those who are good? . . . If someone does not allow that the nature of the greater stands in relation to anything other than the less, it will never stand in relation to the mean. Isn't that

so? Would we not destroy the kinds of *techne* themselves and all their works with this doctrine, including indeed the *techne* of statesmanship that we have been seeking? For all these presumably are on guard against anything that is in excess of or deficient to the mean, which they do not regard as nonexistent but as something difficult that exists in relation to their activity. And when they preserve the mean in this way, all of their works are good and beautiful. . . . For if this [mean] exists those [*technai*] exist, and if those exist this exists also; but neither one of them can ever exist if the other doesn't.[33]

The first of these two components of measurement—"the shared largeness or smallness of things toward one another"—is the kind that enabled the ascent out of the cave. The ascent began with comparison of three fingers, which were large or small in relation to one another, and all the other studies as well involved the measurement of things relatively to one another rather than to an absolute standard.[34] What the *Statesman* account adds to that of the *Republic* is the description of the other (downward) component of measure—the mean—by which *techne* is able to accomplish its beneficent work ("when they preserve the mean in this way, all of their works are good and beautiful"), and which accounts even for our ability to implement the good in our conduct ("in this lies the chief difference between those of us who are bad and those who are good"). This second kind of measure explains how the philosophers can apply their formal contemplative knowledge to practical action and thereby become wise or at least philosophically adept rulers ("the *techne* of statesmanship that we have been seeking"). It "comprises whatever measures things in relation to the mean, the fitting, the *kairos*, the needful, and anything else that dwells in the middle away from the extremes" (284e). The *Laws* reiterates the necessity of the mean for the practice of ruling:

If one gives a greater degree of power to what is lesser, neglecting the mean . . . then everything is upset. . . . There does not exist, my friends, a mortal soul whose nature will ever be able to wield the greatest human ruling power when young and irresponsible, without becoming filled in its mind with the greatest disease, unreason, which makes it become hated by its closest friends. When this comes about it quickly destroys it and obliterates all its power. Guarding against this, then, by knowing the mean, is the task of great lawgivers. [691c]

It is not the concept of a mean in itself that distinguishes the kind of measurement essential to the *techne* of ruling from the kind that is essential to the theoretical studies, for the theoretical studies make use of their own kind of mean. The *Timaeus* tells us, for example, that plane and solid geometry are concerned in an essential way with the single and double mean respectively (32a–b, 36a), and according to the *Symposium* (187b), the *Republic*'s final study, harmony, is a mean between the high and low.[35] The difference between these kinds of mean and the kind that the *Statesman* and *Laws* connect with ruling is that in the mathematical studies the mean is defined by the extremes—it articulates the relationship between integers in arithmetic, shapes or solids in geometry, motions in astronomy, and pitches in harmony—so it is still a kind of relative measure. The mean that is an absolute measure, on the other hand, is itself the defining term, and the extremes are such only in relation to it. What enables the mean to provide the *techne* of ruling with the power to translate goodness into practical action is not that it furnishes us a priori with a precise *prescription* which then must be applied to an imprecise world (as with the nuptial number), but rather that it furnishes us with a power to *perceive* when success has been achieved. We can recognize when something goes too far or not far enough, even when we cannot say in advance precisely what we are looking for.[36]

The doctrine of the mean does not receive the kind of thematic presentation in the *Republic* that it does in the *Statesman*, but it is present both implicitly and explicitly. The doctrine comprises two primary components:

1) Practical goodness is to be conceived as the correct degree between too much and too little, rather than as an extreme that is pursued to the greatest extent possible (we can still, of course, speak of trying to be as good as possible).

2) This mean is inseparable from the attainment of excellence in *techne*: "when the [*technai*] preserve the mean in this way, all of their works are good and beautiful. . . . For if this [mean] exists those exist, and if those exist this exists also; but neither one of them can ever exist if the other doesn't" (*Statesman* 284b,d). It follows that the mean can only be perceived in relation to practical activity, for otherwise the mean could exist independently of *techne*. In other words, the mean, unlike the good, does not exist as a form or Idea in itself, divorced from our activity in the corporeal world. It exists only in the context of that activity, as the mark that we aim at it in our efforts to achieve excellence, rather than going too far or not far enough.

To what extent are these views present in the *Republic*?

The Mean

The view that justice is a mean between extremes appears several times in the dialogue.

a) The most explicit passage is at the very end of the dialogue where goodness and justice are explicitly described as a mean. At the end of the myth of Er, Socrates emphasizes the importance of the study of the good life and says, "each of us must take special care and, being indifferent to the other studies, seek out and learn this study . . . [that provides] the ability and *episteme* of distinguishing the good from the bad life" (618c). This means know-ing how to combine things with one another or separate them. For example,

> knowing how beauty, combined with poverty or wealth and with what kind of character of the soul, produces good or evil, good birth and bad birth, private life and governing, strength and weakness, ease of learning and difficulty of learning, and all such things regarding the soul, both natural and acquired, so that from all these things—and looking at the nature of the soul—he will be able to choose rationally between the better and worse life, calling a life worse which leads him to become more unjust, better if it leads him to become more just, and disregarding all other considerations. . . . *He would know how to always choose the mean*[37] among such lives, and avoid each of the extremes, both in this life and also, as far as possible, in all that come after. For in this way a human being becomes happiest. [618c–619b; emphasis added]

b) The basis for that conclusion lies in Socrates' earlier definition of justice as a harmony among the three parts of the soul, so that a just action is one which preserves this harmony, while an unjust action is one which destroys it (443d–444a). Since a harmony is destroyed when one of the elements is taken too far or not far enough, Socrates' later conclusion follows, that a life of justice requires us to avoid the extremes and pursue the mean.[38]

In the preliminary conversation before Socrates developed his own analy-sis, justice was already adumbrated as a kind of mean. Since the discussion there was governed by the conventional ways of characterizing justice that Glaucon relates, the nature of justice (and therefore of the mean and its extremes) does not necessarily coincide with the way it will appear in Socrates' own investigation.

c) At the beginning of Book 2 Socrates identified justice as an intermedi-ate kind of good: neither the one extreme of a good that is only good for its consequences, nor the other extreme of a good that is intrinsically good but without good consequences, but the middle kind that is good in both ways. Its median nature is emphasized by the fact that Glaucon lists the intermediate type in between his description of the extremes, even though it is more natu-ral to describe each pure type first and then the mixture (357b–358a). It fol-lows that if what we are doing seems good in principle but leads to bad consequences, or at the other extreme it leads to good consequences but is not beneficial itself, then we have gone too far in the direction of either prin-ciple or consequence, and have missed true justice at the mean.

d) In reply Glaucon, speaking as a devil's advocate for Thrasymachus, sug-gests that justice is a different kind of mean: people say that justice amounts to neither doing nor suffering injustice and it is "in between the best, which is to do injustice without paying the penalty, and the worst, which is to be treated unjustly and be unable to take revenge. Justice is a mean (ἐν μέσῳ) between these two" (359a). Although Socrates would dispute the claim that the best lies at one of the extremes rather than with the mean, he would agree that justice is a mean between them: the intention of a just person is neither to do nor suffer injustice, that is, to be neither completely selfish nor completely self-sacrificing, but to take a middle course between these extremes.

e) When Socrates first defined the nature of the original guardians, it turned out to be a mean between excessive spiritedness and excessive gentleness (375a–c).

f) Similarly, the education of the guardians will consist of music and gymnastics, because the former will prevent them from being too savage while the latter will prevent them from being too soft (410c–d).

g) The philosophical nature that is to receive this education must itself be neither cowardly at one extreme, nor savage at the other (486b).

h) It must also be a mean between being too flighty or too stolid (503c–d).

i) And it must be a mean between the character of someone whose love is entirely for physical labor to the exclusion of mental labor and someone whose love is entirely for mental labor to the exclusion of physical labor (535d).

The view of justice as a mean was implicit even in the aporetic arguments of Book 1. The elenctic character of that book makes it impossible to extract any doctrines with assurance, and Socrates himself concluded that it did not lead to an understanding of justice (353e–354a), but nevertheless there were already adumbrations of the fact that justice will turn out to be some kind of mean that is contrasted with one-sided extremes.

j) In the case of the first two interlocutors, we saw that Cephalus' definition of justice seemed to work in peaceful situations but not violent ones, while Polemarchus' worked in war but not in peacetime. Taken together the two showed the need for a mean between those extremes.

k) If the first two arguments showed that justice cannot be one extreme or the other, the subsequent argument with Thrasymachus established that justice must be conceived as the right degree instead of as an extreme. Whereas an unjust person wants to overreach both just and unjust people in order to obtain as much as possible of everything, a just person wants to overreach unjust people but not other just people (349b–c). Injustice aimed at an extreme—as much as possible of everything—while justice aimed at a limit, a correct degree between not going far enough and going too far. In aiming to overreach the unjust but not the just, justice is a mean between the excess of aiming to overreach everyone (i.e., Thrasymachus' view of injustice: 343e–344a), and the deficiency of not aiming to overreach anyone (i.e., Thrasymachus' view of justice: 343c).

l) Earlier in the discussion Socrates told Thrasymachus that even though no *techne* provides what is beneficial to itself but only what is beneficial for its subject, "the *techne* of getting paid" benefits the practitioner (346a–c). If getting paid is a *techne*, then *techne* combines self-sacrifice with self-interest, and so is not an extreme of self-sacrifice, but a mean between selflessness and selfishness.

Techne

Justice is, then, a kind of mean in the *Republic*, both explicitly and implicitly. But does the *Republic* identify the mean with *techne*, as the *Statesman* does?

In the case of the rulers the two coincide, since ruling is *techne* and also aims at a mean in pursuing justice, but it does not follow that it is the nature of *techne* in general to pursue a mean, or that the very concept of a mean implies *techne*. The *Statesman* claimed that the mean is what enables *techne* to make its products good and beautiful (284b)—not as a precise abstract rule, conceived prior to the work and then enforced upon the materials, but rather as a perception of something as neither too much nor too little. The ability to make a table requires only concepts that can then be applied; but to apply the concepts most effectively—to make the table good or beautiful—requires something more. Otherwise all the products of every craftsworker who learned the appropriate concepts would be good and beautiful, and in the case of any product that lacked goodness or beauty, we should be able to point to precisely which rules or concepts were not applied. The reason we cannot do so is that a kind of sensitivity or good taste is involved—analogous to Aristotelian *phronesis* in the realm of ethics—by which the skilled practitioner can recognize when some aspect of the product or its production needs to be increased or diminished.

Do we find this doctrine in the *Republic* as well? The passage cited under a) took the good life to be a mean between extremes, which we can achieve if we engage in a study that produces "the ability and *episteme* of distinguishing the good from the bad life". Not only our life as a whole was conceived in terms of the mean, but so also were the individual elements that make it what it is: beauty, wealth, character, birth, participation in public life, strength, quickness of mind (618b–619b). There is no suggestion here as there is in the *Statesman* that not only ruling, which aims at justice, but every *techne* achieves its purpose through the mean. However, as far as ruling itself is concerned, the essence of the *Statesman* account is already anticipated in the *Republic*: ruling, at least, is a *techne* that aims at a mean. The *Republic*, moreover, gives us something that the *Statesman* does not, namely a concrete image of how this kind of thinking may operate. In explaining the importance of proper musical education Socrates said,

> Isn't it for this reason that nurture in music is most sovereign, namely that rhythm and harmony most of all permeate the soul and most vigorously take hold of it, bringing grace with them, and making it graceful if one is rightly nurtured, and if not, the opposite? And again it is sovereign because the one who was properly nurtured in that way would most sharply perceive when something is left out, or when something was not made beautifully or didn't grow beautifully. And, rightly feeling distaste, he would praise what is beautiful and welcome it and receive it into his soul and, being nurtured by them, become beautiful and good. [401d–e]

This was not an example of the mean, because only one of the two extremes—the deficiency ("when something is left out")—is clearly specified, and it is paired not with its opposite, excess, but with a more general reference to not growing or being made beautifully. Moreover, Socrates later points out that although this training made the guardians harmonious and graceful, it did so on the basis of habit rather than *episteme* (522a), which rules out *techne* as well. Nevertheless, as with the mean, the children recognize when something is left out and when the object is not beautiful, without having a prescriptive rational concept of beauty that they can use to identify what is or is not beautiful—in fact, they are explicitly said to be at a pre-rational age (402a). They do not know what something should contain in order to be beautiful, but they are sensitive to the presence of beauty and its absence because of the grace that their training has instilled in their soul. Even if the training is only in rhythm and harmony, the result is a sensitivity to every kind of beauty and goodness generally. They perceive the beautiful and good not directly and positively in accordance with a pre-given concept or description, but the way we perceive a note as in tune because it does not sound sharp or flat.

Musical training was only the first step in the education of the philosophers. When they have not only been trained in harmony but have also studied it as the last of the five mathematical disciplines preparatory to dialectic, and when they have finally had a vision of the good itself that converts their entire soul to a commitment to goodness, they will be in a situation that parallels at a higher level that of the children trained in harmony and rhythm. The graceful state of their soul, rather than any specific precepts, was what enabled the children to recognize what is beautiful and good. The philosophers' vision of the good has a parallel effect. Their entire soul—not only their faculty of rationality—is turned away from becoming to being (518c–d,

519b), with the result that when they look at those who are still in the cave, nothing could induce them to share their opinions and way of life (516d). The rulers, like the children, must apply this without precepts: their fifteen-year apprenticeship is necessary not in order to teach new precepts but "so that they won't lag behind the others in experience" (539e).[39] Their ability to discern the good in sensible things is formulated in terms of sense experience itself rather than in terms of a concept that tells us what to look for. They have come to understand the good itself through years of contemplation, but only through a lengthy contact with practical experience can a kind of thinking which concludes in forms be applied effectively to things. What the *Statesman* adds to this, or at least presents more explicitly, is that what is gained by that experience is the ability to discern the good as a mean between excess and deficiency in the realm of the greater and lesser.[40]

The perception of justice as a mean aspires to the condition of Socrates' "divine sign", which "always turns me away from what I was about to do but never urges me forward" (*Apology* 31d), and whose absence tells him that what he is about to do is right.[41] Of the five ways that Socrates mentioned by which someone may become a philosopher *without* the active support of the city, his divine sign is the only one that produces practical wisdom (496a–c).[42] By warning him both of his errors of commission (*Apology* 40a) and his errors of omission (*Phaedrus* 242b–c)—that is, when he goes too far or not far enough—it steers him to the mean in every situation. The city is not capable of bestowing Socrates' divine sign on its future rulers, but it can give them a *techne* of ruling that approximates Socrates' gift as far as possible. The numerical and calculative character of *techne* enables the philosophers to cross from the realm of becoming to that of being, where they gain an intuition of goodness itself, while the practical aspect of *techne*, refined by a fifteen-year apprenticeship, enables them to locate the good life in concrete situations as a mean between too much and too little. The rulers are able to recognize goodness within the indefiniteness of particularity not explicitly, by means of a determinate formula, but implicitly by the indefinable concordance between their perception of a situation and their intuition of the ideal.

The Philosophical Nature (535a–541b)

In Book 6 Socrates and Glaucon identified the qualities to be sought in prospective guardians: good memory, quickness to learn, high-mindedness, grace (εὔχαριν), being a friend and kin to truth, being just, courageous, and self-controlled (487a). In light of the new curriculum, Socrates now revisits the question and says that in addition to stability, courage, gracefulness (εὐειδεστάτους), nobility, and toughness, the candidates must also have a keen-ness and facility for learning, good memory, and love of work (535a–c). The new list is odd in that it seemingly identifies as new, qualities that were already specified (facility for learning and good memory), and treats as old, qualities that are now mentioned for the first time (stability, toughness). What is both avowedly and, in fact, new is keenness for learning and love of work. The new curriculum is more demanding than the previous combination of arts and physical training, if only because pain of the soul's labor is felt more intimately than that of the body's labor, and it requires students who would not be daunted by its demands (535b). The current lack of regard for philosophy, by contrast, is explained by the half-measures that its practitioners are satisfied with, such as loving either physical or mental labors but not both, or hating voluntary falsehood but not the involuntary falsehood of ignorance. These illegitimate virtues are described as lame on one side (535c–536b), a criticism that calls to mind the importance of the mean, as does his confession that he has been expressing his disapproval to an excessive degree (536c).

Two other changes from the earlier conception of education were noted ear-lier: now the students must be children rather than the grown warriors con-templated at the end of Book 3, and the learning must not be constrained but free (536d–e). Not that the prospective rulers are free either to learn or not, but that they must be motivated rather than forced (βία) to learn. Just as the com-pulsion imposed on the philosophers to return to the cave was the compulsion of rational persuasion, the compulsion that leads the prisoners out of the cave in the first place takes the form of enticement rather than force. Those who respond will be given honors and chosen for further training, and at the age of twenty they must gather the subjects that they haphazardly studied in child-hood into their interconnection with one another and with the nature of what is—a test of the synoptic powers that are required of a dialectician. At the age of thirty those who have best succeeded will receive further honors and will be tested by the power of dialectic as to how well they can disengage themselves from reliance on the senses, and proceed to being itself and truth (536e–537d).

But this must be done carefully because dialectic can be abused, as it is at present due to the lawlessness with which its practitioners are filled. When young people are asked what is the noble, or the just, or the good, and repeat-edly find that when they give the conventional answer that they have learned they are refuted, they will end up convinced that nothing is any more noble or just or good than anything else. Then, when they are no longer con-vinced by the traditional principles, and unable to discover the true ones, they will likely surrender themselves to a life that flatters them; just as children raised amid wealth and flattery who discover that the people they thought were their parents are not, and are unable to find their real parents, are likely to fall in with those who flatter them and to become lawless (537e–539a). One way to guard against this is not to let the students have a taste of argument while they are young and are likely to turn argument into a game of contentiousness, for then they quickly fall into a vehement distrust of what they used to believe, and both they and philosophy are discredited. This is less likely to be a problem with older people with stable natures (539a–d); here the rule of thumb would seem to be "Don't trust anyone *under* thirty".

After exercising in discourse (λόγων) for five years as an antistrophe[43] to gymnastics, at the age of thirty-five they reverse direction and return to the cave, where they are compelled (ἀναγκαστέοι) to gain experience in the *technai* related to ruling; and once again their stability is put to the test (539e). Then, at the age of fifty those who survive the tests will be compelled (ἀναγκαστέον) to reverse direction a second time and raise the light of their souls to that which furnishes light for all. Once they have seen the good itself they will reverse direction a third time and use the good as a paradigm for setting in order the city, its citizens, and they themselves for the rest of their lives. They will spend most of their time with philosophy, but will rule when their turn comes, regarding ruling not as something fine but as a necessity (ἀναγκαῖον), and after they have educated their replacements they will reverse direction for a fourth and final time, departing for the Isles of the Blessed, where they will thereafter dwell. The quasi-independence of religion, which was affirmed when the Pythian oracle (Apollo's priestess at Delphi) was given veto power over sexual unions (461e), is reaffirmed with similar power given over the possibility that the retired rulers will be memorialized and sacrificed to as divinities, or at least as blessed (539d–540c). Here again we find the effects of the two blindnesses: the rulers still need to be compelled to go in both directions, both back to the cave and up to the light.

But why the fourfold zigzag change of directions? Why could the philosophers not have been brought from dialectic directly up to a vision of the good before they apprentice as rulers? Given the fifteen years of apprenticeship required, perhaps Socrates wants to avoid the dimming of their memory of the paradigm by which they will rule—although it is also possible, as we saw above, 119–22, that the years of apprenticeship are inserted at that point because they will make the philosophers more capable of discerning the Idea of the good than they would otherwise have been. Whatever the reason, the back-and-forth of the philosopher-rulers' education stitches together the two poles of philosophy and ruling.

Socrates concludes that the city and its constitution are not entirely wishful thinking—although it is difficult to bring them about, it is not impossible.

The easiest and quickest way would be to send everyone over the age of ten out into the country, and raise their children in the city away from the influence and ethos of their parents. "By far the easiest", Glaucon replies, "and how it would come into being, if indeed it ever came into being, it seems to me, Socrates that you have described well" (540e–541b). It is hard not to hear irony in this exchange. The third wave made it all too clear in what regard philosophers were held by the general populace, and now we are told that the easiest way to bring the city about, indeed the only way, according to Glaucon, is if the people are willing not only to entrust their children's education to philosophers, but put their children completely and forever into the power of the philosophers, while they themselves abandon their children, their homes, and their livelihoods, and take themselves into permanent exile. Even apart from the disruption of their own lives, it does not take much imagination to envision what the people who found Socrates guilty of corrupting the youth would say if his kindred spirits wanted exclusive custody over their children.

Why does Plato put into the mouths of Socrates and Glaucon the views both that the city is not impossible and that we can never realistically expect it to come into being? It is important to insist that it is not impossible because it is important to acknowledge both that wisdom is possible and that it is possible for wisdom to inform our behavior and the behavior of educators and rulers. It is important to accept that we have the ability to discover the source of all that is and to recognize its goodness, and that we ourselves will be fundamentally transformed by this discovery and achieve true virtue. And it is important to accept that this fundamental transformation need not remain a matter of intellectual virtue—wisdom as a state of mind—but can also translate into moral virtue, virtuous behavior, when through experience we develop a feel for the *kairos* that shows what is right at any given moment. Finally, it is important to accept that this is what rulers can and should strive to attain, whether or not they ever will. If these things were not possible *in principle*, then they could not function as serious answers to the dialogue's question about the nature of justice.

If it is important to believe that all this is possible, it is perhaps no less important to believe that there is no credible series of events by which it can come into being. Our political experience (and Plato's was not any different in this respect) shows that the practice, however well intended, of keeping something hidden away from all but a few people of a certain age and with a certain kind of nature also has the effect of insulating those in power from criticism and renewal. If the rulers are fully wise ex hypothesi as in the *Republic*, then criticism is irrelevant and renewal unnecessary; but redeeming that hypothesis is another matter. For one thing, the dialogues tell us that human beings are not capable of perfect wisdom (*Apology* 23a, *Phaedrus* 278d), and even if we assume that such wisdom is possible, how can we recognize someone who has attained it? There are always many rival claimants. We have all seen too many examples in Western history of ideologically driven tyrannies—whose rulers believe that they are following a higher truth even as they murder and exploit their subjects—not to be aware of the dangers of what Plato is proposing. Plato seeks to minimize that danger by limiting the ideological field to those of proven intelligence and character, and excluding those with tyrannical ambitions from the means to realize them. But in practice how can it be decided politically who is worthy? Socrates himself never claims to be wise, and has just now confessed to a failure of virtue himself, in becoming angry when he should not have (536c).

For the city to come about, two things would be necessary: initial rulers who already are wise, and a way to prove that fact to everyone else. Even if the first is possible, the second is not, and that seems to be Glaucon's point here. The city gives us a model by which we can better understand the nature of justice, and it is not vitiated by the problem of competing visions of the "good", precisely because that very problem will ensure that the city remains a formal ideal rather than a political reality. Only individually can we give content to the formal conception of beholding the good: "the power of dialectic alone can reveal it to someone who is experienced in the things we just went through, and it is not possible in any other way" (533a). There is nothing that Plato can say to persuade those who doubt that there is a single highest good, but neither will that belief ever be imposed on anyone who rejects it, since the city will never be anything but a city in thought.

Notes

1. The pervasiveness of this theme is documented in Edward Andrew, "Descent to the Cave", *Review of Politics* 45 (1983): 510–35, esp. 516.

2. The best known formulation of this accusation is Karl Popper's *The Open Society and Its Enemies* (London: Routledge, 1945). For a more balanced view of the *Republic* conceived in part as a reply to Popper, see Clay 1988.

3. See above, ch. 5 n. 4.

4. Irwin suggests that "The argument has followed an 'upward' path from Cephalus' first thoughts about justice to the Form of the Good, and now it follows a downward path (511b3–c2; cf. Ar., *EN* 1095a30–b4) back to the initial beliefs about justice" (1995, 314).

5. According to Strauss, "the philosophers cannot be persuaded, they can only be compelled to rule the cities [and] the just city is not possible because of the philosophers' unwillingness to rule" (1964, 124, cf. Bloom 1968, 410). But the passages he cites

say only that the philosophers must be compelled, not that they cannot be persuaded; they do not contradict the claim at 520b–c that the compulsion means a compelling argument (cf. Howland 1998, 656). Kraut suggests "that although the philosophers will recognize the justice of the requirement and abide by it, they will do so with appropriate reluctance, for they rightly regard purely philosophical activity as better for them than the activity of ruling the city. . . . So, Plato is apparently saying that in this particular case it is contrary to one's interest to act justly", (1991, 43–44). However, acting altruistically rather than from self-interest does not imply that we are acting reluctantly. Moreover, as Denyer observes, since "the whole upbringing of philosophers in the ideal city has right from birth been calculated to rid them of any concern with particulars in their particularity and to focus them rather upon the general . . . I am incapable of any longer desiring that I . . . as opposed to someone else, should continue to enjoy the intellectual life . . . And so I can have no self-interest which would urge me not to play my proper role in the continuance of that city", (1986, 29). Also see N. White 1979, 192–93. Those who take Socrates' "going down" to the Piraeus, and the compulsion that prevented him from leaving, to foreshadow the compulsion on the philosopher to go down into the cave, may recall that what kept Socrates from leaving was not Polemarchus' playful threat but Adeimantus' persuasion (328a). For discussions of the need to compel the philosophers to rule, see Eric Brown, "Justice and Compulsion for Plato's Philosopher-Rulers", *Ancient Philosophy* 20 (2000): 1–17; and Jiyuan Yu, "Justice in the *Republic*: An Evolving Paradox", *History of Philosophy Quarterly* 17 (2000): 121–41.

6. James Peters points out that when just individuals govern the lower parts of their soul with the highest part, this is not a distraction from contemplation but a precondition for achieving the tranquillity necessary for contemplation. He argues that if that is true of the individual, and the same relations hold in the city as in the individual, then there should be no conflict between the guardians' dual roles of governance and contemplation ("Reason and Passion in Plato's *Republic*", *Ancient Philosophy* 9 [1989]: 173–87). Cf. Kahn 1987, 89; Timothy Mahoney, "Do Plato's Philosopher-Rulers Sacrifice Self-Interest to Justice?", *Phronesis* 37 (1992): 265–82, esp. 271; and John Cooper, "The Psychology of Justice in Plato", in Kraut 1997b, 17–30, esp. 25–7. However, in the individual what rules is rationality (*logistikon*: 439d) and what contemplates truth is reason (*noesis*: 511d). Just as there are different functions within the rational part of the soul that are "theoretical" and "practical", that contemplate and govern, so too different members of the guardian class will contemplate and govern at any given time. But since these individuals will have similar natures, they will all prefer contemplation to ruling. Peters is correct in that one is a precondition for the other; but that does not mean there will be no conflict for those who must occupy themselves with the instrumental good rather than the intrinsic one. Even in the individual the need to govern our appetites distracts us from contemplation (cf. *Phaedo* 66d).

7. At the end of the discussion Socrates repeats that the philosopher must approach ruling "not as a fine thing but as a necessity" (540b). Cf. N. White 1979, "the ruler's position *is just* because an essential part of his task is that very discontent with ruling that might superficially appear to show that his position is *not just*" (191).

8. Cf. Andrew 1983, 529.

9. Henri Bergson, *The Two Sources of Morality and Religion* (Garden City, N.Y.: Doubleday Anchor, 1935 [1932]), 220–21. Cf. Plotinus *Enneads* 3.8.4.

10. A. E. Taylor 1956 (1926), 295.

11. See Richard Kraut, "Return to the Cave: *Republic* 519–521", in Gail Fine, ed., *Plato 2* (Oxford: Oxford University Press, 1999), 235–54.

12. *The Deliverance from Error*, in Hyman and Walsh, eds., *Philosophy in the Middle Ages*, 2nd edition (Indianapolis: Hackett, 1983), 279.

13. Martin Buber, *Tales of the Hassidim*, Book One (New York: Schocken, 1947), 101–2.

14. Cf. *Apology* 31d–e

15. βάναυσοι; cf. 495d–e.

16. Even the ultimate objects of eros, because they are eternal, do not arouse the appetite (*Symposium* 199e–203b & 209a–212a; cf. *Republic* 499b–c).

17. Cf. Aristotle, *Metaphysics* A.1. 981a3–b9.

18. David Roochnik summarizes eight pre-Platonic conceptions of *techne* from Homer to the sophists, and shows that in each case the list of criteria includes both rational principles and a practical application (*Of Art and Wisdom: Plato's Understanding of Techne* [University Park: Pennsylvania State University Press, 1996], 20–21, 26, 31, 41, 44, 50, 52, 70).

19. As we saw in chapter 6, 198–99, the fact that the same studies are both useful in the empirical world and can also awaken us to the intelligible may explain why the Divided Line makes *pistis* and *dianoia* of equal size.

20. ἀξιοῦτε; cf. ὑποθέσεων etc. in the discussion of *dianoia* at 510b5 and following.

21. διανοηθῆναι. Here *dianoia* is contrasted with sight but not with *noesis*.

22. Benardete disagrees: "The sequence that Socrates establishes for the mathematical sciences . . . is not a sequence of ascent. Harmonics is not closer to either being or the good than arithmetic" (1989, 181). But, in fact, harmonics *is* closer to the good than arithmetic in the required sense: it is more synoptic. Harmonics includes arithmetic but arithmetic does not include harmonics. Nettleship similarly observes that "Each step adds something to the complexity of the subject" (1901, 269); cf. Brumbaugh: "the order of the curriculum is one in which each successive science presupposes the principles of the one preceding, but integrates them with new attributes peculiar to its own treatment" (1954, 104–6).

23. E.g., Annas 1981, 275; but cf. Nettleship 1901, 271–73.

24. Cf. Rousseau's "Discourse on the Arts and Sciences."

25. 341d–342e, 374e, 466e, 488d–489a, 493d. Cf. *Statesman* 284a.

26. In the original account, this final training might have been redundant since the philosophers began as warrior-rulers in the transition from the spirited city to the rational (412c–414b), but now that in the kallipolis the students have been reconceived as children ("In the earlier part of our discussion we chose old men, but in this one we cannot accept that. . . . All the preparatory studies for dialectic must be put before them when they are children", 536c–d) they must have additional training in these areas.

27. We saw in the previous chapter that in all five ways that philosophers develop without the intervention of the city, an insulating factor protects them from temptation—whether exile, contempt for one's peers, limitations imposed by sickliness, or the warning of a divine voice (496a–c).

28. There is a well-known problem in the *Nicomachean Ethics* about the relation between intellectual virtue which leads to contemplation, and moral virtue which leads to the mean (see, for example, J. L. Ackrill, "Aristotle on Eudaimonia", in A. O. Rorty, *Essays on Aristotle's Ethics* [Berkeley: University of California Press, 1980], 17–33). I believe that the resolution in Aristotle is analogous to the one I am attributing to Plato. Although it is often argued that the moral virtues in Aristotle are independent of contemplation, only someone who has attained the impersonal consciousness of contemplation will be able to reliably discern the virtuous mean in every situation without the distorting influence of self-interested desires. Otherwise, even if we have virtuous habits, however much we may aim at moral behavior we will have no reliable ability to hit upon it. Only *phronesis*, practical wisdom, unimpeded by irrational desires, can accomplish that (see *Nicomachean Ethics* 1.13, 2.2, 2.6, 6.13), and *phronesis* is connected with contemplation insofar as both are identified with *nous*, reason (compare 6.13.1144b1–13 with 10.7.1177b18–20).

29. Cf. *Symposium* 211d–212a.

30. Adam calls it "notoriously the most difficult passage in his writings" (1963 [1902], 264); Gomperz calls it "the despair of commentators" (1905, 91); Grube says it is "perhaps the most obscure and controversial passage in the whole of Plato's works. Scholars are not even agreed as to whether there is one Platonic number or two" (1974, 197 n. 6); and Cornford omits it from his translation because of its obscurity (1941, 269n3). Brumbaugh's detailed discussion gives a good sense of the difficulties of interpreting it (1954, 107–150). A more technical discussion may be found in Adam (1963 [1902], 201–9, 264–312). Even if we could agree on an interpretation of the passage, it is still far from clear what the components of the number(s) refer to and how it is to be applied. Suppose, for example, that we accept Reeve's interpretation:

> The human geometrical number is the product of 3, 4, and 5 'thrice increased', multiplied by itself three times, i.e., $(3 \cdot 4 \cdot 5)4$ or 12,960,000. This can be represented geometrically as a square whose sides are 3600 or as an oblong or rectangle whose sides are 4800 and 2700. The first is 'so many times a hundred', viz. 36 times. The latter is obtained as follows. The 'rational diameter' of 5 is the nearest rational number to the real diagonal of a square whose sides are 5, i.e., to $\sqrt{50}$. This number is 7. Since the square of 7 is 49, we get the longer side of the rectangle by diminishing 49 by 1 and multiplying the result by 100. This gives 4800. The 'irrational diameter' of 5 is $\sqrt{50}$. When squared, diminished by 2, and multiplied by 100 this, too, is 4800. The short side, 'a hundred cubes of three', is 2700. [1992, 216–17 n. 10]

Even if Reeve has sorted out the mathematics correctly, we still do not know what the numbers refer to and how to apply them. For a more recent discussion see Rod Jenks,

"The Machinery of the Collapse: On *Republic* VIII", *History of Political Thought* 23 (2002): 21–29.

31. Thus it is not the case, as is sometimes supposed, that if moral knowledge is a *techne* in Plato it must consist merely in a calculable application of rules. For related discussions of the *techne* model of knowledge in the *Republic* see Laurence Houlgate, "Virtue is Knowledge", *Monist* 54 (1970): 142–53, esp. 148; Terence Irwin, "Recollection and Plato's Moral Theory", *Review of Metaphysics* 27 (1974): 752–72, esp. 755; R. K. Sprague, *Plato's Philosopher-King* (Columbia: University of South Carolina Press, 1976), 66, 74; Richard Parry, "The Craft of Justice", *Canadian Journal of Philosophy* Supplementary Volume IX (1983): 19–38, and *Plato's Craft of Justice* (Albany: State University of New York Press, 1996); Martha Nussbaum, *The Fragility of Goodness* (Cambridge: Cambridge University Press, 1986), 298; Alexander Nehamas, "Socratic Intellectualism", in John Cleary, ed., *Proceedings of the Boston Area Colloquium in Ancient Philosophy* 2 (Lanham, Md.: University Press of America, 1987), 275–316, esp. 299, 309; John McKie, *LCMD* 20 and 26; Julia Annas, "Virtue as a Skill", *International Journal of Philosophical Studies* 3 (1995): 227–43.

32. I have argued elsewhere against the view that the *Statesman*—together with the *Parmenides*, *Theaetetus*, and *Sophist*—rejects and revises the metaphysics of the *Republic* (Dorter 1994), but even if we accept that view, there is no reason why the *Statesman* might not share and further develop the *Republic*'s conception of the relation between theory and practice.

33. *Statesman* 283d–e, 284a–b, d; interjections omitted.

34. Geometry aims at knowledge of the equal, the double, and other ratios (529e–530a). Pure astronomy too deals with quickness and slowness in relation to each other (529d), and harmony with what relations are harmonious with each other (531c). Even when we give a precise measurement, such as that an object is so many cubits in size, the measurement is in relation to an arbitrarily chosen unit of measure rather than to anything absolute such as the mean, the right degree.

35. Ian Robins concludes that a concept of the mean is central to all the mathematical studies of Book 7:

> Ratios and proportion . . . are the basis of the community and kinship of the sciences [and are what make mathematicians] able to embark on dialectic. . . . Central to the significance of ratios and proportions within plane and solid geometry is the geometric mean. . . . Plato would have such applications of ratios and proportions extended to what he calls astronomy. . . . What in the geometrical sciences and astronomy were studied in their applications are in harmonics studied in themselves. The ratios are now related not only to mean proportionals, the geometric mean, but also to arithmetic and harmonic means.

("Mathematics and the Conversion of the Mind: *Republic* vii 522c1–531e3", *Ancient Philosophy* 15 [1995]: 359–91, esp. 387–88.)

36. Aristotle will resolve the same difficulty in the same way. At the beginning of the *Nicomachean Ethics* he too points out the problem of applying precise concepts to the world of action:

Our discussion will be adequate if it achieves as much clarity as the subject matter allows, for precision ought not to be sought for equally in all discussions, any more than in all the products of craftsmanship. Noble and just actions, which political philosophy investigates, contain much discrepancy and irregularity. . . . And good actions too involve a similar irregularity. . . . We must be content, then, when dealing with such subjects, and drawing inferences from such material, to indicate the truth in a general way and in outline . . . for it is the mark of an educated person to seek the degree of precision in each class of things which the nature of the subject admits. [I.3.1094b11–25]

Like Plato, he responds to the lack of precision in practical affairs by developing the concept of an imprecise "mean" (II.6–9; cf. III.6–IV.9). Also like Plato, he connects the doctrine of the mean with *techne*: see Welton and Polansky 1996, 84. Their defense of the Aristotelian doctrine of the mean against certain ways that it has been misunderstood would apply as well to Plato's formulation.

37. The term used is τὸ μέσον (cf. Aristotle's μεσότης), whereas the *Statesman* and *Laws* use τὸ μέτριον.

38. The Confucian classic, *The Doctrine of the Mean*, apparently written around the time of Plato (legend ascribes it to Confucius' grandson), draws an analogous although not identical connection between harmony and the mean: "Before the feelings of pleasure, anger, sorrow, and joy are aroused the way is called the mean. When these feelings are aroused and each and all attain due measure and degree, it is called harmony" (in Wing-tsit Chan, editor and translator, *A Source Book in Chinese Philosophy* [Princeton: Princeton University Press, 1963], 98).

39. "Critics of Plato frequently overlook the fact that he insisted on practical experience in the training of his rulers. Newman, *Aristot. Pol.* i. p. 5, points out that this experience takes the place of special training in political science" (Shorey 1935, 229).

40. Cf. Aristotle, *Metaphysics* A.7.988a26–7.

41. "The usual prophetic voice of the divinity in previous times always spoke to me very frequently and opposed me even in very trivial matters if I was about to do something that was not right. . . . It could not be the case that the usual sign would not have opposed me, if I was not about to do something good." (*Apology* 40a–c; cf. *Euthydemus* 272e, *Phaedrus* 242b). This infallibility is not achieved by the philosopher-rulers, as the unreliability of the nuptial number showed.

42. Benardete argues that "since in fact the *daimonion* kept Socrates out of politics, the *daimonion* could not be what it was for Socrates and bring about the coincidence of philosophy and power" (1989, 149). However, it was not politics as such that the divine sign kept Socrates out of, but only the Athenian politics of his day: "It is this [divine sign] that opposes my engaging in politics . . . for there is no human being who will survive if he nobly opposes you or any other crowd, and prevents many unjust and illegal things from happening in the city" (*Apology* 31d–e). The populace of the kallipolis is not a "crowd" (πλήθει) that will kill its just rulers, so Benardete's inference does not apply to the *Republic* itself. Later Socrates and Glaucon explicitly acknowledge that a just man who might be unwilling to take part in the politics of his

present homeland would nevertheless be willing to participate in the political life of the city they are constructing (592a).

43. A term that earlier described the relationship between astronomy and harmony (530d). Here it refers to the complementarity of mind and body, there to seeing and hearing.

CHAPTER EIGHT

~

Decline and Fall
(Books 8 and 9 to 575d)

The Decline of Aristocracy (543a–547b)

Socrates recapitulates the three waves and suggests that they recall the point
from which they digressed. Glaucon recalls that prior to the digression of
Books 5–7 Socrates had described both a city and a person that were good,
"although it seemed that you had an even finer city and man to tell of", and
had been about to enumerate four primary species of lesser cities and people
when Polemarchus and Adeimantus interrupted. He suggests that, as in an
interrupted wrestling match, Socrates ought to offer him the same hold as
before and try to give him the same answer that he would have given then
(543d–544b). There was no need for Socrates to refer to Books 5–7 as a
digression (543c5), or for him and Glaucon to characterize the next stage as
a return to the earlier situation as if those books did not exist. Socrates could
simply have said, "Now that we have seen what the best city is like, let us look
at the others". The decline could have been depicted as a decay of the
kallipolis of the philosopher-rulers, rather than the rational city of the complete guardians described in Book 4. The arbitrary description of the next step
as a return to the end of Book 4 is another instance of drawing emphatic
boundaries between adjoining sections of the dialogue in order to emphasize
the passage between levels of the Divided Line, for the discussion is about to
return from *dianoetic* and *noetic* concerns with intelligible reality back to concerns about visible reality (*pistis*), cities whose goals are practical rather than
contemplative.

The four primary types of lesser constitution are the Cretan or Laconian (Spartan), oligarchy, democracy, and tyranny. Just as in Book 4 the apparent rigidity of the tripartite soul was softened by an acknowledgement that there may be other parts in between the three (443d), here too it is acknowledged that there are other constitutions in between these four, such as dynasties and purchased kingships (544c–d). And as in Book 4 the presence of the three characteristics of the city—appetite, spiritedness, rationality—was ascribed to their presence in individuals (435d–e), now the existence of the five constitutions among cities is said to come "from the characters of the citizens which, as if tipping the scales by their weight, pull other things after them" (544d–e). In that case, Socrates concludes, since there are five types of city there must be five types of soul. We shall examine that obscure metaphor after going through Socrates' account of the decline.

When Socrates goes on to say that they have already discussed the type of soul that corresponds to aristocracy ("the rule of the best") he is referring back to Book 4, since they have just agreed to pick up from where they were before the "digression", and in any case the correspondence referred to here between soul and city had been absent from Books 5–7.[1] The next step for Socrates is to discuss the other four constitutions with a view to understanding the nature of the most unjust (i.e., tyranny) in order to compare it with the most just, and adjudicate between the claims of Socrates and Thrasymachus. Plato is interested not only in classifying the different constitutions but also in discovering the process by which one arises out of another, so the first question concerns not only timocracy, the rule of honor or spiritedness, but also its predecessor, aristocracy, and the reasons for the latter's decay. Socrates' guiding principle is that "every regime changes because of its rulers, when dissention arises among them; but when they are of the same mind, even if they are very few, alteration is impossible" (545c–d). The principle fails to acknowledge that regimes can also change when the subjects rebel, and not only does the history of Plato's own society bear ample evidence of that possibility,[2] but Socrates himself will acknowledge it when he comes to the transition from oligarchy to democracy. Perhaps it is a deliberate over-simplification in order to focus on the way one constitution can turn into another by internal necessity rather than external contingencies.

Transition: Weakened Aristocracy (545c–547a)

In language that he self-mockingly compares to Homer and the tragedians, Socrates announces in the personae of the Muses that everything which comes into being must eventually be destroyed, even something as well constituted as aristocracy. During his discussion of the Second Wave—the communities of men, women, and children—Socrates had spoken of the need for selective breeding (458d–460a). We now learn that the decline of the aristocracy will take place when eugenics is improperly managed. The aristocracy of Book 4 has fewer hurdles to surmount than the kallipolis of Books 5–7 in order to come into existence, but if it should come about it will sooner or later fall victim to the difficulties of the nuptial number that we noted in chapter 7. The city would soon begin to decay because "those who were educated to be rulers of the city will not hit upon the fertility and barrenness of our race through calculation together with sense perception, but it will escape them and they will beget children at some time when they should not" (546b). Because sense perception is directed to what is imprecise and constantly changing, there can be no precise rule for the practical application of a formula like the nuptial number even if we knew how to interpret it, and we can only hope for a sensitivity to what the moment requires, *kairos* (546d2), a sensitivity that cannot be taught because it is nonconceptual, and which therefore will sooner or later fail.[3]

When that happens there will be no worthy successors, and the second stage of rulers will have to be the best of a bad lot. As rulers, the Muses continue, they will first neglect the Muses, and education in the arts will suffer, followed by physical training. Since education in the arts was what enabled the children to recognize the difference between the beautiful, rational, and good, on one hand, and the ugly, irrational, and bad, on the other, rulers who lack that training will no longer be able to distinguish among "Hesiod's and our gold, silver, bronze, and iron races" (546d–547a).[4] When Socrates says that the next (i.e., third) stage of rulers would have mixed natures—iron mixed in with silver, and bronze mixed in with gold—this implies that both gold and silver were already present even in the rulers of the second stage. So they had mixed natures as well, not only gold as originally conceived but also silver, which was previously present only in the auxiliaries (415a). In one sense we all have mixed natures, since everyone has all three elements within themselves; but in the present context to say that the natures of the rulers and auxiliaries are mixed is to say that some of the rulers will have natures in which appetite is stronger than reason, and some of the auxiliaries will have natures in which it is stronger than spiritedness. As a result of the mixtures, like-mindedness among the rulers will be replaced with unlikeness and disharmony, the seeds of dissention and instability, which "always beget war and enmity whenever they arise" (547a).

When the nuptial number failed because of the difficulty of employing "rationality together with sense perception" (546b), the implication is that even in our most stable condition the tension between rationality and sense perception,[5] mind and body, cannot be resolved. The incoherence between rationality and sense perception will produce rulers who are subject to the more volatile discordance between rationality and appetite (cf. 439d). Once bronze and iron natures are mixed in the rulers with gold and silver, the city's self-mastery, the control of appetite by rationality that was the basis of all the virtues in Book 4, will deteriorate into a struggle for dominance between the two. "'Of this lineage'",[6] the Muses announce through Socrates, "is dissention, wherever and whenever it arises." Glaucon concludes that "we shall say that the Muses have answered correctly", and Socrates replies, "They must have since they're Muses" (547a). Now that the conversation has returned from the level of *episteme* to that of *doxa*, poets like Homer and Hesiod, and their Muses, take on renewed importance, although, of course, the poets' words would be accepted no more uncritically than they were in Books 2 and 3. The appeal to the Muses also seems to acknowledge that the account Socrates is about to give is not historically factual (as we shall see below, 271–74) but represents the ideal sequence to which the principles on which the city was founded would lead.

Timocracy (547b–550c)

The Timocratic City (547b–548d)

In this generation the rulers of different natures pull in opposite directions, the iron and bronze toward money-making and the acquisition of land, houses, gold, and silver; while those with gold and silver natures, "being rich by nature", pull the souls back to virtue and the old order. They end by agreeing on a middle course—but not every mean is good: they distribute the land and houses privately, enslave the productive class, who had previously been their friends and free, making them serfs and domestic servants, and occupy themselves with war and with defending themselves against those whom they enslaved (547b–c). Like the spirited city of Book 2, its chief characteristic is military force rather than wealth or rationality. There it happened positively, from an unlimited extension of appetite; here it happened negatively, from the escape of appetite from the limitation of rationality. As part of the compromise, the spirited rulers will, like their aristocratic predecessors, refrain from money-making and other kinds of work associated with the productive class (although they will secretly hoard gold and silver) but unlike them they will be afraid to appoint wise rulers. They neglect the true Muse (the companionship of discussion and philosophy), respect physical training more than the arts, and are educated by force rather than persuasion. Because of their spirited natures the city is characterized by the love of honor rather than love of pleasure or truth (547b–548c).

An unmentioned casualty in the decline from aristocracy to timocracy is the equality of women. When Socrates says that the rulers will now amass secret hoards of gold and silver, he adds that they will also have secret love-nests where they will spend lavishly on "women as well as anyone else they wish" (548a–b), so evidently the rulers now are exclusively men. Women must implicitly be numbered among the formerly free friends of the rulers whom they now, in effect, enslave as serfs and domestic servants. The inferior position in which women now find themselves reduces their access to higher things and confines them to a world of petty aspirations. Each of the transitions to a different constitution results from a dialectic between representatives of opposing values, which destabilizes the previous order and leads to a compromise that becomes the next regime. In the case of the aristocratic city, the opposing values, are embodied by different natures (gold, silver, bronze, iron), and in the case of the individual, by the influence of people in different stations. In view of the reduced status of women since the collapse of the aristocracy it is not surprising, although certainly disappointing, that the main dialectic in the corruption of the aristocratic individual is between the father and mother, the latter (together with servants) providing the undermining influence. Women will not, however, contribute to the decline of the oligarchic or democratic person.

The Timocratic Person (548d–550b)

Adeimantus now takes Glaucon's place as Socrates' respondent, after remarking that the timocratic person must be much like Glaucon, with respect to being a lover of victory (548d). In this case only, Socrates describes the characteristics of the type of person before tracing how the person arises from his predecessors. The other accounts, both of city and individual, conform to the model of the timocratic *city*: first the origins are described and then the characteristics.

The timocratic individual, like the city, is governed by love of honor, and so is more stubborn than his predecessor and harsher to his slaves. But he will share with his predecessor a gentleness toward other free people and an obedience to the rulers. Although he will love the arts, his training will be more weighted toward physical exercise. Just as the timocratic city arises from a good constitution (aristocracy) that is badly governed, the timocratic individual originates from a good father who lives in a badly governed city. As people who have escaped the cave and discovered the good are no longer tempted by the pleasures and honors of the prisoners (516d), the father values the life of mind and cares little about honors and money. The mother's life lacks this dimension, and when she sees that her husband does not attain

honors and money, she complains to their son that his father is unmanly, as
do the servants. They view the father with the same contempt with which
Thrasymachus viewed people who are just. Pulled between his father's
encouragement of his rational part, and the others' encouragement of his
honor-loving and money-loving parts, he settles in the middle as a lover of
honor. As a lover of honor he will at first despise money, but because he is not
protected by the best guardian and preserver of virtue, namely rationality
mixed with the arts, as he gets older the money-loving part of his nature will
gradually take control. It will be no easier for rationality to assert its claims,
now that self-mastery has been lost, than it was to bring true aristocracy into
being in the first place.

Oligarchy (550c–555a)

The Oligarchic City (550c–552e)

Oligarchy, "the rule of the few", is used here to mean plutocracy,[7] the rule of
the rich. As the genesis of the first three cities in Books 2–3 was not discontinuous but a gradual evolution in which the higher forms were already
implicit in the lower, here too, once the balance of power begins to shift from
rationality to appetite, all of the regimes are stations along a single road to
ever greater indulgence of the appetites. Even in the timocracy wealth was
hoarded and prized,[8] and once that precedent has been set the shallow but
highly visible rewards of the appetites will gradually blind the rulers to the
rewards of virtue, since wealth is opposed to virtue as much as if they were in
opposite pans of a scale (550e). Eventually the rulers and their wives will
spend money in ways that pervert the laws and even defy them. Again violence comes into play, but this time there is no talk of enslaving the non-
rulers but only using force or threats of force to change the constitution to
disenfranchise all but the rich.

Socrates itemizes the disadvantages that result from a city in which love of
money is the dominant value. First, in an allusion to the allegory of the ship
in Book 6, Socrates reminds Adeimantus of how a ship would fare if the captain were chosen by wealth rather than skill (551c). Second, the city is no
longer unified, which had been one of the essential requirements for a successful city (462a–b), but is now divided rich against poor (551d). Third, it
will be weak externally as well as internally because the oligarchs, unlike the
timocrats, will not be good at war, and not only will they be afraid to arm
their hostile subjects, but their love of money will make them unwilling to
pay mercenaries (551d–e). Fourth, since the same people may be farmers,
money-makers, and soldiers, the principle of specialization, on which the ear-

lier conception of justice was based, will be violated (551e–552a). Finally, the premium placed on wealth will lead to the creation of a class of the destitute, in addition to those of the rich and poor. A society that values money above all else encourages extravagance, which leads to bankruptcy. Under this constitution, for the first time people will be allowed to sell all their possessions and remain in the city as unemployed beggars. Such people made as little contribution to the city when they were spendthrifts as they do when reduced to beggary, for although they seemed to be rulers, they neither ruled nor obeyed but only consumed what was available (552b). Socrates compares them to drones, non-worker bees, and distinguishes them into two species corresponding to the distinction between stingless and stinging drones, namely beggars and evildoers—products of lack of education, bad upbringing, and a badly constituted regime (552e). The importance of drones as a separate category within the class of the poor is comparable to the importance of enslaved priests in Nietzsche's scenario of the resentment and rebellion of slave morality.[9] For Nietzsche, the lingering sense of entitlement in the former priests is what enables them to resist their masters' judgement of them as inferior, and gives them the confidence to oppose and eventually defeat the masters. In the same way, the fact that the drones were not always poor but once were oligarchs themselves gives them a sense of entitlement that fuels their resentment and turns it into destructiveness and rebellion (stings) rather than defeatism.

The Oligarchic Person (553a–555b)

The description of the timocratic city did not itemize its disadvantages the way the description of the oligarchic city did, but we saw that one of them was that timocracy opened out on one side to the love of money and so was always under pressure from the appetites. Another becomes visible in the depiction of the origin of the oligarchic person, with an echo of the ship metaphor:

> A son who has been following in the footsteps of his timocratic father sees him suddenly dashed against the city as against a reef. His father was either a general or holder of some other important office who was accused in court by false witnesses and put to death or exiled or dishonored, and lost all his property. [553a–b]

Since the highest value in timocracy is honor, spirited people will constantly vie with one another for honors and will not hesitate to plot against their rivals and seek to dishonor them. After seeing the fate of his father, and suffering the resulting impoverishment, the son ousts the love of honor from his inner throne and replaces it with the love of money. Just as in the oligarchic city everyone who is not a ruler is reduced to beggary (552d), in the oligarchic person rationality and spiritedness become slaves to appetite, so that rationality is permitted to function only in the service of getting more money, and spiritedness is permitted to honor only wealth and what leads to it (553c–d). But he is still close enough to the timocratic mentality to be thrifty and hard-working, so he will enslave not only rationality and spiritedness but also his unnecessary appetites, which he regards as vain, and satisfy only his necessary ones. What Socrates means by these terms is not explained until the discussion of democracy: "Aren't those [appetites] that we can't desist from, and those whose satisfaction benefits us, rightly called necessary, for we are by nature compelled to satisfy them both?"—for example, the desire for healthy food. Unnecessary appetites, on the other hand, are those that go beyond what is necessary for health and well-being, and are "harmful both to the body and to the soul with respect to wisdom and self-control", like the desire for unhealthy food. Unlike necessary appetites, we can usually train ourselves to be free of the unnecessary ones. Necessary appetites correspond to money-making because they are useful, while unnecessary ones correspond to extravagance (558d–559c).

Although the oligarchic person will keep them under control, he will nevertheless be filled with drone-like unnecessary appetites both of the beggarly and the evil-doer species, because he does not value education. But like the city itself he will be careful to keep them in check, not because he can rule them through rationality as with aristocracy, but he rules them by compulsion and fear because he worries about losing his possessions (554a–d).[10] He is thus divided against himself, necessary against unnecessary appetites, the way the city is divided rich against poor—the second of the five items of indictment against it—and he shares its third weaknesses as well: his fear of spending his money or of arousing his appetites makes him too cautious, and he is often defeated (554d–555a).

Democracy (555b–562a)

The Democratic City (555b–558c)

When Books 2 and 3 traced the evolution of the cities, the healthy city that limited itself to the necessary appetites became fevered and gave itself over to unnecessary appetites as well (373b–d), but subsequently purified itself under the discipline of warrior rule (399e). As the city now devolves, it passes in reverse order through stages that correspond to the earlier ones—but with important differences. Timocracy corresponds in essential ways to the spirited city ruled by warriors, but its successor, oligarchy, does not correspond to the undisciplined feverish city that preceded warrior rule, since oligarchy retains timocracy's discipline. The evolution from the fevered city to the militaristic city would find its symmetrical devolution here only if we bypassed oligarchy and imagined a change from timocracy directly to democracy, in which military discipline is abandoned in favor of a self-indulgence that no longer distinguishes between necessary and unnecessary appetites. The reason oligarchy does not fit into the pattern is that it represents a stage where discipline is retained after militarism has been abandoned, but there was no corresponding stage in the first half of the dialogue where discipline was established before militarism arrived. What corresponds there to the self-limitation of appetite in oligarchy is the self-limitation of appetite in the original healthy city, but that was a product of natural innocence in the service of cooperation, while this is a product of deliberate restraint in the service of competition. Another asymmetry between the stages of growth and decline is the almost complete heterogeneity between the last stage of decline—tyranny—and the first stage of growth—the healthy city. Both series have five stages but they correspond to each other only in part:

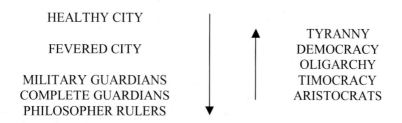

HEALTHY CITY

FEVERED CITY

MILITARY GUARDIANS
COMPLETE GUARDIANS
PHILOSOPHER RULERS

TYRANNY
DEMOCRACY
OLIGARCHY
TIMOCRACY
ARISTOCRATS

The fevered city was characterized by the unlimited (ἄπειρον) desire for money (373d), and now democracy comes about because the honoring of wealth in an oligarchy will lead to an insatiable (ἀπληστίαν) desire to become as rich as possible. That, in turn, leads the rulers to encourage others to waste their substance and go into debt with them, so that in the end they may take over the others' wealth and become even richer, while the others are reduced to drones. The drones with their stings are filled with resentment and plot revenge, lusting (ἐρῶντες: 555e1) for revolution, while the money-makers avert their eyes from them and continue their predatory practices, further swelling the number of drones. Socrates had said that oligarchy is the first of the regimes not to have a law against allowing people to dispose of their property in any way they wish, so one way to prevent the present volatile state of affairs would be to enact such a law, and the second-best way would be to prescribe that most voluntary contracts will be at the lender's own risk so that the debtor's property could not be seized for non-repayment of loans. But any such measure runs counter to the spirit of oligarchy and would not be enacted (556a–b).

The fact that oligarchy is destroyed simply by the excessive pursuit of its defining value of wealth (as will be true of democracy and its defining value of liberty, and was implicitly true of timocracy to the extent that wealth was valued as a badge of honor),[11] resumes two of the leitmotivs that we have been tracing since the beginning of the dialogue, and shows how they are related. On one hand it shows once again the importance of pursuing a good that is self-limiting—a mean rather than one that is unlimited and extreme. On the other hand it shows how pursuing something to its extreme leads to its reversal: in this case the unlimited drive to wealth by the rich will lead to the triumph of the poor.

The rulers and their children who care only about wealth and luxury will become as deficient in physical strength as they are in spiritedness, and when the exploited poor, who are strong and tough from their labors, see this, they will seize the opportunity for revolution. The revolution takes place when the tensions between the two parties are ignited by an external force such as the bringing in of allies by one of the parties, just as a shock from outside may send an unhealthy body into sickness. If the poor are victorious, after eliminating their opponents they will give everyone an equal share in ruling (Athens was a direct democracy rather than a representative one), and the rulers will be chosen by lot. In Book 4 Socrates characterized the aristocracy as being like a statue whose parts are painted in the appropriate colors, rather than in the most beautiful colors without regard for their relation to the whole (420c–d). Democracy turns out to be the exact opposite: "This seems to be the most beautiful of the constitutions; like a multicolored cloak embroidered with all kinds of ornament, this too, embroidered with every kind of character, would appear to be the most beautiful"—so much so that it could serve as an emporium of constitutions that one could visit to decide which kind one prefers (557c–d). With its characteristic emphasis on total liberty "it would be, as it seems, a pleasant constitution, without rulers (*anarchos*) and multicolored, distributing a certain equality to both equals and unequals alike" (558c).[12] The latter words of course also imply one of the flaws of democracy—that it is unable to make distinctions among things that are importantly different. Thus, whether or not people rule has nothing to do with whether they are qualified to rule, and as the term *anarchos* implies, people will not even feel bound to obey the law, and convicted criminals will freely roam the streets (558a): if everyone is equal, then it becomes difficult to insist on obedience from those who disagree with the lawmakers. Clearly, this portrait of toleration in democracies is exaggerated, or Socrates would have died of old age.

In the *Statesman* Plato concedes that in one way democracy can be viewed as the best form of government, namely when we are speaking of governments that are badly run (302b–303b). When the rulers are good and wise, then the more power they have to put their wisdom into effect, the better; so rule by a single person will be best, and rule by a few people second best, while democratic rule, in which the rulers have the least power, will be least good. But when the rulers are bad or unwise, the less power they have, the better off the society will be, so rule by one person will be worst—a tyranny—and democratic rule will be best. In the *Republic* Plato is investigating the case of regimes in their ideal form, so democracy fares poorly.

The Democratic Person (558c–562a)

Previously the mechanisms of transformation in the city and person were described in precisely parallel terms, since the rational, spirited, and appetitive drives in a person exactly corresponded to the rational, spirited, and appetitive classes of the city. But once oligarchy is reached, we are entirely within the realm of the appetite with nowhere further to go, so subsequent distinctions must be made within appetite itself. Now, the fault line within the city is between the rich and poor, but since money has only external existence, whatever corresponds to those two within the individual must do so only analogously. These are the necessary and unnecessary appetites, the former being like money making because they are useful for our works, while the latter resemble impoverishment because unnecessary appetites are like extravagance (559c). The correspondence seems strained since extravagance is not the same as poverty, but what Socrates has in mind is not the poor in general but the most extreme subset of the poor, the drones, whose poverty resulted from extravagance and who are therefore synonymous with unnecessary appetites (554b7). The polarity that will undermine the oligarchic person develops when he gets a taste of the drones' honey, and his necessary desires have to compete with the excitement and variety of the unnecessary ones. As with the city, the crisis is precipitated by an external influence, such as the influence of his oligarchic father and family on one side, or of his dissipated acquaintances on the other. If the drones are victorious, his moderate views are banished and a transvaluation of values takes place: a sense of shame is called foolishness, and self-control cowardice, while on the other hand arrogance is called being well educated, being uncontrolled (*anarchian*) freedom, wastefulness magnificence, and shamelessness courage (560d–561a). If he is lucky and his frenzy does not go too far, he will welcome back some of the exiles, and instead of giving the unnecessary pleasures precedence over the necessary ones, he will put them all on an equal footing, denying that any pleasures are better than any others. His life then flits from one desire to another without distinction, everything from drink to music to philosophy to politics to soldiering, whichever seems pleasant at the time.[13] His constitution is thus full of liberty and multicolored in just the way the city was (561b–562a).

The fact that the defining feature of democracy is the *variety* of its citizens, who are its rulers, and not that the rulers themselves necessarily have democratic characters of the kind just described, is a departure from the previous cases, in which the internal constitution of the rulers paralleled that of the city.[14] It is also a departure from the metaphor of the scale, with which Socrates first introduced the subject, and according to which "regimes are born from . . . the characters of the citizens" (544d). There is some question, therefore, whether Socrates' account as a whole is coherent.[15] The case of democracy is not, however, as different from the others as it at first appears, since the genesis of democracy is from the victory of the working poor (557a) who are the largest group in the city (565a). Just as the rich are the most disciplined of the appetitive people, most of the poor will be appetitive people who lack internal discipline and who are internally democratic, treating necessary and unnecessary appetites as equals. Internally democratic people will therefore be the dominant force in democracies. Although democracy is therefore as compatible with the metaphor of the scale as were the others, there is some question about whether Socrates' accounts of all of them in general are compatible with that metaphor, since he derives each civic constitution from its predecessor rather than from the influence of the corresponding kind of person. We will consider this question after looking at the account of tyranny.

Tyranny (562a–576a)

The Tyrannical City (562a–569c)

Here, again, in the transition from democracy to tyranny, the familiar themes reappear of the importance of the mean and the self-reversal of extremes. As oligarchy's insatiable desire for what it takes to be the good, namely wealth, led to the rule of the poor, democracy's insatiable desire for its own conception of the good, freedom, leads to the enslavement of tyranny (562b–c). Socrates will later repeat this point more emphatically, adding as a general principle that "anything that is done to excess is wont to produce a correspondingly great opposite reaction: in the seasons, as well as in plants, and in bodies, and not least in political constitutions" (563e–564a). As we noted earlier, this general principle was previously instantiated in Book 3, at a point in the rise of the city that corresponds to this point in its decline, when the excessive luxury of the city led to a puritanical reaction (399e).

In a passage that resonates with the recent practice of the radical left of denouncing their opponents, however moderate, as fascists, Socrates says that when a democracy becomes too demanding of freedom, unless the rulers become more and more permissive they are accused of being oligarchs, and law-abiding citizens are called willing slaves. Rulers and subjects end up reversing their roles, as do teacher and student, and parent and child as well, so that fathers fear their children and emulate them, while children behave fearlessly and shamelessly, and slaves behave like the equals of freemen— recall that the dialogue began when Polemarchus' slave grabbed hold of Socrates' clothing. Finally, and ironically, another symptom of the collapse of order is a return to the equality of women (562c–562b).[16] In the kallipolis women were the equals of men because they received the same training and education. In timocracy and oligarchy they no longer received the same benefits as men, and, at least in timocracy, they represented a lower level of values. In the freedom and indiscriminate toleration of a democracy, education is no longer required (558b), so the new equality of the sexes results no longer from women being given the training and education that was otherwise reserved for men, but rather from men no longer receiving the training and education that used to raise them above women. Whereas in the kallipolis they met on the high ground, now they meet on the low.

Thus far we have not yet reached tyranny but only anarchy: "In the end they pay no mind to the laws, whether written or unwritten, in order that no one may in any way be their master" (563d–e). It is at this point that Socrates introduces the principle of opposition quoted above, that anything done to excess sets up an equal and opposite reaction, and accordingly from the most extreme freedom arises the greatest and most savage slavery (563e–564a). In a democracy the drones are no longer disenfranchised as in oligarchy, and the most fierce among them now become rabble-rousing speakers and demagogues. Their chief targets will be the rich, from whom they can extort money by predatory litigation or even by the threat of it (cf. 553a–b), and after keeping most of the money for themselves, the drones use a portion to buy the allegiance of the workers, who are the largest and most powerful of the three classes. When the rich try to defend themselves, the drones accuse them of being oligarchs who are plotting revolution to restore the oligarchy, and at that point the democracy becomes so destabilized by the polarization between the rich and the rest that it can no longer survive. Neither the rich nor the workers want a crisis, but as the drones incite the workers against the rich there will be impeachments, judgements, and lawsuits. If the rich are victorious they reestablish the evil of oligarchy as a matter of self-defense against the drones. If the workers are victorious they set up in power the drone who is their leader, and that is the origin of tyranny (564e–565e).

Socrates refers to the myth of Lycaean Zeus in Arcadia, according to which anyone who tastes human innards cut up with those of sacrificial animals becomes a wolf, and he applies it to the tyrant who kills his opponents, banishing others, and pacifying the rest of the people with promises of land distribution. The killing is his taste of human blood, and if he is not killed himself he must become a wolf.[17] Most of the stages that he goes through are remarkably familiar even today. At the beginning he will deny tyrannical ambitions and be friendly to the general populace, ingratiating himself by making promises, forgiving debts, and distributing land (566d–e), so when those whom he is attacking plot to kill him in self-defense, the people readily grant his request for bodyguards. Now that he has armed supporters, he readily disposes of his enemies, either putting them to death or frightening them into exile, until he consolidates his power as a tyrant (566a–d). Once he has consolidated his power domestically, he will start a war so that the people will still feel the need of a leader, and will use the war to impoverish them by taxes, so that they will have to concern themselves with day-to-day existence and will have less opportunity to plot against him. He will also use wars as a pretext to put his opponents at the mercy of the enemy. As people begin to hate him, and the most courageous openly criticize him, he will kill them as well and get rid of anyone who is courageous, high-minded, wise, or rich. With the best people gone, and the rest increasingly hating him, he will have to enlarge his bodyguard from the only sources he can trust: on one hand foreign mercenaries, and on the other hand slaves to whom he grants freedom in exchange for their service (566e–567e).

In a brief digression, as he calls it (568d4), this gives Socrates further grounds for criticizing the poets. When Euripides said, "Tyrants are wise by associating with the wise", he must have thought that the slaves and mercenaries, whom we have now seen to be the tyrant's associates, are wise. The context from which this quotation comes has been lost, but presumably Socrates is being mischievous, and the words should be taken to mean, "If tyrants associate with the wise they will become wise", not "Because tyrants associate with the wise they have become wise". However much Socrates may have taken liberties with Euripides' words, Adeimantus seems willing to agree that the interpretation is consistent with what the poets say elsewhere: "he praises the tyrant's absolute power as godlike, and in many other ways, and the other poets do the same thing" (568b). The poets ought to understand, then, that they will not be welcome in their city, and indeed their influence tends to support tyrants and democracies.

To maintain his corps of bodyguards the tyrant will loot the city, both public treasury and private wealth, until people begin to complain. When Socrates first described how democracy degenerates into tyranny he said it was characteristic of democracy for fathers to behave like children and children like fathers, and for slaves to behave as equals of freemen (562e–563b). Now things go further, for the tyrant is the creature of the city, and thus stands toward it in the relation of son to father,[18] but it is for a grown son to support his father, not the other way around. Here the grown son, the tyrant, consumes the property of his "father" to support himself. Moreover the citizens are becoming impoverished also in order to support the bodyguard, which is composed in part of liberated slaves, and so not only is the father supporting the grown son, but the free are serving their own slaves. When the people's complaints are ignored and they try to dismiss the tyrant, they will find that the child is now stronger than the father, and their remaining weapons will be taken from them. The democracy is now openly destroyed and replaced by tyranny, ruled by someone who has just shown himself to be a "parricide" (568e–569b).

The Tyrannical Person (571a–576a)

In the context of the city Socrates had distinguished a subclass of drones within the larger class of the poor, and now, within the class of unnecessary appetites, he makes a corresponding distinction of a subclass of lawless appetites. "They are probably in all of us, but when restrained by the laws, and by the better appetites together with rationality,[19] in some people they are gotten rid of completely or only a few weak ones remain, while in others they are stronger and more numerous" (571b–c). When Adeimantus asks what these lawless appetites are, Socrates' reply once again (cf. 485d–e) could almost have come out of Freud:

> Those that are aroused during sleep when the rest of the soul slumbers—the rational, gentle, and ruling part of it—but the bestial and wild part, full of food or drink, springs up and, pushing away sleep, seeks to go and satisfy its dispositions. You know that in this condition it dares to do everything, as though released from and rid of all shame and wisdom. It shrinks from nothing, and

tries to have sex with its mother, as it believes, or with any other person, god, or beast; nor does it shrink from any murder or refuse any food. In a word, it stops short of no folly or shamelessness. . . . There is then a terrible, wild, and lawless form of appetite in each of us, even in some of us who seem to be most moderate, and this becomes clear in our sleep. [571c–d, 572b]

The people who are most likely to apprehend truth and least likely to have lawless fantasies during sleep are those who are healthy and self-controlled, and who, before going to sleep, rouse their rational part and feed it with beautiful words and observations, and feed their appetitive part so that it is neither starved nor satiated (the *Republic*'s emphasis on the mean precludes asceticism), leaving the rational part undisturbed by pleasure or pain to apprehend things past, present, or future that it did not know; and soothe their spirited part so that they do not go to sleep angry (571d–572b).

Socrates reminds Adeimantus that the democratic person came about as a compromise between the thrift of his oligarchic father, who indulged only his necessary appetites, and the profligacy of his dronish associates and their lawless appetites; he enjoys both ways of life in moderation. The son of such a man will no longer have the sustaining influence of an oligarchic father who is rigidly opposed to the unnecessary appetites, but only that of a democratic father who is tolerant of them, even if only moderately so. Consequently he will be an easier prey for the drones. He will be able to hold out for a time with the aid of his father and household, but eventually the drones will seduce him by implanting in him a certain kind of eros, like a great winged drone, to be the leader of his idle and prodigal appetites. The latter will nourish the drone and implant in it the sting of yearning, and madness will be its bodyguard (572b–573a).[20] Socrates' qualification, "a certain kind of eros" (ἔρωτά τινα), reminds us that not all eros is negative, for he had earlier spoken of "a true eros for true philosophy" (499b–c). We might even say that since it is the same nature which is potentially the most just and most unjust, namely the best nature (491d–492a), what determines the course of its development is the direction in which its eros is turned.[21] Socrates re-emphasizes that he is not condemning eros in general here but only a particular kind of eros, by adding, "What else do you think the eros of such people (τῶν τοιούτων) would be" (573a2)?

The reference to madness is another matter, however, for unlike the *Phaedrus* (244a–245a, 249c–d) the *Republic* never regards philosophical eros as a divine species of madness, or makes any reference to madness that is not entirely negative.[22] From the Third Wave to the allegory of the cave it is clear that philosophers may be regarded as mad by others, but Socrates himself never presents them that way. Whether or not the concept of divine madness had occurred to Plato when he wrote the *Republic*, there is another factor as well. In both dialogues, philosophy is connected with achieving proximity to the divine, but the difference between the purposes of the two dialogues leads to a difference in the way that human capability is conceived. The *Republic* aims to discover the nature of justice by a thought-experiment in which a perfectly just city is constructed. If such a city is to be conceived of as possible, we must assume the possibility of a system of calculable eugenics (the nuptial number) and also the possibility of a *techne* (518d3) by which the best and brightest of their generation can be compelled (519c9) to reach the point at which they can behold the Good. In other words, we cannot leave philosophy up to the uncertainty of divine inspiration, but must operate under the hypothesis that the path to philosophy can be made calculable. The *Phaedrus*, on the other hand, is governed by a context in which human nature is not idealized; it shows us as we are rather than as we might be. In our present condition, shorn of hopeful idealization, we cannot reach the highest wisdom in a calculable and sober way. From the perspective of the *Phaedrus*, what the *Republic* calls conversion is not a controlled final step of a *techne* of education, but the turning away from the sober reality of ordinary experience to something extraordinary that is not visible to sobriety and must, by contrast, be conceived as mad.

To return to the genesis of the internally tyrannical person (who except in rare cases has no actual political power), the overmastering passion of his eros will, like the tyrant within the city, destroy and expel its opponents—in this case the self-controlled beliefs and appetites—and fill its host with imported madness. Three examples of overmastering passions are the tyranny of eros, the tyrannical behavior of a drunk, and that of a madman who tries to rule over not only other people but gods (572b–573c). Once we relax control over our appetites and no longer feel shame in pursuing any of them, things that were once unthinkable become at first conceivable and then irresistible, as we become driven by an appetite for the excitement and adventure of novelty. The belief that every appetite, no matter how extreme, deserves to be gratified cannot help but be felt eventually as an insatiable longing.

In Book 2 the healthy appetites of the first city became diversified under the momentum of the desire for novelty, and eventually crossed over into the unnecessary appetites of the fevered city, until the spirited appetite took control and purged its rivals. Now as we move back down the tripartite soul, that purgation is reversed and we are plunged back into the limitless appetitiveness of the fevered city, which now is held in check neither by the austerity of the spirited element nor the innocence of the founding craftspeople. In the downward trajectory it is the limitlessness of appetite, not the discipline of spiritedness, that takes control and purges its rivals. (There will not be a return to the first city, for even if there is such a thing as return to lost innocence, it will not be accomplished by decadence.)

The tyrannical person, like the city, will consume his resources to gratify his ever-increasing appetites, and will eventually turn to theft, not scrupling to steal from his parents, as the political tyrant steals from his "father" the city, or again to do violence to them like the political tyrant. He will not stop at bringing his sexual partners home to live in his parents' house, and expecting his parents to serve them, as in the political analogue the parental city became servants of the tyrants' associates. As his unlimited eros pushes him ever further into the territory of once-forbidden appetites, each one becoming less unthinkable as its predecessors are accommodated, his waking life will become continuously the dissipation that his dreaming life used to be only occasionally (573d–575a).

Finally Socrates combines the two accounts and remarks that the political tyrant will necessarily be this kind of person internally as well. Adeimantus agrees to this easily (575c–d), but it is by no means obvious that a tyrant must be internally tyrannical (at the mercy of his most destructive appetites)—as Socrates himself later acknowledges (579e5–6)—and could not simply be calculatingly ruthless.[23] Had Adeimantus challenged Socrates on this point, there are two answers that Socrates could have given. First, according to the story of Gyges' ring that Glaucon told (359c–360d), power corrupts, especially if the nature is appetitive to begin with; so even if the tyrant started out as an internally orderly person, eventually his inhibitions would fall away according to something like the scenario that Socrates described. Second, tyrants try to impress the world by their public façade, but if we could see them privately we would have a very different picture of the lives and their happiness (577a). This latter argument allows that a tyrant may appear to be internally controlled without being so in reality, but it does not show that this is actually the case. Socrates later implicitly acknowledges that there is still some question as to whether the political tyrant must be internally tyrannical, when he says of the tyrant, "if indeed he resembles the condition of the city that he rules" (579d–e). If we set aside Socrates' claim that the ruler of a tyranny must be internally tyrannical, everything else that he says about political tyranny and about internally tyrannical people may still be true. Insofar as the accounts of the cities and individual souls are treated as parallel counterparts of one another, rather than causally related, there was no reason for Socrates to insist that the ruler of a tyranny must be internally tyrannical. But Socrates' scale metaphor claimed that the character of the city is explained by that of its dominant citizens, so let us look more closely at that metaphor.

The Scale Metaphor

When Socrates began to trace the decline of aristocracy into the four degenerate constitutions, he compared the relationship between the political constitutions and corresponding individual constitutions to a scale and its contents:

> Do you know then that there must be as many character types of people as of regimes? Or do you think that the regimes are "born from trees or rocks" but not from the characters of the citizens which, as if tipping the scales by their weight, pull other things after them?
> There is no way that they could come from anywhere other than there.
> Then if there are five types of cities, won't there be five constitutions of the soul of individuals? [544d–e]

The scale metaphor leads us to expect that Socrates will show how each of the devolutionary cities comes about as a result of being governed by people of a corresponding character; but he all but ignored that model and returned in effect to the enlargement metaphor of the city as the soul writ large, according to which the city and soul have the same internal structure, but which never suggests a causal relationship between them. As in the account of the virtues in Book 4, the city and individual were not treated as causally related but as parallel political and psychological analogues of each other. They were presented as two completely independent sequences, like the parallel causal series in Spinoza's two attributes, that are related isomorphically by virtue of having the same internal relationship of their parts. In both cases, aristocracy meant the governance of spiritedness and appetite by the rational element, timocracy meant governance by the spirited part, oligarchy governance by the rich or by necessary appetites, democracy governance by all equally, and tyranny was the enslavement of all the others by limitless appetite. Thus a city was an aristocracy, timocracy, oligarchy, democracy, or tyranny not because it was ruled by aristocratic, timocratic, oligarchic, or democratic types of people, but because it was ruled by rational, spirited, rich, diverse, or predatory people. Socrates explained the origin of each political constitution not by the character type that corresponds to it but by its genealogical descent from its predecessor.

He introduced the scale metaphor as prima facie evidence that there will be as many types of individual as city, but he did not continue to make use of it because it would have complicated matters in a way that the enlargement metaphor does not. The complications would not arise in aristocracy and timocracy because not only are those individuals and cities isomorphic but equivalent, having the same character of rationality and spiritedness respectively. With the three appetitive constitutions, however, although the city and individual are still isomorphic, they are no longer equivalent. They are both still identified by whether they give power to the rich, the poor, or both equally; but in the case of cities terms like "rich" and "poor" are literal and refer to money, while in the case of individuals they are figurative and refer to necessary and unnecessary appetites. Because the political and individual realms are still isomorphic, they are unproblematic with regard to the enlargement metaphor, but since they are no longer equivalent, they do not obviously fit the scale metaphor. We saw earlier, for example, that the ruling group in a democracy is composed of people with the greatest variety of characters rather than specifically democratic characters. Is the scale metaphor simply misleading, or is Socrates once again beginning with the simplest model while at the same time indicating how it can be supplemented?[24] Because the enlargement metaphor abstracts from any causal connection between the political and psychological realms, it can only give us part of the story, and the influence of psychological factors were barely touched on in Socrates' accounts of the devolutions of the city. If we can apply the scale metaphor to Socrates' accounts it would supply what is missing.

The scale metaphor makes the relevant differences among the types of individuals merely quantitative, degrees of heaviness, and so fits in with the view that the types of people and parts of soul are more like segments on a continuum than discontinuous entities. Moreover, since gold is heavier than silver, and silver heavier than iron or bronze, the translation of quality into quantity captures the hierarchy among the golden guardians, silver auxiliaries, and iron or bronze craftsworkers. But the details of the metaphor are elusive: what do the two pans of the scale represent, and what does the scale as a whole represent? Socrates gave a clue to his meaning when he said about the tension that undermined timocracy, that wealth is opposed to virtue as much as if they were in opposite pans of a scale (550e); earlier he had said that every regime changes because of dissention among the rulers (545c–d). The scale represents the rulers, and their dissention is represented by an imbalance between the pans. One of the pans contains the more valuable metal, the ruling value of the city, and the other contains the rival values in the rulers that are held in check when the constitution is stable. If a city is characterized by self-mastery, and the less valuable is obedient to the more valuable, the scales are balanced. The ruling element does not drag the scale down to its side because it must stay within its own bounds just as the others do; justice is not one-sided but harmonious (443c–e). When the city was first evolving, Socrates compared it to a cyclical growth driven by the alternation between nurture and nature: good nurturing produces betters natures which produce better nurturing, and so on (424a). As the city declines, we witness a reverse cycle: a debased nature in some of the rulers (represented as an imbalance of the scale) leads to a compromised constitution (represented as balancing the scale by adding baser metals to the purer metals pan), which produces even more debased natures, and so on.

The balance was upset in timocracy when some members of the ruling group became more devoted to wealth than to virtue, and the scale became unbalanced in favor of the baser metals pan. The scale becomes rebalanced when, in effect, enough money-lovers move into the purer pan to rebalance the scale, which thereby becomes an oligarchy. Timocracy was itself the result of an imbalance, when the failure of the nuptial number led the gold and silver natures of the rulers (i.e., guardians and auxiliaries) to become mixed with bronze and iron respectively in the next generation (547a). The iron and bronze elements within the rulers pulled them toward money-making and property, while the gold and silver pulled it back to virtue. But too many of the rulers were in the baser metals pan for the scale to be rebalanced by obedience, and balance returned only in the form of the compromise that established timocracy (547b–c), when some of the contents of the baser metals pan were transferred to the other pan. The scale was no longer an equilibrium between the base and the noble, but between the base and the almost-noble. When timocracy in turn became unbalanced and restored equilibrium by becoming an oligarchy, the difference between the two pans is no longer between precious and base metals but between higher and lower grades of base metal.

In the case of democracy, the imbalance is no longer within the ruling group itself but within the city as a whole, as the oligarchy's oppression of their subjects creates an instability that leads to revolution—or at least the threat of it. The unbalanced pans now represent a destabilization between the rulers and their subjects rather than dissention within the ruling group itself—an exception to the claim that political change always results from dissention among the rulers (545c–d). If the democratic nature of the rebelling subjects outweighs the power of the oligarchs, and the oligarchs are unable to reassert themselves, the scale is rebalanced by admitting democratic natures to the purer pan until democratic natures dominate both pans. Finally, if one of the drones and his followers become powerful enough to pull down the baser pan and destabilize the scale again, he will move into the ruling pan and keep those in the subject pan from weighing too heavily against him by ingratiating himself with them (566d–e) until he can control them by force alone.

We are still left with the problem of whether the character of the members of the ruling group is the same as that of the city in all cases, as the scale metaphor requires. Although an aristocracy is defined as rule by rational rulers, not as rule by internally aristocratic rulers, in fact, the only person who will be sufficiently rational in the required sense will be an internally aristocratic person. Again, although a timocracy is defined as rule by spirited rulers rather than internally timocratic rulers, only internally timocratic people will be spirited in this way, rather than rational or appetitive. The appetitive constitutions present more of a challenge, as we saw, because unlike the cases of rationality and spiritedness, the elements are no longer the same in the city and individual, but are money in the former and appetite in the latter. However, even though oligarchy is defined as rule by the rich, not as rule by internal oligarchs (whose unnecessary appetites are subordinated to their necessary ones), the people with the self-discipline to become rich will, in fact, have oligarchic natures (564e). Even in the case of democracy, although it is defined not as rule by internally democratic people but by the entire panoply of internal constitutions, nevertheless the working poor who constitute by far the largest group will in most cases be internally democratic, rather than possessing kinds of discipline necessary to be internally aristocratic, timocratic, or oligarchic. In the case of tyranny, the scale metaphor works with respect to those tyrants who are internally tyrannical, insatiably driven by extreme appetites, but not in the case of any who are internally disciplined. Socrates would presumably classifying these as belonging to the intermediate types that he spoke of earlier (544c–d).

Dialectical Materialism

Is Plato's account of the stages through which the political constitution will pass vindicated by the fact that the actual political stages of European history since the middle ages seems to follow something very like that sequence? Allowing for the inevitable differences between a small polis and a large diverse continent, the formal stages match up remarkably closely. Insofar as the theocracy of the Middle Ages aimed to govern by a divine model, it corresponds to Plato's kallipolis, however great the difference in details. The feudal aristocracy that succeeded it corresponds to Plato's timocracy, the capitalism that replaced feudalism corresponds to Plato's oligarchy, and last in both series comes democracy, which may lead to tyranny in Plato's account, and has actually done so in some cases in European history.

Plato's intention, however, could not have been to provide a predictive model of the inevitable sequence of constitutions, because the Greek history that he himself was acquainted with did not completely conform to this model.[25] If we take the Homeric golden age of demigod kings and divine intervention to be a theocracy, then it was indeed followed by noble aristocracies ruled by kings, and eventually by oligarchies and democracies, and in what Aristotle calls ancient times (*Politics* 5.5.1305a7) tyrannies did arise from democracies; but closer to Plato's day tyrants were no more likely to arise out of democracy than in response to monarchy, by overthrowing the hereditary monarchs, as Aristotle makes clear (*Politics* 5.12). But Plato no doubt saw in the democracy of his day how populists could play on the resentments of the people, and thus how tyrants could arise through that channel as well. And he must have believed that sequence would reflect its inner nature better than one that places them between the nobility of monarchs and the discipline of rich oligarchs. Since the model does not always describe his own nation's history, and is based on a selection of four out of an unlimited number of imperfect constitutions (445c, 544d),[26] it is clearly not meant to be a deterministic one. Moreover, when Socrates discussed how they might bring the kallipolis into existence, he acknowledged the logical possibility that a democracy could in principle go in that direction as well as the two he mentions later, of returning to oligarchy or declining into tyranny.

Although the stages of Christian European history correspond formally to those of Book 8, we need to see to what extent the resemblance is more than a formal one, and whether the internal details and mechanisms of change correspond to Socrates' account as well. Otherwise the formal resemblance may be no more than a coincidence.

1. Europe began to be a theocracy during the three centuries between the conversion of Clovis I to Christianity in 496 and Charlemagne's acknowledgement of Pope Leo III's authority to crown him emperor in 800. By 1077, at the time of the Investiture Controversy, the theocracy was sufficiently established that Pope Gregory VII could force Henry IV to relinquish the power to appoint abbots and bishops. If modern European history begins with the middle ages (i.e., with the birth of Christian Europe), then modern European history begins with a theocracy, and the theocracy came about in accordance with one of Socrates' scenarios, the conversion of someone who was already a ruler (499c).

2. The transformation of the theocracy into the equivalent of Plato's timocracy was largely the result of Philip IV's campaign to undermine papal authority within his kingdom (1285–1314). Between the end of the thirteenth century and beginning of the sixteenth, the power relations between church and state had changed to the point where Henry VIII could dismiss not only the pope (as Philip IV had failed to do) but the entire Catholic church, and Martin Luther could put an end to the political dominance of the church in his own way. This hardly conforms to Socrates' model, in

which the wise rulers become corrupted from virtue by the lure of wealth; but on the other hand, since the theocrats of the Middle Ages were not virtuous in Socrates' sense to begin with, the mechanism of change could not have been the same in any case.

3. The transformation of feudal aristocracy (timocracy) into capitalist plutocracy resulted from the industrial revolution that began in the 1760s with the steam engine, and made it possible for commoners to amass wealth and political influence. Once again, the mechanism of change resulted from challenges from outside the ruling group, rather than from greed within that group as Socrates envisioned it. And once again, given that the wealthy feudal aristocrats were far from starting out like the austere ascetics of Socrates' timocracy, the change could not have come about in the same way.

4. Democracy arose in Europe largely as a result of the labor movement, which began in response to the capitalist exploitation of the workers. One effect was to extend voting privileges to all men, rather than limiting it to those with property. Another effect was the ultimately successful campaign by the women's suffrage movement to extend the vote to women as well. European democracy remained a representative rather than direct democracy (unavoidable given the size of modern societies), and so never achieved the fully democratic or quasi-anarchistic condition that Socrates described, but it is clearly more democratic than it was in the nineteenth century. In this case there was a clear parallel with Socrates' account, in which the exploited workers threaten to rebel against the oligarchs and are granted concessions out of fear.

5. A similar parallel was present in the rise of tyranny from democracy, when the weakness of the democratic governments in Italy, Germany, and elsewhere allowed rabble-rouser "drones" to bring about the tyrannies of Mussolini and Hitler.

For the most part, then, the transformation of European societies arose from external challenges to the ruling group, rather than a dissention within the ruling group itself as Socrates tried to show (545c). Only where he himself departs from it (in the collapse of oligarchy) and where there is no distinction between ruler and subject (democracy) does his account resemble subsequent European history. That does not mean, however, that there is no significance to the correspondence between the stages in Socrates' account and those of European history, for although Socrates did not anticipate the efficient causes, he may have correctly identified the teleology that drives it (i.e., the direction and goal). Socrates' model is an account of how, even if we begin by embracing transcendent values, our commitment to them will be under constant pressure from the appetites that aim at bodily pleasures. It has been a guiding theme of the *Republic* that appetite knows no limits, and unless it is checked it will push to greater and greater extremes. We saw this early on when the first city grew uncontrollably and was checked only by coming into conflict with another like itself, the way the libido in Freud is checked by the reality principle. Whether there is any significance to the formal correspondence between the stages of Socrates' account and European history depends on whether we can regard that history as beginning with an attempt at a politics in the service of transcendent values, which is progressively eroded by our appetite for physical pleasure and the wealth that buys it. If the passing of political power from priests to kings involved not only power struggles among individuals but also the assertion of human authority against purported divine authority, and, in fact, the claims of the body against the claims of the soul; and if the replacement of the prerogatives of hereditary nobility by the prerogatives of money meant that not only transcendent values but now even the concept of nobility in human virtue gives way before the appetites that money can serve; and if the rise of democracy and its liberty means the exalting of pleasure above even the relatively modest human virtue of the discipline that enables some people to become richer than others; then the correspondence between Socrates' account and European history is more than a coincidence.

Socrates' model is an idealization, which is related to any actual political history the way the ideal principles of astronomy are related to their imperfect embodiment in the actual motions of the stars (530a–b).[27] As Socrates said earlier, it is "the nature of practice to attain to truth less than theory does" (472e–473a). By treating the destabilization of the regimes, as far as possible as the result of dissent within the ruling group, Socrates shows how in principle the decline is ultimately driven by the appetites within us, even if in practice external events provide the occasions for it. He is following to their conclusion the implications of the logic by which the just city was created.[28]

Socrates' decision to trace the destabilization of regimes to dissent within the ruling group gives his analysis a dialectical character rather than a linear one. He does not say that once appetite frees itself from obedience to rationality—it pushes the city ever further into the most extreme appetites. Instead of representing each stage as a simple taking of the next step, he represents it as a compromise between the status quo and the pressure to take an even bigger step. In the following summary of the devolutions of cities (the devolution of individual characters will be dealt with below) the left column represents the ruling principle and the right column the principle that undermines it.

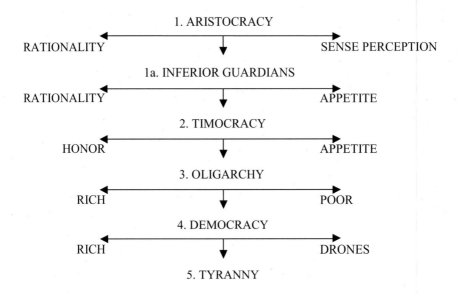

Despite their obvious differences, Plato's model bears a formal resemblance to Marx's insofar as it is driven by materialism and proceeds dialectically by means of class struggle. Unlike Marx, however, Plato sees the dialectic as one of decline rather than ascent, and materialistic only for that reason; an ascent would subordinate materialism to something closer to idealism (not quite in Marx's sense of the word). Related to this is the other most important difference, that for Plato the classless society of democracy, which comes after oligarchy (or its modern counterpart of capitalism), is no less internally contradictory for being classless, and consequently no less insecure. Rather than providing a termination to the dialectic and its violence, it merely offers instability of a different kind. The reason that democracy cannot come to rest in itself is that some people are "by nature most orderly",[29] and will therefore be most successful and become richest (564e), which will create envy among the others. As long as human beings are unequal in their capacity for achievement, democracy can never be fully stabilized. Plato would not agree with Marx that everyone could become willing to contribute according to their ability and to receive only according to their needs. The resentful drones, with their sense of frustrated entitlement, have no interest in contributing to the common good, and in an appetitive climate those who make the most money would not be content with only enough to satisfy their basic needs. It took the austere apparatus of the kallipolis, which denied any but the most basic kinds of property to the guardians and auxiliaries, to produce characters that would be satisfied with minimal materialistic gratification and wealth. In a democracy stripped of those restrictions, Socrates would not expect to see many exhibitions of selflessness, and does not share Marx's optimism that an elimination of political inequality will result in the elimination of selfish behavior.

Beyond the Pleasure Principle

The dialectic of the personal decline precisely echoed that of the political decline in the first two stages because of the parallel tripartite constitutions of rationality-spiritedness-appetite. But when appetite is triumphant in the form of oligarchy, and the political dialectic is between the rich and poor, there are no longer any precisely corresponding elements within the person, and the dialectic was polarized between the necessary and unnecessary appetites. As the class of the poor was further polarized between the workers and the drones, the unnecessary appetites were polarized between the lawful appetites (the necessary appetites together with the less harmful of the unnecessary ones) and unlawful ones. For the oligarchic person the necessary appetites are dominant, for the democratic person all appetites are of equal value, and for the tyrannical person the unnecessary appetites are dominant, especially the unlawful ones. In the following diagram, as before, the left column represents the ruling principle and the right the challenger.

In at least three places the *Republic* describes the appetites in ways that are similar to Freud's. 1) In Book 4 Socrates presented all our motivations, from carnal appetites to the rational love of learning, as different outlets for one and the same motive force: "when the appetites strongly incline

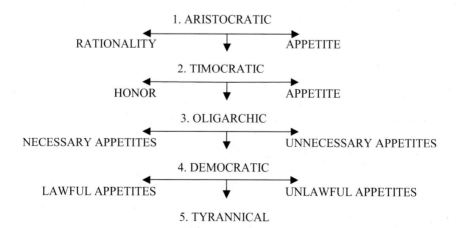

1. ARISTOCRATIC

RATIONALITY   APPETITE

2. TIMOCRATIC

HONOR   APPETITE

3. OLIGARCHIC

NECESSARY APPETITES   UNNECESSARY APPETITES

4. DEMOCRATIC

LAWFUL APPETITES   UNLAWFUL APPETITES

5. TYRANNICAL

toward some one thing they are thereby weakened toward others, like a stream from which there is a diversion into another channel" (485d). 2) Previously, at the beginning of his account of the soul writ large, Socrates showed how appetite pursues pleasure insatiably until it is thwarted externally, like the Freudian relationship between the pleasure principle (libido) and reality principle. Only when appetite was thwarted in its quest for pleasure was it channeled into spiritedness and rationality, along the lines of Freud's concept of sublimation. 3) Earlier in this chapter we noted Socrates' description of what Freud calls the repressed desires that reveal themselves when our subconscious is active in our dream states (571c–572b). Now in Book 9, four pages after the description of the tyrannical person, Socrates reiterates that the motive forces of all three parts of the soul are varieties of appetite (580d).

If even rationality is a species of appetite, how can Socrates' model avoid the Freudian conclusion that appetite is our fundamental nature, and rationality is only a derivative form of appetite? How can his condemnation of the unnecessary appetites amount to anything more than Freud's condemnation of the id: an acknowledgement that this is what we are by nature, but that for practical reasons (the reality principle) it must be repressed? At the beginning of Book 2 Socrates' rejection of the social contract theory advanced by Glaucon was an implicit rejection of the view that our truest nature is the lawless appetites. He replaced it with a conception of the city as having its origin in the necessary appetites, a cooperative supplying of the necessities of life. But there it would have remained if the unnecessary appetites did not make an appearance and drive to city to feverish expansion (373b–d). We saw that they were not introduced from outside, but were already implicit in the artisan's appetitiveness, kept in check at first only by the more pressing need to supply the necessities of life. Once those have been assured, the others can clamor for attention. If our appetitive drives were confined to what is necessary for life, we would still be living the primitive corporeal existence that Glaucon derided as piggish (372d).[30] If the kallipolis grows out of our pursuit of unnecessary appetites, in accordance with Socrates' account, and if rationality itself is in some sense an outgrowth of appetite, how can Plato escape a Freudian hedonistic materialism?

The answer is that although for Plato, as for Freud, rationality emerges on a continuum that begins in corporeal appetite, it is not a sublimation of corporeal appetite, which expresses our fundamental nature less directly than bodily pleasure-seeking does, but an emergence of what was always implicit in appetite and indeed the consummation, which alone can satisfy our appetitive urges (586d–e). Whereas on Freud's original account,[31] whatever in us is not the pleasure principle is that principle disguised, for Plato the truth-seeking channel of our appetite is as primordial as the pleasure-seeking one. In contrast with Freud's reductionistic monism, Plato analyzes the world of our experience into elements of rational regularity and irrational contingency, which have their source in the two fundamental principles of intelligible being and corporeal becoming. These antithetical principles can be combined only by a third principle that is commensurate with both of them (*Timaeus*, 31b–c), in this case a principle that imparts rational motion so that, as rational, it is commensurate with the forms and, as motive, commensurate with what is always changing. That is the function of soul. "Soul" (*psuche*) traditionally meant the principle of motion: something was alive, "ensouled" (*empsuchon*), if it had an internal principle of motion—the criterion that we still use today—which led Thales to conclude that magnets have soul because they move iron.[32] Accordingly, when Plato wanted to speak about what we call energy he uses the term "world soul" (*Timaeus*, 41d). The world is not only constantly changing, but it is changing in a knowable way, a rational way, as the *Timaeus* attempts to demonstrate.

The principle of motion is at the same time the active principle of rationality, without which the forms would have no efficacy. In the *Phaedo* the forms are called the true causes, but there are also active conditions called "that without which the cause would never be a cause", like the muscles and bones that enable us to act (99a–b). Muscles and bones are products of the formative activity of soul, and the ability to move them is another function of the soul. In Book 1 of the *Republic* Socrates had argued that the successful functioning of something is its virtue or excellence, and the function of the soul is life,[33] while its virtue or excellence is justice (353d–e). That conclusion is reaffirmed in Book 10 when Socrates proposes a demonstration of the soul's immortality based on the premise that the good of the soul is justice and the other moral virtues. It follows, then, that the individual soul, like the world-soul in the *Timaeus*, is not merely the principle of motion but the principle of *good* motion. In contrast to the soulless disorderly motion of the *Timaeus*,[34] soul itself can be given a unitary definition as "the principle of orderly motion". Because order is already implicit in it, it is a bridge between the changeable and the eternal. We begin in the visible world of change because we rely on our senses before we can rely on rationality,[35] but we develop rationality not as a mere sublimation of carnal appetite, as with Freud, but as a progression along the bridge that begins with the bodily and leads to the intelligible.

Notes

1. There is no equality of women, community of wives and children, or philosopher within the individual soul, and there was no discussion of the individual that corresponds to the kallipolis of Book 7, but only the disingenuous remark, "No doubt it's also clear what we'll say the individual is like" (541b).

2. See Aristotle's historical survey in *Politics* 5.12.

3. Aristotle overlooks this when he accuses Socrates of giving no cause of change that is specific to the first city (*Politics* 5.12.1316a1–17). Again, since the problem is that sensitivity to *kairos* cannot be assured, it is misleading to describe this as an "inevitable change . . . *in the cycle of fertility*" (Dennis Blackwood, "The Decline of Man and State in Books 8–9 of the Republic: Devolution and/or Instability Argument?" *American Catholic Philosophical Quarterly* 75 [2001]: 1–24, esp. 20; emphasis added). Blackwood's recapitulation is more to the point: "All states and all things will decay owing to soul-caused 'secondary' motions and the basic impermanence and imperfection of the material substrate" (23). There is certainly no justification for Rosenstock's claim that the reason for the kallipolis' downfall is misogynistic: "so long as the male must join himself with a woman (old or new) to perpetuate himself, he must forgo any dream he has of mastering the changes wrought by time on all that exists" (1994, 382).

4. Friedländer suggests that Socrates' reference to Hesiod's four races—gold, silver, bronze, iron (546e–547a)—implies that "Hesiod's myth of the five ages of man [gold, silver, bronze, demigods, iron (*Works and Days*, 109–201)] serves as the prototype for the process of corruption" (1964, vol. 3, 118). If so, it is only a general prototype, since the characteristics of Socrates' types are different from those of Hesiod, and Socrates' choice of a five-part classification has an independent internal basis: the three types of city/person, with the third subdivided into the three possible relations between rich and poor citizens or between necessary and unnecessary appetites.

5. See, for example, *Phaedo* 65a–b.

6. Cf. Homer, *Iliad* 6.211.

7. The latter term is used by Xenophon in *Memoribilia* 4.6.12.

8. Guthrie writes: "Rather confusingly, Gk τιμή meant reward as well as honour, and τίμημα (about to be used at 550d11 [evidently a typo for c11]) is an assessment of property" (1975, 529).

9. *Genealogy of Morals*, First Essay.

10. Cf. *Phaedo* 68b–69b.

11. Recall the use of τιμημάτων (honor, value) to mean assessment of wealth at 550c11.

12. It is not surprising that democracy's claim to beauty is qualified by "seems to be" (κινδυνεύει), but why it is not even truly pleasant but only "seems" so (ἔοικεν) will not be clear until the discussion of pleasure in Book 9.

13. See Santas' comparison of this with modern theories of "desire satisfaction" (2001, 65–71).

14. It might be argued that the same was true of oligarchy since the ruler of an oligarchy need only be rich, not internally oligarchic (appetitive but disciplined); but Socrates does claim that there is a connection between being disciplined and becoming wealthy (564e).

15. Williams (1973) and Annas (1981, 301) take the apparently anomalous relationship between democracy and its rulers to be a sign of incoherence in Plato's general position. Lear (1992), Santas (2001), and Ferrari (2003) attempt in various ways to resolve the tension.

16. If the description of the behavior of slaves had its basis in Plato's Athens, that could hardly be said about the status of women, who were far from equal, as we saw in chapter 5 (139–43).

17. Thrasymachus was compared to a wild beast just before he launched into his defense of tyranny (336b).

18. Cf. the city as "mother" in the Myth of Metals (414e).

19. The restraint of the unnecessary desires by the better desires as well as by rationality is paralleled in the *Phaedrus* by the way the lawless appetites of the black horse are held in check by the white horse as well as the charioteer, who is identified with rationality (253d). Much else in the present discussion has its counterpart in the *Phaedrus* as well.

20. The theme of the tyrannical madness or eros was foreshadowed in Book 1 with Cephalus' endorsement of Sophocles' characterization of eros as a wild and raving despot within us (329b–d).

21. Cf. 508c–d.

22. See 329c, 331c, 341c, 359b, 382c, 382e, 396a–b, 400b, 496c, 539c, 573c, 578a.

23. Annas (1981, 303–5) and Frede (1997, 262) point out that Socrates' account fits later tyrants like Caligula and Nero better than cases in Plato's own experience like Dionysius I of Syracuse, who had a stable regime for 38 years.

24. The two dissimilar types of explanation that intersect here—isomorphism and causality—may both have been implicit in the question that introduced the scale metaphor. When Socrates asked Glaucon, "Do you think that the regimes are 'born from trees or rocks' but not from the characters of the citizens?" the context of the internal quotation from Homer's *Odyssey* (19.163) suggests an alternative to the answer offered ("from the characters of the citizens"). Penelope is asking Odysseus, who is disguised from the suitors, who he is and where he comes from, and Odysseus replies with an account of his ancestry and his adventures. His (fabricated) account shows that the kind of answer Penelope is looking for as an alternative to "born from trees or rocks" is "born from such and such a father and shaped by such and such experiences". So when Socrates presents Glaucon with the alternatives that cities are born "from trees or rocks" or from the characters of their citizens, Glaucon could have rejected both alternatives and replied, on analogy with Odysseus, that "they are born from their predecessors and further shaped by events", an answer that would, in fact, precisely reflect the genetic explanations that Socrates was actually about to give. In the case of the accounts of the constitutions in *individuals* it is fully explicit that their

origin is explained, like that of Odysseus, in terms of their father and their interactions with others.

25. Socrates' audience would have known that he was not describing the actual course of Greek history, and therefore would not have taken this account to be a kind of historical determinism. Cf. Dorothea Frede, "Die ungerechten Verfassungen und die ihnen entsprehenden Menschen", in Ottfried Höffe, *Platon Politeia* (Berlin: Akademie Verlag, 1997), 253–54.

26. Cf. Frede 1997, 254–55.

27. If we think of it in those terms, as ideal classification rather than as historical prognostication, the Socratic hierarchy parallels the hierarchy of traditional Indian castes: theocratic philosopher-rulers (or complete guardians) and theocratic priests (*brahmins*), warrior timocrats and warrior-kings (*ksatriyas*), moneyed oligarchs and moneyed merchants (*vaisyas*), democratic workers and the worker caste (*sudras*). There is no evidence that the Greeks were aware of Hindu culture prior to Alexander's Indian expedition in 326–325 BCE, two decades after Plato's death.

28. I agree on the whole with Nettleship's conclusion, "These books therefore put before us an ideal history of evil, as the previous books put before us an ideal history of good" (1901, 295), although I would prefer the words "irrationality" and "rationality" to "evil" and "good". Cf. Cross and Woozley 1964: "In both cases he is observing an order, but not a chronological order" (263). Other readers see it as an attempt at "a systematic philosophy of history" (Gomperz 1905, 91), an ethical and in no way political analysis (Taylor 1956 [1926], 295), "the outline of a political science" (Bloom 1968, 414), and a typological classification (Torsten Andersson, *Polis and Psyche: A Motif in Plato's Republic* [Stokholm: Almqvist & Wiksell, 1971], 157). Eric Voegelin recognizes both the limitations and value of Socrates' account:

> Plato does not claim that every historical polity is bound to pass through the sequence of forms. On the contrary, the selection of examples, as well as the surrounding remarks, seem to exclude the notion. As examples of timocracy are mentioned the constitutions of Crete and Sparta; but there is no suggestion that either of them has fallen off from a previous more perfect form, nor that they will have to develop into oligarchies, democracies, and tyrannies . . . [Nevertheless,] [n]ot only Hellenic civilization, but civilizations in general, show something like a sequence of political forms which begins with heroic monarchy and aristocracy, then moves on to the rise of the Third Estate with its oligarchic problems, further on to the entrance of the masses into politics, and issues forth into the forms of plebiscitarian democracy and tyranny. However blurred the pattern may be in the various civilizations, it nevertheless is there. Moreover, the sequence is, on the whole, irreversible. Civilizations do not begin with a plebiscitarian tyranny and then move on to heroic aristocracy; they move from the rule of the Third Estate to mass democracy, but not in the opposite direction, and so forth. Obviously an irreversible pattern exists. [*Plato* (Baton Rouge: Louisiana State University Press, 1957), 123, 128]

29. κοσμιώτατοι φύσει (564e6). What he means by orderly was explained in Book 4: "Self-control is surely some kind of order (κόσμος), the self-mastery of certain pleasures and appetites. . . . When the part that is better by nature is master of the worse, this is what is meant by speaking of being master of oneself" (430eB431a). There self-mastery refers to the control of appetite by reason; here, since everyone is driven by appetite of one kind or another, a more modest kind of internal order or self-mastery is involved: the dominance of the necessary appetites over the unnecessary ones. In that case, among people who are driven by a desire for money, the ones who succeed are more likely to be self-disciplined only in the sense of following their necessary appetites rather than their unnecessary ones, while the others are more likely to be self-indulgent—that is, more at the mercy of their unnecessary appetites.

30. Cf. Clay 1988: Plato "forces upon us the reflection that all civilization rests on injustice and the uncontrolled need of the lowest and most passionate element of the soul to violate the frontiers of what is necessary to life for what is thought to be necessary to the good life" (28).

31. Prior to 1920. In *Beyond the Pleasure Principle* (1920) he saw the need to balance the pleasure principle with a nearly antithetical drive toward destructiveness, the death wish. The death wish, like the pleasure principle, does not have its origin in a non-materialistic principle, but involves a retreat to a lower form of organization of that principle.

32. See Aristotle, *De Anima* 405a19–21, and Book 1 chapter 2 generally, for his discussion of this theme in other pre-Socratic philosophers as well.

33. Cf. the identification of soul as the principle of motion in the *Phaedrus* (245c–e) and *Laws* (895e–897b), and in the *Phaedo* as that without which the form of Life could not be a cause (105c–106d).

34. In the *Timaeus*, before the introduction of soul, "all that was visible was not at rest but moving discordantly and in a disorderly way" (κινούμενον πλημμελῶς καὶ ἀτάκτωσε 30a). The reason that the myth of the *Timaeus* can speak of motion without soul (a logical impossibility according to other dialogues) is that it is hypothesizing a world from which soul has been abstracted, in order to highlight the rationality that soul then brings to it. But such a world could never, in fact, exist, and when Timaeus goes on to speak of the world-soul he says that even though he spoke of a soulless corporeal world first, for the sake of a clear exposition, soul is always prior to body (34b–c).

35. 402a, 514a–516c, cf. *Timaeus* 44a–b.

~

CHAPTER NINE

The Superiority of Justice (Book 9 from 575e)

First Argument: Fitness to Rule (575e–580c)

Book 7 represented the climax of the dialogue from the point of view of the Divided Line, since it is there that the highest kind of thinking was described as far as possible; but the climax of the question of justice is only now coming into view. Socrates will give three arguments for the superiority of justice over injustice, only the first of which follows from the previous discussions.

The first argument is based on the life of an unjust person as portrayed in the investigation into tyranny. From the standpoint of the *Republic*, the identification of perfect injustice with tyranny is reasonable since Thrasymachus himself had identified the tyrant as the archetypal unjust person (344a). The tyrant, Socrates and Adeimantus conclude, is incapable of true friendship or true freedom. Not freedom because either he behaves like a slave when he needs people's support, fawning and debasing himself, or treats everyone else like slaves once he no longer needs them. And because this makes him unreliable he is not capable of real friendship either. The tyrant then is the most unjust and worst kind of person, and the longer he is a tyrant the more his life will resemble the nightmare described at 571c–d. There is no reason to suppose that Adeimantus would not have assented to this last point since he readily assented to everything leading up to it, but before he can reply Glaucon takes over the argument and agrees (576b). The argument reaches its conclusion in the next line, when Glaucon and Socrates agree that the tyrant will be not only most vicious but most miserable.

The preceding stage of the argument referred to the political tyrant regardless of whether he is also internally tyrannical. The next stage examines the internally tyrannical person independently of whether or not he happens to be a political tyrant, but it begins by looking at the tyrant writ large, the tyrannical city: "Would the tyrannical person resemble anything other than the tyrannical city?" (576c). Asked to compare the tyrannical city and the city ruled by kings, Glaucon contrasts them as the worst and the best, and Socrates asks him to compare them also with respect to their happiness. Since a city takes its character from the inner relations of its parts rather than from the character of the dominant citizens,[1] they must continue to formulate separate but parallel accounts of the city and person. If they resist being "dazzled by looking at one man, the tyrant, or the few who surround him" and look at the city as a whole, it is obvious that tyrannies are the most miserable of cities, and those ruled by kings (aristocracies) the happiest. It should follow on the basis of their isomorphic constitutions that the internal tyrant will be the most miserable of people: as with the tyrannical city, his most decent parts are enslaved to the most vicious and mad. He will be full of confusion and regret, poverty and unfulfillment, and fear and grief.

Socrates would have preferred not to simply transfer that conclusion from their evaluation of the tyrannical city, but to obtain independent confirmation of it from someone who can see into people without being fooled by outward show, and who has lived with a tyrant and has observed what he is like in private when he is not putting on an act (577a–b). But since no one like that is present "we must examine them very well with an argument (*logos*) like this one, for our examination is concerned with the most important thing, good and bad life" (578c). Socrates' preference for an eyewitness over rational argument is another indication that the dialogue has returned along the Divided Line from the intelligible to the visible, from an investigation into intelligible forms to an investigation of visible cities and individuals.

The internal tyrant will be even more miserable if he is also the ruler of a political tyranny. Whereas Thrasymachus had maintained that when a tyrant "in addition to the property of the citizens, kidnaps and enslaves them as well, instead of these shameful names he is called happy and blessed" (344a–b), Socrates reminds Glaucon that the tyrant must live in constant fear of the people he has enslaved. He will have to ingratiate himself with some of his slaves and even free them in order to maintain his own security, and so rather than being free he will find himself forced to do things against his will for the sake of survival. Not even his movements are free since he will not be able to show himself too openly, and his life will be lived largely within the walls of his house (578c–579b). This picture is not unfamiliar to us today.

On the basis of the tyrant's inherent insecurity and need to flatter and appease those who are threats to him, Socrates concludes:

> In truth then, even if some do not think so, the one who is in reality a tyrant is in reality a slave to the greatest flattery, slavery, and fawning before the vilest men; and since his appetites do not get any satisfaction whatever, he is in need of most things and appears in truth to be poor, if one knows how to observe the entire soul. And throughout his life he is full of fears and filled with convulsions and pains, if indeed (εἴπερ) he resembles the condition of the city that he rules. [579d–e]

There are two parts to this conclusion, the first stated confidently ("In truth then, even if some do not think so") and the second more cautiously ("if indeed he resembles the condition of the city that he rules"). The cautious nature of the latter shows that Socrates is under no illusions about the fact that he has not demonstrated that the ruler of a tyrannical state must have an internally tyrannical constitution. The most he can conclude is that *if* that should be the case, then the indictment against the most unjust life is even stronger. For those who are not convinced, however, he has offered an independent argument based on political necessity (that being a tyrant entails living in fear) together with the psychological extrapolation.

Second Argument: Criteria of Truth (580c–583a)

The second argument could hardly begin more hesitantly: "Look at this second one if indeed you think there's anything in it" (580d). All three parts of the soul have their proper pleasures, desires, and ruling principles. The first part is that with which we learn, the second that by which we get angry, and the third is multiform but is named appetite because the appetites are the largest and strongest members of that multiplicity; it is also called the money-loving part because it is by means of money that the appetites are most easily gratified. Since its pleasure and love (*philia*) are for gain we can designate it as the money-loving or gain-loving part. Now that the terms "pleasure" and "*epithumia*" (appetite or desire) are used generically of the whole soul, the lowest part can no longer be distinguished from the others by calling it appetitive or pleasure-loving. The spirited part is victory-loving and honor-loving, and the part with which we learn is learning-loving and wisdom-loving (*philosophon*). Because different parts rule in different people, the three primary kinds of people are lovers of wisdom, lovers of victory, and lovers of gain, each with their distinctive kind of pleasure. If we ask all these people which of the three kinds of life is most pleasant, they would each choose their own. Those whose primary love is for money are not going to care much about learning or victory except where they are profitable; lovers of honor have contempt for money (which they consider vulgar) and for learning (which they consider smoke and nonsense) except where money and learning can bring them honor; and lovers of wisdom would regard the others not as true pleasures but only necessities, which they would ignore if possible. The question, then, is which one of the three speaks most truly (580c–582a).[2]

It is odd that Socrates would introduce the subject of pleasure at all, since he was challenged to show only that just people are happier than unjust ones, not that they live more pleasantly, and Socrates is the last person to equate happiness with pleasure, especially after he pointed out that some pleasures are bad (505c).[3] It would be more in keeping with the preceding analyses for him to maintain that even if the life of a voluptuary is more pleasant than that of the philosopher, the philosopher's life is more noble, and nobility is closer to the good (and happiness) than is pleasure. Socrates rules out that kind of answer, however, by insisting that the present argument is not about which life is more noble or base, or better or worse, but only about their pleasantness or painlessness (581e–582a).

Socrates is meeting the hedonists on their own grounds: he has just awarded the victory to philosophy over appetite on the basis of his own terms of reference, and now demonstrates that even if he accepts those of the lovers of appetite, his conclusion still follows. When people object to hedonism by protesting that they are not motivated by pleasure but by nobility or morality or anything else, hedonists reply that those are false oppositions: it is not that the moralists have chosen morality instead of pleasure, but that the gratification of self-love that morality produces in them gives them the *most* pleasure. People who say they prefer something else to pleasure are really saying that that they prefer a less common pleasure to a more common one. For the sake of argument Socrates accepted this frame of reference at the beginning of this second demonstration, when he dropped his earlier classification of appetite or desire as only one of three competing parts of the soul, and instead classified all three parts of the soul as species of appetite or desire that pursued corresponding species of pleasure (580d). Doing so enables him to show that even if he entertains the hedonistic analysis of motivation and argues on the hedonists' own terms, the philosophical or just life will turn out to be the best (i.e., most pleasant) life, and the unjust the most unpleasant. Moreover, where the first argument presupposed the tripartite model of appetite, spiritedness, and rationality, this one is closer to the model of love of pleasure, honor, and truth as three channels through which a single stream of eros flows (485d).

Although it may seem that Socrates is begging the question in favor of hedonism, he can also be accused of begging it in favor of philosophy. "How can we know which is speaking most truly?" (582a1), Socrates had asked; but caring about truth pertains only to the philosopher (581e1), so by putting the question in these terms Socrates may be prejudicing the outcome. That may be why the demonstration began with the cautionary advice to Glaucon to see if he thinks there is anything in it. As we saw earlier, in the *Philebus*, when the life of reason and that of pleasure compete for supremacy, and Socrates proposes that they decide between the two rationally, Philebus replies that as far as he is concerned pleasure will be the winner regardless of what happens in the argument (12a–b), and refuses to take any further part in the proceedings. It is the correct course for him, for why should the competing claims of hedonism and rationalism be adjudicated by the criteria of reason? If Philebus finds the pursuit of pleasure more pleasant than the pursuit of truth, then for him that is the only criterion that counts. Before considering this objection let us look at the argument more fully.

Socrates suggests three criteria for determining the truth of the matter: experience, intelligence (φρόνησις), and rationality (λόγος) (582a). In all three cases there is once again a prima facie prejudice in favor of the love of knowledge, but only prima facie because there is nothing in principle that would prevent our rational faculties from judging corporeal pleasures to be more satisfying than rational ones.

The main part of the argument deals with the criterion of experience. Socrates asks which of the three types of people has had the most experience of all three kinds of pleasure. In Book 4 when Glaucon agreed with Socrates' distinction between rationality and spiritedness, he pointed out that children are spirited from birth, but not rational until much later if at all (441b–c); now he points out that lovers of wisdom have tasted the pleasures of appetite and spiritedness since childhood, while there is no need for lovers of gain to have experienced the pleasure of learning the nature of reality, even if they are able to do so. Similarly, both lovers of wisdom and lovers of gain will have experienced the pleasures of being honored when they have been successful, but only the lover of wisdom knows the pleasure of contemplating reality (582a–d). Philosophers, then, are the only ones who are in a position to compare the three from a position of experience, and so their verdict must be considered to have the greatest claim to truth; someone who has had a certain kind of experience is in a better position to measure it against other kinds of experience than someone who has not.[4]

Socrates' point is only that lovers of wisdom have more complete experience than the other two kinds of people, and that they do, in fact, pronounce their distinctive pleasure to be superior to the others. But would he go as far as Mill would do two millennia later, and deny that it is even possible for someone who has experienced the pleasure of learning to prefer those of the body? After stating that "it is an unquestionable fact, that those who are equally acquainted with and equally capable of appreciating and enjoying both do give a most marked preference to the manner of existence which employs their higher faculties", he raises the objection that "many who begin with youthful enthusiasm for every thing noble, as they advance in years sink into indolence and selfishness"; but dismisses it with the words, "I do not believe that those who undergo this very common change voluntarily choose the lower description of pleasures in preference to the higher. I believe that, before they devote themselves exclusively to the one, they have already become incapable of the other".[5] If this is construed as a purely logical argument, it is clearly circular since it identifies goods by means of experts and experts by their choice of goods; but not if it is construed as something to which he is bearing witness on the basis of his own experience, namely that the experience of truth is incomparably more satisfying than any other kind of pleasure. Mill's need to fall back on personal testimony may compromise his project of providing an objective empirical basis for ethics, but it does not falsify this particular claim. Presumably Socrates would make the same answer, given his belief that once we have experienced the highest kind of knowing and look back at the people still in the cave, nothing could tempt us to live as they do (516d).

We saw that the attitude favoring the pursuit of knowledge was already implicit in Socrates' choice of experiential knowledge, intelligence, and rationality, as the criteria by which to evaluate the competing claims of the three kinds of pleasure, and that now becomes more evident as he turns to the second and third criteria, intelligence and rationality. Alone of the three kinds of people, the experiences of lovers of wisdom are accompanied by intelligence, so their way of life contains greater intelligence as well as greater experience. And the same is true of rationality, since it is the proper instrument of the lover of wisdom (582d). If wealth and gain were the best criteria by which to make judgements, the things praised and censured by the lover of gain would be the truest; and if honor, victory, and courage were the best criteria the preferences of the lover of honor and victory would be truest; but since experience, intelligence, and rationality are the proper criteria, the preferences of the lover of wisdom and rationality are most true. On the basis of the preferences of the lovers of wisdom, Socrates concludes that their life is best, the life of the warrior and lover of honor is second because it is closer to that of the lover of wisdom than is the life of the money-maker, and that of the lover of gain is last (582d–583a).

Does the argument beg the question by its reliance on the criteria of experience, intelligence, and rationality? That would be the case only if the criteria were arbitrary ones, whereas they are, in fact, the most reasonable ones that could be appealed to. It could still be claimed that choosing them on the basis of reasonableness already prejudices the argument in favor of rationality, but the only alternative would be to follow Philebus into misology. The assumption would beg the question only if some other set of criteria for choosing among competing claims seems superior or at least equal in value, and leads to a different conclusion; but there are no obvious candidates. The most that can be said against Socrates' procedure is that he has not demonstrated all of his premises, but it is never possible to demonstrate all premises, and we must be satisfied if we begin with what is self-evident in the sense that to deny it is to deny the possibility of rational inquiry; Socrates' assumption meets that standard of self-evidence. As for those who would maintain that it is an unwarrantable assumption to think that rational inquiry is better than any other basis for making choices, there is no common ground on which Socrates can meet them, and in the *Philebus* Plato shows that he understands this.

If this argument appeals to the standards of rationality in a way that hedonists might not be willing to accept, that will not be true of the next one, which proceeds not from the character of knowledge but from the character of pleasure itself. In fact, the three arguments by which the just life of the philosopher will defeat the unjust life of the tyrant correspond to the three values manifested by the three parts of the soul and city. The first argument was based on a civil-war model wherein not only do the three parts of the city and soul compete for supremacy, but a further power struggle takes place within the appetitive part—either between rich and poor classes or between necessary and unnecessary appetites. In the end the just life is preferred, because in the unjust soul the better parts are enslaved by the worse, and because the life of the tyrant is under continual threat from his victims. There the question was looked at according to the categories of spiritedness, as a question of warfare, enslavement, and domination. In the present argument the categories of rationality are employed, and it becomes a question of ascertaining the truth of competing claims. In the third and final argument that we turn to next, the categories of appetite come to the fore, and it becomes a question of ascertaining which life has the most pleasure and the least pain. So if the present argument privileges rationality the other two restore the balance.

Third Argument: True and False Pleasure (583b–588a)

Socrates dedicates the final argument to Olympian Zeus the Savior and predicts that it will be the greatest and most masterful of the just person's three victories over the unjust.[6] It is based on something that Socrates thinks he has heard from one of the wise men (σοφῶν), namely that the pleasures of someone who is not wise (φρονίμου) are not completely true nor pure but like "shadow paintings", paintings that use shading to give the illusion of three-dimensionality. Socrates distinguishes three conditions: the opposites pain and pleasure, and an intermediary state neither pleasant nor painful but calm. When people who are sick or in pain speak of how pleasant it is to be healthy or free of pain, they are identifying the intermediate calm with pleasure; as they move from the bottom to the middle they mistake the middle for the top (583d). But it is also true that when someone ceases to feel pleasure the state of calm feels painful (this, as we know, is the psychological basis of addiction); as they move from the top to the middle they mistake the middle for the bottom (583e). It follows from this that the intermediate state can be both painful and pleasant, but it is not "possible for what is neither to become both" (583e), so this state is not true pleasure.

The argument so far recognizes two kinds of pleasure: true pleasures that leave us with a painful feeling when they depart, and false pleasures that are only relief from pain. Socrates now points to a third kind of pleasure that is neither false nor leads to painful deprivation when it departs, such as the pleasures of smell. "Then let us not be persuaded that pure pleasure is the departure of pain, or pain the departure of pleasure" (584b–c). Pure (καθαρὰν) pleasure is thus a true pleasure which does not leave us feeling painfully deprived when it departs. There are, then, true but fleeting pleasures (followed by pain), false pleasures (preceded by pain), and pure pleasures (neither preceded nor followed by pain). The olfactory pleasures are only a transitional example to a more important kind of pure pleasure.[7] Greater than any pleasure of the body, including the pure pleasures of smell, are the pleasures of knowledge, because the mind is in relation to a more pure (καθαρᾶς) being than the body is (585b), and its pleasures stable and pure (καθαρᾶς) (586a).[8] Thus the just life of the philosopher will be the most pleasant since it is filled with the truest pleasures, while the unjust life of the tyrant will be the most unpleasant because its appetitive pleasures are most inseparable from pain (586e–587b).

It is often objected against this argument that if people feel relief of pain as pleasure, it makes no sense to tell them they are not truly feeling pleasure: pleasure is a subjective state and only the subject can pronounce on its presence or absence.[9] But we shall see that the argument rests on something more than telling people that they do not feel what they think they feel. Even in the present context, Socrates' point is that because these felt pleasures depend on a prior condition of pain, a life that is devoted to them is equally a life devoted to pain, and thus only an apparently pleasant life.

It is not clear, however, what Socrates meant when he said that the intermediate state cannot be pleasure or pain because "the coming to be of pleasure and pain in the soul are both a kind of motion" (583e) while their absence is a state of calm. If he means that the motion of pleasure and pain is their coming to be in the soul, then same would be true of the intermediate state, which also comes to be in the soul. But if he means that the actual state of pleasure and the state of pain are motions in themselves, in that respect at least they cannot be the same as the intermediate, which is a state of calmness. The pleasures of smell are motions because they are caused by particles that enter our nose. On that model pleasures would be motions because they necessarily involve our being acted on by something; there is always an agent that acts on us or within us when we feel pleasure or pain, and when the agent ceases we are in a state of calm.[10] In the pleasures of thinking we are moved by reality itself. Similarly, in the case of pain there is always an interactivity between ourselves and something else. On this view we would have to say that if we cut our finger, the reason that the pain persists after the cut has been made is that our body is still under the influence of the incursion. Most bodily pleasures, however, are not like the pleasure of smell, but are pseudo-pleasures that are really relief from pain; and the same is true of the pleasures and pains of anticipation, the pleasant expectation of future pleasure and painful expectation of future pain (584c). If most bodily pleasures are returns to calm, while true pleasures are motions, then most bodily pleasures are not true pleasures.

To return to the objection that was mentioned above, we might wonder what difference any of this makes. If one person is content because of pseudo-pleasures like relief from pain, and another is content because of real pleasures like pure sensations, both are nevertheless content. If ignorant people are happy because they do not know any better, are they any less happy than wise people? The answer becomes clearer in the next stage of the argument, where the relevant motions of pleasure are characterized as "being filled". Ignorance and being unwise (ἀφροσύνη) are empty states of the soul, as hunger and thirst are of the body, the second of which is filled by eating food, and the first by getting rationality (νοῦν). Now Socrates adds that we are more truly filled when we are filled with what more truly is, and asks which kind participates in purer being: the class (γένη) of food, drink, delicacies, and nourishment in general; or the form (εἶδος) of true opinion, knowledge, reason (νοῦ), and in short all of virtue.

Judge it this way: that which is related to what is always the same, and immortal, and true, and which because it itself is of this kind comes to be in what also is of this kind; does it seem to you that this is more than what is never the same, and mortal, and which because it is of that kind comes to be in what also is of that kind?

That which is related to what is always the same goes far beyond the other. [585b–c]

The next line appears to be textually corrupt. The manuscripts have the following exchange:

Does the being (οὐσία) of what is always the same participate any more in being than in knowledge?

Not at all.

Or more than in truth?

Not that either.

If less in truth, won't it also be less in being?

Necessarily.

Isn't it true in general that the kinds concerned with care of the body participate less in truth and being than the kinds concerned with care of the soul? [585c–d]

For Socrates to be arguing that "the being of what is always the same" does not participate fully in being and truth, would neither follow from what he has just said nor lead to what he is about to say; it has been proposed to emend c7 from "what is always the same" (ἀεὶ ὁμοίου) to "what is not the same" or "never the same" (ἀνομοίου or ἀεὶ ἀνομοίου).[11] In that case Socrates, having just shown that "what is always the same" is connected with knowledge (585b14), and by implication reaffirming the previously established corollary that "what is not the same" is not connected with knowledge (479c–480a), now says that "what is not the same" is no more connected with being or truth than it was with knowledge. And this enables him to conclude that that which is concerned with care of the body (that which is not the same) "participates less in truth and being than what is concerned with care of the soul" (585d1–3). As emended the argument is coherent, but the manuscript version makes it a double non sequitur.

Regardless of how we amend 585c7 to function coherently within the series of inferences, the argument supplies the answer to our question about what difference it makes whether what gives us pleasure is a pure pleasure or only a relief from deprivation. It is not enough to say that as long as we feel pleasure the basis of that feeling is unimportant, for pleasure turns out to be not just a feeling but a state of being. The feeling of pleasure is a felt, naturally appropriate (φύσει προσηκόντων: 585d11) change in our condition, and we can scarcely say that changes in our condition make no difference as long as what we feel is pleasant. The argument answers our question, but only indirectly. Its primary point is that pleasures of the mind are superior to pleasures of the body because they change our condition by the addition of true being (what is always the same) rather than by the addition of something ephemeral (which is always altering). But the same reasoning enables us to see that even in the case of corporeal pleasures pure pleasures are superior to the pleasures of relief because they add something to our being (they "fill" us) while the pleasures of relief must be preceded by deprivation and therefore merely leave us where we started. Those without experience in wisdom and virtue spend their lives wandering back and forth between the lower part and the middle, without ever looking up at what is truly above or being brought to it, nor do they become filled with what really is or taste pleasure that is stable and pure (586a).[12] It was suggested in the Introduction that although the dialogue moves back down the Divided Line after Book 7, it does so with the higher levels still in sight. The present passage is one of the places where that is evident.

The second argument provided us with one reason why, even if the pleasures of the mind are more stable and pure than pleasures of the body, they are not the ones that most people think are best—namely that most people have had little or no experience of them. Socrates' next remark provides the additional explanation that the very impurity of the bodily pleasures is a source of their appeal: because the pleasures that such people live with are mingled with pains, they take on color from the contrast between them, which gives them an added intensity that inspires a mad eros in those who are without wisdom (586b–c). The same is true of spiritedness when its pleasures are pursued without rationality and reason (λογισμοῦ τε καὶ νοῦ): the love of honor in such cases leads not only to pleasure (when it is successful) but also to the pain of envy; its love of victory leads to the pain of violence as well as the pleasures of its satisfaction; and its bad temper leads to the pain of anger (586c–d).

The qualifications "without wisdom" and "without rationality and reason" imply that as long as we follow rationality and wisdom we can reduce this problem to a minimum. Guided by rationality, we will be able to pursue the pleasures that appetite and spiritedness have to offer and enjoy them in their truest forms; and since what is best for something is what is most its own, the truest pleasures of appetite and spiritedness are also those that most belong to them (586d–e). Presumably this is because under the guidance of rationality spiritedness and appetite will devote themselves to pursuits that are most likely to achieve the desired results, rather than if our spirited pursuits were reckless and self-defeating, or our appetitive pursuits sought pleasure in ways that bring the most pain. Socrates is proposing the conception of pleasure maximization through rationality that was later championed by Epicurus.[13] The most pleasant life, then, is under the governance of rationality, and thus corresponds to the most just life as described in Book 4. This is reflected in the language now used:

> When the entire soul, then, follows the wisdom-loving part without rebelling, the result for each part is that in all other matters it does its own work and is just, and it enjoys the pleasures which are distinctively its own, and the best, and as far as possible the truest.
> Absolutely.
> But then when one of the others takes control, the result for it is that it does not find its proper pleasure and it also compels the others to pursue an alien pleasure and not a true one. [586e–587a]

This compulsion that leads to alienation is most likely to come from the parts that are furthest from philosophy and from rationality, and thus from law and order, namely the erotic and tyrannical appetites; and least likely to come from those that are kingly and orderly. Consequently the life of the king (the aristocratic person of Book 8) will be most pleasant and the tyrant's life least so.

In this argument Socrates is nothing if not precise: the life of the most just person, the king, is not only more pleasant than that of the most unjust person, the tyrant; it is precisely 729 times more pleasant. This number, he says, "is true and fitting, and appropriate to our lives, if indeed days and nights and months and years are appropriate to them" (588a). The reference to days, nights, months, and years seem to allude to the calculations of the Pythagorean philosopher Philolaus, who estimated that there are 364½ days in a year, from which it follows that there are 729 days and nights, and on the basis of this he also posited a "great year" consisting of 729 months.[14] Socrates evidently wants to suggest that the king is happier every day of the year.[15] Socrates clearly had that number in mind from the first, rather than discovering at it as the result of an open-ended calculation, but it is not easy to determine exactly how he arrives at it. The calculation is based on the number 3 that was provided by the tripartite soul, and it reaches its goal by arguing that the just person's life is $(3 \times 3)^3$ more pleasant than the tyrant's, but what the numbers stand for is not always clear.

The first step of the calculation is to count the tyrant as third from the oligarch since the democrat is between them. The tyrant lives with a semblance of pleasure that is a third removed from the oligarch's with respect to truth (587b14–c10) presumably because 1) the unmixed oligarchic pleasures of necessary appetites are truer (less attended by pain) than 2) the mixed democratic pleasures of necessary and unnecessary appetites together, which in turn are truer than 3) the unmixed tyrannical pleasures of unnecessary appetites.

The oligarch in turn is third from the (aristocratic) king, with the timocrat between them, so the tyrant is 3×3 times removed from true pleasure (thrice from the oligarch who is thrice from the king: 587c12–d4). No doubt if Socrates had wanted to work from a base number of 5 he would simply have said that the tyrant is five times removed from the king because after the king comes the timocrat, oligarch, and democrat, and then the tyrant, who is thus in the fifth place. But Socrates wants to work from a base number of 9, so he multiplies the two triads instead of combining them. The question is whether there is any plausible basis for Glaucon's acquiescence in the switch from addition to multiplication. Since the first triad represented only subdivisions within appetite (oligarch, democrat, tyrant), while the second represented the main triadic divisions of the soul as a whole (appetite, spiritedness, rationality) the implicit justification for Socrates' procedure may be that the difference between the three fundamental parts of the soul must be on a greater scale than any subsequent distinctions within any of the parts. In that case, if the distances among the first triad are *additive*, the distances among the second might be represented as *multiple* relative to the first.[16]

Finally, now that we have arrived at the number 9, Socrates says that the tyrant's semblance of pleasure, which this number represents, is a plane number that must be squared and cubed in order to discover the distance between his life and that of the king. The final calculation then is 9 cubed, which equals 729 (587d6–e4). Socrates does not explain why the number needs to be cubed. It is sometimes suggested that it is because we live in a three-dimensional world; but the same is true of the tyrant, in which case the number representing the tyrant's life should already have been a cube.[17] The clue to Socrates' intention may be his reminder here that the tyrant's pleasure that is represented by the plane number 9 is only a semblance (εἴδωλον) of pleasure (587d6). We may recall that Socrates had also established three distinct levels of pleasure in a way that had nothing to do with the tripartite soul: 1) false pleasures of relief that are preceded by pain, 2) true pleasures of the body (which are usually followed by pain but need not be, as in the pure pleasure smell), and 3) pure pleasures of the mind (583c–584b, 585b). The pure pleasures of philosophy are related to the intelligible realm, while the true pleasures of the body are related to the sensible one, but the tyrant's pleasure does not even properly belong to the sensible world since it is a false semblance of pleasure (584d–e). Because it is only a semblance it is as far below true sensible corporeal pleasure as the latter is beneath pure intelligible pleasure. This gives us a triad of a different dimension than the previous two: intelligible, sensible, illusory.

In the first triad the subdivisions within one of the parts of the soul (appetite) were measured additively, and in the second triad the three parts themselves were measured as multiples of the former. So it is plausible to represent the crucial distinctions within this more fundamental triad as a difference of powers: intelligible reality as a cube; sensible reality, which is an image of intelligible reality (510a); as a square and false semblance, which is an image of sensible reality, as a line (the shadow of a cube is a square, and in principle the shadow of a square is a line). The calculation would then work as follows: The distance between the tyrant and oligarch within appetite = 3; multiplied by the distance (3) between appetite and rationality = 9; to the power of the distance (3) between illusion and intelligible truth = 729.

If the good and just life defeats the bad and unjust one by such a margin with respect to pleasure, Socrates concludes, the margin by which it would defeat it with respect to grace, beauty, and virtue would be incalculable (588a).

The Beast and the God: Return to *Eikasia* (588b–592b)

Socrates begins his concluding remarks by returning to the problem with which they began in Book 2, and recalling that "it was said that injustice profits a completely unjust man as long as he is believed to be just".[18] Socrates proposes to reply now with an image of the soul that will bring home to the proponents of this view the implications of what they are saying. The image adds nothing substantive to what has already been said, but the answers so far have been either in terms of intelligible reality (Book 7) or *pistis* (the images of justice and injustice in the cities and lives described in Books 8–9); now Socrates is going to repeat them in an image composed of words (εἰκονα . . . λόγῳ: 588b10) for those at the level of *eikasia*.

The image is of a creature that outwardly looks like a human being, but is inwardly composed of three parts. The first is a variegated beast with a ring of heads from different beasts, some gentle and some savage, and with the power to change and grow all of them from itself. This obviously corresponds to appetite, which Socrates had earlier described as not really a single thing but multiform (580d11), and the ability to grow the heads and change them from one to another recalls Socrates' earlier image of appetite as a stream that can be diverted among different channels (485d). The second and third parts of the beast, in descending order of size and corresponding respectively to spiritedness and rationality, are a lion and a human being (588d). It obviously invites an infinite regress to have a human being as a component part of human beings: if a human being is composed of three things of which a human being is one, the internal human being must also be composed of three similar parts, and so on in infinitum. Socrates did not say, however, that the entire creature was a human being, but only that "to someone who is not able to see inside but sees only the outer covering, it appears as a single animal, a human being" (588d11–e1). He seems to be anticipating what he will say later, that our soul in its pure form, abstracted from the influence of the body, is not tripartite but purely rational (611b–c). The internal human being here corresponds to that pure self (rationality), while the tripartite animal that is outwardly human corresponds to our true self in conjunction with the body. It is a recurring theme in the dialogues that our truest self is not tripartite but only appears so in conjunction with our body. Thus the *Timaeus* calls rationality the immortal part of the soul, and spiritedness and appetites the mortal parts (i.e., the parts that depend on the body) (90b–c). And the *Phaedo*, which is concerned only with what is immortal in the soul, ascribes only rationality to the soul, and appetite and spiritedness to the body (68b–c, 82b–c).

This ambiguity, about whether we ought to say that our nature is that of the composite or only of what is best in us, becomes more pointed when Socrates goes on to say that perhaps the part within us that he has been calling human ought to be called divine instead (589d1, e4). The dual formulation gives us two ways to look at ourselves, corresponding to the difference between the *Phaedo*'s limitation of "soul" to rationality, and the *Republic*'s use of the term in Books 4 and 8 to include appetite and spiritedness as well: if "human" means what is best in us, then our embodied nature as a whole is only nominally human; but if "human" refers to our embodied nature as a whole, then something in us is more than human—divine.

In either case, this image provides the champions of injustice with a graphic illustration of what they are advocating: first, that we nurture and strengthen what is beastlike within us, while starving and weakening what is distinctively human and godly, so that the latter is dragged around by the other two; second, that instead of fostering friendship among the three we leave them to fight each another. The advocates of justice, on the other hand, seek to give the human part control over the others and to have it care for the multiform beast as a farmer does his animals, cultivating the tame heads while hindering the savage ones. Moreover, they would have the human part make the lion its ally, and would seek to bring all three into friendly concord (588e–589b). In this way the defenders of justice can be seen to have a better understanding than the defenders of injustice, who think that gold can compensate us for enslaving the best part of ourselves to the worst, the most godly part to the most godless (589d–e). Moreover the belief that injustice is profitable as long as we are believed to be just, and are rewarded accordingly, is the opposite of the truth: having our injustice go undetected makes us worse, while having it discovered and punished weakens what is bestial in us and frees the gentle part from its servitude, so that the soul settles into its best nature and acquires self-control, justice, and wisdom (591a–b). Thus Socrates maintained in the *Gorgias* (480a–b) that someone who is unjust ought to seek out a judge to impose punishment the way someone who is sick seeks out a doctor for treatment.

The image not only illustrates the errors of the iconoclastic defenders of injustice, but also the basis for the traditional attitudes about the noble and base. The things we consider noble are those that subordinate the bestial parts of our nature to the divine, while those we consider base do the reverse (589c–d). In particular, licentiousness is blamed because it gives too much freedom to the multiform beast; as are stubbornness and irritability because they excessively strengthen and stretch the part that is like a lion and snake; and luxury and softness are blamed because they slacken and relax this same part when they introduce cowardice into it.[19] Again, flattery and illiberality are blamed when they subject the spirited part to the rule of the mob-like beast so that it becomes more of an ape than a lion.[20] The image further illustrates why people tend to look down on manual workers, namely that their lives are devoted to serving the needs of appetite rather than what is best in us, and the presumption is that the latter is not strongly enough developed in them to command their attention (590a–c).

Because it is important not to have too much wealth—as well as not having too little, and because it is important to accept only those honors that make us better but not those that throw us off balance, Glaucon concludes that someone with understanding will not want to take part in politics. Socrates agrees that this may be true of the politics of the just person's native city unless he meets with some divine chance (presumably the chance to transform the city along the lines proposed in the earlier discussion), but not that of his "own" city, which Glaucon justifiably understands to mean "the city whose founding we just went through, the one that lies in words, for I think it is nowhere on earth". Socrates replies: "But perhaps there is a pattern (παράδειγμα) lying up in heaven for the one who wants to see it and who, after seeing it, wants to found a city within himself. It makes no difference whether it is or will ever be somewhere, for he will take part in the affairs of this one alone, and of no other" (592a–b).

When Socrates says that there is a pattern not only in words but in heaven, he is emphasizing that its primary realm is not that of *eikasia* (only in words) but *noesis*. In that case the key to understanding what Socrates means by saying that there is a paradigm in heaven which we can use to create a just city, both in ourselves and in the world, is his earlier remark that the philosopher looks upon and contemplates what is organized and eternally the same, which neither commit injustice nor are treated unjustly by one another, but which all are orderly in accordance with rationality, and he imitates them and assimilates himself to them as far as possible. . . . Associating with the divine and orderly, the philosopher becomes orderly and divine as far as is possible for a human being. . . . Do you think he would be a poor crafter of moderation, justice, and all of popular virtue? . . . [Consequently] a city will otherwise never be happy unless it is drawn by artists who use a divine pattern (παραδείγματι). [500c–e]

A different interpretation takes "heaven" (οὐρανῷ) to indicate not the *noetic* realm of the forms but the visible sky (therefore by implication the realm of *pistis*), and to refer back to Socrates' remark that we should study the heavenly (οὐρανόν) bodies with a view to using them as patterns (παραδείγμασι) of the rational principles that underlie them (529d).[21] In that passage, however, the heavenly bodies are used as a paradigm for understanding intelligible principles, not as models for ourselves. Nor is it clear how they could be used directly as models for ourselves: we are not going to be able to understand how to achieve just lives simply by looking at the stars. They can only become models for us indirectly, by first awakening in us an awareness of a deeper and more pervasive kind of rationality that the movements of the stars imperfectly reflect. That deeper rationality is what can become our guide, but it is not something visible in the sky; it is only intelligible to our mind. In that case, even if we take the present passage to be referring to the visible heaven that is the place of the stars, rather than to the intelligible heaven that is the place of the forms, it still must be understood as pointing eventually to the intelligible realm. The passage thus refers to the intelligible heaven either in the first instance or the second, and so, in accordance with Aristotle's Razor, "it is better to say the first".[22]

Does it make sense to conceive of this pattern as something like a form of the just city? If the forms are offsprings of the Idea of the good, they might seem more likely to be forms of natural things rather than humanly constructed ones such as a city. But, in fact, Socrates is only eight short speeches away from saying that there is a form for every group of things to which we apply the same name (i.e., for every universal), and from giving as the only two examples the forms of a couch and a table (596a–b). In that case there is nothing to prevent him from referring here to the form of a different kind of human artifact, a just city. Since a form is neither spatial nor composite, the form of a just city would not have to be conceived (in a reductio ad absurdum) as composed of additional forms of houses, people, and laws, any more than the form of couch or table would be a composite containing forms of legs, planks, and other elements. If there is a form of a just city, we should conceive it rather as that aspect of reality by the contemplation of which we could understand the nature of a just city and how it might be constructed. On the other hand, Socrates does not say that the pattern is a pattern of the city, but only that it is a pattern, so it may be that what he is referring to is not the form of the just city at all, but the ultimate paradigm, the Idea of the good. For when he stipulated the kind of education that the prospective philosopher-rulers were to receive, he said that "they must be compelled to turn the bright vision of their souls upward and look toward that which provides light for all things, and when they have seen the Good itself they must use it as a pattern (παραδείγματι) for putting in order the city, citizens, and themselves" (540a–b).

Notes

1. This was true according to the enlargement metaphor on which Socrates' account was modeled, although not according to the scale metaphor.

2. The statement that philosophers prefer their own pleasure is textually ambiguous if not corrupt. See the discussion by Michael Stokes in "Some Pleasures of Plato, *Republic* IX", *Polis* 9 (1990): 2–51, esp. 2–22.

3. Cf. Murphy 1951, 209–211, 223; and Annas 1981, 306–314.

4. Nettleship believes that the argument is unsatisfactory because "a man who had no experience of a kind of pleasure which he was asked to believe was better than his own could not be convinced by the experience of another" (1901, 321). However, the goal of the argument is not to convince appetitive and spirited people that their belief about what is most pleasant is wrong, but to show which of the three beliefs has a stronger claim to truth. Gomperz claims that the argument "overlooks the fact that greater susceptibility to one kind of pleasure is usually coupled with a smaller capacity for enjoying other kinds" (1905, vol. 3, 100), but far from overlooking that point, it forms the foundation of Socrates' argument. Appetitive people are less susceptible to the pleasures of learning because they are less capable of them, and philosophers are less susceptible to the lure of appetites because they have found something better.

5. Stuart 1979, chapter 2, par. 6–7.

6. At banquets the first libation was offered to Olympian Zeus and the Olympian gods, the second to the heroes, and the third to Zeus the Savior (see Adam 1963 [1902], 348). The present dedication to "Olympian Zeus the Savior" combines the first and third oaths but omits the oath to the heroes, perhaps because the argument aims at the immortal (585c2) and disparages the spirited (586c7–d2). His acceptance of the first and third dedications and rejection of the second foreshadows the argument itself, in which the first and third species of pain/pleasure will be true, but the middle one false.

7. For this reason among others, Stokes questions whether the term καθαράν (pure) is even appropriate in the case of the olfactory pleasures, and should not be

deleted as a later addition (1990, 23–28, 42). It is certainly true that the reference to pure pleasures of smell complicates the argument's contrast between intellectual and corporeal pleasures, but if "pure" means neither preceded nor followed by pain, then the adjective does apply to that example. If the anomalous example of smell softens the boundaries between the intelligible and corporeal realms, it fits a pattern of such softening that we have seen since Book 6.

8. There may be an allusion to the allegory of the cave when Socrates says that those who confuse the intermediate state with pleasure are like people who are brought from the depths up to a point intermediate between the bottom and the top, and because they look downward to where they came from and do not realize that there is a higher place in the other direction, they think that the midpoint is the top (584d–e).

9. Cf. Cross and Woozley: "The question 'which is the most pleasant life?' unless it means 'which would *you* prefer?' is not a properly formed question at all" (1964, 266); cf. Guthrie 1975, vol. 4, 541. But as Annas points out, "it is up to us to argue, and not just assert, that pleasantness can *never* be an objective matter" (1981, 314; see her discussion at 308–314). Also see Stokes 1990, 39–40.

10. On this view the problems do not arise that Aristotle mentions in *Nicomachean Ethics* 10.3.

11. E.g., Karl Friedrich Hermann in his edition of the *Republic* (Leipzig: Teubner, 1884), cf. Adam 1963 (1902), 354, 381–83. G. R. F. Ferrari, on the basis of a different way of construing the logic of the argument, suggests an emendation that gives the sense, "Well, does anything have a greater share in the being of what is always the same than knowledge does?" ("Plato, *Republic* 9.585c–d" *Classical Quarterly* NS 52 [2002]: 383–88).

12. Nettleship suggests a different way of construing the argument. He translates πληροῦσθαι (filled) as "satisfied" (1901, 324) and remarks that "The only test we can apply to different forms of satisfaction of ourselves is the question, How far is each, when we have obtained it, a permanent element in ourselves?" (330).

13. Also see Irwin 1995, 293–94. Nettleship takes Socrates to be making a stronger claim, and suggests the following illustration: "A person who could say with St. Paul, 'whether I eat or drink, I do all to the glory of God', might mean: That in the most trivial satisfactions there may be a sense of serving something wider and higher than animal appetite; that this gives to the satisfaction of appetite a permanence and a satisfactoriness which by itself it cannot have; and yet that in this lies the only appropriate satisfaction of appetite, or, as Plato says, its 'own' (οἰκεῖον) satisfaction" (1901, 331).

14. Cf. Adam 1963 (1902), 361.

15. And perhaps every day of his life, given Socrates' reference to "days and nights and months and *years*", if a great year (i.e., sixty years, nine months) was considered a normal life span. That seems unlikely, however, since the Psalms, written at about the same time, puts the normal life span at seventy to eighty years (90:10), much as we do. Nor is it likely that a great year represents the *average* life span of the time, since not only would Philolaus have had no access to those statistics, but modern

computations of the average life span in ancient Greece puts it at twenty years (Dilip Jeste and Rodrigo Muñoz, "Preparing for the Future", *Psychiatric Services* 50:9 [September 1999]: 1157). The reference to "years" in the above passage may be explained by the reference to 729 days and nights (i.e., a year). Neither is it necessary to account for it by assuming with Adam that Philolaus may also have posited 729 years = 1 greatest year (1963 [1902], 361).

16. Alternatively, Adam suggests that since the five types that are mentioned include the beginning and end of the series (king and tyrant), the total number of nine can be explained on the assumption that four additional types are implicit as intermediate stages in the decline (1963 [1902], 360). Following up Adam's suggestion, Brumbaugh attempts to identify the additional four lives by matching the five-part descending classification of lives in the *Republic* with the nine-part descending classification of lives in the *Phaedrus* (1954, 152–54, 158). The first three lives of the *Republic* (aristocrat, timocrat, oligarch) match up well with the first three lives of the *Phaedrus* (philosopher, general, citizen-merchant), and both series conclude with the tyrant, but other cases are less convincing. The *Republic*'s fourth life, the democrat, has to be paired with the *Phaedrus*' sixth life, which is a poet (there seems to be an error in Brumbaugh's citation of 557c as showing that "in *Republic* ix" Socrates emphasizes an equivalence "of the democratic character and the mimetic artist's occupation"; 661c–d would suit the purpose better but still not very well, and, in fact, both passages are in Book 8 rather than 9, so perhaps Brumbaugh has some place different in mind); and nothing in the *Republic* would explain why the life of a citizen-merchant would be followed (as it is in the *Phaedrus*) by that of a gymnast, prophet, and poet, respectively, or why an artisan would come in seventh while the citizen-merchant was third.

17. Brumbaugh bases the cube on the triad of experience (*empeiria*), intelligence (*phronēsis*), and reason (*logos*) at 582a (1954, 155), but since that triad was already used as evidence for the second argument it is unlikely that it would be pressed into service for this purpose as well.

18. Socrates uses the passive voice ("it was said") rather than attributing it to Glaucon and Adeimantus, who introduced it, because they did not put the view forward as their own belief.

19. These last two taken together reaffirm the importance of the mean, as will Socrates' later remark that we must guard against having either too much wealth or too little: 591e.

20. Are we meant to think of the snake as an image of an excessively spirited lion, and the ape an image of a deficiently spirited one? The imagery points in that direction, but it is difficult to think of a snake as emblematic of extreme spiritedness.

21. See, for example, Guthrie 1975, vol. 4, 543–44, Burnyeat 1999, 299, and Ferrari 2003, 106.

22. Aristotle, *Metaphysics* Λ.6.1972a15, cf. *Physics* 8.6.259a6–13.

~

CHAPTER TEN

Art and Death
(Book 10)

Creation and Imitation: Painting (595a–598d)

The final book of the *Republic* begins with a critique of poetry and ends with one of Plato's greatest poetic achievements, the myth of Er. One advantage, then, in revisiting in Book 10 the criticisms of poetry that were put forward in Book 3, is that along with a discussion of the kinds of poetry that are to be prohibited Plato can display a kind of poetry that would be permissible. For this reason our consideration of Socrates' critique of poetry (which applies to all forms of literature) will not be complete until the end of the chapter.

Socrates begins by saying that despite the love and admiration he has always felt for Homer, one of the many reasons he is convinced that they founded the city correctly is that the tripartite division of the soul in Book 4 confirms the decision they made in Book 3 to banish tragedians and other imitative poets (595a–b). Socrates not only reaffirms their previous conclusions but extends them. Previously, only imitators of unhealthy states of mind were banned, while a poet who imitated the speech of a good person, and said things in accordance with the patterns that they established earlier, would be allowed (395d–398b). However, that was before they distinguished the parts of the soul, and established that a devotion to pleasure is always less worthy than a devotion to rationality, even when the pleasure is not necessarily unhealthy in itself. It was also before they distinguished the four levels of the Divided Line and established that a devotion to sensuous appearances is always less worthy than a devotion to the intelligible. Since artistic imitation calls attention to sensuous appearances, works of art may draw us to the lower part of the Divided Line. And because imitative works of art are often designed to give pleasure through their imitations, they may strengthen the irrational part of our soul. Consequently, imitation is now seen to be potentially dangerous to rationality even when what is imitated is not objectionable in itself. Because of the *Republic*'s evolving point of view, it is not surprising that the value of the arts is assessed differently in Book 9 than it was in Book 3.

The condemnation of imitation is ironic in a dialogue where Socrates himself imitates all the speakers in the course of his narration, replicating the speeches of Cephalus, Polemarchus, Thrasymachus, Cleitophon, Glaucon, Adeimantus, and Er. Perhaps we are meant to notice that the arguments that follow do not, in fact, implicate Plato's own kind of imitation. If so, once again the *Republic* begins with an oversimplification and refines it in the subsequent course of the discussion. Socrates does not make explicit that the objection to poetry has now become more far-reaching, but the subsequent arguments provide justifications for the broader condemnation.[1] In Books 2 and 3 the positive value of poetry and the other arts was explicitly acknowledged as well as their dangers, on the basis of which the arts became a primary educational tool; here the emphasis will be almost entirely on the dangers of the arts, and their redeeming features will be referred to only in the most oblique ways. The one-sidedness of the arguments has led to a number of different conclusions on the part of Plato's readers.[2]

The concern about imitative art leads Socrates to ask about the nature of imitation itself, and when Glaucon declines to venture an explanation Socrates begins by formulating what is both the most concise and broadest description of the theory of forms anywhere in the dialogues: "we posit one form (εἶδος) for every plurality to which we give the same name" (596a). Thus there are many couches and tables but only two Ideas (ἰδέαι), one each of the couch and table, for if there were two forms there would have to be a third form for what they have in common, and that would be the true form (597b–c).[3] The individual artifacts come into being when an artisan makes them in accordance with the corresponding Idea. If I want to build a couch I must first understand what a couch is, and then make something that accords with that understanding. When Socrates goes on to say, "Surely no maker makes the Idea itself, for how could he?" (596b), the implication is that the form is something beyond what even an inventor can create. Whoever invented the first couch or table was only formulating one version of a possibility that existed all along: "a surface for reclining on" or "a raised surface on which objects can be placed". All inventions are instantiations of a possibility inherent in the nature of things, and only the latter, strictly speaking, are forms: the form of a couch is the "couch in nature" (597b6, c2).

In the case of a couch or table there are at least physical precedents in nature, flat surfaces that we can lie on or raised surfaces that we can place things on; but how can we deny that an inventor makes the form of something that had no preexisting counterpart in the physical world, such as a wheel?[4] Insofar as we call many things wheels there must be a form of wheel, and if the form of the wheel is the "wheel in nature" how can there be something in nature of which there can be no natural instantiations? A spinning top, which Socrates himself used as an example in an earlier context (436d), has concrete natural counterparts like a spinning rock, but the axle of a wheel sets it apart from anything in corporeal nature, including logs that were used as rollers. Nevertheless, what he says about the top can be extrapolated to the wheel. He showed that there is nothing contradictory about the fact that a top is both spinning and standing still, because it is the circumference that is spinning and the axis that is standing still. We could say, then, that whereas in the case of a top the circumference is parallel to the ground and the axis perpendicular to it, the form of a wheel is "a spinning circumference that is perpendicular to the ground, with an axis that is parallel to the ground and provides a basis for supporting and carrying something in the direction of the spin". The invention of the wheel is, in fact, a discovery of this principle which was always "there". All inventions, no matter how complicated, could be shown in this way to be discoveries of the forms or possibilities (see above, 199–200) inherent in the nature of things, made not by the inventor but by a god, as Socrates puts it a page later (597b), an image of the Idea of the good (509b).

By choosing the problematic examples of artificial things, Socrates is able to locate the imitator in relation not only to the form, but also in relation to the artisan. His subsequent argument will depend in part on comparisons between the artisan and the artist with respect to the form, which requires him to refer to forms of artifacts. The two examples that he chooses here, the couch and the table, were the first two items whose absence Glaucon complained about in the original healthy city (372d7–8) and the first two that Socrates subsequently introduced into the feverish city (373e6–a2). They were the original examples of unnecessary appetites, and Socrates' reference to them here foreshadows the connection that he will establish by the end of the arguments, between imitation and irrational appetite.

What would Glaucon call artisans who can make all things, Socrates asks— not only the usual artifacts but all plants and animals including themselves, and even earth, heaven, and the gods? Glaucon replies that this artisan is "A most wondrous sophist" (596d1)—a remark that links the present discussion of art with the sophistical arguments of Book 1—but what Socrates has in mind turns out to be not so wondrous after all: Glaucon himself would be able to do it if he were willing to carry around a mirror (596d–e). We are back in the realm of *eikasia*, a kind of thinking that is the equivalent of looking only at the visible images (*eikones*) of things, like shadows and reflections (509e–510a).

Painters are comparable to Glaucon with his mirror, for they make only the appearance of a couch. The carpenter makes a particular couch but not the form, for the form is what it is to be a couch (ὅ ἔστι κλίνη), or the couch in nature, which we would presumably say is made by no one but a god.[5] Since the carpenter does not make what it is to be a couch, he makes not the being (τὸ ὄν) of the couch but only something that resembles the being, which is dimmer than the true couch (597a). Just as the carpenter does not make the form but only an individual couch, someone who paints a picture of a couch makes neither the form nor a particular couch, but an imitation of a particular couch (597e–598a). There are three couches then: the form made by a god, the physical couch made by a carpenter, and the picture of a couch made by the painter. And just as the individual couch is "dimmer" than the form, the painting represents only a single aspect or perspective of the object, so it does not even imitate the being of the physical couch but only its appearance. It is therefore far from the truth, and the painter, like the man with a mirror, can produce everything only because it is produced at the most superficial level (598b–d). At this point, what "imitation" refers to is not quite the same as in Book 3. There imitation referred to copying within ourselves particular kinds of behavior (394d–396e), whereas here it means copying in pictures (or words) particular things.[6] The difference is that the present discussion applies the concept to a broader range of instances; in the final two arguments it will be applied in much the same sense as in Book 3 (603c–606c).

When Socrates asked what the relationship is between the painter and the couch, it was Glaucon who said, "He is an imitator of what those others make" (597e2). But now Socrates raises another possibility:[7] "Does the painter seem to you to try to imitate each thing itself as it is in nature, or the works of the artisans?" (598a1–3). Since Glaucon had already said that the painter imitates what the artisans make, the only thing that is accomplished by Socrates' repetition of the question is to point out that there was another possible answer: the painter might conceivably imitate not the thing but the form (each "thing itself"). Glaucon reasserts his earlier answer, although without giving any reason for rejecting the other alternative, and the possibility that has just been raised is never mentioned again. In an earlier passage, however, Socrates himself seemed to suggest that a painter might in principle imitate something like a form, when he conceived of a painter who paints "a pattern (*paradeigma*) of what the most beautiful human being would be like" (472d).[8] "*Paradeigma*" is one of Plato's words for the forms, and it is hard to see a difference between being able in principle to imitate this paradigm in a painting, and to imitate the paradigm of couch or table.

In fact, the art historian J. J. Pollitt argues that "Greek artists tended to look for the typical and essential forms which expressed the essential nature of classes of phenomena in the same way that Platonic 'forms' or 'ideas' expressed essential realities underlying the multiplicity of sense perception".[9] Pollitt's description of the statuette of the bronze horse in Figure 1, for example, as "an attempt to get at the 'horseness' which lies behind all particular horses" (*ibid*) is more convincing than a Glauconian claim that the sculptor was trying to imitate the outward appearance of a particular horse. Plato speaks about painting rather than sculpture here, but almost nothing has survived of Greek painting, except for vase painting, which was intended primarily to decorate household objects (*ibid* 61). Consequently, we have to generalize from what sculpture shows us about Greek artistic practices.

Closer to Plato's own day is the "severe" style represented by the Aphrodite Sosandra in figure 2, in which naturalistic imitation is sacrificed to a geometricizing abstraction of the human form. "The effect produced is that of a geometric shape, a polyhedron . . . with only the toes projecting from beneath to give a human dimension. The somber, hooded face . . . also has a geometric exactitude" (*ibid* 39). The aim is clearly to capture an ideal rather than to imitate the appearance of a particular person.

Not only artworks themselves, but even the art theory that Plato would have known contradicts Glaucon's assurance that art is imitation. One of Pythagoras' homonymous contemporaries (sixth century BCE) was Pythagoras of Rhegium "who appears to be the first to aim at rhythm and symmetry",[10] which is quite a different matter than slavish imitation. Polykleitos of Argos, who flourished in the second half of the fifth century and was evidently influenced by Pythagoreanism, wrote a treatise on *symmetria* in art called the *Canon*, according to which the "aim was to express what Polykleitos himself called *to eu*, 'the perfect' or 'the good', and what others seem to have called *to kallos*, 'the beautiful'. . . . The goal of his system of *symmetria* was to describe an ideal nature in man".[11] In a later and more detailed survey of this aspect of Greek art, Pollitt writes with regard to Greek artists who aimed at "making forms", that their basic approach "was to pare away details which seemed inessential in a form in order to bring out its underlying geometric structures, and then to reassemble these structures into a new proportional harmony".[12]

*Fig. 10.1. Bronze Horse, c. 750 BCE. Berlin, Staatliche Museen Preussischer Kulturbesitz.
Photo Credit: Bildarchiv Preussischer Kulturbesitz / Art Resource, New York*

As someone who has shown himself earlier in the book to be well informed about music theory (and in the *Phaedrus* theories of rhetoric), Plato can hardly have been unaware of the styles and theories of Greek painting mentioned above. In fact, Socrates may have been alluding to Polykleitus' theory in Book 3 when he said that like music and the other arts, painting is full of qualities like harmony, grace, and rhythm that follow a character that is perfect (*eu*) and beautiful (*kalos*) (400d11–401a1).

Fig. 10.2. Aphrodite Sosandra. c. 460 BCE Museo Archeologico Nazionale, Naples, Italy
Photo Credit: Scala / Art Resource, New York

Since Plato must have been aware that there is more to painting than the imitation of outward appearances, why does he have Glaucon answer so simplistically? In a passage of the *Timaeus* previously cited in chapter 3, we are told:

> However much of music in sound is useful for hearing is given for the sake of harmony. And harmony, which has motions akin to the revolutions within us of our soul, was given by the Muses to him who makes use of it with intelligence, not for irrational pleasures, such as now appears to be its use, but as a co-fighter against the disharmoniousness of the revolution of the soul which has come about in us, to bring it into order and concordance with itself. [47c–d]

The reason for Glaucon's answer may lie in the words "irrational pleasures, such as now appears to be its use". For in Plato's own day the idealization characteristic of the works shown above was replaced by a new emphasis on emotion and sensuousness.[13] The objection against art is a simplification, as are many moments in the dialogues, but as in the other cases we have seen, complicating factors will be introduced once the basic point has been made, and if we remove the hyperbole by defining the claim more narrowly, the point turns out to be a reasonable one. Given the artistic practices of the day, if Socrates had asked Glaucon not about what "the painter" does but about how "painters now" appear to use their art, Glaucon's answer would seem to be justified—much in the way that Schopenhauer complained of composers of his day who wrote "program music" that illustrated events in the world of phenomena, imitating outward appearances instead of exploiting music's ability to express the in-itself of the will. Socrates' strategy throughout the founding of the city has been to minimize the risk of corrupting influences (e.g., 490e–493a), and so art is here judged by the damage it can do rather than the good it can accomplish. Accordingly, the emphasis here is not on the ability of art to convey the intelligible by means of the sensible (an ability that was already indicated in Book 3 and will be alluded to again), but on the danger that it will make the sensible an end in itself and focus our thoughts within the realm of *doxa*. All art, as we shall see, functions as a bridge between sensuousness and intelligibility, but the bridge can be crossed in both directions. Artistic idealization leads us from our senses to something intelligible, but sensuous or emotional art uses beauty to enhance the pleasures of sensation, as in the passage cited from the *Timaeus*.

Imitation and Implementation: Poetry (598d–601b)

During the discussion of painting Socrates had anticipated the critique of poetry. After Glaucon agreed that what a painter makes is only an imitation three times removed from nature (i.e., from the form), Socrates added, "This then will also be the case with a tragedian if indeed he is an imitator. He is third from the king and the truth by nature, and so are all other imitators" (597e).[14] Given the mythic paradigms on which the tragedies were based, however, it is hard to believe that Socrates or Plato would seriously think that the characterizations were nothing more than slavish imitations of particular individuals. It is hard to believe that the person who says "Whoever arrives at the gates of poetry without the madness of the Muses, convinced that he will be an adequate poet by means of *techne*, is unsuccessful" (*Phaedrus* 245a)[15] would disagree with Aristotle's claim that poetry is more philosophical than history because it is concerned with universals rather than particulars (*Poetics* 9)—that poets are interested in the individuals they imitate not ultimately for the sake of biographical accuracy but as vehicles by which to express something universal. But even if poetry is more philosophical than history, it is not as philosophical as philosophy, and that is where Socrates' emphasis lies here (607b).[16]

The first argument that is specifically directed against poetry takes as its target "tragedy and its leader Homer" (598d). The reference to Homer shows what we have already seen in the case of painting—that the present critique applies to a broader conception of imitation than did that of Book 3. There only the directly imitative poetry of drama came under attack, but now it includes even the indirect imitation of narrative epitomized by Homer.

The critique of poetry takes a different form than the argument against painting, because the products of poetry are composed of words rather than visual images, and can thus be taken as providing literal guidance to life—which is why poetry is the only art form that is a direct rival to philosophy (607b). There were intimations of this in the beginning of the first and second books. In Book 1 Cephalus presented his views in the words of Sophocles (329b–d) and Pindar (331a), and Polemarchus did so in the words of Simonides (331d–e); while at the beginning of Book 2 Adeimantus shows how the words of the poets encourage people to believe that justice is profitable only for its reputation while injustice is profitable inherently (363a–368a).[17] Socrates' argument attacks the common belief that if poets create beautiful poetry they must have knowledge of the subjects they write about, and since they write about all things including the crafts, human virtue and vice, and even the gods, they must have knowledge of all things, and could not be mere imitators three times removed from the being of things (598d–599a). The argument is not presented as sequential inference, but it implies the following steps:

1. Someone who truly understands actions could perform them as well as imitate them.

2. Actions have more value and benefit than images of them do.

3. Therefore if poets understood the actions they imitate they would prefer to be remembered for doing noble deeds rather than for imitating them—to be praised rather than to praise.

4. There is no record of such accomplishments by the great poets.

5. Therefore they do not have genuine knowledge of the things they imitate.

The third premise is obviously contentious since poets would not accept the description of their work as mere imitation. But Socrates is taking this point to have been established by the previous argument and in need of no further discussion—even though in that argument he applied the conclusion to poetry only in tentative terms: "if indeed (εἴπερ) he is an imitator" (597e). The third premise stands or falls with the validity of the first argument, and our conclusion about the first argument was that its claims are true selectively but not universally.

Before we consider the extent to which those reservations undermine the present argument, let us look more closely at step 4, the premise for which Socrates provides the most detailed argument. He alludes in passing to the kind of argument he makes in the Ion (537a–540e),[18] to the effect that poetic imitators lack expert knowledge of the crafts they imitate. He says he will not ask about crafts like medicine and whether poets have cured people or had medical disciples (although to raise the question is to answer it), but only about the most important crafts like those of war, government, and education. None of the great poets have benefited their cities as lawgivers the way Lycurgus, Charondas, and Solon did, or devised useful inventions like Thales and Anacharsis, or had followings as educators like Pythagoras, or like Protagoras and Prodicus. Since Protagoras and Prodicus were sophists, this is a strange argument from the mouth of Socrates, who excoriated the sophists in no uncertain terms three books earlier (492a–495a). Are we really to suppose that the poets' lack of wisdom can be proven by the fact that they are not as politically successful as sophists?

Equally puzzling is the goal of "being praised" that Socrates appeals to in step 3. The corrupt nature of public praise and blame was graphically exposed in Books 6 (492b–c), 7 (516c–d), and 8 (449c–550a), and will soon be identified as a factor in undermining the virtue of playwrights (605a). Given Socrates' own fate in the court of public opinion, it is a strange court for Plato to have him appeal to now; it inspires as little confidence as a goal of wisdom as does the success of the sophists. If this argument were offered as a freestanding demonstration, it would be hard not to regard it as proposed in bad faith, since it uses premises that Socrates cannot have believed to be true.

However, it is not offered as a free-standing demonstration but as a refutation of an objection to the previous argument. It began with the words, "we hear from some people that [Homer and the tragedians] know all the crafts, all human affairs concerning virtue and vice, and the affairs of the gods as well" (598d). The argument refutes this claim on its own terms, appealing in passing to the concepts of popularity and praise that the objectors presumably accept, even if Socrates does not. It loosely takes the form of a reductio ad absurdum: assuming that the poets have the kind of knowledge you attribute to them, they would have used it to benefit public institutions, but they did not do so, so your assumption must be false.[19]

Socrates reaffirms their previous conclusion that the poet, like the sculptor, does not need to have knowledge of his subjects but only of how to imitate their outward appearance, so that people will be impressed who, like the poet, form opinions by seeing things through words (i.e., by *eikasia*). What impresses them, however, is not only the skillfulness of the imitation, but also the fact that the poet "speaks in meter, rhythm, and harmony . . . So great is the enchantment that these very things have by nature" (601a–b). In the first argument Socrates simplified the indictment against painting by making no mention of the important positive qualities of harmony, grace, and rhythm that gave the arts importance in the education of the guardians (400d11–401a1). Now he shows that he has not forgotten the power of these attributes, but they do not testify to wisdom on the part of artists if wisdom means understanding the world of action. An understanding of meter, rhythm, harmony, and beauty generally is no small thing in the context of the *Republic*. But it is not the same as the practical wisdom that is also attributed to the poets as an extension of it by audiences who fail to make the distinction.[20]

Acquaintance and Imitation: Painting (601b–602c)

The first argument put visual artists as makers of imitations in third place with respect to truth, behind the maker of the form and the maker of the thing that participates in the form and is imitated by the painting. The new argument puts visual artists in third place again, but this time not ontologically with respect to the truth of the work of art, but epistemologically with respect to the knowledge of the artists themselves. Socrates begins with the example of knowledge regarding the reins and bit of a horse. The painter imitates them, and the cobbler and smith make them, but neither the painter nor the cobbler and smith understand their use as well as the rider. In all cases there are these three kinds of *techne*—that of the user, the maker, and the imitator—and it is the user who knows the thing best because the excellence (*aretē*), beauty, and rightness of a thing refer to its use. Thus the user reports to the maker what is good or bad about the way the object performs (601b–d).

Socrates now changes his example. A flute player tells the flute maker what is good and bad about the flutes he makes, and instructs him as to what kind to make, and the maker follows his instructions. The one who knows about the goodness and badness of flutes, then, is the user (χρώμενος)—in fact, the terms "good" (ἀγαθός) and "useful" (χρηστός) are used interchangeably here (601d–e)[21]—while the maker has a correct conviction about what is fine or bad about them. Imitators, however, neither know from their own experience whether or not what they imitate is fine or correct, nor do they have correct opinion as a result of consulting those who do use the artifact. Having neither knowledge nor correct opinion that something is bad or good, what they imitate is what appears beautiful to the multitude, who do not know anything. Imitation, then, is a kind of playing rather than a serious matter. Once again the conclusions drawn from the example of painting are extended to poetry: tragedians, whether they write in iambics or epics (like Homer) are all imitators to the greatest possible degree (601d–602b).

The charge of a lack of seriousness, which was previously made in the second argument (599a–b), is also leveled in the *Phaedrus*, but against the writing of philosophy (276b–277a). If the writing of philosophy is no better than poetic imitation, Plato is not in a strong position to be condemnatory. The difference between seriousness and play is always a comparative one, however. In the *Phaedrus* writing is play compared to the seriousness of oral dialogue; and in the second argument above, poetry is not as serious as reforming society. From the standpoint of the *Republic*, where the highest knowing cannot be put into words (533a), the *Phaedrus*' attitude toward written philosophy would not be out of place, especially since written philosophy too is an *imitation* in words. But the philosopher, when writing about the experience of thinking or virtue, is a user as well as an imitator, and so written philosophy is at least more serious than poetry, according to the present argument. The characterization of artists as imitating not the being of a thing but only the way it appears to their audience recalls other passages of the *Phaedrus*, where rhetoricians are condemned for caring not about the way things really are but only the way their audience thinks that they are (260b–d, 272d–273c). Since what painters do is comparable to what manipulative rhetoricians or even sophists do (cf. *Sophist* 235b–236b), the initial comparison of artists with sophists at 596d1 should not be taken lightly.

But there is another side to this argument. Why did Socrates change his example from reins and bits to flutes? All of the points that are made in terms of the new example could have been made in terms of the first one. The most obvious difference in the new example is that now the *techne* associated with the most complete knowledge is that of a musician. In an argument devoted to denying to artists any true knowledge, it is surprising to find knowledge attributed to the musician at the same time that it is denied to the painter. The first argument described the artists' work only in terms of the imitation of outward appearances, and without any reference to the important contribution that they were earlier acknowledged to make in terms of harmony, grace, rhythm, and beauty generally (400d–402a). The second argument, in turn, reminded us explicitly of the power of the poet's knowledge of meter, rhythm, and harmony (601a–b). If we now ask what kind of knowledge flute players have that enables them to tell the maker what is good and bad about flutes, most obviously they must have some understanding of goodness (ἀγαθά: 601d9), which involves an understanding of beauty (κάλλους: 601e8). They must also have knowledge of *harmonia* or tuning, in order to judge whether the instrument is in tune. And as for the poets, Socrates reminds us again of their knowledge of rhythm when he says that they are imitators whether they write in iambics or epic hexameters. There is a tacit acknowledgement once again that although artists may have no knowledge of the kinds of things they imitate, they have another kind of knowledge whose importance cannot be overestimated, although it is not of a conceptual nature.

There has been an ascent through the stages of the tripartite soul in the examples that Socrates has chosen: the couch and table were allusions to the unnecessary appetites (372d–373a), horses are first mentioned in the *Republic* in the spirited context of competition, a horse race (328a), and later serve as an explicit example of spiritedness (375a),[22] while the flute example implies rationality (*harmonia*: 530d).

Art and the Divided Line: Painting (602c–603b)

Painting is an art of illusion, and its power to produce illusions is what makes it bewitching and awe-inspiring. But this power is of questionable benefit if, as Socrates points out, it is rooted in the propensity of sight to harbor inconsistent impressions, as when the same thing seems unequal to itself in size when seen from different distances,[23] or the same stick looks both straight and bent depending on whether it is in or out of water, or something looks both concave and convex because of its colors. The corrective of these confusions is rationality, which resolves the equivocality of sensation by means of measuring, counting, and weighing (602c–d). Socrates points out that when we believe one thing on the basis of rationality, such as that a stick is straight, and the opposite on the basis of sight, such as that the stick is bent, it cannot be the same part of us that believes both, since as they said before (436b–c) the same thing cannot have contradictory beliefs at the same time. The part that trusts in measurement and rationality is the best part of the soul, while the one that contradicts it is inferior. In that case, not only are the products of painting and imitative art in general far from the truth, but the part of us that they consort with is also inferior; and the offspring of these two inferior parents—the effect of painting on an inferior part of our soul—is inferior as well.[24] As in the first and third arguments Socrates extrapolated the conclusion from painting to poetry (597e, 602a), here too he asks whether it applies not only to the imitations that we see but also those that we hear, and thus to poetry as well as painting; and Glaucon replies that it probably does (603b). We shall see, however, that the way poetry consorts with an inferior part of us is not the same as the way painting does.

This discussion of the effect of painting on us is reminiscent of Socrates' description in Book 7 of how perceptual contradictions could be used to turn the soul from the realm of *doxa* to that of reason (523e–524c), but here it seems that these same contradictions contribute to the power of art to appeal to *doxa rather than* reason. This fundamental difference is reflected in the fact that here Socrates appeals to the examples of shadow painting and the way distance fools us about the size of an object (602c–d), whereas in the earlier passage when Glaucon suggested those very examples Socrates said that he was missing the point (523b). The tension between these passages, which refer to the same phenomenon of inconsistent sense impressions but which derive opposite results from it, is analogous to a tension we have witnessed before. The second argument above reminded us that rhythm and harmony have so powerful an effect on us that they can make mediocre products seem exciting and profound (601a–b); but these same qualities formed the basis of the children's first education to goodness (400d–401a). Both of these tensions show how the appearance of the rational within the perceptual realm (whether symbolically in rhythm, harmony, and beauty, or directly in calculation) sets up a pressure that can push us toward either pole. It can make us dissatisfied with the perceptual realm because of that realm's self-sufficiency and thus point to something beyond sense perception. Or we can find the unresolved tension exciting in itself and thus have our pleasure in the perceptual realm enhanced, like the intensity of the false pleasures that results from the juxtaposition of pleasure and pain (586b–c), or Socrates' example in the *Philebus* of inexpressible pleasures produced by the juxtaposition of the pain of an unquenchable itch and the pleasure of the partial relief brought by scratching it (46e). The alternatives are reminiscent of the alternative uses of music mentioned in the *Timaeus* passage cited above: it can be used either for irrational pleasures, "such as now appears to be its use", or to bring the soul into harmony with the rational basis of reality (47c–d).

We can summarize this fourth argument, then, by saying that painting, and the arts in general, use elements of our experience, such as optical illusions, to make our perceptual experience more exciting and thus tie us even more closely to it, instead of using them to expose the insubstantiality of the world of the senses and turn us toward what is in truth substantial.[25]

Art and the Tripartite Soul: Poetry (603b–605c)

When the previous argument extrapolated the criticism of painting to poetry, Glaucon expressed his agreement by saying, "It is likely" (*eikos*, 603b8). Socrates now replies, in words that recall the stages of the Divided Line but without observing the distinctions among them, that they should not have *pistis* (trust) in *eikasia* (what is likely) on the basis of painting, but should go to that part of *dianoia* (the mind) with which poetic imitations consort and see whether it is inferior or something to be taken seriously (603b9–c2). The four levels of the Line are divisions of the rational part of the tripartite soul— they are ways by which we hold something for true rather than pleasant or honorable. Until now the arguments have been based on the Divided Line's distinction between originals and imitations or images, and have criticized art for being satisfied with imitations. The common theme of all the criticisms was that art devotes itself to appearance and the senses rather than to reality and reason. Art was not charged with being inimical to rationality as such, but only with emphasizing rationality's lowest levels. The fifth argument, on the contrary, will conclude that poetry destroys rationality (ἀπόλλυσι τὸ λογιστικόν) in the soul (605b), and so for the first time the critique moves from the epistemological considerations of the Divided Line to the motivational, implicitly moral distinctions of the tripartite soul.

"Mimetic poetry imitates people acting under compulsion or voluntarily, and, as a result of their actions, believing that they acted either well or badly, and in all these cases feeling either sorrow or gladness" (603c).[26] Whenever we do something, we subsequently form a belief about whether what we did was good or bad, and this leads to a feeling of pain or pleasure. Presumably we would normally feel pleasure when we think we have done well, and pain when we think we have done badly, but when we are compelled by force to do something that we think is wrong, we might feel glad if our actions failed, or regret if they succeeded. And there are more subtle forms of compulsion, such as when we are too weak to resist temptation and we act against our better judgement. Then too we feel pained by the result of our action, as when Leontius cursed his eyes for their inability to resist looking at the corpses (439e–440a). The connection is made explicit between this discussion and that earlier one where the tripartite soul was demonstrated: in all such cases we are not in agreement with ourselves, but different parts of us have different opinions and engage in civil war with one another, as we amply agreed in our earlier accounts (603c–e). In what follows, however, Socrates will speak of only two parts of the soul, a rational and irrational one, which has led some readers to see a tension between this discussion and that of Book 4, either resolvable or not.[27] Since the fifth and sixth arguments criticize art for undermining the rule of rationality within us, what is at stake here is the relationship between the part of us that is rational and the part of us that is not, and there is no reason to keep in view the distinction within our irrational nature between appetite and spiritedness. Whatever nourishes either one of them at the expense of reason is equally blameworthy. When Socrates speaks of pleasure (603c7, 606d1–2), laziness (604d10), or appetite (606a5–6, d2) the appetitive part of the soul is implied, while when he speaks about fighting against pain (604a2), or about cowardice (604d10) or anger (606d1), the spirited part is implied; but to distinguish the two explicitly in this context would be cumbersome and irrelevant.

In Book 3 when they discussed education in poetry, and scrutinized the *Iliad* and *Odyssey* for unwholesome passages, Socrates mentioned that if a good man suffers the loss of a son or something else dear to him he will bear it more easily than other people (387e). Socrates now adds that such a man will be torn between his emotion, which pushes him to give vent to his pain, and rationality and law or convention (λόγος καὶ νόμος), which push him toward restraint, with the result that he will be more likely to give way to his grief in private because he would be ashamed to do so in public. The law or custom that Socrates refers to says that it is best to accept misfortunes as quietly as possible for several reasons: the good and bad of such things is not clear; there is nothing to be gained by taking them hard; nothing mortal deserves to be treated with great seriousness; and grieving impedes the very thing that we most need, namely to deliberate about what happened and arrange our affairs in the way that rationality determines to be best (603e–604c).

The best part of us is the one that is willing to follow rationality and devote itself to healing rather than bewailing, while the part that wants to indulge in self-pity is irrational, lazy, and a friend of cowardice. The latter, however, admits of many and varied imitations, while the former is difficult to imitate and difficult for the varied multitude of theater-goers at a festival to understand. Accordingly, since the poets depend on the approval of the spectators they naturally work in relation to the excitable and variegated character rather than the controlled and rational one.[28] Like the painter, then, the poet's creations are inferior with respect to truth, and they appeal to a correspondingly inferior part of the soul rather than the best part.

Moreover, the poet destroys the rational part of the soul by strengthening the irrational part, the way strengthening the worst people in a city leads to the ruination of the best people (604d–605c).

Art and the Corruption of Virtue (605c–608a)

The consideration introduced in the previous sentence was presented as an extension of the previous argument, but it is also a bridge to the next one, which shows how poetry, by appealing to a lower part of our soul, also strengthens it against rationality. This, Socrates says, is the most serious of the charges against imitation (605c). Part of being virtuous is the ability to control our emotions, to bear our suffering with dignity and strength rather than giving vent to self-pitying exhibitions of grief. But although we may be ashamed to indulge our emotions in this way, we enjoy seeing this kind of behavior in tragic heroes. On one hand the part of us that by nature desires to give vent to grief takes vicarious pleasure in watching others behaving in this way; while on the other hand the part of us that is by nature best, if it has not been adequately educated by rationality or habit, regards this as a harmless pleasure and allows it to be indulged. It does not recognize that when we enjoy something in others, that necessarily has an effect on us, and once the emotion of pity is nourished in us in relation to others, it is more difficult to restrain in relation to ourselves (605c–606b).

Comedy is as dangerous in this respect as tragedy, for just as in tragedies we allow ourselves to indulge in the pleasure of pity toward tragic figures, vicariously sharing their self-pity, in comedies we permit ourselves to enjoy and vicariously share in the clownishness of the characters even though we would be ashamed to behave that way ourselves. In both cases we nourish what is irrational in us and strengthen it against the control of the rational. The principle that operates in the case of pity and clownishness operates also with respect to our other appetites as well—sex and anger and all the others. In the final analysis, then, only by excluding all imitative poetry from the city, and limiting poetry to hymns to the gods and encomia to good men, can pleasure and pain be prevented from gaining an excessive level of influence over us (606c–607a). Hymns to the gods and encomia to good men consort with the highest part of our soul, rationality—the former directing our thoughts to the gods, and the latter directing them to manifestations of the good.[29]

The philosophical condemnation of poetry is nothing new, for there is a quarrel of long standing between philosophy and poetry,[30] and the poets speak equally harshly of philosophers, comparing them to dogs yelping at their masters, babbling fools, and self-styled wise men, among other things. Socrates puts the onus of proof on poetry, however: now that he has advanced his arguments against the imitative poets, it is up to the poets or the lovers of poetry (φιλοποιηταί) to refute them, and Socrates and his allies will willingly listen to the refutations because they would be glad to believe that these works, which give so much pleasure, might also be beneficial. But if no convincing rebuttals are brought forward, they must regard the love (ἔρωτα) of imitative poetry that was instilled in them by their upbringing, the way lovers (ἐρασθέντες) do who realize that their love (ἔρωτα) is not a healthy one, and force themselves with difficulty to refrain from it (607b–608a). The emphasis on eros throughout this passage helps underscore the importance of what is at stake from Socrates' point of view: since what distinguishes the best and the worst people from each other is not their fundamental nature (one and the same nature can be fulfilled or corrupted) but the direction in which their eros is turned,[31] if the love of poetry carries within it a love of the objects of appetite and sensuousness, it is a dangerous love.

By limiting the field of battle to arguments, Socrates is open once again[32] to a charge of begging the question in favor of rationality. Just as Philebus refused to allow the value of pleasure to be decided by its rival, rationality, poets may similarly refuse to accept any judgement upon poetry by its rival. If they find poetic thinking more rewarding than philosophical thinking, Socrates' arguments may be dismissed as irrelevant. But there is no common denominator between art and rationality that would enable us to find a neutral tool of adjudication, and there is nothing arbitrary about asserting the value of rational inquiry. The only alternative, as before, is the misology of a Philebus.

Socrates' Criticisms of the Arts

The three criticisms of painting were all extrapolated against poetry (597e, 602a, 603b), but the criticisms of poetry were not extended to painting, most significantly in the case of the "greatest accusation" against poetry, its ability to seduce even the best of us into unhealthy emotions like self-pity. Accordingly it is only the poets who are banned from the city, not the painters and musicians (398a, 595a, 607a–b).[33] In the *Laws* the Athenian says that it is difficult to understand the meaning of music without words (669e), and with painting it is almost as difficult. Because the language of paintings, like that of music, is not as explicit as that of poetry, it cannot influence our attitudes the way literary arts can.

Socrates' arguments point to real dangers in the arts. Works of art can indeed be created without 1) looking to true reality, 2) displaying wisdom regarding the subject matter, 3) having personal acquaintance with it, 4) rising above the pleasures of illusion, 5) rising above tawdry emotionality, or 6) governing our irrational emotions. However, nothing valuable is without danger, including philosophy—a view of philosophy voiced not only by Socrates' jurors but by the narrator of the *Republic* himself. He warned earlier that if young people are given a taste of argumentation they are likely to develop an excessive distrust of traditional beliefs, and discredit both themselves and philosophy generally (537e–539d). The arts are no more invalidated by their possible misuse than is philosophy, and together with his criticisms we saw that Socrates also alluded to art's positive potential. In the first argument he raised the possibility of the painter imitating the forms rather than particular things (598a), echoing the possibility he raised earlier of a painter painting "a pattern of what the most beautiful human being would be like" (472d), a potential that accrues to poetry as well when Socrates extrapolates the argument from painters to poets (597e). The second and third arguments, in turn, showed how poets and musicians have their own kind of access to truth through their relationship with harmony, rhythm, and beauty.

Socrates does not fail to appreciate the value of the arts, and shows more respect for them than do those who treat them more tolerantly because they consider them harmless. His criticisms are aimed not primarily at the arts but at their practitioners, like Adeimantus' earlier criticism of philosophy: most of those who pursue philosophy become completely strange, or even vicious, and at best useless (487c–d). Socrates had replied that this was not the fault of philosophy but of those who practice it in a manner that degrades it (494a–496a). In the same way his criticisms are not an indictment of art so much as of those who abuse its potential. The passage quoted above from the *Timaeus* is Plato's clearest description of this abuse: music is being wrongly employed for irrational pleasures instead of being used to make us internally harmonious and open to truth (47c–d). The power of the arts lies in the relation between the universal and the individual—between intelligibility and sensibility or between rationality and emotion. When the arts use what is universal and transcendent to enhance our enjoyment of the concrete, the works that result are open to Socrates' criticisms; but when they use the concrete to awaken us to the possibility of something more, they become the powerful instruments of education and enlightenment that Socrates welcomed in Book 3.

Virtue and Immortality (608b–613e)

The unifying theme of Book 10, and indeed that of the *Republic* as a whole, is the importance of justice. All of the criticisms of the arts in one way or another build toward the charge that the arts reinforce our devotion to the sensual world and interfere with the passages from *eikasia* to *noesis* and from appetite to rationality, which are indispensable to human excellence and justice. That theme now carries into the issues of immortality and afterlife: if our existence does not come to an end with the death of our bodies, then the struggle to be good is of far greater importance than we think, and we must not let honor, wealth, political power, or even poetry deter us from caring about justice and virtue as a whole. In fact, the greatest rewards and prizes for virtue have not yet been discussed, Socrates says, for so far they have talked about it only in relation to the length of a human life, which is insignificant in relation to all of time (607b–c).

This leads to the strangest of all Plato's proofs for the immortality of the soul, which is so oddly introduced as to lead us to wonder how seriously it is meant to be taken. Socrates casually asks, "Have you never perceived that our soul is immortal and never perishes?" When Glaucon responds with amazement, Socrates assures him that it is not difficult to show (607d). To anyone familiar with Socrates' labors to convince his audience of the soul's immortality in the *Phaedo*, at the end of which Simmias still has reservations (107a–b), Socrates' assurance here of the simplicity of the task cannot be taken seriously, as readers have long noted. The misgivings set up by this introduction do not diminish when the proof itself is unveiled:

1. What destroys and corrupts is always the bad or evil, while what preserves and benefits is the good (608e).

2. There is a good and bad for everything: ophthalmia is the distinctive evil of the eyes, disease that of the body, mildew of grain, rot of wood, rust of bronze and iron, etc. (608e–609a).

3. If something cannot be destroyed by what specifically makes it bad then it must be indestructible, since that is by definition (from 1) what is most capable of destroying it (609a–b).

4. What makes the soul bad is injustice, intemperance, cowardice, and ignorance (609b–c).

5. Although they corrupt the soul the vices do not lead it to death and separation from the body (609d).

6. If the body dies it will be because it has been infected with its own proper evil; but since the soul is not destroyed by the evil proper to it (from 5), it will hardly be destroyed by the evil proper to the body or anything else, so it is indestructible (609d–610a).

7. Only if our souls became more unjust as our body died would we have any reason to fear that the death of the body would entail the death of the soul (610b).

Step 5 is puzzling at first because the soul's separation from the body defines the death of the body, not the soul. The point seems to be that if the soul died so would the body because the soul would no longer be present in it, so the fact that the body is still alive shows that the soul is still active within it. But that is the least of the problems with the proof. The reason that this final argument of Book 10 leaves us feeling unpersuaded, and that Socrates may have introduced it with tongue in cheek, can be seen by comparing it with the final argument of Book 1, with which it shares some crucial features:

1. The function of a thing is what one can do only with it, or best with it. For example, we see only with the eyes and hear only with the ears, and although we can prune a vine with any kind of knife we can best do so with a pruning knife (352e–353a).

2. A thing can perform its function well only if it has the associated virtue or excellence rather than the corresponding evil; in the case of the eyes, for example, sight rather than blindness (353a–d).

3. The functions which pertain to the soul include caring for things, ruling, deliberating, and living, which it will do well if it has its proper virtue, but badly if it has the corresponding evil (353d–e).

4. The virtue of the soul is justice and its evil is injustice (353e).

5. Therefore a just person lives well (353e).

6. To live well is to be happy (354a).

7. Therefore a just person is happy and an unjust person is wretched (354a).

The two arguments agree in assigning a distinctive evil to things, including the soul, but this argument from Book 1 never claimed that the distinctive evil might destroy the thing in question, much less that it is the only thing that might destroy it, but only that it prevents it from functioning well (step 3). The virtue of a pruning knife would be sharpness, for example, but a dull knife is not destroyed by its badness. It would be destroyed instead by things like breakage or rust (cf. the reference to rust at 609a2, step 2 in the immortality argument). Socrates began the earlier argument by securing Thrasymachus' agreement that a horse has a function (352d). They do not specify what the horse's function is, but if, for the sake of argument, we say that the function of a horse is to have a spirited nature, and its virtue to be strong, then if it has an injury or deformity that diminishes its strength, that evil will not thereby make it cease to exist. It may on the other hand be destroyed by something unrelated to its distinctive evil, such as a fire or predators. This argument gives us ample reason, then, to reject the crucial step 4 in the proof of immortality:

there is no basis for the claim that a thing can only—or even at all—be destroyed by its proper evil. The soul might conceivably be destroyed by something quite different from the evil of injustice and the other vices, just as a knife can be destroyed by something quite different from dullness, or a horse by something quite different from slowness or weakness. Just as a sharp knife may be destroyed by a rock without ever losing its sharpness, nothing in the logic of the argument rules out the possibility that the soul might be destroyed by the body's fatal illness without ever losing its justice.

We can see the problem in another way. How do we know that premise 5 of the immortality argument is true (i.e., that the soul of an unjust person is not, in fact, dead)?[34] Only by the fact that the body is still alive, in which case we must believe that the primary function of the soul is to impart life to the body.[35] But if the virtue and vice of something are that by which it performs its function well or badly, then the moral virtues and vices do not seem to be the distinctive virtues or vices of the soul, because the body is equally alive when the person is moral and immoral. In that case it would make more sense to say that the virtue and vice of the soul are vigor and torpor, respectively, and it is not at all self-evident that the soul could not be destroyed by torpor. More fundamentally, if Socrates does not know what the true nature of the soul is (611b–d), how will he know what is good or bad for it (cf. 354c)?[36]

If the argument is entirely without cogency, as is generally agreed,[37] and if Socrates' offhand introduction of it is a sign of his own recognition that it cannot be taken very seriously, what is its purpose? Why did Plato not use the kinds of arguments that he uses throughout the *Phaedo* and in the *Phaedrus* (245d–e) and *Laws* (895e–897b), which, whatever their limitations, cannot be dismissed as simple non sequiturs? The answer seems to be that Plato wants to establish a connection between virtue and immortality, to suggest that the soul is immortal in a way that depends on its moral virtue. It is a connection that we have met before in the *Republic*. In Book 6, for example, Socrates said that the philosopher

> looks upon and contemplates what are organized and eternally [ἀεί] the same, which neither commit injustice nor are treated unjustly by one another, but which all are orderly in accordance with rationality, and he imitates them and assimilates himself to them as far as possible. . . . Associating with the divine and orderly, the philosopher becomes orderly and divine as far as is possible for a human being. [500c–d]

By contemplating what is divine, eternal, and just, philosophers themselves become as divine (immortal) as possible. In Book 7 Socrates goes on to say that the philosophers who attain to a vision of truth and the good would not want to take their turn ruling because they would "believe that they had arrived at the Islands of the Blessed while still alive" (519c), in other words that they had attained eternal happiness while still alive. In the present passage Socrates says that if we wish to know the true nature of the soul we cannot restrict ourselves to observing it in its present condition, where it is disfigured by its association with the body. Reaffirming the transcendentalism of the middle books he says that we must look instead "to its love of wisdom and understand what it grasps and what it longs to associate with, as being akin to the divine and immortal and to eternal being" (611e). There is a kind of eternality that does not depend on the endless continuation of existence. Although Socrates' proof of immortality, predicated on the claim that things can be destroyed only by their most distinctive evil, cannot be taken seriously at its face value, if we consider its broader claim that only injustice can prevent the soul from being immortal, its conclusion accords with the passages reviewed from Books 6 and 7: the soul's proper good is justice, which is eternal, and we ourselves can experience eternality during our lifetimes by assimilating ourselves to the justice of eternity. Looked at in this way, Socrates' introduction may not be so strange after all: when he asks whether Glaucon has not perceived (ᾔσθησαι) that the soul is immortal, rather than whether he has not understood it, Socrates may well be implying that our immortality is not something to be inferred by demonstration, but to be discerned by looking within ourselves.

This sense of immortality is explicitly maintained in the *Symposium*, a dialogue which the *Republic* recalled in a number of passages,[38] when Socrates asserts that if someone can apprehend and contemplate the eternal form of beauty, then "if indeed it is for any human being to be immortal, it will be so for him" (211d8–212a7). Again in the *Republic*'s sequel, the *Timaeus*, we are told that if someone devotes himself to appetites and victory-loving activities, all of his beliefs will necessarily become mortal and he himself will become as completely mortal as possible; but if he devotes himself to the love of learning and true wisdom, he will think what is immortal and divine, if he touches upon truth, and will necessarily possess as much immortality as is possible for a mortal nature (90b–c).

If Socrates says this clearly in the *Symposium* and *Timaeus*, why not be as explicit in the *Republic*? Why present in the form of a charade a view that he is capable of presenting openly? The purpose of this argument is a moral one. The argument was introduced in support of Socrates' claim that the struggle to live a life according to justice rather than injustice is more important than people realize, because it has implications for eternity, and not only for the comparatively short span of a human life (608b–c). If the inner meaning of this claim is that those who devote themselves to what is eternal achieve a kind of eternality themselves, while those who devote themselves only to transient things are deprived of the ultimate goal toward which human life aims, it is not a message that would be believed by and would motivate most listeners, any more than the appetitive classes of the aristocracy and kallipolis would accept the natural differences among kinds of people, without the noble lie or similar religious doctrines. The noble lie (414b–415c) was noble because it was not a "true lie", a story that produces falsehood within the soul (382a–d), but rather one that presented as if it were literally true a story that was metaphorically true: that there are natural differences among us but that we are brothers and sisters who owe filial devotion to the land that produced us. It is easier to believe that in a similar way Socrates' strange argument for immortality based on virtue, with its odd introduction, is a metaphorical truth (devotion to justice brings us into contact with eternity) that is presented as if literally true (only injustice could have ended our continued existence), than to believe that it is intended as a serious argument.

There is another level of interpretation on which the argument makes sense as well, but it requires going beyond anything that is explicit in the *Republic*, to the conception of soul in its most fundamental manifestation as the world-soul or the energy system of the cosmos. This conception goes back to Thales,[39] although it is not explicitly present in Plato until the *Timaeus*. There the world-soul appears as the driving force of the world's rationality (35a–36e), and in that sense there is something to be said for the claim that it could not be destroyed unless it ceased to be rational (i.e., became unjust). Elements of this doctrine appear in the *Republic*, even if not the doctrine as such. We are told, for example, that the number of souls is constant, for not only do souls never perish but neither can new ones be created, because they would have to be created from a mortal source that would eventually become depleted (611a). This sets the stage for the doctrine of reincarnation that will follow shortly in the myth of Er, according to which not only do the same souls cut across the boundaries between individuals and take on different human lives, but also cut across the boundaries between species so that the same soul may serve to animate all forms of life (620a–d) from the lowest animals to the quasi-divine life of the philosopher. The soul appears as a kind of continuous medium by which the corporeal realm is connected to the intelligible. That is why in its pure state, abstracting from all corporeal manifestations, the soul will be seen to be not only uniform rather than tripartite,[40] but divine and eternal (611a–e). Given the connection between divinity and eternity, it would not be going too far to say that as long as the soul retains its divine nature it is immortal; that the only thing that could conceivably deprive it of that nature would be the contamination of mortal corporeality; that the sign that it has been corrupted is an unjust character; and that therefore the fact that injustice does not kill the principle of life within us shows that that principle is indestructible.

Until now Socrates' defense of the just life was conducted under the condition imposed upon him by Glaucon and Adeimantus: that the just person would have a reputation for injustice and be treated accordingly, while the unjust person would not only have a reputation for justice but would also be in a better position to secure the favor of the gods (362c, 365e). Now that Socrates has established his claims to their satisfaction in the face of that handicap, he asks that the artificial condition be removed, since, in fact, the just and unjust person will normally be recognized as such and rewarded accordingly, and by gods as well as by other people (612b–e).[41] In a powerful analogy, Socrates suggests that the seductiveness of the unjust life lies only in its short-term results, which are more than paid for in the long term, like a runner who sprints ahead in the first part of a race but cannot sustain the pace and finishes ignominiously in exhaustion, passed by the rest of the field. In the same way the advantages of injustice appear immediately while those of justice are built up slowly over time, but unjust people who secure early advantages are usually greeted in the end with contempt and punishment (613b–d).

The Myth of Er (614a–621d)

The consequences of justice and injustice that they have been considering are nothing, Socrates says, compared to those which await us after death. He illustrates this with the story of Er, a warrior who was found ten days after being killed in battle, and came back to life two days later on the funeral pyre. Er recounts that after his death he came to a place where the souls of the dead were judged and sent through one of two doors: the good to heaven to be rewarded, the bad to the underworld to be punished. Through two other doors those who had already served their thousand-year term were returning, and they told of the beauties of heaven and the sufferings of the underworld. After seven days the souls left the plain, and at the end of a four-day journey (an apparent image of the Divided Line), they came to the shining spindle of Necessity, to which the orbits of the solar system were attached, as to an axis. A Siren sat on each orbit singing one note, all together producing a single harmony,[42] and the three Fates sang along with them. At that point the souls were assigned lots, and in the allotted order they chose their next life from patterns on the ground in front of them that showed everything that would

→ all animals have human souls?

occur in each life. Both animal lives and the whole variety of human lives were represented, and those who had been animals similarly chose from among both kinds of lives. Each soul was assigned a guardian spirit to fulfill what was chosen, and the Fates then ratified the choices of the lives and made them irreversible. Finally all the souls except Er drank a measure of the waters of forgetfulness and went to sleep. At midnight they all were carried up in different ways to their birth, like shooting stars.

At the beginning of this chapter I mentioned that the inclusion of the myth of Er within the same book that contains Socrates' criticisms of poetry has the advantage of providing a positive model of a kind of poetry that can be powerful without relying on any of the features to which Socrates objects. At the end of the myth he says, "And thus myth was saved and not destroyed" (621b8). His words are grammatically ambiguous. The primary meaning is that "Er's story (*mythos*) was preserved because he did not drink a full measure of forgetfulness", but it admits of a secondary meaning: "We have just seen how mythology can be permitted to exist in our city".[43] The myth of Er is, in fact, free from all six of the elements that were targeted by Socrates' criticisms of art: 1) It does not primarily imitate the visible world (it does talk about meadows, doors, lights, writings, water, and so on, but its primary subjects are not visible: disembodied souls, divinities, heaven, and Hades); 2) It provides us with moral guidance in life; 3) It is presented as the testimony of someone who has direct personal experience of the subject; 4) It appeals to us at the level of thought rather than sensuality; 5) It nourishes rationality rather than emotion; 6) It strengthens our self-control rather than undermining it. To put the contrast between this kind of poetry and the conventional kind in general terms, whereas most poetry makes use of the extraordinary to enhance our enjoyment of the ordinary (see especially the fourth argument), the myth of Er uses images of the ordinary (meadows, doors, lights, writings, water) to enable us to conceive of the extraordinary. As with Plato's other myths, it functions at the level of *dianoia*, which uses visible images to convey the intelligible (510d–e), rather than *eikasia*, which takes the images as pleasurable ends in themselves, as in the kind of poetry that Socrates objects to. It cannot function at the level of *noesis* since it is wedded to the use of images (510b), so its function is pedagogical rather than strictly philosophical—there would be no reason for philosophers at the level of *noesis* to speak to each other in myths. Even in the most *noetic* parts of Plato's writing, however, artistic poetic elements play such an important part that his criticisms of poetry are often thought to be either not serious or self-refuting. But once again we can see that they are free from all the elements that call down Socrates' criticisms on traditional poetry.

There is a puzzling discrepancy between the myth of Er and the myth of the metals at the end of Book 3,[44] when Socrates proposes to tell the populace that they are all brothers and sisters because they were gestated in the earth and so have a common mother, but they do not all have the same natures because Mother Earth mixed into them different proportions of gold, silver, iron, and bronze. Where the implications of this "noble lie" most differ from those of the myth of Er is that it absolved us of responsibility for our individual differences by making them dependent on the proportions of metals introduced into us by the goddess Earth. According to the myth of Er the different proportions of greed, hunger for power, and love of truth within us were chosen not by a god but by ourselves. Our character is for us to choose: we choose our guiding spirit; it does not choose us (617e). By choosing a certain kind of life we choose a certain kind of character: "The internal ordering of the soul", Socrates tells us, "was not [one of the variables] in the lives to be chosen, because choosing a different life necessarily meant the internal ordering would be different" (618b). In other words, our choice of actions presupposes a certain moral nature, and the actions themselves contribute to the further development of that character.

To choose to live a particular life means to choose the kind of desires by which we will be driven, such as whether the eros that motivates us will be for appetitive money-making, for spirited competition, or for wisdom. As Diotima says in the Symposium, although we tend to reserve the term "eros" for the love between people, the desire for anything we consider good, like money, athletic competition, or philosophy—in other words appetite, spiritedness, and wisdom—is a kind of eros as well (205b–d).[45] Since the myth of Er ('Ηρός) is an account of the basis of this eros (ἔρως), we may wonder whether Plato intended his audience to hear echoes of the word erōs in the name Ēros, and chose Ēros as his protagonist as a way of encouraging us to use the accounts of eros and Er to complete each other.[46] If so, this would be another place where the Symposium and Republic intersect.

Our choice of a particular life entails the choice of a particular character (618b), but any choice we make is already determined by our present character, and if we must choose our future character on the basis of the character we already have, there seems to be an infinite regress. At any moment the character on the basis of which we make our choices is already given, so we are never in a position to make a clean choice. In that case, the myth of the metals seems to be the truth after all: we cannot be entirely responsible for our character. Socrates is often tentative and hesitant when putting claims forward, and emphasizes his ignorance and lack of certainty, but on the matter of the conclusiveness with which our past determines our present course

he is anything but tentative (at least on Er's behalf). After the soul has chosen its future life, one of the three Fates, Lachesis, assigns to it the guardian
spirit of that life "to fulfill the choice". The guardian spirit then takes the soul
under the hand of Lachesis' sister-Fate, Clotho, as she turns the spindle of
Necessity, in order to ratify the fate it had chosen. Next the soul is brought to
the third Fate, Atropos, who makes the weave of its destiny irreversible. As if
all this were not enough, the soul must then pass beneath the throne of
Necessity (620d–e). Our future is conclusively and irrevocably determined by
our previous choice of our present life. Moreover, for most of us the prenatal
choice of our present life is determined by our previous life (620a), so the pre-
determination of our choices regresses indefinitely. The rewards and punishments that we are assigned in the afterlife also influence our choice of the
next life, but they too were determined by our previous life, so the nature of
our responsibility for our lives remains problematic. *influenced, but not det?*

In the *Nicomachean Ethics* Aristotle argues that since our moral choices
follow from our character, then if we can be held morally responsible for the
kind of person we are, we must somehow be the cause of our own character.
Otherwise virtue and vice are involuntary, merely the necessary consequences of the accident of our birth, in which case we cannot be held responsible for our behavior:

> Suppose someone were to say that all people seek what appears good to them,
> and have no control over the appearance; but rather, the sort of person one is
> determines how the end appears to him. In that case, if each person is somehow
> responsible for his own character, he will also be responsible for how things
> appear to him. If not, no one is responsible for his own evildoing, but he does
> these things through ignorance of the proper end, thinking that by these
> actions the greatest good will come to him. And the way we aim at the end is
> not voluntary, but we have to be born with something like an eye by which we
> can judge well and choose what is truly good, and someone has a good nature
> in whom this is well developed by nature. For he will have the greatest and
> finest possession, which cannot be acquired or learned from anyone else; and to
> be well and finely possessed of this by nature would be the most perfect and true
> good nature. But if this is true, how will virtue be any more voluntary than
> vice? [3.5.1114a31–b8]

Aristotle's remarks can be taken as a demythologization of the myth of Er. If
the myth is the first explicit formulation of the problem of freedom of will
generally,[47] Aristotle here has produced the first conceptualized statement of
the problem (not until the eighth tractate of Plotinus' sixth Ennead does the
issue receive anything like the kind of thorough analysis that we have since

come to expect). Aristotle does not resolve the problem any more than Plato does. Like Plato, he seems to believe that one of the alternatives—that "no one is responsible for his own evildoing"—is a reductio ad absurdum, and so the other alternative must somehow be true, even if we cannot explain how it is true.

The myth of Er functions with respect to morality the way the doctrine of recollection (which seems to be alluded to at the end of the myth when the souls drink the water of forgetfulness before they are reincarnated)[48] functions with respect to knowledge. Recollection is meant to account for the non-empirical element in knowledge: absolutes like perfect equality are never given in experience, so why does the mind even form such concepts? If they are not given through the senses, then they must be given to the mind independently of the senses; that is, they are given to the mind prior to the mind's union with the body, and this logical priority is illustrated by the temporal priority of a soul that is between incarnations. The soul is depicted as "seeing" the forms before its present incarnation, and then forgetting them when it enters a body, but becoming at least partially aware of them again when instances of them "remind" us of the forms.[49] Accordingly, our knowledge of the forms is comparable to our knowledge of something that we have forgotten but not completely forgotten. That is, we can be guided by that knowledge even though we are not able to articulate it,[50] as when we know, for example, that a name we have forgotten starts with the letter A. Just as the doctrine of recollection provides us with an image of how we can have knowledge of absolutes even though we perceive only particulars, the myth of Er provides us with an image of how we can have responsibility even though all of our choices follow from our preexisting character. If our choices are determined by our character, we have no ability to choose otherwise, and consequently the idea of praising good behavior and censuring bad behavior becomes problematic except on instrumental grounds. Reward and punishment can still be justified for the sake of positive reinforcement and deterrence, but this is a matter of social manipulation, not morality—we simply reward someone for doing what we like, and punish others for doing what we dislike. If goodness or badness of character are no longer at issue, however, then it is the power-relation models of Thrasymachus and Protagoras rather than the morality models of Socrates and Plato that win out. Plato must obviously swim against that current: if we are morally responsible only for what we choose, and we are somehow responsible for our character, then in some sense we must choose our character. But since in our empirical choosing our character is always already given, we must make that choice at a pre-empirical level. Here, as in recollection, the logically prior is represented by the temporal priority of a soul that is between incarnations (as later it would be defended by Kant in terms of a pre-empirical noumenal realm that is exempt from the paradoxes of the causal account of free will).[51] Just as knowledge of absolutes cannot be accounted for empirically, and is a kind of a priori foundation for knowledge that the doctrine of recollection illustrates with the story of a temporally prior event; so too moral responsibility is problematic because choices seem empirically to be nothing more than results of causal determinism, and yet responsibility is also a presupposition for our moral consciousness that the myth of Er illustrates with the story of a temporally prior event.

If the post-mortem temporality of the myth is itself one of the mythical elements, then the strange proof of immortality that preceded it becomes more comprehensible, for we saw that it pointed to immortality not in the sense of indefinite continuation of existence, but in the sense of an eternality that we can achieve while we are alive. Moreover, if the indefinite continuation that is presented in the myth can be understood as an image of a timeless immortality, and the prenatal choice that the souls make in the myth can be understood as an allegory of our present responsibility for our lives,[52] a major difficulty in the myth disappears. Since the souls drink the water of forgetfulness before they are reborn, and no longer remember their past lives, in what sense can we be said to be the same soul as before? If there is no continuity of memory, it is hard to see either how there can be continuity of identity or any reliable sense of profiting from our past experiences. But if that scenario is an allegorical representation of the eternality that accrues to us by virtue of our reason, as well as a representation of our unity with all living things, then there is no difficulty: if immortality is timeless eternity in the present rather than sequential continuation of the past, then memory of our past lives becomes irrelevant. On that interpretation the myth of Er, like the constructed city, can be regarded as the soul writ large—but expanded temporally rather than spatially—as an image of the inner condition that corresponds to the life we live and the choices we make. However, it is not only enlarged but poeticized, perhaps to convince "the child in us" who responds to stories rather than reasoned arguments (*Phaedo* 77e), or the appetitive part of our soul that can only be moved by images (*Timaeus* 71b–e)—in other words that part of us which needs to hear a noble lie.

Socrates' mythic explanation of personal responsibility in terms of a prenatal choosing of our future life is hard to reconcile with lives that seem illstarred from the beginning. If children die in infancy we lament the waste of potential, and would not be reconciled to the deaths by an assurance that it was probably their own fault for not looking carefully enough at their lives before they chose them. Socrates seems to be aware of the problem, for he teasingly remarks that "The other things he said, about those who had just been born and lived only a short time, were not worth remembering" (615c). Why were they not worth remembering? Is it because they were unconvincing or because they were somehow distasteful? If they were unconvincing it would be an admission by Plato that the myth of Er is fatally flawed in its inability to deal with the fact of infant mortality. More likely, we are meant to assume that there is an explanation, but one that Plato would prefer us to ferret out ourselves; and there are, in fact, passages in the dialogues that provide an explanation. Plato could have avoided the problem by making the number of lives equal to the number of souls, so that the last souls to choose might have found nothing better; but in that case evil people too may simply not have had any moral lives left to choose from, and need bear no responsibility for their present actions. Consequently, Socrates says instead that according to Er there are far more lives than souls, and even the one who chooses last can find one that is rewarding and not bad (619b). In that case the explanation not worth remembering must be that some people prefer to die in infancy. The ancient Greek proverb, "Best of all is never to have been born, second best is to die early",[53] is not without its echoes in Plato. The dialogues tell us repeatedly that since the body is an impediment to the soul, the soul's fulfillment is possible only in its disembodied state, and therefore death can be considered superior to life.[54] It is not inconceivable, then, that some souls, if they must return to bodies, would prefer to do so for as short a time as possible before returning to heaven for another thousand years. In a dialogue that emphasizes the importance of making dangerous doctrines as inaccessible as possible (378a), it is understandable that Plato may have chosen only to hint at a doctrine that makes death superior to life, and which might therefore encourage thoughts of impious suicide. When this doctrine was presented in the *Phaedo*, it was presented with a great deal of caution and indirection (61e–63b). In that passage it is also suggested that by our life here we perform some service to the gods, so conceivably even someone who shared the view that death is superior to life might, in terms of the myth of Er, choose a lengthy life for unselfish reasons.

Nevertheless, why are there such lives to be chosen at all? Why are not all lives more rewarding? An answer can be inferred from the way the harmony of the spheres functions in the myth. The harmony of the spheres passage, together with the discussion of the Idea of the good, is the closest the *Republic* comes to the *Timaeus'* depiction of the world as created in accordance with the principles of reason and goodness. Some reference to the creativity of the good, which the dialogue represents by the sun (506d–517c), is suggested by the myth's depiction here of the solar system as appearing from a distance as "a straight light, like a pillar, resembling most of all the rainbow but brighter and purer" (616b). The harmony of the spheres is connected not only with the underlying eternal structure of the universe, but also with temporal events. On each orbit stands a Siren who sings a single note, all of which blend in harmony. The spindle to which all the orbits are attached "turned on the knees of Necessity", and around the whole sat the daughters of Necessity, the three Fates, who sing along with the harmony of the Sirens—Atropos singing of the future, Clotho of the present, and Lachesis of the past (617b–c). Thus not only the timeless metaphysical structure of the universe, but the past, present, and future events of our world are determined in accordance with the harmony of the whole as well, and in that case so must be our individual destinies. In fact, the myth pointedly intertwines the destinies of the individual lives with that of the cosmos as a whole. Not only do we choose our fates at the very spot where the cosmic spheres' Spindle of Necessity begins, but the lots and patterns of lives are taken from the lap of Lachesis as she helps turn the spindle, and the individual choices of lives are ratified by the three Fates as they turn the spindle, after which the souls pass beneath the throne of Necessity, on whose knees the spindle is turning. The interconnection between individual and cosmic destiny could hardly be more explicit than when we are told that the guardian daimon "first led the soul to Clotho, under her hand and her turning of the whirling spindle, which ratified the fate of its lot and choice" (620). In that case the deterministic details of our lives as individuals are a matter not just of causal necessity, but of rational necessity. Even if our choices are always determined by an indefinite regress of previous choices, at least it seems that this chain of causality is not an empty, meaningless, blind necessity, but a necessity that follows from the rational nature of the universe. Our lives, and even the lives of those who die in infancy, somehow play a necessary part in the harmonious fabric of the whole. Like musicians who may have only one note to play in a symphony, we all nevertheless contribute something without which the whole could not be what it is.

This connection between the life of the individual and the order of the universe may be the significance also of the mysterious remark in the *Timaeus* that when the creator created individual souls, he created them in the same number as the stars, and assigned each one to a particular star (41d–e). The destiny of the microcosm of each individual is intimately bound up with the destiny of the macrocosm of the universe as a whole. Plotinus' view seems to be an elaboration of this:

[The universe] completes its course periodically according to everlastingly fixed rational principles, and everlastingly returns to the same state . . . in proportionate succession of defined lives, these here being brought into harmony with those there and completed according to them, everything being ordered under one rational principle. . . . The harmonious adjustment of the souls to the order of this universe of ours witnesses to this; they . . . make one harmony with its circuit, so that their fortunes and their lives and their choices are indicated by the figures made by the heavenly bodies and they sing, as it were, with one voice and are never out of tune. . . . And the individual, which is subordinated to the universal, is sent according to law. For the universal bears heavily upon the particular, and the law does not derive from outside the strength for its accomplishment, but is given to be in those themselves who are subject to it, and they bear it about with them. And if the time comes too, then what it wills to happen is also brought about by beings themselves in whom it is present, so that they accomplish it themselves because they bear it about; . . . it makes itself a sort of weight in them and implants a longing, a birth pang of desire to come there where the law within them as it were calls them to come.[55]

Plato would not go quite so far, however. Because there are many more lives than souls who choose, there is an element of indeterminacy in Plato's model that is absent from Plotinus'. Plato is a dualist rather than a monist, and unlike Plotinus he sees the universe as permeated by a certain degree of contingency. When the creator makes the cosmos out of "discordant and disorderly" material (*Timaeus* 30b), he is able to persuade the irrational necessity of the errant cause to accept the governance of reason and lead things to the good, only "for the most part" (47e–48a). The firm distinction at the end of Book 5, between the stable intelligible realm of forms, about which we can have knowledge, and the ever-changing perceptual realm of individuals, about which we can only have opinion, is a reflection of this ultimate incommensurability between being and becoming. Perhaps this is also the implication behind the fact that the subsequent details of the myth of Er that include the human element (616c–e) turn out to be incommensurable with the myth's description of the heavens at 616b.[56] Plato does not subscribe to rational determinism as completely as Plotinus; his views coincide with Plotinus' only "for the most part".

Plato's recognition of the regress of responsibility is apparent when Socrates says that "most people chose [their future lives] according to the habit of their previous lives". Orpheus, for example, who had been killed by women, chose to become a swan rather than be born to a woman. Telemonian Ajax, transferring his anger at Achilles to humanity in general, chose the life of a lion instead of a human. The final example is Odysseus, who was tired of the life of spirited struggle and, in the spirit of the *Republic*'s model of justice, chose the life of an ordinary man who minded his own business (ἀπράγμονος, 620a–c).[57] Moreover, those whose previous lives did not call down punishment afterward tended to choose carelessly, while those who suffered punishment for their past lives tended to take great care over the next one, "so that there was an interchange of good and bad for most of the souls" (619d). Both of these passages—the description of choices made from past habits and the description of choices made as a result of reward or punishment—speak only of "most people" or "most of the souls". Who were the others, the exceptions? Were they souls that were influenced by one of these two—our habits, and the rewards and punishments to which they lead—but not the other? Or were they souls that were somehow able to overcome the influence both of past habit and of the consequent reward and punishment, and to achieve some sort of absolute liberty of choice? Evidently both. If the punishments that we suffer and the rewards that we desire succeed in breaking our old habits of behavior, then we will be exceptions to those whose future is determined by past habits. Conversely, if our old habits are so strong as to withstand the normal influence of reward and punishment, we will be exceptions to those whose future is determined by punishments and rewards. Since there are two variables rather than one, no straightforward prediction is possible.

But there is also a third factor beside our habits and the rewards and punishments that they lead to, so there may be people whose choices are determined by something other than either their past habits or the consequences of their actions. At the end of the myth the souls returning to earth drink a measure of water from the River of Unheeding (*Ameleta*) on the Plain of Forgetfulness (*Lethe*), "but those not saved by wisdom drink more than the measure, and the one drinking forgot everything" (621a). What is this wisdom, and what is the "everything" that the others forget? What they forget is more than just the events of the afterlife, for those are already wiped from memory by the normal measure of the water, as was its purpose. Since the complete forgetfulness is determined not by chance but by the presence or absence of wisdom, it must have something to do with wisdom itself. Our habits, and the desires and fears produced by the prospect of punishment and reward, belong to the irrational parts of our soul—appetite and spiritedness. Wisdom belongs to the third and most important part of our soul, rationality, which enters into the myth in three places. First, we must choose our life with reason ($\nu\hat{\omega}$) (619b). Next, in the course of our life we must philosophize soundly (619e). Third, we must be saved by wisdom ($\phi\rho\acute{o}\nu\eta\sigma\iota\varsigma$) from drinking too much oblivion and forgetting everything (621a)—perhaps a suggestion that a lack of wisdom is equivalent to the lack of a capacity for "recollection".[58]

If the meaning of our lives is connected with the meaning of the whole, that connection is only extrinsic in the case of the two factors in our decisions that were discussed previously. Our habits, and the influence of rewards and punishments, do not form a link in any essential way between our personal goals and the good of the whole. The most that can be said of them is that lives based on habit and obedience are related to the good of the cosmos as parts to a whole, where the nature of the whole is not directly perceivable in that of the individual parts. It is the third factor in our choices, reason, that is our bridge from partiality to the rationality of the whole; there alone is the nature of the whole visible in the individual part. When we base our decisions on our habits, we uncritically follow pathways whose origins we do not know, and our choices are determined by factors that are not subject to present evaluation. In the myth, "those who in the previous life lived in a well-ordered society, and partook of virtue by habit without philosophy"—like the non-philosophers in the just city (442b11–c3, c10–d1)—are most likely to choose the illusory rewards of injustice when the opportunity presents itself (619c–d). Their choices are not made rationally, but on the basis of an uncritical response to what has happened to them in the past, and they are not so much acting as reacting. Their choices are at the mercy of other people's actions and treatment of them. The same is true when we uncritically respond to the lure of reward and the threat of punishment—which are, after all, intended to produce new habits—without first determining in the light of reason whether the rewards and punishments lead us toward what is good, or are only arbitrary devices of societal manipulation.

Habits represent the determination of our choices by the retained past, while reward and punishment are the determination of our choices by the expected future. Only reason has its source in the present, that is, in a present examination of the situation. And only reason is free from external constraints, for even though reason may constrain us to choose a particular alternative, the constraint is not an external one because reason is, in fact, our truest self (611b–e). We may still be determined to make a particular choice by what reason tells us is right, and if we think rationally perhaps it is because we were determined to do so by prior causal factors. But once we have begun to choose rationally, the choice itself is free in the sense that matters: it is chosen in the present and by our truest self.[59] Rational choice is the one freedom that is compatible with causal determinism, as the Stoics were the first to point out, followed more recently by compatibilists like Spinoza, Leibniz (and perhaps Descartes), and their philosophical descendants. Our empirical selves are not free from the law of cause and effect, but our truest self, reason, is free from the domination of the irrational, and from the unconscious domination of habit and manipulation.

But while reason and philosophy may be sufficient causes of our freedom, they turn out to be insufficient to guarantee our happiness. At first it seems otherwise. We were told that even the one who chooses last can find a life that is rewarding and not bad (ἀγαπητός, οὐ κακός, 619b), so it sounds as though the souls who choose rationally and wisely can always be authors of their own happiness. The account apparently confirms what Socrates seems to have been insisting on in the first nine books—that if we live our life in the right way, in accordance with philosophy, we can find complete happiness regardless of any external factors; our happiness depends entirely on ourselves and our intellectual virtue. But now he tells us that "if someone philosophizes soundly, *and the lot of his choice does not fall out among the last*, we may assume . . . that not only will he be happy here, but that also the passage from here to there and from there back will not be through the earth and rough, but smooth and through heaven" (619e; emphasis added). Why does it matter whether the lot of our choice falls out among the last, since we can still find a life that is "rewarding and not bad", and we can still "philosophize soundly"? The implication is that even philosophers can become overwhelmed by the events of their life and prevented from achieving perfect happiness—their life may be rewarding but without achieving complete consummation and true happiness. Has Plato exaggerated the apparent optimism of the earlier books in order to give as much courage as possible to Glaucon, Adeimantus, and the rest of us in the face of the adverse circumstances of our lives, and buried the tempering of that optimism deep in the concluding myth?

The main argument of the *Republic* began at the start of Book 2, when Glaucon rebuked Socrates for his sophistical refutation of Thrasymachus, and he and Adeimantus challenged Socrates to argue in good faith for the superiority of justice over injustice. Until 612c–d they insisted that he not only show that a just person is happier than an unjust one, but that he do so in a way that compensates for the fact that just people receive many advantages because their behavior is approved of by others, while the reverse is true for unjust people. In order to show that it is *being* just that provides the advantages, rather than only *appearing* to be just, Socrates had to show that the just person is happier than the unjust person, even when the just person is believed to be most unjust and the unjust person is believed to be most just. The unjust person had to be granted every possible social reward that life has to offer, and the just person had to suffer every possible social affliction, even if that means "being whipped, stretched on the rack, bound in chains, having his eyes burned out, and finally, after suffering every evil, being run through with nails" (361e). Not even Job had to endure this much before he cried out in protest, and Epictetus' ability to achieve happiness in the life of a slave does not seem like much of an accomplishment by comparison.

Because the terms of the challenge were so extreme, it is easy to believe that Socrates defended the position that a just person will be happy no matter what—that absolutely nothing life can do to us can prevent us from being happy if only we are just. But as we saw in Book 2, Glaucon and Adeimantus require Socrates to show only that the just person, in no matter what condition, will be happier than the unjust person, in no matter what condition; not that the just person will be fully happy in any circumstances. Socrates complied by arguing that injustice so perverts our inner self that no extrinsic benefits can possibly compensate for that damage. Compared with this condition, the just person's life turns out to be clearly preferable, but preferable does not necessarily imply being *truly* happy in the most horrible circumstances; it means only that they will still be *more* happy than unjust people, even when the latter are in the most favorable circumstances. Socrates never claims in answer to Glaucon and Adeimantus' challenge that justice by itself is sufficient to guarantee happiness, and now, tucked into an unobtrusive sentence of the myth, he tells us that, by itself, philosophy—that is, complete justice—results in happiness only if a certain amount of luck is present as well. We do not need a lot of luck, but we do need some.

We saw that immediately before the myth Socrates reminded Glaucon that they have now agreed it is better to be just than unjust regardless of any superiority in extrinsic advantages that the unjust person might enjoy, and he got Glaucon to acknowledge in addition that the just person will, in fact, get most of the extrinsic advantages as well as the intrinsic ones, for it is the just person who will ultimately be rewarded by gods and humans (612b–e). "This is the position we must take on the just man. If he falls into poverty or disease or any other of the apparent evils, for him these things will eventually be something good, both when he is alive and also when he has died" (613a). Suffering ennobles, but it only ennobles a good nature; otherwise it embitters. While this does not mean that the ability of just people to make the best of misfortune will enable them to achieve true happiness even in face of the greatest misfortunes, it does mean that it is always in our power to achieve a *relative* happiness in which "these [bad] things will eventually be something good".[60]

How does that happen? The reason that the souls coming up from Hades generally make better choices than those who have just come down from heaven is that suffering forces us to think; it makes us consider how to bring the suffering to an end. Comfort and pleasure, on the other hand, anesthetize us from thinking; they give us no incentive to make an effort. The souls who are in heaven because they had "lived in an orderly society, partaking in virtue by habit, without philosophy" (619c), and who now have spent a thousand years enjoying the glories of heaven, had no more occasion to make an effort at reflective thinking than Adam and Eve before the fall. We learn far more from failure than from success. In the case of the souls in Hades the nature of their thinking may be shallow and instrumental, just an effort to replace pain with pleasure. But for people who have rational natures rather than appetitive ones—people who care more about what is right and true than about what is pleasant—the thinking that their suffering impels them to will be of another kind. It will help them see the fragility of a satisfaction that is built on external goods, and will turn them inward to apprehend the deeper and stable happiness that results from goodness of character. Being perfectly happy may not always be in our power, but being more or less happy always is.

In the final analysis the myth of the metals and the myth of Er complement rather than contradict each other. The myth of the metals emphasizes the limitations of our freedom to choose our character, and the myth of Er emphasizes the freedom that remains to us in spite of those limitations. Even if we are appetitive by nature it is open to us to discover the transitory illusory character of the rewards of appetite that is documented in Book 9, and to base our future choices on reason. We may continue to love pleasure more than truth, but we will be able to pursue that goal more intelligently.

The myth of Er adds to the previous discussions a meditation on our responsibility for our own lives; but it also can be seen as a kind of mythic microcosm of the *Republic* as a whole.[61] The two correspond formally insofar as Er's narration of his experiences in a transit camp beyond the realm of the living, attended by the divine, parallels Socrates' narration of his experience in a port beyond the walls of Athens with a backdrop of religious ceremony.[62] And they correspond in content insofar as Er's account, like that of Socrates, speaks of the blessings of being just and the misery of being unjust (615a–c, 578b–589b); the importance of the mean (619a, 443d); the virtue of minding one's own business (620c, 433a–b); astronomy and harmony as primary manifestations of the highest principle (616b–617b, 528e–531c); and the supremacy of philosophy (619c–e, 474b–501d).

Notes

1. Also see Rohatyn 1975, 319–21. Views on the compatibility of the two accounts vary. J. Tate argues that the banishment of imitative poets here refers only to the kind of imitation that was already banned in Book 3 ("Imitation in Plato's Republic", *Classical Quarterly* 22 [1928]: 16–23, and "Plato and Imitation", *Classical Quarterly* 26 [1932]: 161–69), but the evidence does not support that solution; see Alexander Nehamas, "Plato on Imitation and Poetry in *Republic* 10", in Moravcsik and Temko, eds., *Plato on Beauty, Wisdom, and the Arts*, (Totowa, N.J.: Rowman & Littlefield, 1982), 47–78, esp. 49–50. Gerald Else (1972) believes that the accounts are so incompatible as to argue for a much later date for Book 10 than Book 3 (55–56). Annas (1981), too, believes it is impossible to reconcile the differences between the two

accounts (336), but Reeve (1988) disagrees: "when Plato tells us at the beginning of Book 10 that all T[echnically]-imitative poetry has been excluded from the Kallipolis, he is referring to the effect that the philosopher's truth-guided, censoring hand has had on all the poetry that has been allowed to remain there" (228).

2. For Hans-Georg Gadamer ("Plato and the Poets" [1934] in Gadamer 1980) it is a deliberate position that Plato takes toward poetry "in the conviction that philosophy alone has the capacity to save the state" (47) from the decadence of sophistry; Annas (1981) considers it to be a "hysterical attempt to show that the poet is not really creative [which] shows that Plato was in fact aware of the nature of the poet's creativity" (344); Charles Griswold sees the arguments as caricaturing the poets' own schema of interpretation ("The Ideas and the Criticism of Poetry in Plato's *Republic*, Book 10", *Journal of the History of Philosophy* 19 [1981]: 135–50). Jeff Mitscherling sees it as a critique of poetry only insofar as poetry is conceived as a *techne* (specifically of imitation) and not as inspiration (*The Image of a Second Sun: Plato's View of Poetry*, dissertation, 1983); Stephen Halliwell suggests, "One possible function of this style is to provoke the lovers of poetry into defining much more rigorously the value which they attach to it" (*Plato: Republic 10* [trans. and ed.], [Warminster: Aris & Phillips, 1988], 6); Roochnik (2003) argues that "Socrates' critique of poetry in book 10 manifestly contradicts his own use of narrative and imitation in books 8 and 9" (118) which "leads to a conception of philosophy as including within it a poetical moment" (130).

3. Cf. *Timaeus* 31a. This is sometimes thought to be a version of the Largeness regress in the *Parmenides* (132a–b) which leads to an infinite regress, but there is the important difference that, whereas here the third form unites two other *forms*, in the *Parmenides* the third form is posited as what the form and the *thing* have in common, and so a new ontological level must be posited each time, that grounds both that of the thing and the previous form(s). Thus, whereas Socrates here considers the argument to be a reductio against the possibility of more than one form, Parmenides presents it as a reductio against the theory of forms generally (see Dorter 1994, 32–34).

4. Or a shuttle, to cite the example at *Cratylus* 389b. The following discussion applies especially to wheels on vehicles—other kinds of wheels, like potter's wheels, would have to be discussed somewhat differently.

5. For a discussion of this passage and the history of its interpretation, see Harold Cherniss, "On Plato's *Republic* X 597 B", *American Journal of Philology* 53 (1932): 233–42. For more recent discussions see Reale 1997 (1991), 314–20, and Kahn 1996, 363.

6. Cf. Halliwell 1988, 105; Naddaff 2002, 136n8.

7. Cf. Gallop 1965, 120.

8. Cf. Morriss Partee, "Plato's Banishment of Poetry", *Journal of Aesthetics and Art Criticism* 29 (1970): 209–222, esp. 217; and Nehamas 1982, 58–64.

9. J. J. Pollitt, *Art and Experience in Classical Greece* (Cambridge: Cambridge University Press, 1972), 6.

10. Diogenes Laertius, 8.47.

11. Pollitt 1972, 106, 108.

12. "Early Classical Greek Art in a Platonic Universe" in C. Boulter (ed.), *Greek Art: Archaic into Classical* (Leiden: Brill, 1985), 96–111 and plates 79–96.

13. Pollitt 1972, 143–64.

14. "The king" refers in the first instance to the god who makes the form, but since the term was most recently used to refer to the philosopher (580c, 587b–d) and is here conjoined with "the truth", there may be an implication that the imitator is also third from the philosopher. Adam 1963 (1902) takes it to refer ultimately to the Idea of the good, but adds that "it is possible enough that the expression itself was half-proverbial in Plato's time and referred originally to the person who stood next but one in order of succession of the Persian throne" (vol. 2, 392, 464–65). Cf. Halliwell 1988, 116.

15. Cf. Murdoch 1977: "Surely art transforms, is creation, as Plato's own praise of the 'divine frenzy' must imply" (7).

16. Cf. Murphy 1951, 229.

17. Cf. Stephen Halliwell, "The *Republic*'s Two Critiques of Poetry", in Höffe 1997, 313–32, esp. 314–15.

18. Cf. *Gorgias* 453d, *Protagoras* 311b, 318c.

19. Gallop points out that the charge of "mere word painting, if it disqualifies the poet, [need not] disqualify the philosopher. Since the latter depicts Forms and not phenomena, the fact that he merely paints need not debar him from pronouncing upon morals and statecraft. For his words, unlike the poet's, lay more hold upon truth than action" (1965, 127).

20. J. O. Urmson shows how this issue is as relevant today as it was then ("Plato and the Poets", in Kraut 1997, 223–34).

21. χρηστός is used throughout the *Republic* (and elsewhere) as a synonym for ἀγαθός ("good"): 334c–e, 396d, 401b, 403d, 409d, 424a, 438a, 475b, 478e, 531b, 573a, 602b, 608b, 618b. Cf. Guthrie: it is an "old Socratic dictum" that "the excellence and beauty of everything . . . consists in its fitness to perform its proper function" (1975, 546).

22. Cf. Benardete 1989, 215, although he is mistaken in thinking that this is the first mention of horses (cf. 335b and 352e2).

23. Descartes will use the same example to similar purpose. See *Meditations* 3, AT39L/31F.

24. Shorey points out the resemblance of this line to 496a (1935, 450).

25. Cf. Murdoch on Plato: "Art makes us content with appearances, and by playing magically with particular images it steals the educational wonder of the world away from philosophy and confuses our sense of direction toward reality and our motives for discerning it" (1977, 66). For Murdoch's defense of art see *op. cit.* 82–89.

26. Else points out the resemblance between this passage and Aristotle's *Poetics* (1972, 43–54).

27. Cf. Annas 1981, 339–40; Elizabeth Belfiore, "Plato's Greatest Accusation against Poetry", *Canadian Journal of Philosophy* 9 (1983): 39–62, 152–56; Halliwell 1988, 134–35; Naddaff 2002, 162n6.

28. Apart from the competition to win a prize, the pressure on dramatic poets to please the theater-going crowd was evident in Book 6, when Socrates remarked that in theatres and other public gatherings people object so aggressively to what they dislike and approve so loudly what they like that it is hard not to be swept away by their views (492b–c).

29. Cf. Gadamer 1934, 65–66.

30. 607b. Cf. Xenophanes fr. 11. For a survey of where Plato's and Homer's world-views coincide and where they differ, see Charles Segal, "'The Myth was Saved': Reflections on Homer and the Mythology of Plato's Republic", *Hermes* 106 (1978): 315–36.

31. Compare 491d–492a with 485d–e and 572e–573e.

32. Also see chapter 9, 291–93.

33. Cf. Nehamas 1982, 47.

34. Cf. Adam 1963 (1902), vol. 2, 423; Halliwell 1988, 160–61.

35. Cf. *Phaedrus* 245c, *Timaeus* 89e, *Laws* 894b.

36. Cf. Strauss 1964, 137–38.

37. Friedländer (1964), after noting Socrates' ironic preface, calls the proof itself absurd (129), Guthrie (1975) remarks that "for Plato's sake one would hope that it was not very seriously meant" (555), and Annas (1981) calls it "one of the few really embarrassingly bad arguments in Plato" (345). Naddaff (2002) regards it as "seemingly parodying any logical proof . . . [of] the soul's immortality" (129).

38. See chapter 3, n. 12.

39. See Aristotle, *De Anima* 1.2.405a19–21 and 1.5.411a7–8.

40. Socrates puts it more ambiguously: "We must not believe that the soul in its true nature is full of variety, dissimilarity, difference toward itself. . . . It is not easy for what is eternal to be composed of many parts if it is not composed in the most beautiful way, as the soul now appeared to us" (611b). If we take this to mean that in its true (disembodied) form the soul does not combine reason with appetite and spiritedness, then there is no ultimate difference between the way the soul is conceived in the *Republic* and the *Phaedo*. For further discussion of this issue see T. M. Robinson, "Soul and Immortality in *Republic* X", *Phronesis* 12 (1967): 147–51; W. K. C. Guthrie, "Plato's Views on the Nature of the Soul", in Vlastos 1971 (1), 230–43; Roger Shiner, "Soul in *Republic* X 611", *Apeiron* 6 (1972): 23–30; Thomas Szlezak, "Unsterblichkeit und Trichotomie der Seele in zehnten Buch der Politeia", *Phronesis* 21 (1976): 31–58; Lloyd Gerson, "A Note on Tripartition and Immortality in Plato", *Apeiron* 20 (1987): 81–96; James Robinson, "The Nature of the Soul in *Republic* X", *Journal of Philosophical Research* XVI (1990–1991): 213–22.

41. Simone Weil succinctly formulates both the problem that led to the separation of justice from its appearance, and the problem that resulted from that separation: "If justice is apparent, it is veiled in appearance, enveloped in prestige. If it does not appear, if no one knows that the perfectly just man is just, how can he serve as model?" ("The 'Republic'", in *Intimations of Christianity Among the Ancient Greeks* [London: Routledge, 1957], 142).

42. Brumbaugh suggests that Socrates does not give the spheres the names of the planets because they represent the pure astronomy of which planetary astronomy was only an approximation (529c–d). He also sees an "intentional echo here of the earlier image of political organization as a harmony of the classes in the state . . . like the fixed notes of a scale". The Sirens thus personify "the projection of social harmony into the relation of parts of the cosmos itself" (1954, 175). It was also his suggestion that the four-day journey is an allusion to the Divided Line (177).

43. Cf. Segal 1978, 330.

44. Moors (1988) suggests that the three myths of the *Republic* form an ascent through the tripartite soul, from appetite (Gyge's Ring) to spiritedness (the myth of the metals) to "the necessity of pursuing the rational" (the myth of Er) (240). But the myth of the metals is introduced after the rational guardians have been set over the spirited auxiliaries, so it is more naturally associated with rationality than spiritedness.

45. Cf. Segal 1978: "The natural language for ἔρως is myth, and perhaps only myth can effectively express its nature. Hence the *Symposium* relies more heavily on mythic discourse than any other of Plato's dialogues. . . . [In the *Phaedrus*] another discourse of love and another great myth of Eros unfolds" (331).

46. In the original myth the name may have been Ara. Arthur Platt (1911) writes: "the modern commentators are as much in the dark about Er as were the ancients. Illumination may be shed upon him by [the Armenian History] of Moses of Chorene . . . Ara was son of Aram, who succeeded his father as King of Armenia. . . . It certainly looks as if this Ara was the original of Plato's Er; each of them is a valiant Armenian killed in battle, and each is said to be restored to life. For I think that τοῦ Ἀρμενίου originally meant 'the Armenian;' but Plato, having somehow got hold of him under that title, then added in his playful manner τὸ γένος Παμφύλου, because Er in this myth is a type of 'all nations and kindreds and tongues'. . . . But it is also possible to suppose that Ἠρός τοῦ Ἀρμενίου means 'Ara the son of Aram', and so the scholiast, who did not see what Παμφύλου meant, explains it as 'son of a man named Armenius'" (13–14). But cf. Halliwell 1988, 170.

47. David Gallop reminds me that one might trace it back at least to Heracleitus' statement, "A person's character is his *daimon*" (DK B119).

48. Cf. Bosanquet 1906, 415; and Halliwell 1988, 21.

49. *Phaedo* 74a–75c, *Phaedrus* 247c–250d.

50. *Meno* 81d–86c.

51. Also see J. A. Stewart, *The Myths of Plato* (London: Centaur, 1960 [1904]), 177.

52. Cf. Brumbaugh 1954, 162; Annas 1981, 351 and 1982, 137–38; Halliwell 1988, 22.

53. E.g., Theognis, I.425, repeated by others such as Sophocles and Herodotus.

54. *Apology* 40b–41a, *Cratylus* 403a–404a, *Phaedo* 64a–68b, *Laws* 838d.

55. Plotinus, *Enneads*, IV.3.12–13, Armstrong translation (substituting "universe" for "All").

56. See Adam 1963 (1902), vol. 2, 441 and vol. 2, 447. For an examination of the more technical details of the myth see *ibid.* vol. 2, 470–79, Stewart 1960 (1904),

170–75; Brumbaugh 1954, 174–208; J. S. Morrison, "Parmenides and Er", *Journal of Hellenic Studies* 75 (1955): 59–68, esp. 65–8.

57. Cf. Victor Ehrenberg, "Polypragmosyne: A Study in Greek Politics", *Journal of Hellenic Studies* 67 (1947): 46–67, esp. 60. Brumbaugh (1954) points out that "the souls changing into animals (Orpheus, Thamyras, Ajax, Agamemnon, Atalanta, and Epeius and Thersites) represent, as Proclus and Adam have noted, the musician-ruler-athlete-artisan-mimetic artist of the *Phaedrus* list, and they are presented in almost the same order" (287n76, cf. 152–55 and 204–8).

58. Cf. *Phaedrus* 248c–250a, and n. 48 above.

59. In the *Sophist* the Eleatic stranger calls philosophy "the *episteme* of free people" (253c). By contrast, those who are governed by irrational passions are the least free (*Republic* 576a).

60. This may be all that Socrates means in the *Gorgias*, when he says that "the good and noble man or woman is happy, and an unjust and evil one is miserable" (470e)—a passage that is often interpreted as implying that a good person can be perfectly happy regardless of circumstances. Cf. George Klosko: "Decisive evidence that Socrates does not *always* regard virtue as a sufficient condition for happiness is found in the *Crito* at 47d–e, and the *Lysis* 220a7–b3 ("Socrates on Goods and Happiness", *History of Philosophy Quarterly* 4 [1987]: 251–64, esp. 259, emphasis in original).

61. Also see Brumbaugh 1954, 167–68.

62. Cf. Baracchi 2002, 18, and Peter Warnek, "Saving the Last Word: Heidegger and the Concluding Myth of Plato's *Republic*", *Philosophy Today* 46 (2002): 255–73, esp. 255.

CHAPTER ELEVEN

~

The Limits of the *Timaeus*

On the above account of the dialogue as a whole, Plato's philosophy is not foundational but instrumental. It is not intended to present us with finished doctrines, but rather with models to focus our thinking, which are progressively transformed into something less rigid and more subtle. The *Republic's* sequel, the *Timaeus*, begins by disclaiming the authoritativeness of its account. Timaeus acknowledges that "To discover the maker and father of the universe would be quite a job and, if we discovered him, to tell everyone about him would be impossible" (28c). Moreover, not only in the case of the creator but also in the case of his creation, we are told that an accurate account is not possible, because only what has being is susceptible of stable and rational accounts, while the universe belongs to the realm of becoming and therefore can only admit likely and unstable accounts (28b–29c)—which follows also from the Divided Line's contention that the visible world is accessible only to *doxa*, not *episteme*. Accordingly, the dialogue is presented as a *mythos* rather than a *logos*.

Nevertheless, the *Timaeus* is sometimes thought to demonstrate the opposite, that Plato had a foundational metaphysics in mind to which the other dialogues allude in various ways. For after these initial disclaimers, the narrative proceeds like a confident description of the nature of things, so there is some justification for the usual practice of downplaying the disclaimers and reading the subsequent account as a work of foundational metaphysics, a myth that may be translated into concepts as fully as the myth of the metals. Both before and after the disclaimers quoted above, however, there are other

351

indications that the account is not meant to be taken as definitive, although the indications are of a more indirect nature. If Plato wants us to take the metaphysics of the *Timaeus* seriously but not dogmatically, its limitations are better revealed only after we have had time to reflect on it, the way the tripartite soul and two-world models of Books 4 and 5 were tacitly softened after their initial appearance. He does this in the *Timaeus* not only by putting the teaching in the form of a myth, with the above disclaimers, and by putting the myth in the mouth of someone other than Socrates, but also by presenting an account that is self-consciously incomplete, and indicating the missing elements in a way that becomes apparent only after repeated readings.

Its incompleteness is signaled in the opening line, which must be the strangest opening line in Plato: "One, two, three, but where is the fourth, dear Timaeus, of those who were our guests yesterday and are now our hosts?" The strangeness of this line lies chiefly in the fact that the fourth person in this presumably fictitious gathering is in principle impossible to identify.[1] "Yesterday" refers to the day that Socrates narrated the events of the conversation of the day before yesterday, that narration being the *Republic*, much of which is summarized at 17c–19b.[2] But since the *Republic* is a monologue without a dramatic frame—there is no setting of the stage in an introductory scene—it gives no indication of who the audience was to whom Socrates was speaking. We could not possibly have known that Socrates was speaking to four people, let alone who they were. Why would Plato invent an unknowable member of the *Republic*'s audience to be absent from the *Timaeus*? The problem is not diminished if the reference was to some other occasion than the narration of the *Republic*. If the referent of Socrates' question is in principle unidentifiable, then the only meaning that Socrates' question can possibly have for us is simply that there is a missing fourth member. If we read the dialogue with the possibility in mind that the opening words are meant to alert us to a corresponding incompleteness in the account that is to follow, we will find that there are four passages in which a fourth member is missing from a series. In each case what is missing is a mediating term between the realm of individuals and the source from which they derive. The incomplete mediations mean that the metaphysics of the *Timaeus* is not a conclusive metaphysical system, and if Plato chose the opening words in order to signal the omissions, then the inconclusiveness was deliberately built into the metaphysics.

That momentary suggestion of a missing fourth is soon reinforced by a more elaborate one. We know now that Socrates' audience for the previous day's narration consisted of the three who are present for the *Timaeus*, and the absentee; and today's gathering consists of Critias, Timaeus, Hermocrates, and Socrates. Timaeus agrees that in exchange for Socrates' having enter-

tained them the day before with his narration, the rest of the four will enter-
tain Socrates in kind (17a–b), an offer that Hermocrates expressly seconds
(20c). Later, however, when Critias tells Socrates how they plan to put this
into effect, he mentions Timaeus' speech, and then his own, but makes no
reference to Hermocrates (27a–b). This omission is not redressed later, nor is
there any record of a dialogue called the *Hermocrates*, to accompany the
Republic, *Timaeus*, and *Critias*. That Plato never wrote such a dialogue can be
explained in any number of ways,[3] but Critias' failure to anticipate the fourth
dialogue here, in the very dialogue where it is proposed, is surprising. Once
again an impression is created that something is missing, again the fourth
member of a series.

Groups of three and groups of four figure prominently in the *Timaeus*. Even
on a casual reading the prominence of the number three is obvious: the world
is composed of the triad form-body-soul, the soul itself is tripartite, and body is
composed of triangles. Moreover, since the *Republic* like the *Timaeus* opens
with a reference to the previous day ("I went down yesterday"), if we count
Socrates' conversation with Glaucon, Adeimantus, and the others as the first
day, the present conversation of the *Timaeus* takes place on the third day. But
the number four makes frequent appearances as well. Socrates classifies people
into four groups: ordinary people (like himself), poets, sophists, and philosophers (like Timaeus, Critias, and Hermocrates) (19c–20a); Critias' story is
now in its fourth telling (after an Egyptian priest told it to Solon, Solon to
Critias' grandfather,[4] and Critias' grandfather to Critias himself: 20d–e, 22b);
there are four elements (fire, air, water, earth: 31b–32b); four types of sentient
beings (gods, birds, fish, and land animals: 39e–40a); and, just as the dialogue
opens with a reference to a group of four members, it ends with a list of the four
species into which men devolve in their next life (90e–92b).

There are four passages, however, that present a threefold classification
where we would expect a fourfold one, and in each case the fourth member is
called to our attention in a different context. Since each missing member is
one of the two terms by which contrasting realms are mediated, their absence
produces fundamental aporias in the metaphysics of the dialogue, but in an
implicit way that does not threaten to undermine at the outset the value of
the metaphysics as *one* way of conceiving the teleological nature of reality.

Human Vocations (17b–24d)

Socrates begins his recapitulation of the *Republic* conversation with the
words, "Did we not first separate in it the class of workers of the land, and the
other crafts, from the class of defenders?" (17c). In the *Republic* there was an

ambiguity as to whether the city is divided into three classes or four. Although Socrates usually spoke of only three classes, that was because the two lowest classes, the farmers and craftspeople, are taken together; in some places, however, he kept them distinct, calling them the iron and bronze classes, while the auxiliaries are silver and the guardians gold (e.g., 415a–b). Where the *Republic* tended to collapse the distinction between the farmers and craftspeople, in the *Timaeus* Socrates preserves that distinction but collapses the one between the guardians and auxiliaries, so that we are left with three classes where we would have expected four. The *Republic* had made that distinction when the city evolved from spirited to rational (412d–414b), in order ultimately to distinguish the philosopher from the warrior. Here the distinction is never made, and the guardians are said to be both extraordinarily spirited *and* philosophical (18a). This position corresponds not to the philosopher-rulers of the kallipolis in Book 7, or even to the complete guardians of Book 4, but to the more primitive warrior society (375e) that preceded the separation of the philosophers and warriors.[5]

The omission of the distinction between spiritedness and philosophy is further emphasized by a second omission. In the *Republic* Socrates warned of three waves of criticism that his proposals about the guardians would provoke: one against the proposed equality of women (457b), a second against the replacement of families by communal equality (457c), and the third and greatest against the recommendation that there be philosopher-rulers (473c–d). Here Socrates repeats the first two waves (18c–19a), and then asks, "Then have we now gone through yesterday's discussion, as far as a review of the main points is concerned? Or do we still miss anything that was said, dear Timaeus, which has been omitted?" (19a). "Not at all", Timaeus replies; so the dialogue proceeds without reference to the third wave, in which the rulers would have been clearly distinguished from the spirited warriors by virtue of being philosophers. In this opening discussion then, the question "Where is the fourth?" could be applied to the class of philosophers, which remains submerged in the class of warriors from which the *Republic* had disengaged it.

The collapsing of the distinction between these two classes does not imply a recantation by Plato of the difference between spiritedness and reason, for they are clearly distinguished in what follows, reason being located in the head and spiritedness in the chest (44d, 69d–70a). In fact, shortly after the passages mentioned above, Socrates proceeds to praise Timaeus for 1) his wealth, 2) his status (offices and honors), and 3) his command of philosophy (20a). Those are the three distinctive orientations of the tripartite city and the tripartite soul, and are here once again treated as distinct. Most telling of all is that the middle section of the *Timaeus* will recapitulate the road to philosophy that is described in the middle of the *Republic*, but was omitted from this summary at the beginning of the dialogue. In training the warriors to become philosophers, the *Republic* had advocated using astronomy and harmony as propaedeutics to philosophy, since the two disciplines respectively use the eyes and ears to awaken reason to rational order and goodness (529c–531d). The *Timaeus*, leaving behind its earlier failure to distinguish between the practitioners of war and philosophy, now precisely recalls the teaching of the *Republic* in saying that the senses of sight and hearing, and the sciences of astronomy and harmony that they make possible, lead us "to the genus of philosophy, and no greater good than this has or will ever come to the mortal race by the gift of the gods" (47a–e). Why then is philosophy omitted from the earlier summary?

After that summary Critias relates a story about the founding of Athens that he heard at the age of ten from his ninety-year-old grandfather, who had heard it from Solon long before, who, in turn, heard it from a priest in the Egyptian city of Sais (20d–22b). The priest claims that many of the laws of present-day Sais resemble those of ancient Athens, in particular the division of the populace into four classes: 1) priests; 2) craftspeople; 3) shepherds, hunters, land workers; and 4) warriors (24a–b). Here the fourfold classification of the *Republic* is restored, except that now the ruling class is comprised of priests rather than philosophers. The priests assimilate to their own role the function of philosophers—the pursuit of wisdom (24b–c), just as in the *Republic* the philosophers appropriated to themselves the function of priests—the founding and supervising of the people's religion (379a *ff*, 414b–415c). The reason that each can appropriate the role of the other is that both mediate between the divine and human realms, the priests working downward from the divine by purporting to convey the will of the gods, the philosophers working upward from the human.

The discrepancy between the threefold division of farmer-artisan-warrior (17c–18a) and the fourfold division of farmer-artisan-warrior-priests (24a–b) leaves philosophy in an ambivalent position. In neither classification does philosophy appear as itself: in the former it is not yet separated from spiritedness; in the latter it is already absorbed into priestliness. This progression parallels the trajectory of philosophy in the *Republic*, where the philosopher originally emerges from the warrior class and eventually develops into something like a priest who rules with infallible divine wisdom. In their own way both roles are relevant to philosophy. Philosophy may begin in wonder, but it will not get far if the wonder is not accompanied by a fighting spirit that struggles against difficulties and against conventional beliefs—Socratic "irony", in its original sense, means the false modesty that cloaks hubris.[6] But together with that false modesty and its presumptuousness is a genuine humility. Philosophers, like priests, must ultimately subordinate themselves to something higher than themselves. The goal of philosophy, if it is ever to become simple love of wisdom, must be to overcome the vanity of personal achievement that is, however, one of its original driving forces. Whatever wisdom we attain must initially be purchased with a spirited struggle; otherwise our conclusions will be indistinguishable from divine inspiration, and the philosopher indistinguishable from the priest. To the extent that philosophy is only polemical argument, as it was for the sophists, then the philosopher is engaged in just another form of competition or polemic; but if that element is missing entirely, wisdom will collapse into uncritical piety.

Nowhere in the dialogues does Plato claim to give an adequate account of what philosophy is. The second and seventh letters (314a–c, 341c–d) echo the *Republic*'s (533a) insistence on the impossibility of a verbal presentation of philosophy at its highest level; and in the *Timaeus* Socrates is so far from claiming to be capable of such a presentation that he does not even profess to be a philosopher himself—unlike Timaeus, Critias, and Hermocrates, on whom he ironically bestows that title, he is only an ordinary person (19c–20a). The difficulty of discerning the necessary and sufficient conditions that distinguish the philosopher from the warrior-like sophist on one hand, and the priest-like statesman on the other,[7] may be inferred from Plato's failure to write the promised dialogue, the *Philosopher*, which was supposed to succeed the *Theaetetus*, *Sophist*, and *Statesman*.[8] We are given no dialogue in which philosophy appears directly as itself, rather than indirectly in its examination of a particular question. The *Timaeus*' absorption of philosophy into the class of warriors in the three-part classification, and into that of priests in the four-part classification, reflects the same unstable polarity of philosophy between spiritedness and wisdom that the *Republic* and the unfinished Eleatic tetralogy reflect in their own ways.

Elements and Gods (31b–32c, 39e–41a)

Normally we think of a mean as a single mediation between two terms, but Timaeus points out that when the two terms are solids, like fire and earth, a double mean is necessary—a third and fourth term, one from the side of each of the extremes (32b). Thus the fire and earth are mediated by both air and water, air on the side of fire ("As fire is to air, air is to water") and water on the side of earth ("As air is to water, water is to earth") (31b–32b). The technique of synthesis by a double mean is often at work in the dialogues if we take it in an extended sense that is not always mathematical. The *Republic*'s Divided

Line, for example, mediated between the *eikastic* Cave and the *noetic* Isles of the Blessed by means of *pistis* from below and *dianoia* from above. In the *Sophist* the Eleatic visitor effects a double reconciliation between the "friends of the forms" and the materialists, from above by collecting their respective principles within the comprehensive genus of "power" (247d–e), and from below by having both parties recognize something of their opponents' claims (246e–247c, 248e–249d). And in the *Statesman* the Eleatic stranger says that the statesman will have to use a double bond—divine and human—in order to weave together the courageous and the moderate citizens (309b–c): the divine bond is a common belief in the nature of the good (309c–e), and the human bond is intermarriage (310a–b).

Shortly after the passage in which the *Timaeus* presents the doctrine of the double mean to link fire and earth by air and water, we are told that corresponding to those four elements and their regions are the four fundamental species of beings: gods, winged animals, aquatic animals, and land animals. The gods are mostly fire (40a), but Timaeus also mentions gods associated with other elements: the first and eldest of the gods within Ouranos (heaven, the province of fire) is Gaia (earth) (40b–c), and these two, Ouranos and Gaia, give birth to Oceanus (ocean) and Tethys (queen of the sea) (40e), parents of all the rivers of the world. After them are mentioned only Phorcys, who is associated with sea monsters, and Kronos, Rhea, Zeus, and Hera, all of whom are associated with heaven, Ouranos. Just as Timaeus' cosmogony began with heaven (fire) and earth, his theogony begins with the gods of heaven and earth. But whereas the cosmogony described two means that join the extremes (air and water), the theogony mentions, besides the gods of heaven and earth, only gods associated with water (Ocean, Tethys, Phorcys); and then, instead of proceeding to gods of air (such as Aeolus, Boreus, and Zephyrus), who are never mentioned, returns to those of heavenly fire. Gods of three of the elemental levels are mentioned, but not the fourth. Coming so soon after the explanation of a need for air and water as means between fire and earth, the reference to only three of these four in their divine personae is surprising.

In the first passage that we looked at, the class of philosophers was suppressed, who mediate between the divine and human from the side of the human, and only the class of priests was mentioned, who mediate between the divine and human from the side of the divine. Here again it is one of the means between two poles that is left out, but this time it is the upper mean, the one closest to heaven that is omitted, rather than the mean closest to us. Whether the opposition is between humanity and the gods, as in the first pair of classifications, or heaven and earth, as here, the implication is, once again, that there is an incompleteness of mediation, a threefold classification where we have been led to expect a fourfold one.

Causes of the Cosmos (48c–53b)

The previous discussion, Timaeus says, divided the universe into two forms, paradigmatic form that is intelligible, and an imitation of it that is generated and visible. Now a third must be added, the receptacle that receives the imitation (48e–49b). Once again a fourth member is missing. In the previous discussion that Timaeus is referring to, there were three terms, not two. Not only did he distinguish between the model of intelligible being and its imitation in sensible becoming (27d–28c), but he twice added that there must also be a third term, the cause by which becoming is brought into its imitative existence: "everything that comes to be necessarily comes to be by a cause" (28a); "in the case of what comes to be we say that it is necessary that it come to be by some cause" (28c). But there is no mention here of that fourth principle, the cause by which what comes to be in the receptacle is brought into existence in imitation of paradigmatic form.

A section of the *Philebus* corresponds remarkably closely to the present passage. That passage too begins by saying, "Let us divide everything that now exists in the universe into two parts, or rather, if you like, into three" (23c). The three parts are limit, the unlimited, and the mixture of the two. In the *Timaeus* paradigmatic form corresponds to limit in the *Philebus*, the imitation of form in the realm of becoming corresponds to the mixture of limit and the unlimited, and the receptacle corresponds to the unlimited. But the *Philebus* then adds the fourth principle that the present passage of the *Timaeus* omits, and does so in almost precisely the same words that Timaeus used at 28a and 28c. Socrates says that we must consider not only the two elements and the mixture that arises from them, but we must also seek a fourth factor, the cause of the mixture, for "it is necessary that all things that come to be, come to be by a cause" (*Philebus* 26e).

The emphasis in the two dialogues is different. In the *Philebus* what is sought is the mixture of limit and unlimited, and its cause. The problem is to mediate between limit and unlimited, and the mixture ("becoming") functions as a mean between them on the side of the unlimited, while the cause of the mixture functions as a mean on the side of limit. Here in the *Timaeus* the problem is to meditate between the eternal and the temporal, that is, in the language of the *Philebus*, between limit and the mixture, not limit and the unlimited. These two—the eternal and temporal, form and becoming—like the two in the *Philebus*, are mediated in one way from below and in another way from above. The receptacle is the mean from below, on the side of the becoming,⁹ but there must also be a mean from above, on the side of being. Why is there no discussion here of that fourth term, the cause that mediates downward by bringing becoming into existence in imitation of being? Its absence is accounted for by something that Timaeus said just prior to this passage: "We shall not now explain the principle or principles—or however we conceive them—of all things, for no other reason than because of the difficulty of making our beliefs clear according to our present type of method" (48c).¹⁰ He had made the same point after mentioning the importance of the causal principle in the earlier passage as well, quoted at the beginning of this chapter: "To discover the maker and father of the universe would be quite a job and, if we discovered him, to tell everyone about him would be impossible" (28c). But the fact that a principle resists explanation does not mean that it should not be counted among the relevant principles and that the remaining principles are by themselves sufficient, as Timaeus claims here (48e, 49a).

Mythically, the first principle is represented by the divine demiurge (28c, 53b) but we are given no precise conception of what this mythological characterization represents in purely conceptual terms. We are told that, being good, he is not jealous and therefore made the world as much like himself as possible (29e–30a), but we are not told what it means to call him good, what goodness is. In his productive aspect he is creative mind, and since mind operates by reason rather than force his creative shaping of material necessity is described as persuasion (47e–48a), but the metaphor of persuasion does not generate clear and distinct concepts when applied to cosmogony. We saw in chapter 6 that the explanation of creation as a lack of jealousy suggests an emanation theory—in the absence of a deliberate withholding (jealousy) the world naturally follows from the creative principle—but Timaeus nowhere makes this explicit. What we are told is that the individuals that populate the world are created only indirectly by the demiurge, for all his direct creations must be eternal, and directly by the eternal gods that the demiurge creates. The necessarily immortal cannot generate the mortal except through the medium of the contingently immortal (41a–b). But the creative operations of the gods are no less mysterious and no less in need of demythologization than those of the demiurge, if we are to be able to distinguish philosophy from piety and philosophers from priests.

Since Plato usually calls the material imitation of paradigmatic form "participation", the entire creation myth of the *Timaeus* can be regarded as an image of the phenomenon of participation, in which temporal priority stands for ontological priority. But if, like Parmenides in the first part of his eponymous dialogue, we ask precisely what is meant by participation, which is after all only a metaphor, we will find no answer in Plato. The concept of participation is one of the fundamental aporias in Platonic philosophy. Accordingly, whether we ask the question in mythic or conceptual terms, we will find no real answer to the question, "Where is the fourth?" (i.e., if the upward mediation between divine creativity and mortal createdness is the receptacle, where is the downward mediation, the cause of participation)?

Levels of Soul (69c–73a)

When the demiurge turns over the creation of all that is mortal to his offspring, they take the immortal soul, reason, which the demiurge had created from the not quite pure residue of the world-soul (41d), create around it the human body, and within the body add a mortal soul comprising spiritedness and appetite (69c). Reason was housed in the head (44d), and now the spirited element is housed between the neck and the midriff (i.e., in the top third of the torso) and the appetitive part occupies the middle third of the torso, the lower thorax between the midriff and the navel (70a–e).[11] But what about the fourth part of the body, the abdomen? This case is not problematic in the way the previous ones were, where the fourth member of a quartet is omitted altogether, for Timaeus does go on to discuss the abdomen after the discussion of the midsection is complete, but it is the one part of the central body that is never connected with soul. At that point he says, "The next subject . . . is the way the rest of the body has come to be" (72e). "The rest of the body" turns out to include only two categories, the abdomen on one hand, and the marrow and its products on the other, for the marrow is the originating principle of "bones, flesh, and all such natures" (73b). Marrow combines in itself all three types of soul and is therefore able to produce not only flesh and bones, but structures as different as the brain and the sperm, and the spinal cord in between (73c–d).

Thus the head, thorax, and midriff are each the seat of a particular kind of soul, while marrow combines all three. Only the abdomen, the fourth part of the body, seems to have no distinctive soul nature. It is a kind of counterpart to marrow in that, while only in the function of marrow are all three parts of the individual soul combined, only in the function of the abdomen are all three absent. Marrow bonds the soul to the body in life (73b), but three-dimensional kinds require two means to bind them (32b), and a second mean is never mentioned. Can the second bond between soul and body be found in the function of the abdomen?

A distinctive kind of motion does, in fact, take place in the abdomen, and that is a prima facie indication of the presence of some kind of soul, since soul is the principle of motion. The distinctive motion of the abdomen is neither rational nor spirited nor appetitive—does it therefore imply a fourth kind of soul? Timaeus describes the function of the abdomen as follows:

> Those who were constructing our race knew the incontinence that would be in us for drinks and food, and that through greed we would consume far more than what is moderate and necessary. In order, then, that they not be swiftly destroyed by diseases and the mortal race come to an immediate end without reaching its end, foreseeing these things they set what is called the abdomen as a receptacle to hold superfluous drink and food. And they coiled the formation of the intestines around, so that the nourishment would not pass through quickly and force the body to quickly again require more nourishment, bringing about insatiability and, by virtue of gluttony, making the whole race end up unphilosophical and uncultured, and disobedient to the most divine part that we possess. [72e–73a]

Left to its own devices, then, appetite is subject to incontinence and greed. Spiritedness too is subject to a pair of "unwise counselors", the extremes of boldness and fearfulness (69d), but since appetite is further both in nature and location from reason than is spiritedness, it is even less obedient (70a) and more susceptible to unwise counsel. The purpose of the abdomen is to curtail our tendency to insatiable cravings, making us moderate and subduing the importunity of the body sufficiently to allow us to respond to the promptings of divine reason. Whereas spiritedness' tendency to excess need only be countered by the dictates of reason coming from above, the stronger tendency to excess in the appetitive part must be countered both from above by the alliance of reason and spiritedness (70a), and from below by the abdomen.[12] The fourth part of the body, then, becomes an additional ally of reason against the unlimited greed of appetite, and functions as a fourth player in the game, in addition to the three parts of the soul.

But Plato usually characterizes the body as being by nature opposed to the mind, the irrational to the rational.[13] In that case how can the mechanical body function here as the ally of reason? Is it only because of a design extrinsically added onto the body, by which reason uses the resistance of matter to its own advantage—or is there also some as yet unspecified *intrinsic* soul at work, a principle of motion not reducible to the other three? If so, the tension between the three-part division of the soul and the four-part division of the body will once again point to an unmentioned fourth category.

There is no obvious principle of motion in the abdomen. It seems that either the waste material would be conceived as being forced through the intestines by the new food entering from above, analogously to the case of urination where downward pressure is exerted by air pressure from the lungs (91a), or else since it is akin to earth it naturally moves in the direction of earth (cf. 81a). Even mechanical processes like these are not entirely soulless, however, as they follow from the laws of nature (φύσεως . . . νόμους: 83e), that is, the world-soul. By denying any part of the tripartite soul to the lowest quarter of the body, Plato displays there the operation of the world-soul without the overlay of the vegetable (appetitive), animal (spirited), or human (rational) souls.

The cosmos as a whole is a single animal in which all other things, living and nonliving, are contained as parts.[14] Since nothing exists outside of it, its own waste provides its nourishment (33c). This refers not only to the fact that all living beings are subject to inflow and outflow (42a, 43a) so that the by-products of one are the nourishment of another, but also to processes among nonliving things, such as the interchange of fire, air, and water (49c, 54b–55c). That is what Timaeus means by saying that when the created gods made mortal animals out of the material of the cosmos' body, it was with the intention of paying it back (42e–43a): the natural elements appropriated by living bodies are returned to nature through elimination and exhalation while the organism is alive, and by decomposition after death. In fact, the two types of processes, living and nonliving, follow precisely the same laws. Speaking of the human body, Timaeus says:

> The manner of filling and evacuation comes about just as everything in the universe is carried out, in accordance with the principle that all that is akin is carried toward its kin. For the elements that surround us without always dissolve and divide us, distributing to each species its own kind. [81a]

It is on this principle of like returning to like that all bodily inflow and outflow is based. On one hand growth depends on food being converted to add bone to bone, flesh to flesh, and blood to blood. On the other hand, not only is our body worn away by its interaction with our environment, but our breath joins with outside air and our waste products with earth and water. Our feces and urine are expelled at a lower point than our breath because the natural places of water and earth are lower than the natural place of air (63c–e). The motions of elimination derive, then, not from the sentient soul of the individual (whether rational, spirited, or appetitive) but from the laws of nature. The continuing separation of the four kinds into their respective places is due to the fact that the receptacle, the site of becoming, is not evenly balanced, and therefore sways and shakes, its shaking separating the heavier and lighter elements the way a winnowing fan separates the wheat from the chaff (52e–53a). The motion of the receptacle is a purely mechanical motion, unlike the goal-directed motions of vegetative, animal, and rational souls, but it is not a soulless motion, since soul is the source of all motion—or at least all motion that is not irrational.[15]

The motion of the receptacle cannot exist without soul, since the reason why the elements came to be mixed together in the first place, and why they do not remain in their places once separated, is that

> the revolution of the universe, since it comprehends the kinds, and since it is circular and naturally wants to come together with itself, squeezes them all and allows no empty space to remain. . . . The coming together of the compression pushes the small elements into the interstices of the large ones. [58a–b]

We already know that this revolution of the universe is produced by the circular motion of the world-soul (36e), so the ultimate cause of the shaking of the receptacle is the world-soul, which forces unlikes together and thus creates the imbalance that results in the shaking. In fact, since the motion of the world-soul is a double circle—the circle of the same and the circle of the different (36c)—not only the centripetal motion that forces together the different, but also the shaking motion that separates the same must have its source in the motion of the world-soul. The receptacle itself and the differing weights of the elements are necessary causes of the motions of nature, but they are not sufficient causes. They are what in other contexts Timaeus calls contributing or subordinate causes (46c, 68e), the necessary cause rather than the divine (68e).[16]

Our question was whether in the function of the abdomen we can see the second bond between soul and body, the fourth element in the mediation, as in marrow we saw the first bond. Marrow is the means by which the three parts of the soul act on the physical world; for the double mediation to be complete there must also be a means by which the physical world acts on the soul. If we turn our attention outside the body, the most obvious example of this is sense perception (43b–e),[17] but if we confine ourselves to what takes place within the body itself, the clearest example of the activity of the body on the soul is the intestines' mechanical alliance with reason against the excesses of appetite (69d–72d). Within the human body the "soulless" abdomen is the only part where, in default of the presence of any of the three parts of the individual soul, the operations of the world-soul appear beside them as a fourth.

Conclusion

The four passages we have been considering are all characterized by a tension between a triadic classification and a quadratic one, and in each case the omitted term was one of the two means between the source from which we come and the realm of becoming in which we live—either between truth and thought, gods and earth-dwellers, creator and creation, or whole and parts. 1) The philosopher is the upward mean between human thought and divine truth, as the priest is the downward mean. 2) The gods of the air mediate downward between the element of the gods and the element of humans, fire and earth (39e–40a), as the gods of water mediate upward. 3) The cause of the mixture of the rational and irrational is the downward mean between being and becoming, as the receptacle is the upward mean. 4) The world-soul is the downward mean between the cosmos and the individual—the whole and parts (30d)—as the individual soul is the upward mean.

As I suggested in the beginning, these four lacunae point to fundamental aporias in the *Timaeus'* account. 1) We are told that philosophy is the greatest gift that ever has or will be bestowed upon us by the gods (47b); however, what exactly philosophy is, not only is never explained (nor did the promised dialogue, the *Philosopher*, materialize), but is continuously conflated with mythology throughout the *Timaeus*. 2) From beginning to end the dialogues repeatedly emphasize our relationship to the gods; but how we are to conceive of the gods or their patronization of us is never explained in a non-mythic way. 3) The causality of the good and the forms appears throughout at least the middle and late dialogues; but we are given no conceptual metaphysical account of what that means—only mythic accounts like the *Timaeus*, or metaphors like "participating", "partaking", "imitating", and "striving towards". 4) The ascetic element in Plato that points us away from the body is balanced by the reminder that we should not turn our back too hastily on the corporeal world because we are also natural beings with a role to play in the natural world;[18] but how is that to be conceived? How can we understand ourselves as parts of a greater whole, when our appetite and spiritedness continually insist on our egocentricity? Plato provides us with no foundational metaphysics to complement the myth of Er and show how our physical life is entirely a product of the world-soul, the laws of nature, any more than he shows how our rational life is a product of divine reason.

In recent decades the *Timaeus* has frequently been linked with the *Parmenides* over the question of whether Plato repudiated his earlier theory of forms. The criticisms of that theory, which appear in the *Parmenides*, lend themselves to this interpretation, but the theory reappears intact in the *Timaeus* which, by all stylistic measures, was written after the *Parmenides*.[19] I would like to suggest a different way to understand their complementarity. To repeat what I said earlier, metaphysics functions in Plato instrumentally rather than dogmatically, as a means of thinking about the intelligible, not as a definitive account of truth. The *Parmenides* reminds us of the doctrinal inadequacy of metaphysics by showing the aporias in the metaphysical theory of forms; but it reaffirms the instrumental value of the theory in a brief passage that appears to be a mere afterthought of Parmenides:

> Only a man of very great natural ability will be able to understand that there is a certain genus and essence, itself-by-itself, for each thing, and only a still more amazing man will be able to discover all these things and teach someone else to evaluate them properly. . . . But if anyone, in view of these and other such difficulties, will not permit the existence of forms of things or mark off a single form in each case, he will not have anything on which to fix his thoughts, as long as he does not permit the idea of each thing to be always the same, and in this way he will utterly destroy the power of discourse. You seem to me to have been well aware of this. [135a–c]

The *Timaeus* is the counterpart of the *Parmenides* in this respect. Whereas the *Parmenides* emphasized the limitations of metaphysics while reminding us, almost as an afterthought, of its importance, the *Timaeus* shows us the value of metaphysics by giving us the most ambitious metaphysical account in all of Plato, while at the same time reminding us almost inconspicuously—both by its mythic form and by its missing mediations—of the limitations of such an account.

Notes

1. For some of the historical speculation regarding this question see Sallis 1999, 10–11.

2. Not everyone agrees that the *Timaeus* is a sequel to the *Republic*, since some doctrines central to the *Republic* are left out of the *Timaeus'* summary. Some readers have suggested instead that the *Timaeus* was written after an early version of the *Republic* which did not include those doctrines, and before the version that we know: A. E. Taylor mentions Henry Jackson and R. D. Archer-Hind as defenders of this view (*A Commentary on Plato's Timaeus* [Oxford: Clarendon Press, 1928], 27). But there is no evidence for this claim and it is rejected not only by Taylor (32) but by everyone since, as far as I know. Others make the opposite claim: not that the *Republic* (as we know it) supersedes the *Timaeus*, but that the *Timaeus* supersedes the *Republic* (i.e., that the abbreviated summary is meant to repudiate by their absence those doctrines of the *Republic* to which Plato no longer subscribes). W. K. C. Guthrie, for example, writes, "Plato is telling us explicitly that in the years since he wrote it his interests have veered from an idealistic view of society towards practical policy" (*A History of Greek Philosophy*, Vol. 5 [Cambridge: Cambridge University Press, 1978], 245). Still others consider the summary not to refer to the *Republic* at all, but to some other conversation. Thus F. M. Cornford argues that because matters that are important in the *Republic* have been left out, and because "Plato [gives] his own clear indication . . .

that the summary actually given is complete . . . Plato could not have stated more plainly that Socrates is not to be supposed to have narrated the whole conversation in the *Republic* as we have it. It follows at once that he did not intend the *Republic* to stand as the first dialogue in his new series. . . . [However,] no ground remains for any inference that Plato meant the contents of the later books of the *Republic* to be super-seded or corrected by the *Timaeus*" (*Plato's Cosmology* [London: Routledge, 1937], 4–5). But Plato does not give a "clear indication" that the summary is complete—that judgement is made only by Timaeus (19a–b), the very person who requested the sum-mary because of his inability to remember the conversation adequately (17b). Brann believes that Socrates' remark at about celebrating the festival of the goddess (*Timaeus* 26e) is a reference to the Lesser Panathenaea, "which occurred two months later". She suggests that "Socrates proposed this city on various occasions and that it was known as 'his'" (1967, 21). Also see Sallis 1999, 22–23. Be that as it may, Plato could hardly have written this part of the *Timaeus* without expecting his readers to be reminded of the *Republic*, so I shall treat it that way to see what follows from the comparison.

3. See, for example, Cornford 1937, 7–8 & n. 2; Guthrie 1978, 246n1.

4. Taking the subject of εἶπεν ("told") in 20e4 to be Solon (with Cornford and Jowett). The referent of the verb is grammatically ambiguous and is sometimes taken to refer to Dropides, Critias' great-grandfather, but Critias later refers to this as the story "that old Critias [the grandfather] heard from Solon" (25e).

5. In the timocracy that is the first stage of the degeneration (547b) the philoso-phers are still distinct from the warriors although they are now politically subservient to them.

6. Cf. Aristotle, *Nicomachean Ethics* 4.7.

7. Cf. *Statesman* 303b, 309c. The role of actual priests in the *Statesman* is more cir-cumscribed, however: 290c–d.

8. *Statesman* 257a–258a; cf. *Sophist* 216e–17a.

9. The receptacle is ontologically an extreme but cosmologically a mean. Onto-logically it is an extreme because it is the least determinate level of reality, as being (form) is the most determinate. But cosmologically it is a mean because individuals could not come into being if there were not already a receptacle. The *Timaeus* pre-sents the cosmological side, the *Philebus* the ontological side. A similar duality arises in Plotinus, where matter must emanate from the One prior to individuals because it is the principle of individuation (a mean), and yet it must be considered as the last emanation of all (an extreme) because it is least determinate.

10. Even as he refuses to discuss the principle [ἀρχήν] he makes that omission as conspicuous as possible by using the same word in a different sense throughout the passage, as, for example, in the following sentence: "But holding to what I said at the beginning [κατ' ἀρχάς] about the efficacy of likely accounts, I shall try to give one no less likely than others, but more so as before, and speak from the beginning [ἀπ' ἀρχῆς] about each thing and the totality of all things" (48d). Also see Cornford 1937, 161. So far is Timaeus from explaining this principle, that there is little agreement among commentators as to even what he is referring to. It has been taken to mean

that "what he is going to take as the ABC of things may be capable of further analysis, only 'for our present purposes' we shall not try to analyse any further" (Taylor 309). Or that Timaeus is employing "a method which aims only at 'probability' or 'likelihood': to attain to 'first principles' we should need to employ the 'dialectic' method" (R. G. Bury ed., *Timaeus* etc. [London: Heineman, 1929], 110n2). Or "This warning may mean that the elementary triangles themselves are reducible to numbers, and number perhaps to be derived from unity; but he will not here push the analysis so far. Or it may mean that no one can ever really know the ultimate constitution of body, because there can be no such thing as physical science, but only a 'probable' account" (Cornford 1937, 162.). But once we notice that the three-part classification of being (form), becoming, and the receptacle, omits a fourth term—the cause or principle which had been mentioned at 28c and 48c, and which corresponds to the fourth term in the *Philebus* classification—we can see that this is the principle that Timaeus is refusing to bring into his account.

11. This classification has a certain figurative plausibility even today: reason in the brain, spiritedness in the heart (as the etymology of "courage" testifies), and appetite in the stomach.

12. And even from within by the liver (71a–d).

13. Most notably in the *Phaedo*: see 64d–67a, 80a–b. In the *Republic* this opposition is expressed in terms of the conflict between rationality and appetite.

14. 30d, 32c, 39e, 69c, 92c.

15. *Phaedrus* 245c–e, *Laws* 10.895b–897b. Whether soul is also the source of irrational motion is a matter of continuing controversy; see Richard Mohr's survey of the literature (*The Platonic Cosmology* [Leiden: Brill, 1985], 116–19). Guthrie (1978) rejects the view that soul is the source of irrational motion, which dates back to antiquity (see Taylor 1928, 155 ff), and which has more recently been defended by Cornford (1937, 205), J. B. Skemp (*The Theory of Motion in Plato's Later Dialogues* [Amsterdam: Hakkert 1967], 3–5, 76), Leonardo Tarán ("The Creation Myth in Plato's *Timaeus*", in Anton and Kustas, *Essays in Ancient Greek Philosophy* [Albany, N.Y.: State University of New York Press, 1971], 372–407), and J. S. Clegg ("Plato's Vision of Chaos", *Classical Quarterly* [1976]). Mohr, on the other hand, defends something like Guthrie's position. Guthrie's reason for rejecting the traditional view is that "even a myth (if this is all mythical) should be internally consistent, and in Timaeus' story the disorderly motion was there before the world-soul was created". Timaeus explicitly says, however, that although this was true of the order of his presentation, the opposite was true in the order of actuality:

> With regard to the soul, it is not the case that since we are now undertaking to speak of it after [the body], it follows that the god planned it to be younger. For when uniting them he would not have allowed the elder to be ruled by the younger. But we [humans], participating greatly in the accidental and random, also speak that way. But the god made the soul earlier and more venerable than the body, since soul was to be master and ruler, and body the subject. [34b–c]

Body could not have existed prior to soul, then, despite the sequence of Timaeus' narrative, and if not body then not motion.

16. Cf. *Phaedo* 99b.

17. Here again the law of nature that like goes to like is at work (e.g., 45b–d).

18. See, for example, *Phaedo* 61b–67b.

19. For details see Dorter 1994, 1–9.

~

Conclusion

Throughout our examination of the *Republic* we noticed the way Plato employs sharply delineated models that maximize contrasts and enable us to make useful distinctions as clearly as possible, but then proceeds to transform those simplified models into something that captures more of the nuance and ambiguity of the world. The models, in other words, have an instrumental rather than dogmatic function.[1] The two most dramatic examples were the tripartite soul, and the "two world" view of reality (being and becoming) with its cognitive counterpart (knowledge and opinion). Both began as rigid tri- or dichotomies, whose lines of demarcation almost immediately began to blur, until they both began to resemble continuums rather than discontinuities— in one case a stream that flowed into different channels (485d–e), in the other a continuous line. The line is divided first once, then twice, then sub-divided five more times in one of its segments (523a–531d) and three more in another (511b–c, 532d–533a), and we saw that there were borderline cases within all of the boundaries. Not only did the formal models turn out to be more fluid than their initial appearance indicated, however, but the converse was also true: the apparently casual elements of the dialogue—the order in which subjects were covered and the apparently random lists and sets of examples—displayed underlying formal order and patterns. In Plato's art, as in his ontology, rational structure and the fluidity of appearances interpenetrate each other.

The *Republic*'s distinctions between appetite and reason, and between being and becoming—which are seriously meant, however much they may be oversimplified—show that the relative value of living a just or an unjust life cannot be measured by the gratification of our appetites, which involve self-cancelling pleasures and fill us with an insubstantial kind of reality. The supposed advantage of injustice, insofar as it may bring us more rewards of that kind, turns out to be illusory, like that of runners who fail to pace themselves and start the race impressively but finish in disgrace. On the other hand, because the distinction between the substantiality of being and the insubstantiality of becoming can never be as absolute as it seemed, there is no purely rational calculation that can provide us with the right course of action. We must combine a rational understanding of the being of goodness with an ability to recognize the mean in the sensuous play of becoming. The latter is achieved through long experience, while the former is achieved though a discipline that weakens our devotion to unnecessary appetites and divisive pleasures, and intellectual study that strengthens our rationality. To apprehend the principle which gives rise to our own reality and that of the world is to find a fulfillment that makes all other kinds of gratification insignificant by comparison (516d), and thus quiets our rebellious impulses and brings us into harmony with ourselves (518c–d).

The implications of the purely political aspect of the *Republic* have been much debated, with the proposed city conceived at one extreme as nothing more than a metaphorical device by which to display the nature of the soul, and at the other as an earnest blueprint for an ideal government. The first view is supported by Socrates' own description of his project as psychological rather than political in character (368c–369a) and his seeming indifference to whether it can actually exist (472e, 592a–b); but when the development of the city leaves the parallel with the soul behind, as in books 5–7, and Socrates takes the trouble to insist that it is not impossible for it to come into being (540d), it is hard to dismiss the kallipolis as unintended to have political as well as psychological relevance. It seems then that the political dimension serves two functions. The first is to make observable our inner life in general, and the nature of justice in particular, by constructing a visible analogue in the form of a city. The other is to show how the image of political justice thus achieved can serve as a model for a society that promotes the ability of its citizens to achieve the highest level of human fulfillment (500d–501b). The negative effort of disciplined abstention and the positive effort of pursuit of knowledge, which we make as individuals, can be institutionalized respectively through censorship and education. Protected from corrosive influences, and directed toward the highest forms of knowledge and reality, we become free to focus our energies on the pursuit of wisdom. But censorship can only be justified hypothetically, where the wisdom of the rulers is assured. In other societies the Socrateses of the world become not the authors but the victims of censorship.

Note

1. I have discussed this strategy more extensively in "Three Disappearing Ladders in Plato", *Philosophy and Rhetoric* 29 (1996): 279–99.

Bibliography

Adam, James. 1963 (1902). *The Republic of Plato*, 2nd edition. Cambridge, Mass.: Cambridge University Press.

Algazali. 1983. "The Deliverance from Error". In *Philosophy in the Middle Ages*. 2nd ed. Edited by Hyman and Walsh. Indianapolis, Ind.: Hackett.

Allen, R. E. 1987. "The Speech of Glaucon in Plato's *Republic*". *Journal of the History of Philosophy* 25: 3–11.

Alperson, Philip. 1994. "Music as Philosophy". In Alperson, ed., 1994, 193–210.

———, ed. 1994. *What is Music?: An Introduction to the Philosophy of Music*. University Park, Penn.: Pennsylvania State Press.

Andersson, Torsten. 1971. *Polis and Psyche: A Motif in Plato's Republic*. Stockholm: Almqvist & Wiksell.

Andrew, Edward. 1983. "Descent to the Cave". *Review of Politics* 45: 510–35.

Annas, Julia. 1981. *An Introduction to Plato's Republic*. Oxford: Clarendon Press.

———. 1982. "Plato's Myths of Judgement". *Phronesis* 27: 119–43.

———. 1986. "Plato, *Republic* V-VII". In Bambrough 1986: 3–17.

———. 1995. "Virtue as a Skill". *International Journal of Philosophical Studies* 3: 227–43.

Anton, John, and G. Kustas, eds. 1971. *Essays in Ancient Greek Philosophy*. Albany, N.Y.: State University of New York Press.

Anton, John, and Anthony Preus, eds. 1989. *Essays in Ancient Greek Philosophy III: Plato*. Albany, N.Y.: State University of New York Press.

Apel, Willi. 1944. *Harvard Dictionary of Music*. Cambridge, Mass.: Harvard University Press.

Assagioli, Roberto. 1965. "Music as a Cause of Disease and as a Means of Cure". Reprinted as Chapter VII of *Psychosynthesis*. New York: Viking.

Austin, J. L. 1979. "The Line and the Cave in Plato's *Republic*". In *Philosophical Papers*, 3rd ed. Edited by J. O. Urmson and G. J. Warnock. Oxford: Oxford University Press.

Bambrough, Renford, ed. 1986. *Philosophers Ancient and Modern*. *Philosophy* Supplementary Vol. 20.

Baracchi, Claudia. 2002. *Of Myth, Life, and War in Plato's* Republic. Bloomington: Indiana University Press.

Belfiore, Elizabeth. 1983. "Plato's Greatest Accusation against Poetry". *Canadian Journal of Philosophy* 9: 39–62.

Benardete, Seth. 1989. *Socrates' Second Sailing: On Plato's* Republic. Chicago: University of Chicago Press.

Bergson, Henri. 1935 (1932). *The Two Sources of Morality and Religion*. Translated by R. Ashley Audra and Cloudesley Brereton, with the assistance of W. Horsfall Carter. Garden City, N.Y.: Doubleday Anchor.

Billings, Grace Hadley. 1920. *The Art of Transition in Plato*. Menasha, Wisc.: George Banta. A facsimile reprint has been issued by New York: Garland, 1979.

Blackwood, Dennis. 2001. "The Decline of Man and State in Books 8–9 of the *Republic*: Devolution and/or Instability Argument?" *American Catholic Philosophical Quarterly* 75: 1–24.

Blondell, Ruby. 2002. *The Play of Character in Plato's Dialogues*. Cambridge, Mass.: Cambridge University Press.

Bloom, Allan. 1968. *The* Republic *of Plato* (translation and commentary). New York: Basic Books.

Bluestone, Natalie Harris. 1987. *Women and the Ideal Society: Plato's* Republic *and Modern Myths of Gender*. Oxford: Berg.

Bobonich, Christopher. 2002. *Plato's Utopia Recast: His Later Ethics and Politics*. Oxford: Clarendon Press.

Bosanquet, Bernard. 1906. *A Companion to Plato's Republic*. London: Rivingtons.

Bosley, Richard, R. Shiner, and J. Sisson, eds. 1996. *Aristotle, Virtue, and the Mean*. Edmonton: Academic Printing & Publishing.

Boulter, C., ed. 1985. *Greek Art: Archaic into Classical*, Leiden: Brill.

Brann, Eva. 1967. "The Music of the *Republic*". *Agon* 1: i–vi and 1–117.

Brown, Eric. 2000. "Justice and Compulsion for Plato's Philosopher-Rulers". *Ancient Philosophy* 20: 1–17.

Brumbaugh, Robert. 1954. *Plato's Mathematical Imagination*. Bloomington: Indiana University Press.

———. 1989. *Platonic Studies of Greek Philosophy*. Albany, N.Y.: State University of New York Press.

Buber, Martin. 1947. *Tales of the Hassidim*. New York: Schocken.

Burnyeat, M. F. 1999. "Utopia and Fantasy: The Practicability of Plato's Ideally Just City". In Fine 1999, 297–308.

Bury, R. G., ed. 1929. *Timaeus, Critias, Cleitophon, Menexenus, Epistles*. London: Heineman.

Calvert, Brian. 1975. "Plato and the Equality of Women". *Phoenix* 29: 231–43.

Carone, Gabriela Roxana. 2001. "*Akrasia* in the *Republic*: Does Plato Change His Mind?" In *Oxford Studies in Ancient Philosophy* XX. Edited by D. Sedley. Oxford: Clarendon Press, 107–48.

Chan, Wing-tsit, ed. and trans. 1963. *The Doctrine of the Mean*. In Chan, Wing-tsit, *A Source Book in Chinese Philosophy*. Princeton: Princeton University Press.

Chappell, T. D. J. 1992. "The Virtues of Thrasymachus". *Phronesis* 38: 1–17.

Cherniss, Harold. 1932. "On Plato's *Republic* X 597 B". *American Journal of Philology* 53: 233–42.

Clay, Diskin. 1988. "Reading the *Republic*". In *Platonic Writings, Platonic Readings*. Edited by Charles Griswold. New York: Routledge 1988. Reprinted University Park: Pennsylvania State University Press 2002.

Cleary, John, ed. 1987. *Proceedings of the Boston Area Colloquium in Ancient Philosophy*. Vol. II. Lanham, Md.: University Press of America.

Cleary, John, and Daniel Shartin, eds. 1988. *Proceedings of the Boston Area Colloquium in Ancient Philosophy*. Vol. IV. Lanham, Md.: University Press of America.

Cleary, John, ed. 1991. *Proceedings of the Boston Area Colloquium in Ancient Philosophy*. Vol. VII. Lanham, Md.: University Press of America.

Cleary, John, and Gary Gurtler, eds. 1999. *Proceedings of the Boston Area Colloquium in Ancient Philosophy*. XIII. Leiden: Brill.

Clegg, J. S. 1976. "Plato's Vision of Chaos". *Classical Quarterly* 26: 52–61.

Cooke, Elizabeth. 1999. "The Moral and Intellectual Development of the Philosopher in Plato's *Republic*". *Ancient Philosophy* 19: 37–44.

Cooper, John. 1984. "Plato's Theory of Human Motivation". *History of Philosophy Quarterly* 1: 3–22.

———. 2000. "Two Theories of Justice". *Proceedings and Address of the American Philosophical Association* 74: 5–27.

Cooper, Neil. 1966. "The Importance of *ΔΙΑΝΟΙΑ* in Plato's Theory of Forms". *Classical Quarterly* New Series 16 (1966): 65–9.

Cornford, F. M. 1912. "Psychology and Social Structure in the *Republic* of Plato". *Classical Quarterly* 6: 246–65.

———. 1937. *Plato's Cosmology*. London: Routledge.

———, trans. 1941. *The Republic of Plato*. Translated with Introduction and Notes. London: Oxford University Press.

Craig, Leon. 1994. *The War Lover: A Study of Plato's* Republic. Toronto: University of Toronto Press.

Cross, R. C., and A. D. Woozley. 1964. *Plato's* Republic: *A Philosophical Commentary*. London: Macmillan.

Demos, Raphael. 1964. "A Fallacy in Plato's *Republic?*" *Philosophical Review* 73: 390–5. Reprinted in Vlastos 1971: 52–6.

Denyer, Nicholas. 1986. "Ethics in Plato's *Republic*". In Bambrough 1986, 19–32.

Desjardins, Rosemary. 2004. *Plato and the Good: Illuminating the Darkling Vision*. Leiden: Brill.

de Stryker, Emile. 1966. "The Unity of Knowledge and Love in Socrates' Conception of Virtue". *International Philosophical Quarterly* 6: 428–44.

Devereaux, Daniel. 1979. "Socrates' First City in the *Republic*". *Apeiron* 13: 36–40.

Dorter, Kenneth. 1982. *Plato's* Phaedo: *An Interpretation*. Toronto: University of Toronto Press.

———. 1992. "A Dual Dialectic in Plato's *Symposium*". *Philosophy and Rhetoric* 25: 253–70.

———. 1994. *Form and Good in Plato's Eleatic Dialogues: the* Parmenides, Theaetetus, Sophist, *and* Statesman. Berkeley: University of California Press.

———. 2001. "Philosopher-Rulers: How Contemplation Becomes Action". *Ancient Philosophy* 21: 335–56.

———. 2004. "The Divided Line and the Structure of Plato's Republic". *History of Philosophy Quarterly*.

Dover, Kenneth. 1974. *Greek Popular Morality in the Time of Plato and Aristotle*. Berkeley: University of California Press.

Ehrenberg, Victor. 1947. "Polypragmosyne: A Study in Greek Politics". *Journal of Hellenic Studies* 67: 46–67.

Else, Gerald. 1972. *The Structure and Date of Book 10 of Plato's* Republic. Heidelberg: Carl Winter.

Ferrari, G. R. F. 2002. "Plato, *Republic* 9.585c–d". *Classical Quarterly* NS 52: 383–88.

———. 2003. *City and Soul in Plato's* Republic. Sankt Augustin: Academia Verlag.

Fine, Gail. 1978. "Knowledge and Belief in *Republic* V. *Archiv fur Geschichte der Philosophie* 60: 121–139.

———. 1990. "Knowledge and Belief in *Republic* V-VII". In *Epistemology*. Edited by S. Everson. Cambridge: Cambridge University Press, 85–115.

———. 1999. *Plato 2*. Oxford: Oxford University Press.

Flew, Antony. 1995. "Responding to Plato's Thrasymachus". *Philosophy* 70: 436–47.

Friedländer, Paul. 1964. *Plato*, 3 Vols. Translated by Hans Meyerhoff. Princeton: Princeton University Press.

Fries, Horace. 1940. "Virtue is Knowledge". *Philosophy of Science* Vol. VIII: 89–99.

Gadamer, Hans-Georg. 1934. "Plato and the Poets". In Gadamer 1980, 39–72.

———. 1980. *Dialogue and Dialectic*. Translated by P. C. Smith. New Haven: Yale University Press.

Galis, Leon. 1974. "The State-Soul Analogy in Plato's Argument that Justice Pays". *Journal of the History of Philosophy* 12: 285–93.

Gallop, David. 1965. "Image and Reality in Plato's *Republic*". *Archiv für Begriffsgeschichte* 47: 113–31.

Gerson, Lloyd. 1986. "Platonic Dualism". *Monist* Vol. 69: 352–69.

———. 1987. "A Note on Tripartition and Immortality in Plato". *Apeiron* 20: 181–96.

———. 2002. "The development of the doctrine of the Good and Plato's development". In Reale and Scolnicov 2002, 379–91.

Gifford, Mark. 1999. "Dramatic Dialectic in *Republic* I". Paper presented to the Pacific Division meeting of the American Philosophical Association.

Gilbert, Paul. 1988. "Emotional Disorders, Brain State and Pyschosocial Evolution". In W. Dryden and P. Trower, eds., *Developments in Cognitive Psychotherapy*. London: Sage Publications.

Gill, Christopher. 2002. "A critical response to the hermeneutic approach from an analytic perspective". In Reale and Scolnicov 2002, 211–222.

Gomperz, Theodor. 1905. *Greek Thinkers: A History of Ancient Philosophy*, Vol. 3. Translated by G. G. Berry. London: John Murray.

Gonzalez, Francisco. 1996. "Propositions or Objects?: A Critique of Gail Fine on Knowledge and Belief in *Republic* V". *Phronesis* 41: 245–75.

———. 1998. *Dialectic and Dialogue: Plato's Practice of Philosophical Inquiry*. Evanston, Ill.: Northwestern University Press.

Griffith, Tom, trans. 2000. *Plato: The Republic*. Cambridge: Cambridge University Press.

Great Learning, The. 1963. In Chan, Wing-tsit, *A Source Book in Chinese Philosophy*. Princeton: Princeton University Press.

Griswold, Charles. 1981. "The Ideas and the Criticism of Poetry in Plato's *Republic*, Book 10". *Journal of the History of Philosophy* 19: 135–50.

———, ed. 1988. *Platonic Writings, Platonic Readings*. New York: Routledge 1988. Reprinted University Park: Pennsylvania State University Press 2002.

Grube, G. M. A. 1974. *Plato: The* Republic (translation and notes). Indianapolis: Hackett.

Guthrie, W. K. C. 1971. "Plato's Views on the Nature of the Soul". In Vlastos 1971 (1) 230–43.

———. 1975. *A History of Greek Philosophy*. Vol. 4. Cambridge: Cambridge University Press.

———. 1978. *A History of Greek Philosophy*. Vol. 5. Cambridge: Cambridge University Press.

Hadgopoulos, Demetrius. 1973. "Thrasymachus and Legalism" *Phronesis* 18: 204–8.

Halliwell, S., trans. and ed. 1988. *Plato Republic 10*. Warminster: Aris & Phillips.

———, trans. and ed. 1993. *Plato Republic 5*. Warminster: Aris & Phillips.

———. 1997. "The *Republic's* Two Critiques of Poetry". In Höffe 1997, 313–32.

Hanslick, Eduard. 1957. *The Beautiful in Music*. Translation of *Vom Musikalisch-Schönen* (1854) by Gustav Cohen. Indianapolis: Bobbs-Merrill.

Hardie, W. F. R. 1936. *A Study in Plato*. Oxford: Clarendon Press.

Henderson, T. Y. 1970. "In Defense of Thrasymachus". *American Philosophical Quarterly* 7: 218–228.

Hermann, Karl Friedrich, ed. 1884. *Platonis Rei publicae*. Leipzig: Teubner.

Hoerber, Robert. 1944. *The Theme of Plato's Republic*. St. Louis: Washington University.

Houlgate, Laurence. 1970. "Virtue is Knowledge". *Monist* 54: 142–53.

Hourani, George. 1962. "Thrasymachus' Definition of Justice in Plato's *Republic*". *Phronesis* 7: 110–120.

Howland, Jacob. 1993. *The Republic: The Odyssey of Philosophy*. New York: Twayne.

———. 1998. "*The Republic's* Third Wave and the Paradox of Political Philosophy". *Review of Metaphysics* 51: 633–57.

Hyland, Drew. 1988. "Commentary on Moors". In Cleary and Shartin 1988, 248–255.

———. 1990. "Plato's Three Waves and the Question of Utopia". *Interpretation* 18: 91–109.

Irwin, Terence. 1995. *Plato's Ethics.* Oxford: Oxford University Press.

———. 1974. "Recollection and Plato's Moral Theory". *Review of Metaphysics* 27: 752–72.

Jenks, Rod. 2002. "The Machinery of the Collapse: On *Republic* VIII". *History of Political Thought* 23: 21–29.

Jeste, Dilip, and Rodrigo Muñoz. 1999. "Preparing for the Future". *Psychiatric Services* (50:9): 1157.

Joseph, H. W. B. 1935. *Essays in Ancient & Modern Philosophy.* Oxford: Clarendon Press.

Kahn, Charles H. 1966. "The Greek Verb 'to be' and the Concept of Being". *Foundations of Language* 2: 245–65.

———. 1968. Review of Gilbert Ryle's *Plato's Progress. Journal of Philosophy.*

———. 1972. "The Meaning of 'Justice' and the Theory of Forms". *Journal of Philosophy* 69, 567–79.

———. 1981. "Some Philosophical Uses of 'to be' in Plato". *Phronesis* 26: 105–134.

———. 1987. "Plato's Theory of Desire". *Review of Metaphysics* 41: 77–103.

———. 1996. *Plato and the Socratic Dialogue: The Philosophical Use of a Literary Form.* Cambridge: Cambridge University Press.

Karasmanis, Vassilis. 1988. "Plato's *Republic*: The Line and the Cave". *Apeiron* 21: 147–71.

Kelly, John. 1989. "Virtue and Inwardness in Plato's *Republic. Ancient Philosophy* 9: 189–205.

Kerferd, G. B. 1947. "The Doctrine of Thrasymachus in Plato's *Republic*". *Durham University Journal* n.s. 9 (1947): 19–27.

———. 1964. "Thrasymachus and Justice: A Reply". *Phronesis* 9: 12–16.

Kivy, Peter. 1994. "How Music Moves". In Alperson 1994, 147–163.

Klein, Jacob. 1965. *A Commentary on Plato's* Meno. Chapel Hill: University of North Carolina Press.

Klosko, George. 1986. *The Development of Plato's Political Theory.* New York: Methuen.

———. 1987. "Socrates on Goods and Happiness". *History of Philosophy Quarterly* 4: 251–64.

Kraut, Richard. 1999. "Return to the Cave: *Republic* 519–521". In Fine 1999, 235–54.

Lachterman, David. 1989–1990. "What Is 'The Good' of Plato's *Republic?*" *St. John's Review* 39: 139–71

Langer, Susanne. 1953. *Feeling and Form.* New York: Scribner's.

Lear, Jonathan. 1992. "Inside and Outside *The Republic*". *Phronesis* 37: 184–215.

Lesses, Glenn. 1987. "Weakness, Reason, and the Divided Soul in Plato's *Republic*". *History of Philosophy Quarterly* 4: 147–61.

Levenson, R., P. Ekman, and W. Friesen. 1990. "Voluntary Facial Action Generates Emotion-Specific Autonomic Nervous System Activity". *Psychophysiology* 27(4): 363–383.

Lindsay, A. D., trans. 1935. *Plato's Republic*. London: Dent (Everyman's Library).

Lizano-Ordovás, Miguel. 1995. "'Eikasia' und 'Pistis' in Platons Höhlengleichnis". *Zeitschrift für philosophische Forschung* 49: 378–97.

Lykos, Kimon. 1987. *Plato on Justice and Power: Reading Book 1 of Plato's Republic*. Albany, N.Y.: State University of New York Press.

Mahoney, Timothy. 1992. "Do Plato's Philosopher-Rulers Sacrifice Self-Interest to Justice?" *Phronesis* 37: 265–82

Malcolm, J. 1962. "The Line and the Cave". *Phronesis* 7: 38–45.

Margolis, Joseph. 1994. "On the Semiotics of Music". In Alperson 1994, 211–36.

McKie, John. 1994. "Linguistic Competence and Moral Development: Some Parallels". *Philosophical Inquiry* XVI, 20–31.

Mill, John Stuart. 1979. *Utilitarianism*. Indianapolis: Hackett.

Miller, Mitchell. 1985. "Platonic Provocations: Reflections on the Soul and the Good in the *Republic*". In O'Meara 1985, 163–193.

Mitscherling, Jeffrey. 1983. *The Image of a Second Sun: Plato's View of Poetry*. Dissertation, University of Guelph.

Mohr, Richard. 1985. *The Platonic Cosmology*. Leiden: Brill.

Moors, Kent. 1988. "Mythologia and the Limits of Opinion: Presented Myths in Plato's *Republic*". In Cleary and Shartin 1988, 213–47.

Moravscik, Julius. 2001. "Inner Harmony and the Human Ideal in *Republic* IV and IX". *Journal of Ethics* 5: 39–56.

Moravscik, Julius, and Philip Temko, eds. 1982. *Plato on Beauty, Wisdom, and the Arts*. Totowa, N.J.: Rowman & Littlefield.

Morrison, J. S. 1977. "Two Unresolved Difficulties in the Line and the Cave", *Phronesis* 22: 212–31.

Murdoch, Iris. 1977. *The Fire and the Sun: Why Plato Banished the Artists*. Oxford: Clarendon Press.

Murphy, N. R. 1951. *The Interpretation of Plato's Republic*. Oxford: Clarendon Press.

Naddaff, Ramona. 2002. *Exiling the Poets*. Chicago: University of Chicago Press.

Nails, Debra. 2002. *The People of Plato: A Prosopography of Plato and Other Socratics*. Indianapolis: Hackett.

Nehamas, Alexander. 1982. "Plato on Imitation and Poetry in *Republic* 10". In Moravcsik and Temko 1982, 47–78.

———. 1987. "Socratic Intellectualism". In Cleary 1987, 275–316.

Nettleship, Richard Lewis. 1901. *Lectures on the Republic of Plato*, second edition. London: Macmillan.

Nichols, Mary. 1984. "The *Republic's* Two Alternatives: Philosopher-Kings and Socrates" *Political Theory* 12: 252–74.

Nicholson, P. P. 1974. "Unravelling Thrasymachus' Arguments in 'The Republic'". *Phronesis* 19: 210–232.

Nussbaum, Martha. 1986. *The Fragility of Goodness*. Cambridge: Cambridge University Press.

Okin, Susan Moller. 1991 (1977). "Philosopher Queens and Private Wives: Plato on Women and the Family". In Carole Pateman and Mary L. Shanley, eds., *Feminist Interpretations of Political Thought*. Oxford: Blackwell, Polity Press, 11–31.

O'Meara, Dominic, ed. 1985. *Platonic Investigations*. Washington, D.C.: Catholic University of America Press.

O'Neill, Basil. 1988. "The Struggle for the Soul of Thrasymachus". *Ancient Philosophy* 8: 167–85.

Oxford Classical Dictionary. 3rd edition. 1996. Oxford: Oxford University Press.

Page, Carl. 1990. "The Unjust Treatment of Polemarchus". *History of Philosophy Quarterly* 7: 243–67.

———. 1991. "The Truth About Lies in Plato's *Republic*". *Ancient Philosophy* 11: 1–35.

Parry, Richard. 1983. "The Craft of Justice". *Canadian Journal of Philosophy* Supplementary Volume IX, pp. 19–38.

———. 1996. *Plato's Craft of Justice*. Albany, N.Y.: State University of New York Press.

Partee, Morriss. 1970. "Plato's Banishment of Poetry". *Journal of Aesthetics and Art Criticism* 29: 209–22.

Penner, Terry. 1971. "Thought and Desire in Plato". In Gregory Vlastos, *Plato*, Vol. II. Garden City, N.Y.: Anchor Books, 96–118.

Phillips, D. Z. 1994. "Glaucon's Challenges". *Philosophical Investigations* 17: 536–51.

Planinc, Zdravko. 1991. *Plato's Political Philosophy: Prudence in the Republic and the Laws*. Columbia: University of Missouri Press.

Platt, Arthur. 1911. "Plato, *Republic*, 614B". *Classical Review* 25, 13–14.

Pollitt, Jerome J. 1972. *Art and Experience in Classical Greece*. Cambridge: Cambridge University Press.

———. 1985. "Early Classical Greek Art in a Platonic Universe". In Boulter 1985, 96–111 and plates 79–96.

Popper, Karl. 1945. *The Open Society and its Enemies*. London: Routledge.

Rauscher, Frances, Gordon Shaw, Linda Levine, Eric Wright, Wendy Dennis, and Robert Newcomb. 1997. "Music training causes long-term enhancement of preschool children's spatial-temporal reasoning". *Neurological Research* 19: 2–8.

Rawson, Glenn. 1966. "Knowledge and Desire of the Good in Plato's *Republic*". *Southwest Philosophy Review* 12: 103–115.

Reale, Giovanni. 1997 (1991). *Toward a New Interpretation of Plato*. Translated and edited by John Catan and Richard Davies. Washington, D.C.: Catholic University of America Press.

———. 2002. "The One-Good as the load-bearing concept in Plato's protology". In Reale and Scolnicov 2002, 29–48.

Reale, Giovanni, and Samuel Scolnikov, eds. 2002. *New Images of Plato: Dialogues on the Idea of the Good*. Sankt Augustin: Academia Verlag.

Record of Music, The. 1964. *The Sacred Books of the East*, Vol. 28. Translated by James Legge. Delhi: Motilal Banarsidass.

Reeve, C. D. C. 1988. *Philosopher Kings: The Argument of Plato's* Republic. Princeton: Princeton University Press.

———. 1992. *Plato: Republic.* Translated by G. M. A. Grube and C. D. C. Reeve. Indianapolis: Hackett.

Robins, Ian. 1995. "Mathematics and the Conversion of the Mind: *Republic* vii 522c1–531e3". *Ancient Philosophy* 15: 359–91.

Robinson, James. 1990–1991. "The Nature of the Soul in Republic X". *Journal of Philosophical Research* XVI: 213–22.

Robinson, Jenefer. 1994. "Music as a Representational Art". In Alperson 1994, 165–92.

Robinson, Richard. 1953. *Plato's Earlier Dialectic.* 2nd edition. Oxford: Clarendon Press.

Robinson, T. M. 1967. "Soul and Immortality in Republic X". *Phronesis* 12: 147–51.

Rohatyn, Dennis. 1975. "Struktur und Funktion in Buch X von Platons Staat: Ein Überblick". *Gymnasium* 82: 314–30.

Roochnik, David. 1999. "Images as Images: Commentary on Smith". In Cleary and Gurtler 1999, 205–9.

———. 1996. *Of Art and Wisdom: Plato's Understanding of Techne.* University Park: Pennsylvania State University Press.

———. 2003. *Beautiful City: The Dialectical Character of Plato's "Republic".* Ithaca: Cornell University Press.

Rorty, Amélie Oksenberg. 1970. "Plato and Aristotle on Belief, Habit, and *Akrasia*". *American Philosophical Quarterly* 7: 50–61.

———. 1987. "The Limits of Socratic Intellectualism: Did Socrates Teach Arete?" In Cleary 1987, 317–30.

Rosen, Frederick. 1980. "Contemplation and Virtue in Plato". *Religious Studies* 16: 85–95.

Rosen, Stanley. 1988. *The Quarrel Between Philosophy and Poetry.* New York: Routledge.

Rosenstock, Bruce. 1994. "Athena's Cloak: Plato's Critique of the Democratic City in the *Republic*". *Political Theory* 22: 363–390.

Ross, David. 1951. *Plato's Theory of Ideas.* Oxford: Clarendon Press.

Rudebusch, George. 2002. "Dramatic Prefiguration in Plato's *Republic*". *Philosophy and Literature* 26: 75–83.

Sachs, David. 1963. "A Fallacy in Plato's *Republic*". *Philosophical Review* 72: 141–58. Reprinted in Vlastos 1971, 35–51.

Santas, Gerasimos. 1964. "The Socratic Paradoxes". *Philosophical Review* 73: 147–64. Reprinted in Sesonske and Fleming 1965: 49–64.

———. 2001. "Plato's Criticism of the 'Democratic Man' in the *Republic*". *Journal of Ethics* 5: 57–71.

———. 2002. "Plato's Idea of the Good". In Reale and Scolnikov 2002, 359–78.

Saxonhouse, Arlene. 1997 (1976). "The Philosopher and the Female". In Kraut 1997, 95–113.

Sayre, Kenneth. 1995. *Plato's Literary Garden: How to Read a Platonic Dialogue*. Notre Dame: University of Notre Dame Press.

Scolnicov, Samuel. 1978. "Reason and Passion in the Platonic Soul". *Dionysus* 2: 35–49.

———. 1988. *Plato's Metaphysics of Education*. London: Routledge.

Segal, Charles. 1978. "'The Myth was Saved': Reflections on Homer and the Mythology of Plato's Republic". *Hermes* 106: 315–36.

Seifert, Josef. 2002. "The Idea of the Good as the sum total of pure perfections: A new personalist reading of *Republic* VI and VII". In Reale and Scolnicov 2002, 407–424.

Sesonske, Alexander and Noel Fleming, eds. 1965. *Plato's Meno: Text and Criticism*. Belmont, Calif.: Wadsworth.

Shiner, Roger. 1972. "Soul in Republic X 611". *Apeiron* 6: 23–30.

Shorey, Paul, ed. and trans. 1930. *Plato's Republic*. Vol. 1. London: Heinemann.

———, ed. and trans. 1935. *Plato's Republic*. Vol. 2. London: Heinemann.

Skemp, J. B. 1967. *The Theory of Motion in Plato's Later Dialogues*. 2nd ed. Amsterdam: Hakkert.

Smith, Nicholas. 1996. "Plato's Divided Line". *Ancient Philosophy* 16: 25–46.

———. 1999. "How the Prisoners in Plato's Cave are 'Like Us'". In Cleary and Gurtler 1999, 187–204.

———. 2000. "Plato on Knowledge as a Power". *Journal of the History of Philosophy* 38: 145–68.

Sparshott, Francis. 1966. "Socrates and Thrasymachus". *Monist* 50: 421–59.

Sprague, Rosamond Kent. 1976. *Plato's Philosopher-King*. Columbia: University of South Carolina Press.

Sterling, Richard, and William Scott, trans. 1985. *Plato: The Republic*. New York: Norton.

Stewart, J. A. 1960 (1904). *The Myths of Plato*. London: Centaur Press.

Stocks, J. L. 1912. "The Divided Line of *Plato Rep. VI*". *Classical Quarterly* 6: 73–8.

Stoichita, Victor I. 1997. *A Short History of the Shadow*. London: Reaktion.

Stokes, Michael. 1990. "Some Pleasures of Plato, *Republic* IX". *Polis* 9. 2–51.

———. 1992. "Plato and the Sightlovers of the *Republic*". *Apeiron* 25. 103–32.

Strabo. 1928. *Geography*. Vol. 5. Loeb Classical Library. London: William Heinemann.

Strauss, Leo. 1964. *The City and Man*. Chicago: Rand McNally.

Stumpf, Carl. 1883–1890. *Tonpsychologie*. 2 Vols. Leipzig: Weigel.

Szlezak, Thomas. 1976. "Unsterblichkeit und Trichotomie der Seele in zehnten Buch der Politeia". *Phronesis* 21: 31–58.

Tarán, Leonardo. 1971. "The Creation Myth in Plato's *Timaeus*". In Anton and Kustas, 1971.

Tate, J. 1928. "Imitation in Plato's *Republic*". *Classical Quarterly* 22: 16–23.

———. 1932. "Plato and Imitation". *Classical Quarterly* 26: 161–69.

Taylor, A. E. 1956 (1926). *Plato: The Man and His Work*. 6th ed. Cleveland: World.
———. 1928. *A Commentary on Plato's* Timaeus. Oxford: Clarendon Press.
Teloh, Henry. 1976. "Human Nature, Psychic Energy, and Self-Actualization in Plato's *Republic*". *Southern Journal of Philosophy* 14: 345–358.
Thesleff, Holger. 1967. *Studies in the Styles of Plato*. Helsinki: Societas Philosophica Fennica.
———. 1982. *Studies in Platonic Chronology*. Helsinki: Societas Scientiarum Fennica.
Urmson, J. O. 1997. "Plato and the Poets". In Kraut 1997, 223–34.
Vlastos, Gregory. 1968. "The Argument in the *Republic* that Justice Pays". *Journal of Philosophy* 65, 665–74.
———. 1969. "Justice and Psychic Harmony in the *Republic*", *Journal of Philosophy* 66, 505–21.
———, ed. 1971(1). *Plato*, Vol. 2. Garden City, N.Y.: Doubleday Anchor.
———. 1971(2). "Justice and Happiness in the *Republic*". In Vlastos 1971(1) 67–95.
———. 1991. *Socrates, Ironist and Moral Philosopher*. Ithaca: Cornell University Press.
———. 1997 (1986). "Was Plato a Feminist?" In Kraut 1997, 115–28.
Voegelin, Eric. 1957. *Plato*. Baton Rouge: Louisiana State University Press.
Wang Yang-ming. 1963. *Instructions for Practical Living*. In Chan, Wing-tsit, trans. and ed., *Instructions for Practical Living and Other Neo-Confucian Writing by Wang Yang-ming*. New York: Columbia University Press.
Warnek, Peter. 2002. "Saving the Last Word: Heidegger and the Concluding Myth of Plato's *Republic*". *Philosophy Today* 46: 255–73.
Warren, Edward. 1989. "The Craft Argument: An Analogy?" In Anton and Preus 1989, 101–115.
Wedberg, Anders. 1955. *Plato's Philosophy of Mathematics*. Stockholm: Almqvist & Wiksell.
Weil, Simone. 1957. "The 'Republic'". In *Intimations of Christianity Among the Ancient Greeks*. Translated by Elisabeth Chase Geissbuhler. London: Routledge.
Welton, William, and Ronald Polansky. 1996. "The Viability of Virtue in the Mean" in Bosley 1996: 79–102.
Wessler, R. L. 1988. "Affect and Nonconscious Processes in Cognitive Psychotherapy". In W. Dryden and P. Trower, eds., *Developments in Cognitive Psychotherapy*. London: Sage.
White, F. C. 1988. "Justice and the Good of Others in Plato's *Republic*". *History of Philosophy Quarterly* 5: 395–410.
White, Nicholas. 1979. *A Companion to Plato's* Republic. Indianapolis: Hackett.
Williams, Bernard. 1973. "The Analogy of City and Soul in Plato's *Republic*". In E. N. Lee, A. P. D. Mourelatos, R. M. Rorty, eds., *Exegesis and Argument*. New York: Humanities Press, 196–206.
Wren, Chase. 2000. "Being and Knowledge: A Connoisseur's Guide to Republic V.476e ff". *Apeiron* 33: 87–108.
Yu, Jiyuan. 2000. "Justice in the *Republic*: An Evolving Paradox". *History of Philosophy Quarterly* 17: 121–141.

~

Platonic Dialogues Cited

Apology:
    23a: 246;
    31d–e: 242, 248n14;
    40a–41a: 251n41, 348n54
Charmides, 199
Cratylus:
    389b: 345n4;
    390c: 9;
    398d: 9;
    403a–404a: 348n54
Crito:
    47d–e: 349n60;
    50a–52d: 218
Euthydemus:
    272e: 251n41
Euthyphro:
    6d–7c: 199, 209n10
Gorgias, 57–58;
    428b: 72n21;
    453d: 51n14, 346n18;
    462b–c: 208n5;
    480a–b: 302;
    492a–b: 71n17, 106;
    494c–e: 183;
    513c: 17, 215n52
Hippias Major, 199

Ion:
    532d–533c: 82;
    535b–e: 220;
    537a–540e: 51n14, 316;
    542a–b: 82
Laches, 199;
    91c–e: 130n11
Laws, 141;
    633c–d: 130n11;
    691c: 236–37;
    740d: 129n6, 160–61n17;
    838d: 348n54;
    894b: 347n35;
    895e–897b: 285n33, 328, 367
Letters:
    7.337c: 160–61n17
Lysis, 199;
    220a–b: 349n60
Menexenus:
    235e: 140
Meno, 195–96, 199;
    75d: 9;
    77b–e: 209n11;
    78d–e: 129n7;
    80a: 10;
    80d: 80;

Index